Integrating Behavioral and Social Sciences With Public Health

Integrating Behavioral and Social Sciences With Public Health

Edited by
Neil Schneiderman, Marjorie A. Speers,
Julia M. Silva, Henry Tomes, and Jacquelyn H. Gentry

American Psychological Association
Washington, DC

First Printing October 2000
Second Printing April 2001
Third Printing December 2004
Fourth Printing April 2006
Fifth Printing March 2008
Sixth Printing October 2009

Published by
American Psychological Association
750 First Street, NE
Washington, DC 20002

Copies may be ordered from
APA Order Department
P.O. Box 92984
Washington, DC 20090-2984

In the U.K., Europe, Africa, and the Middle East, copies may be ordered from
American Psychological Association
3 Henrietta Street
Covent Garden, London
WC2E 8LU England

Typeset in Goudy by EPS Group Inc., Easton, MD

Printer: United Book Press, Inc., Baltimore, MD
Cover Designer: NiDesign, Baltimore, MD
Technical/Production Editor: Jennifer Powers

The opinions and statements published are the responsibility of the authors, and such opinions and statements do not necessarily represent the policies of the APA.

Library of Congress Cataloging-in-Publication Data
Integrating behavioral and social sciences with public health / edited by Neil
Schneiderman . . . [et al.].
      p. cm.
   Includes bibliographical references and index.
   ISBN 1-55798-721-1 (alk. paper)
   1. Public health—Social aspects.   2. Public health—Psychological aspects.
3. Social medicine.   I. Schneiderman, Neil.

RA418.I522 2000
362.1—dc21

00-033179

British Library Cataloguing-in-Publication Data
A CIP record is available from the British Library.

Printed in the United States of America

CONTENTS

III. Conceptual and Methodological Considerations in the Integration of
Behavioral and Social Sciences With Public Health

CONTRIBUTORS

Diane M. Becker, ScD, MPH, Center for Health Promotion, School of Medicine, Johns Hopkins University, Baltimore, MD

Nancy Breen, PhD, Division of Cancer Control and Population Sciences, National Cancer Institute, Bethesda, MD

Margaret A. Chesney, PhD, Prevention Sciences Group, University of California—San Francisco

Sarah L. Cook, PhD, Department of Psychology, Georgia State University, Atlanta, GA

Cathy A. Coyne, MPH, DrPH, Department of Community Medicine, West Virginia University, Morgantown, WV

Don C. Des Jarlais, PhD, Chemical Dependency Institute, Beth Israel Medical Center, New York, NY

David Fetterman, PhD, School of Education, Stanford University, Stanford, CA

Samuel R. Friedman, PhD, National Development and Research Institutes, New York, NY

Jacquelyn H. Gentry, PhD, Public Interest Directorate, American Psychological Association, Washington, DC

Andrea Carlson Gielen, ScD, ScM, Center for Injury Research and Policy, School of Public Health, Johns Hopkins University, Baltimore, MD

Deborah C. Girasek, PhD, MPH, Department of Preventive Medicine, Uniformed Services University of the Health Sciences, Bethesda, MD

Robert M. Goodman, PhD, Department of Community Health Sciences, School of Public Health and Tropical Medicine, Tulane University, New Orleans, LA

David R. Holtgrave, PhD, Division of HIV/AIDS Prevention-Intervention Research and Support, Centers for Disease Control and Prevention, Atlanta, GA

Seth C. Kalichman, PhD, Center for AIDS Intervention Research, Medical College of Wisconsin, Milwaukee, WI

Robert Karasek, PhD, Department of Work and Environment, University of Massachusetts—Lowell, Lowell, MA

Mary P. Koss, PhD, University of Arizona Prevention Center, Tucson, AZ

Julie Legler, ScD, Division of Cancer Control and Population Sciences, National Cancer Institute, Bethesda, MD

Raymond P. Lorion, PhD, Psychology in Education Division, Graduate School of Education, University of Pennsylvania, Philadelphia, PA

John Lynch, PhD, MPH, Department of Epidemiology, School of Public Health, University of Michigan, Ann Arbor, MI

Helen Meissner, ScM, National Cancer Institute, Division of Cancer Control and Population Sciences, Bethesda, MD

David M. Murray, PhD, Department of Psychology, University of Memphis, Memphis, TN

Steven D. Pinkerton, PhD, Center for AIDS Intervention Research, Medical College of Wisconsin, Milwaukee, WI

Pekka Puska, MD, MPolSc, PhD, Department of Epidemiology and Health Promotion, National Public Health Institute, Helsinki, Finland

Barbara K. Rimer, DrPH, Division of Cancer Control and Population Sciences, National Cancer Institute, Bethesda, MD

Neil Schneiderman, PhD, Department of Psychology, University of Miami, Coral Gables, FL; and Behavioral Medical Research Center, Miami, FL

Kathleen Sikkema, PhD, Department of Psychiatry, Yale University School of Medicine, New Haven, CT

Julia M. Silva, Public Interest Directorate, American Psychological Association, Washington, DC

Anton Somlai, EdD, Center for AIDS Intervention Research, Medical College of Wisconsin, Milwaukee, WI

Marjorie A. Speers, PhD, Centers for Disease Control, Atlanta, GA

Katrina A. Thomas, Prevention Sciences Group, University of California—San Francisco

Rebecca C. Thurston, Duke University Medical Center, Durham, NC

Henry Tomes, PhD, Public Interest Directorate, American Psychological Association, Washington, DC

Antti Uutela, PhD, Health Education Research Unit, Department of Epidemiology and Health Promotion, National Public Health Institute, Helsinki, Finland

Abraham Wandersman, PhD, Department of Psychology, University of South Carolina, Columbia, SC

PREFACE

HENRY TOMES AND JACQUELYN H. GENTRY

Behavioral and social scientists have had long-standing interest and involvement in health research and health service delivery, but the integration of behavioral and social sciences in the core medical and public health research institutions and funding portfolios is a relatively new phenomenon. Over the past half century, an ever-widening realization has evolved that prevention of disease and injury is possible and is far more effective and economical for improving public health than are advances in treatment and rehabilitation. Scientists have identified many risk factors associated with specific diseases, disabling conditions, and injuries. Furthermore, they have recognized that behavioral changes can alter a significant proportion of those risk factors so that either an individual or a population may reduce the likelihood of suffering a debilitating condition. Additionally, behavioral factors frequently have a critical influence on an individual's recovery when treatment is necessary.

Science has provided useful technological advances that have the potential to prevent or control diseases, yet when applied to communities and populations, the actual outcomes sometimes are significantly less successful than expected. Psychological and social factors operating within specific community or cultural contexts can and often do influence human behavior in ways that limit the effectiveness of technological and biomedical advances in prevention and treatment.

Clearly the methods and findings of research on individual behavior, family and community characteristics, cultural influences, and social conditions are critical to effective prevention strategies for improving health, and they are essential for successful treatment and rehabilitative interventions.

Over many years, the American Psychological Association (APA) has explored the relationship of behavior and health in collaboration with other professional organizations, universities, private foundations, and federal agencies, and the APA divisions cover a number of health-related interests such as addictions, health psychology, neuropsychology, aging, developmental psychology, and rehabilitation. Specific activities have included sponsoring scientific conferences, creating special work groups, publishing scientific books and journals, developing research agendas, and educating the U.S. Congress about applications of behavioral research in health issues.

This book is one outcome of the 1998 conference Public Health in the 21st Century: Behavioral and Social Science Contributions, an event organized by APA in collaboration with 13 professional organizations and funded by the Centers for Disease Control and Prevention (CDC) and other federal agencies. This sampling of public health issues in the spotlight at the conference is a testament to the importance of multiple perspectives and methodologies in fully understanding the development, prevention, and treatment of disease and disability, as well as the emergence of illness. At a time when prevention strategy is moving in new directions recognizing the effectiveness of community-based interventions, behavioral and social sciences can contribute to understanding the role of risk behaviors and risk-group characteristics in health interventions. Behavioral and social scientists view people as members of complex and dynamic social units, including acquaintances, friendships, social systems, and multiple generations within families; these scientists have been at the forefront in the development of community approaches to public health interventions. Behavioral and social scientists recognize and incorporate differences across individuals, socioeconomic status, cultures, and generations into their explanations of behavior. Focusing on connections among a person's physical, behavioral, emotional, cognitive, and social characteristics, they examine the individual, community, and cultural factors that foster and sustain healthy or high-risk behaviors. Furthermore, they have applied these understandings to the development and assessment of interventions for many of the public health problems facing the nation.

This volume is offered not only as a showcase for successful examples of integrated research, but also as a challenge to public health specialists and to behavioral and social scientists. We trust that lessons learned from these examples will inform public health efforts to prevent disease, injury, illness, and disability and will strengthen interventions for various populations, diseases and disorders, and settings. Furthermore, we trust that behavioral and social scientists who have not worked in public health may appreciate the individual and public benefit to be gained from their involvement in this area and that they recognize that public health concepts can enhance their own scientific theories and methods.

Users of the book owe a significant debt of gratitude to the former CDC director David Satcher (now surgeon general and assistant secretary of health, U.S. Department of Health and Human Services); to Raymond D. Fowler, chief executive officer, American Psychological Association; and to Neil Schneiderman, conference chair, whose respective efforts facilitated collaboration between the CDC and the APA to convene a multidisciplinary meeting in which behavioral and social scientists could address public health issues of the 21st century.

ACKNOWLEDGMENTS

The production of this edited volume, as well as the conference that inspired it, resulted from the collaborative work of a large number of people and the contribution of resources from several organizations. Although many more individuals worked on the project than we can name here, we want to express our gratitude to some of the key figures that made it possible.

Credit for initiating the APA–CDC collaboration goes to David Satcher, MD, PhD, former director of the Centers for Disease Control and Prevention (CDC), and to Raymond Fowler, PhD, chief executive officer of the American Psychological Association (APA). It was their intention that this project would intensify efforts to meld behavioral and social sciences with public health research and practice.

To develop the 1998 conference, Public Health in the 21st Century: Behavioral and Social Science Contributions, the collaborating professional organizations sent representatives to a long series of planning meetings and contributed substantive content and expertise to the conference program and design, as well as to the identification of speakers. In addition to the APA, those organizations included the American Academy of Nursing; the American Anthropological Association; the American College of Epidemiology; the American Evaluation Association; the American Psychological Society; the American Public Health Association; the American Sociological Association; the Association of American Geographers; the Consortium of Social Science Associations; the Federation of Behavioral, Psychological, and Cognitive Sciences; the Society of Behavioral Medicine; the Society for Public Health Education; and the Society for Psychological Study of Social Issues.

Major financial support for the conference was provided through a cooperative agreement from the CDC. The APA received supplemental funding for the conference from several units of the National Institutes of

Health: the Office of Behavioral and Social Science Research, the National Institute on Drug Abuse, the National Institute of Environmental Health Science, the National Institute of Mental Health, the Office of AIDS Research, the National Institute on Alcohol Abuse and Alcoholism, and the Office of Research on Women's Health. Also contributing to the conference were the Office of Juvenile Justice and Delinquency Prevention of the U.S. Department of Justice and the Substance Abuse and Mental Health Services Administration of the U.S. Department of Human and Health Services.

The Robert Wood Johnson Foundation contributed funds to support dissemination of information from the conference, including a conference web site and the development of this scholarly volume based largely on conference presentations.

Production of this volume has been handled through the APA Books program, with leadership and assistance from Mary Lynn Skutley, editorial manager, and Edward Meidenbauer, development editor.

We are very grateful to the expert reviewers who provided insightful comments and substantive suggestions that enhanced the quality of our manuscripts. They included Craig Ewart, PhD, from Syracuse University and John Allegrante, PhD, from Columbia University. David Sleet, PhD, from the CDC generously contributed comments and suggestions to the chapter on unintentional injury prevention.

Neil Schneiderman
Marjorie A. Speers
Julia M. Silva
Henry Tomes
Jacquelyn H. Gentry

I

INTRODUCTION

1

BEHAVIORAL SCIENCE, SOCIAL SCIENCE, AND PUBLIC HEALTH IN THE 21ST CENTURY

NEIL SCHNEIDERMAN AND MARJORIE A. SPEERS

The purpose of this volume is to provide a capsule view of the relationship of the behavioral and social sciences to public health as we enter the 21st century. Historically, the genealogical tree of Western medicine often is traced to Hippocrates, who held a holistic concept of health and disease: "Health depends upon a state of equilibrium among the various internal factors which govern the operation of the body and the mind; the equilibrium in turn is reached only when man lives in harmony with his external environment" (cited in Dubos, 1959, p. 114). Thus, although physicians before the Age of Enlightenment attempted to treat wounds, burns, and fractures with practical remedies, the emphasis in healing was on health preservation rather than on curative processes. There was also emphasis on the interactions between cognitive–affective processes and bodily processes and between the individual (i.e., the host) and the environment.

In the 17th century, emerging notions of scientific thought shifted the balance in favor of reductionist as opposed to holistic approaches to health and disease and curative medicine over the preservation of health.

One major impact on 17th-century thought was Newton's demonstrations that nature's laws could be understood according to exact, specifiable physical principles. If an apple falls to earth, its single cause is the gravitational pull of the earth, which can be studied precisely. A second major impact was Descartes' *Traite de l'homme*, which posited a dichotomy between mind and body, thought and matter (Eaton, 1927). This encouraged a reductionist viewpoint in which thoughts and emotions were held to have nothing to do with bodily processes; the secrets of health and disease could be understood solely in terms of physical processes.

The 19th century established that microorganisms cause certain diseases and that pathogenic effects could be avoided or reversed by antitoxins and vaccines (King, 1982, p. 796). By the end of the century Koch's postulates were firmly entrenched. Briefly, Koch's postulates state that the etiological microorganism must be present in every case of the disease; the microorganism is not found in any other disease; and the isolated microbe reproduces the disease when administered to a new host.

The last two decades of the 19th century saw an explosion of scientific discoveries by Koch, Pasteur, Jenner, and others, which led to the identification of a plethora of infectious diseases. These included cholera, diphtheria, leprosy, malaria, pneumococcus, staphylococcus, streptococcus, tetanus, and tuberculosis. With the development of immunizations and antibiotics, the tools now exist for preventing and treating most infectious diseases.

Although the development of an understanding of bacterial and viral agents in disease processes, along with the development of vaccines and antibiotics, represents a monumental achievement in the world of science, it is not the whole story. As the 20th century unfolded, it became apparent that few diseases besides tuberculosis and tetanus seemed to satisfy Koch's postulates completely. Even in the case of tuberculosis, transmission depends on the existence of a vulnerable host. Thus, the ability of the tubercle bacillus to infect the host depends on multiple variables including host nutrition, actions of leukocytes, and responses of body tissues to counteract the bacillus at the site of potential infection.

In a provocative analysis, McKinlay and McKinlay (1997) observed that the precipitous declines in infectious disease rates in the United States preceded the development of immunizations and antibiotics by several decades. They observed that for each of nine infectious diseases, including diphtheria and scarlet fever, the incidence rate dropped precipitously long before pharmacologic interventions were developed to counteract the responsible microorganism. Based on the published work of McKeown (1976) and others, McKinlay and McKinlay attributed the decline in infectious diseases to improved nutrition and decreased exposure to infection through improved hygiene. McKinlay and McKinlay concluded that only about 3.5% of the total decline in mortality since 1900 could be attributed to medical interventions. Thus, they argued that changes in environmental conditions, not the control of disease-causing microorganisms, were responsible for the dramatic improvements in public health that occurred during the first half of the 20th century.

In any event, as infectious diseases declined as the leading causes of mortality in the United States, they were eclipsed by chronic diseases such as coronary heart disease (CHD), cancer, and stroke, which by 1990 accounted for more than 60% of the death rate (Centers for Disease Control and Prevention [CDC], 1996). As scientists attempted to find specific causal agents in the development of cancer and CHD throughout most of the 20th century, they became increasingly frustrated. Unable to identify single causes that could satisfy Koch's postulates, attention shifted from the search for single causative agents to the role of the environment and host in the pathogenesis of chronic diseases.

The landmark study for the rethinking of the pathogenesis of chronic diseases was the Framingham heart disease study initiated in the early 1950s. Using a prospective, longitudinal research design, the investigators collected behavioral, clinical, and demographic information on more than 6,000 men between ages 30 and 60 years (Dawber, Meadors, & Moore, 1991). Within 10 years, the investigators prospectively identified three leading risk factors for CHD as smoking, elevated cholesterol, and high blood pressure (Kannel, Dawber, Kagan, Revotskie, & Stokes, 1961). Whereas the single cause-and-effect model had proven successful in studying the genesis of infectious disease, an explanation for the causes of chronic diseases has had to turn to probabilistic models based on the presence of risk factors. The identification of risk factors makes the prediction of chronic diseases more likely, but individual risk factors cannot be seen as necessary and sufficient causes of disease. Scientists are still searching for primary causes of some diseases, but there is increasing recognition that to understand any disease, the interactions among agent, host, and environment are critical.

At the outset of the risk-factor revolution, it was widely thought that the causes of chronic diseases such as CHD could be explained in terms of a few biological (e.g., high cholesterol, high blood pressure) and lifestyle (e.g., smoking) risk factors. This was not the case. For example, the relationship between cholesterol and CHD soon led to a need to distinguish between low-density and high-density lipoprotein cholesterol. Likewise, the search for lifestyle risk factors led to an expanded list of risk factors including physical inactivity and a variety of consummatory activities. In addition, experimental behavioral research using appropriate animal models of human pathology, clinical studies of individuals predisposed to disease, and population-based studies of associations between behavioral–psychosocial variables and disease have extended the list of risk factors for

TABLE 1.1

Average Annual Number of Deaths in the United States, 1988–1992

Rank	Cause of Death	No. of Total Deaths	%
1	Heart disease	723,636	34
2	All cancer	497,545	23
	Lung	(138,742)	(7)
	Colorectal	(56,616)	(3)
	Prostate	(31,658)	(1)
	Breast	(42,551)	(2)
3	Stroke	143,284	7
4	Unintentional injuries	89,395	4
5	Chronic obstructive pulmonary disorder	86,470	4
6	Pneumonia and influenza	76,338	4
7	Diabetes	45,937	2
8	Suicide	29,872	1
9	Liver disease	25,303	1
10	HIV/AIDS	25,175	1
11	Homicide	23,632	1
	Firearm homicide	(15,769)	(1)
	All causes	2,131,977	

Note. Reprinted from *Atlas of United States Mortality* (DHHS Publication No. PHS-97-1015), by Centers for Disease Control and Prevention, 1996, p. 13. Hyattsville, MD: Author.

disease to include multiple psychosocial and behavioral variables (National Heart, Lung, and Blood Institute [NHLBI], 1998).

Behavioral, psychosocial, and sociocultural factors associated with lifestyle are major contributors to morbidity and mortality in the United States and significantly contribute to the leading causes of death (U.S. Surgeon General, 1990). As seen in Table 1.1, the 11 major causes of death are heart disease, cancer, cerebrovascular disease (stroke), unintentional injuries, chronic obstructive pulmonary disease, pneumonia and influenza, diabetes, suicide, chronic liver disease and cirrhosis, HIV infection, and homicide (CDC, 1996).

Death rates from heart disease have declined during the past 30 years, but it remains the leading cause of death in the United States (American Heart Association, 1996). Of these deaths, two thirds are attributable to CHD. The responsible behavioral and lifestyle factors include cigarette smoking, diet high in saturated fat, physical inactivity, obesity, and excess consumption of alcohol. Individual characteristics such as anger and depression also have been implicated, as have social and environmental variables including socioeconomic status, ethnicity, lack of social support, and occupational stress (NHLBI, 1998).

Age-adjusted death rates for all cancer sites combined have changed little in the United States during the past two decades (CDC, 1996), but incidence rates have increased about 1.3% per year (Kosary, Ries, & Miller, 1996). During the past 30 years, lung cancer has been the leading cause of cancer mortality in men; for the past decade, it has been the major cause of cancer deaths in women (American Cancer Society, 1994). The primary risk factor for lung cancer is cigarette smoking, which is associated with such factors as number of cigarettes smoked, duration of smoking, and use of unfiltered cigarettes (Ginsberg, Kris, & Armstrong, 1993).

The third leading cause of death in the United States is stroke, which has steadily declined throughout the 20th century (NHLBI, 1994). Risk factors associated with lifestyle include untreated hypertension, cigarette smoking, obesity, and excessive alcohol consumption.

The fourth leading cause of death in the United States is accidents, which peak between ages 15 and 24 years, then rise again after age 60 (CDC, 1996). Nearly half of all deaths in young people are motor vehicle-related, whereas falls are the leading cause of unintentional injury among older people. Young people, particularly young men, are prone to unintentional injuries often related to high-risk behavior (Baker, O'Neill, Ginsberg, & Li, 1992). This often is exacerbated by the use of alcohol.

Behavioral, psychosocial, sociocultural, and lifestyle factors are related to the other major causes of mortality as well. Among cases of chronic obstructive pulmonary disease, 90% are caused by smoking (NHLBI, 1998). Major risk factors for pneumonia are related to disruptions of natural pulmonary host defense mechanisms, which can include cigarette smoking and alcohol abuse (Donowitz & Mandell, 1995). Approximately 90% of all cases of diabetes mellitus consist of noninsulin-dependent diabetes in which obesity, often linked to poor diet and physical inactivity, is a major factor (Pareschi & Tomasi, 1989). Suicide has been related to alcohol abuse, depression, and stressful life events including loss of a spouse (Monk, 1987). Heavy use of alcohol is a major risk factor for chronic liver disease and cirrhosis (CDC, 1993). In the United States, infection from HIV is primarily spread through high-risk sexual practices and the sharing of contaminated drug paraphernalia (Auerbach, Wypijewska, & Brodie, 1994). These risks are exacerbated by alcohol or drug abuse. Finally, homicide is a leading cause of death within the United States and the leading cause of death in Black men between ages 15 and 24 (CDC, 1996). Major behavioral and psychosocial factors associated with homicide include poverty, firearm availability, alcohol and drug abuse, and cultural acceptance of violent behavior (CDC, 1990).

CONTROLLING MORBIDITY AND MORTALITY

The remarkable medical accomplishments of the late 19th century led to the identification of the primary etiological microorganisms responsible for almost all known infectious diseases. Use of immunizations and antibiotics produced impressive results in reducing disease burdens. They also led to the reductionist belief that if only we "knew enough," medical and biological concepts would be fully explicable in physicochemical terms. A more contemporary version of this argument would be that if only we had increased information about the fundamentals of cellular and molecular biology and fully understood the human genome, the illnesses that still plague us could be eradicated.

In contrast to this pure reductionist approach, a complementary view has emerged that it is not only etiologic agents that must be identified, but also the interactions among these agents, the host, and the environment; these must then be understood and controlled to prevent and cure most human afflictions. According to Engel (1981), for example, "the biochemical effect constitutes but one factor among many, the complex interaction of which may culminate in active disease or manifest illness" (p. 131). Thus, contemporary approaches to medicine and public health have begun to include the study of risk factors as well as interactions, often behavioral, that occur among agents, host, and the environment. Further, emphasis has shifted in public health from a focus on the individual to a focus on the population or community.

Individual Versus Population-Based Approaches to Disease Prevention

The control over most causes of morbidity and mortality has been dichotomized into a clinical or high-risk approach on the one hand and a population-based strategy on the other. Consistent with this distinction is the view that individual health care providers place a higher value on providing help to those who need it most, leading these providers to focus on individual patients at high risk for disability and death. Conversely, public health providers are essentially committed to primary prevention to provide the most benefit to the most people. Part of the justification for the population-based strategy can be seen in the example of CHD, in which most coronary events and deaths attributable to the disease occur in people with only a moderate elevation of risk (Rose, 1992).

Although there is some utility in distinguishing between high-risk and population-based strategies, there is also some agreement that individual- and population-based strategies are complementary because neither approach is effective for all behaviors or all target groups (Jeffery, 1989). Thus, it may be argued that an important task is to identify which risk behaviors are most amenable to individual-based versus population-based interventions and how to make these interventions synergistic with one another. With such thoughts in mind, Schneiderman and Orth-Gomér defined *behavioral medicine* as the interdisciplinary field concerned with the development and integration of biomedical, behavioral, psychosocial, and sociocultural science knowledge and techniques relevant to the understanding of health and illness, and the application of this knowledge and these techniques to disease prevention, diagnosis, treatment, rehabilitation, and health promotion. (1996, p. 280)

The key features of the definition are twofold. First, it defines an interdisciplinary field encompassing biomedical, behavioral, psychosocial, and sociocultural science. Second, it encompasses approaches to health and illness that include both clinical, high-risk (e.g., diagnosis, treatment, rehabilitation) and population-based (e.g., disease prevention, health promotion) strategies.

In terms of prevention, the concepts of primary, secondary, and tertiary prevention are often distinguished (Last, 1988). *Primary prevention* refers to measures taken to reduce the incidence of disease. In the case of CHD, for example, individuals may be encouraged to quit smoking, decrease intake of dietary fat, and increase physical activity. *Secondary prevention* involves reducing the prevalence of disease by shortening its duration and limiting adverse physiological and psychological effects. Screening programs are examples of secondary prevention strategies. Breast cancer mortality is decreased by the early detection of breast cancer through the use of mammograms. *Tertiary prevention* involves reducing the complications associated with the disease process and minimizing disability and suffering. In patients with chronic AIDS, for example, medication adherence training may be considered as a form of tertiary prevention.

Sometimes the boundaries of prevention strategies are indistinct, and a given intervention may address a combination of primary, secondary, and tertiary interventions. Figure 1.1 shows how a group-based cognitive–behavioral therapy intervention may address primary and tertiary prevention needs in HIV/AIDS-infected men and women (Schneiderman, 1999). In this instance, the group-based intervention is intended to improve adherence to highly active antiretroviral medication therapy (tertiary prevention) both by providing skills training in adherence and by decreasing distress. Concomitantly, the intervention is intended to promote harm reduction (primary prevention) by educating participants about the increased risk to themselves and others caused by continuing to engage in risky sex or share drug paraphernalia. Because these participants with HIV infection are already seropositive, improved harm-reduction behaviors have a high likelihood of penetrating the community of those already infected and significantly decreasing the incidence of new infections.

In addition to the concepts of primary, secondary, and tertiary prevention, Strasser (1978) coined the term "primordial prevention" to refer to activities that can prevent the penetration of risk factors into the population. An example of this would be the prevention of cigarette sales into

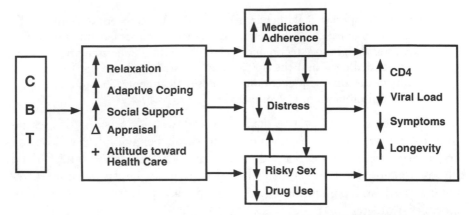

Figure 1.1. Conceptual diagram describing some possible pathways by which elements of the cognitive–behavior therapy (CBT) intervention may influence proximal (distress, medication adherence, substance abuse, risky sex) and distal (HIV disease progression) endpoints. Adapted from *Behavioral Medicine and the Management of HIV/AIDS* by N. Schneiderman. Copyright 1999 by the International Journal of Behavioral Medicine. Reprinted with permission.

countries where cigarette smoking has not yet begun. This issue is discussed further by Lynch in chapter 3.

Intervention Levels

The application of the behavioral and social sciences to improve health and combat disease occurs at many levels and requires the application of different skills both within and across levels. At the individual or interpersonal level, counseling of a suicidal patient, a violent sex offender, or a person recovering from cancer or who has just received a positive diagnosis of HIV infection are examples of such an intervention. Genetic counseling and screening for couples, family counseling to reduce substance abuse or intrafamilial violence, or group counseling to cope with issues such as myocardial infarction, HIV/AIDS, or violent behavior exemplify interventions at the interpersonal level. At the organizational level, individual or interpersonal interventions, as well as media communication, have been organized in schools, prisons, work sites, and community centers. Finally, societal type interventions involving the development of social norms through media and policy actions can occur at the community, state, or federal level.

To achieve public health objectives, it may be necessary to attack many intransigent problems at multiple levels. In this volume, for example, Chesney, Thurston, and Thomas in chapter 2 argue that to deal successfully with the problem of obesity, it is necessary to provide interventions at several levels. Chesney and her colleagues point out that although behavioral interventions administered at the individual level tend to produce successful weight loss in the short-term, they fail to produce sustained long-term weight loss in many cases. They suggest that for individual-based interventions to succeed, such interventions should take place in a socio-cultural environment that is supportive of healthful eating and conducive to exercise. According to Jeffery (1998), this could be accomplished by (a) improving the quality of the food supply, (b) enhancing accessibility of physical activity, (c) increasing advertising for healthy food options, (d) initiating mass-media campaigns supporting a healthy lifestyle, and (e) providing economic incentives for healthy eating by selective taxation (e.g., taxing sugar and some fats). In chapter 4, Puska and Uutela describe how such a multilevel approach reduced morbidity and mortality from CHD in North Karelia, Finland.

Although there is widespread agreement that multilevel approaches may be necessary to solve major public health problems, there is less agreement concerning the sequencing of the various interventions and how they reasonably can be assessed. Several clinical trials, for instance, have obtained mixed or inconclusive results, which at least in part have been attributed to secular trends or contextual factors (e.g., Multiple Risk Factor Intervention Trial [MRFIT], 1982). These factors may have been associated either with the trial itself or with other, possibly multilevel, intervention efforts.

Both the Oslo Heart Study in Norway (Hjermann, Velve-Byre, & Holme, 1981) and MRFIT (1982) in the United States identified high-risk individuals by screening and then intervened to reduce risk factors and CHD incidence. Whereas the Oslo Heart Study convincingly demonstrated significant differences between the intervention and control group in terms of risk-factor reduction and CHD incidence, the MRFIT did not. Both the Oslo Heart Study and the MRFIT, however, were successful in demonstrating evidence of risk-factor reduction associated with a significant decrease in CHD incidence when compared with previous population norms.

A problem with interpreting the MRFIT (1982) data is that many of the high-risk men in the control group apparently reduced risk behaviors on their own. Explanations for these findings have been attributed to several possible variables. First, having been labeled as high risk, some of the men may have responded by changing their behavior. Second, participating in a clinical trial in which they received physician and nurse attention may have provided some of these comparison group members with better medical monitoring than they otherwise might have received. Third, during the course of the MRFIT trial, substantial efforts were made concomitantly by the National High Blood Pressure Education Program (Roccella & Horan, 1988) and the pharmaceutical industry to increase the number of hypertensive individuals under adequate blood pressure control. Fourth, mass-media coverage of the ongoing MRFIT trial and its objectives was widespread, which may have convinced a significant number of comparison group participants to modify target risk factors. In any event, by the sixth annual examination in MRFIT, 47% of the comparison group members were taking antihypertensive drugs (which was considerably higher than expected), compared with 58% in the intervention group. With relatively small differences observed between the intervention and control groups, statistical significance was not achieved between groups for either risk-factor modification or CHD incidence.

The results of the Oslo Heart Study (Hjermann et al., 1981) suggest that behavioral interventions can reduce risk factors and decrease the incidence of CHD. Conversely, the findings from MRFIT (1982) provide a caution that before initiating a large-scale clinical trial, the interventions used should have sufficient power to provide a high likelihood of success. Fortunately, in the two decades since these pioneering behavioral intervention trials, important knowledge has emerged concerning behavioral and psychosocial risk factors on the one hand and behavioral techniques for modifying risk factors on the other (NHLBI, 1998). At the same time, the results of the Oslo and MRFIT studies provide a useful caution about the design of clinical intervention trials. In this volume, Murray (chapter 15) outlines strategies that are likely to be useful in designing group randomized trials in health promotion and disease prevention research. Goodman's discussion (chapter 14) provides a consideration of other design options that may be pursued when experimental designs may not be feasible.

EXPERIMENTAL DESIGN IN HEALTH AND BEHAVIOR RESEARCH

Flay (1986) described multiple steps in health promotion and disease prevention research ranging from basic research through efficacy and effectiveness trials to demonstration studies. One often-used, basic distinction is between efficacy trials and effectiveness trials. Briefly, efficacy trials are designed to test whether an intervention causes an observed effect under carefully controlled conditions. In this case, the investigator would have control over the content of the intervention, its delivery, and context. Conversely, treatment effectiveness trials are used to determine whether the treatment will remain effective when implemented under more natural or realistic conditions.

An example of an efficacy trial would be a cognitive–behavioral therapy intervention for individuals with HIV infection conducted in an academic setting with monetary incentives for participants, PhD-level therapists, and a retention specialist keeping track of participants throughout the study (Schneiderman, 1999). Once efficacy is established, an effectiveness trial might assess whether the intervention effects generalize when extended to multiple community health centers that do not use monetary incentives, a retention specialist, and imported PhD-level psychotherapists. To the extent that patients are used to coming to community health centers to meet their medical needs and transportation and other benefits may be available through the centers, the use of community health centers offers important trade-offs that could facilitate an effectiveness trial. Once effectiveness is established, a demonstration project could be created without the need for a randomized control group. At this stage, the intervention itself would be under community center control, although rigorous evaluation of the type suggested by Goodman should be required (chapter 14).

Design Issues

A major goal of science is to be able to make strong inferences concerning causality. The strongest inferences can be made with those designs that best limit alternative interpretations of results. In experiments, alternative interpretations are limited through stratified sampling, random assignment to groups, and rigorous specification of the independent and dependent variables (Campbell & Stanley, 1966; Cook & Campbell, 1979). These are the objectives for which scientists strive in randomized clinical trials.

Sometimes, however, the randomized clinical trial may severely limit the nature of the scientific question under examination. For example, if one wishes to know whether a particular initiative can modify the health behavior of an entire population, the randomized clinical trial design may not be appropriate. In this case a quasi-experimental design may be more useful. In this volume, Puska and Uutela (chapter 4), describe a population-based intervention for reducing CHD risk factors, morbidity, and mortality in North Karelia, Finland, that has provided more than a quarter century of experience (Puska, 1996). The project used lay-leader training, television programs, stop-smoking contests, school and work-site interventions, and collaboration with housewives' organizations, the food industry, and supermarkets. Initially, comparisons were made between the target area (North Karelia) and a comparison area (Kuopio), although after 10 years the interventions became part of a national policy and took on more of the characteristics of a demonstration project. The basic findings of the study were that serum cholesterol and smoking decreased more rapidly in North Karelia than in Kuopio during the first 10 years of the study; this was accompanied by a concomitant decrease in CHD mortality (Tuomi-lehto et al., 1989).

Quasi-experimental designs are attractive because they allow us to address important population-based questions. They must be approached with caution, however, because lacking rigorous experimental control, it is difficult to rule out alternative hypotheses as a way of understanding the factors that influence the dependent variables. Thus, for example, in comparing the impact of a needle-exchange program on injection-needle use practices among drug abusers, comparisons may be drawn between a community with a needle-exchange program and one without such a program. Even after using logic, reasoning, and knowledge of the experimental domain to rule out obvious confoundings, including community attitudes and police practices, confidence in the results would tend to become more robust as the number of intervention and control communities studied increases. When only one site or a small number of comparison sites is used, the possibility of a secular trend, an unexpected happening (e.g., a police crackdown), or obscure variables confounding the results may limit confidence in the results.

APPLICATION OF THEORY TO HEALTH AND BEHAVIOR PROBLEMS

Theories and models are helpful in health and behavior research to inform the design of intervention approaches and to guide the implementation of interventions. Many of the theories and models in common use have been described by Glanz, Lewis, and Rimer (1997).

Several prominent theories will be reviewed here. One of the first models specifically developed to explain health behavior was the health belief model (Becker, 1974; Rosenstock, 1966). This model was originally developed to explain adoption or nonadoption of preventive health behaviors, such as checkups and immunizations, but was later applied to sick-role behavior, adherence to medical regimens, and health promotion behaviors. The basis of the theory is that knowledge of perceived susceptibility, severity, benefits, and barriers jointly predict health behaviors. When the model has been used to predict the types of behavior for which it was originally intended (e.g., checkups and immunization), it has been successful (Cummings, Jette, Brock, & Haefner, 1979). In contrast, when more complex behaviors, such as smoking initiation, have been studied, beliefs about the severity of smoking-related disease and the benefits of smoking do not predict which adolescents will start smoking (Flay, 1985).

Social–cognitive theory as developed by Bandura (1986) assumes that healthy functioning is determined by the interactions among behavioral, physiological, and cognitive factors and the environment. The theory assumes that self-efficacy is the perception of being able to accomplish objectives necessary to obtain a desired outcome. Attainment of this goal leads to increased positive feelings toward oneself, which can serve as a motivation for change. The theory has been useful in predicting maintenance of physical activity (Sallis, Hovell, & Hofstetter, 1992), smoking relapse (Condiotte & Lichtenstein, 1981), and other health behaviors.

To the extent that stress may influence health behaviors and disease processes, cognitive–behavioral therapy has provided a theoretical model for teaching individuals to reduce their stress, evaluate their appraisals of potentially stressful situations more accurately, and improve coping skills. According to Beck (1976) systematic negative distortions about the future, the self, and others cause many of the components of depression and maladaptive coping responses. Specific applications of cognitive–behavioral therapy have been used in the management of asthma (Bartlett, 1983), rheumatoid arthritis (Parker et al., 1989), low-back pain (Turner, 1982), postmyocardial infarction (Friedman et al., 1986), HIV (Esterling et al., 1992), and malignant melanoma (Fawzy, Fawzy, Hyun, Guthrie, Fahey, & Morton, 1993). The study by Fawzy and colleagues is particularly noteworthy because it demonstrated that the intervention not only influenced affective state and coping positively, but also melanoma recurrence and the 6-year survival rate. It should be noted that many recent applications of cognitive–behavioral therapy to health problems have used a group format and have been concerned not only with the appraisal and management of stress responses but also with promoting self-efficacy, providing social support and health education, and offering adaptive coping, life skills, and harm-reduction training (Schneiderman, 1999). The use of a group format not only permits the therapist to reach more individuals, thus providing improvements in cost–benefits and diffusion of behavior change innovations into the community, but also provides interpersonal and intrapersonal approaches to treatment.

The theory of reasoned action (Ajzen & Fishbein, 1980) and its more recent variant, the theory of planned behavior (Ajzen, 1988) are concerned with the role of anticipated material and social consequences in people's decisions and intentions to engage in health-related behaviors. Briefly, the theory states that intentions are the most immediate influence on behavior. Intentions are influenced by attitudes and subjective norms. Attitudes are determined by the most prominent beliefs about what would happen as a consequence of behavior. Subjective norms are affected primarily by pressures from significant others. Finally, intentions to perform a behavior become stronger once people perceive that they have control over that behavior. The theory of reasoned action has been used to predict smoking and exercise behaviors (Carter, 1990) but has not yet provided explicit strategies for changing behavior.

The transtheoretical model (Prochaska & DiClemente, 1984) was based on the observation that people appear to go through similar stages of change no matter what therapy is applied. The basic theses of the model are that (a) different intervention approaches are needed for people at different stages of behavior change and (b) different processes of change may be occurring at each stage. Briefly, Prochaska and DiClemente distinguished six stages in the process of behavior change. These are precontemplation, contemplation, preparation for action, action, maintenance, and relapse.

Prochaska and DiClemente (1984) used the term *transtheoretical* to indicate that people in different stages of change have to be approached with different intervention strategies, based on different theories, because they have different needs. Thus, precontemplators need to receive information concerning the disadvantages of maintaining current risk behavior and the advantages of changing behavior. Once having reached the contemplation stage, these individuals should be motivated to make specific plans to change behavior and set goals. During the preparation stage, people should be offered interventions that increase self-efficacy, skills, and social support. At the action stage, people need motivation and reinforcement to maintain their changed behavior. During the maintenance stage, relapse prevention strategies should be implemented to prevent backsliding. Finally, in the relapse stage, people must learn to treat this as a limited, minor setback rather than as a defeat; strategies need to be implemented to get the person to return to the contemplation, preparation for action, or action stages. The transtheoretical model has been studied extensively in smoking cessation (DiClemente, Prochaska, Fairhurst, Velicer, Velasquez, & Rossi, 1991) and also in promoting exercise (Marcus, Selby, Niaura, & Rossi, 1992), weight control (O'Connell & Velicer, 1988), alcohol treatment (DiClemente & Hughes, 1990), and mammography (Rakowski, Fulton, & Feldman, 1993).

Because public health problems may be best addressed at multiple levels (i.e., intrapersonal, interpersonal, organizational, and societal), social action theory was developed specifically to integrate social–cognitive models into a public health framework (Ewart, 1991). Briefly, the theory is designed to (a) analyze health behaviors (e.g., unprotected high-risk sex), (b) integrate individual self-change processes (e.g., problem anticipation, planning, role playing) that may be initiated to generate desired patterns, and (c) coordinate the self-change processes with contextual factors (e.g., school-based education, increased condom availability, public health messages) that support self-protective activity.

The models that we have described thus far offer theories of behavior change. Once a program has been demonstrated to be effective, the question is how to get it to be used widely so as to benefit the health of larger populations. Thus, McGuire (1981) has developed a communication–behavior change model describing how to sequence a media campaign and Rogers (1983) has presented a diffusion of innovations model to describe the channels that can be used to communicate health innovations. Finally, Green and Kreuter (1991) have created the PRECEDE–PROCEED model to provide a framework for putting health behavior programs together in a manner that can be delivered to a large number of people at a realistic cost.

McGuire's (1981) communication–behavior change model suggests that to design an effective public communication campaign, one should consider five input and 12 output factors. The five input factors that need to be considered are source, message, channel, receiver, and destination. In considering the *source*, attention must be paid to the credibility of the spokesperson and his or her ability to relate to the intended audience. *Message* factors include what and how the message is presented. The *channel* is the medium through which the message is transmitted and involves cost, number of people to be reached, and whether a "sound-bite" or a more complex message is to be sent. *Receiver* refers to the target audience and involves knowledge of their characteristics, likes, and dislikes. Finally, the *destination* is the intended outcome desired, such as actually placing infant car seats in the rear of vehicles rather than just knowing that it is a good idea.

The output factors in McGuire's (1981) model involve specifying a 12-step sequence of events: exposure to the situation, attending to it, becoming interested in it, comprehending, skill acquisition, attitude change, memory storage of content, information retrieval, deciding on basis of information retrieval, behaving in accord with the decision, reinforcement of desired acts, and finally the maintenance of the behavior. Examination of the communication–behavior change model provides important insights into the difficulties posed in using the media to develop a stable new habit. Thus, for example, even after attracting a receiver's attention, 10 more steps are still needed before the new habit is consolidated. Various aspects of McGuire's model have been tested in communication campaigns to reduce tobacco consumption, improve use of family planning services, and prevent heart disease (Rice & Atkin, 1989).

Rogers' (1983) diffusion of innovation model is similar to the stages of change concept insofar as it suggests that different groups of people require different strategic approaches if they are to adopt a particular health behavior. Thus, Rogers suggested that potential adopters include innovators, early adopters, early majority adopters, late majority adopters, and laggards. The model has been used widely in a variety of disease prevention programs, and Howze and Redman (1992) used the model to implement a strategy for diffusion of health promotion throughout Virginia.

The PRECEDE–PROCEED model (Green & Kreuter, 1991) is intended as a guide for designing and evaluating health promotion programs intended to change the health behaviors of large groups. The model first asks planners to determine if a program is needed (phases 1–5) and then decide how they would go about implementation (phase 6) and evaluation (phases 6–9).

Phase 1 (social diagnosis) involves determining if a problem exists that disrupts the quality of life of the target group. In phase 2 (epidemiological diagnosis), the question is couched in terms of health problems.

Phase 3 (behavioral and environmental diagnosis) asks what behavioral and environmental factors are related to the epidemiological diagnosis. In phase 4 (educational and organizational factors), questions are raised about the predisposing, reinforcing, and enabling factors that are likely to have the most direct effects on the target behaviors. Phase 5 (administrative diagnosis) asks what resources, time constraints, and abilities must be considered in carrying out the program.

Phase 6 (implementation) consists of a detailed plan including the behavior change intervention procedures, how the population will be engaged, what organizations will need to be involved, and what administrative structure will be required. Phase 7 (process evaluation) is the assessment of whether the intervention changed the predisposing, reinforcing, and enabling factors. Phase 8 (impact evaluation) asks whether the important behavioral and environmental variables were changed. Finally, phase 9 (outcome evaluation) addresses the issues of whether the target population improved in terms of quality of life and physical health as a consequence of the intervention. Aspects of the PRECEDE–PROCEED model have been applied in numerous community, occupational, school, and health care settings (Green & Kreuter, 1991).

ABOUT THIS VOLUME

Toward the end of the 20th century, the need for better integrating behavior and social sciences into public health was increasingly recognized. In fact, coursework in social and behavioral sciences was a mandated component of the core curriculum in all schools of public health in the United States that sought accreditation. The integration of sociology, political science, and health economics provided a relatively easy fit into public health training because of the traditional public health emphasis on populations. In contrast, the application of behavioral science expertise into public health research and practice may have lagged somewhat because of its emphasis on the individual. By the end of the 20th century, however, it was apparent that many important public health problems require behavioral change in populations. Thus, there has been increasing awareness that the solution of many public health problems probably will require the use of interdisciplinary strategies focused on multiple levels (i.e., intrapersonal, interpersonal, organizational, and societal).

The selection of chapters and the organization of this volume presented the editors with a challenge. Although the behavioral, social science, and public health communities appear to be eager for further integration among disciplines, they tend to know different things. Thus, some information presented to behavioral scientists may seem redundant to those already trained in public health and vice versa. We hope, however, that the following messages will be conveyed to both constituencies: (a) knowledge and methods gained from the scientific study of individual behavior can be applied to public health problems, and (b) the resolution of many health problems requires attention to the organizational and societal level, as well as to the individual level.

Another problem posed in the development of this book was that the field has not yet absorbed a multilevel, interdisciplinary approach to public health issues. Therefore, instead of attempting to squeeze each chapter into a common template, we have provided the individual authors with an individual platform on which to address important behavioral and social sciences issues as they pertain to public health. At the same time, we have paired some chapters to explore the diversity of approaches used in various areas. Thus, in Part II, "Applying Behavioral and Social Science Approaches to Selected Public Health Problems," chapter 2 (obesity), chapter 9 (breast screening), and chapter 10 (unintentional injury) stand alone. Conversely, chapters 3 and 4 both deal with cardiovascular disease prevention: Chapter 3 focuses on the socioeconomic and psychosocial epidemiology of cardiovascular disease and chapter 4 on the most celebrated first-generation effort to alter community-wide risk for cardiovascular disease. Similarly, chapters 5 and 6 both deal with the topic of violence: Chapter 5 argues for moving beyond a focus on the individual to an ecological approach, and chapter 6 looks broadly at the issue of violence against women. Whereas chapters 7 and 8 both deal with HIV/AIDS, chapter 7 explores what is known about the link between HIV infection and injection drug use, and chapter 8 provides examples of community efforts that have been launched to stem the epidemic through behavioral change in high-risk populations. Considered as a group, the first six chapters of this volume provide a basic introduction to public health concepts and issues for those whose primary background is in behavior, whereas the next four chapters elucidate important public health problems and emphasize a community perspective.

Part III, "Conceptual and Methodological Considerations in the Integration of Behavioral and Social Sciences With Public Health," comprises seven chapters that address a variety of topics central to the integration of social science and behavioral approaches to public health issues. Among the topics discussed are the thorny methodological issues that must be addressed in evaluating behavioral and social science interventions. These include the need to develop and utilize alternative models of evaluating public health programs and the value of group randomized controlled trials in the evaluation of efficacy and effectiveness of health promotion and disease prevention programs. The chapters by Karasek (chapter 13) on the work environment and by Becker (chapter 17) on spirituality in public health are interesting thought pieces that are designed to expand our intellectual horizons.

In the design of the present volume, this chapter (by Schneiderman and Speers) is intended to provide a historical overview of the role of the behavioral and social sciences in public health and to develop the context for the chapters in the next section on "Applying Behavioral and Social Science Approaches to Selected Public Health Problems." Chapter 2 by Chesney, Thurston, and Thomas, using obesity as an example, addresses the issue of moving beyond individual-level behavior change to the broader goal of developing interventions at social and environmental levels. In chapter 3, Lynch explores how socioeconomic factors influence psychosocial risk and public health. Using cardiovascular disease as an example, Lynch persuasively argues that social conditions are a powerful determinant of health and disease throughout the life span. Chapter 4 eloquently describes the conceptual elements of the North Karelia Project, which was designed to reduce cardiovascular morbidity and mortality. Puska and Uutela do a fine job of considering individual-level theories and demonstrating their relevance to a community-wide intervention.

Chapter 5 focuses on pervasive community violence and how community-level efforts can be used to stem this violence. Lorion suggests a number of ways in which theory and methods used in psychology might be applied to public health issues while still attending to the multilevel nature of the problem. Chapter 6 is a clearly written review of violence by men against women. Cook and Koss indicate what needs to be done in the future, with consideration of opportunities to apply behavioral strategies. In chapter 7 Des Jarlais and Friedman provide a useful orientation to the risk of HIV infection among intravenous drug users and describe issues related to increasing the effectiveness of needle exchange programs. Similarly, in chapter 8 Kalichman, Somlai, and Sikkema outline a history of HIV prevention efforts at the community level. Although chapters 7 and 8 do not focus on the individual level, within the context of the present volume the reader can see where opportunities for individual- and community-level interventions could be interactive.

In chapter 9, Rimer, Meissner, Breen, Legler, and Coyne deal with social and behavioral interventions in breast cancer screening, providing an exhaustive literature review of an important topic. In chapter 10, Gielen and Girasek use the classic epidemiological framework of host-agent-environment analysis to demonstrate how behavioral interventions can be applied to preventing unintentional injuries. On the one hand, the chapter clearly addresses the relevance of approaches derived from psychology; on the other hand, it does an outstanding job of conveying an important public health tradition (host-agent-environment analysis) to readers who may be new to the field.

The final section of the book, titled "Conceptual and Methodological Considerations in the Integration of Behavioral and Social Sciences With Public Health," begins with chapter 11, which deals with community mobilization for disease prevention and health promotion. An objective of Wandersman is to show that community mobilization and participation can be an important cornerstone of public health initiatives and that such initiatives can be objectively evaluated. In chapter 12 Holtgrave and Pinkerton describe the major issues in cost-documentation, cost-benefit, and cost-effectiveness analyses of behavioral interventions. The next chapter, chapter 13, offers an intellectually compelling change of pace in the form of a provocative essay about the need to expand the role of psychology and sociology in the study of work environments. Karasek makes a challenging call to action for public health scientists to expand their horizons.

Chapter 14 by Goodman provides an important perspective on how community-level interventions can be evaluated when classical experimental designs are not feasible. Conversely, chapter 15 by Murray provides an excellent discussion of the design of trials to assess efficacy and effectiveness. Whereas scientists from a behavioral background are trained in randomized designs in which the unit of randomization is the individual, chapter 15 introduces the reader to the randomization of groups, which is often appropriate in large-scale public health trials. Thus, chapters 14 and 15 together provide important building blocks for constructing a multilevel public health model for research and practice.

In chapter 16 Fetterman provides a detailed presentation of the principles and conceptual underpinnings of empowerment evaluation followed by a case example. Finally, chapter 17 explores relationships among spirituality, religion, and public health. Becker does a fine job of reviewing the evidence base of research in the area. Although this base is somewhat weak and uneven, the author has been able to pinpoint important issues that deserve further study.

It is clear from this introduction that this book is not intended to provide an exhaustive review of behavioral science, social science, or public health. Because the chapters are written from the perspectives of various disciplines, they are by no means uniform. Thus, some of the chapters work well at one level, and others work well at another. Our hope is that when readers are finished with this volume they will appreciate the direction that science has taken in moving toward interdisciplinary, multilevel approaches to public health research and practice.

A basic thread running through this volume is that the solution to important public health problems depends on these interdisciplinary, multilevel approaches. The public health community already has a rich tradition of epidemiological analysis of host–agent–environmental interactions. Behavioral scientists can contribute to these analyses by providing insight into behavioral change occurring at different levels of analyses. Similarly, social scientists provide important insights into organizational structure at the community level, including the utilization of community action, government, and health economic strategies. This volume represents an early attempt to call attention to the feasibility of these joint efforts among behavioral, social sciences, and public health perspectives.

SUMMARY AND CONCLUSION

This chapter has attempted to show why and how the behavioral and social sciences are making major contributions to understanding and solving the important public health problems confronting us as we enter the new millennium. During the first half of the 20th century, the occurrence of many infectious diseases declined in the United States, and chronic diseases replaced them as the leading causes of mortality. Most of these chronic diseases appear to be multiply determined and involve lifestyle risk factors that have major behavioral, psychosocial, and sociocultural contributions. Thus, to understand almost all major causes of mortality in the United States, it is necessary to study the behavioral, psychosocial, and sociocultural variables that contribute to these deaths.

The control over most causes of morbidity and mortality involves the use of behavioral–social sciences interventions. Application of these interventions occurs at many levels and requires the application of different skills both within and across levels. Thus, for many individual-based (i.e., intrapersonal, interpersonal) interventions to succeed, they may have to take place in a sociocultural environment that also involves concomitant population-based (i.e., organizational, societal) interventions. This is discussed explicitly in this volume in chapters 2 and 4 but appears implicitly throughout the volume in discussions of community interventions for cardiovascular health promotion, cancer screening, and decreasing urban violence.

This volume reflects the current state of public health practice by focusing primarily on behavioral and social factors that prevent disease through the use of community-based interventions. As discussed earlier, the epidemiological transition from infectious to chronic diseases in the U.S. population was accompanied by a delayed shift from primarily clinical interventions targeted to individuals to behavioral and social interventions targeted to populations. As we enter the 21st century, in which the contribution of environmental and social factors (e.g., poverty, illiteracy) on health is likely to increase, community-based behavioral and social interventions will become even more essential to preventing disease and improving quality of life.

Although the emphasis of this particular volume is on primary prevention, it should be pointed out that many people can benefit from secondary and tertiary prevention. As pointed out in chapter 8, there are 31 million persons infected with HIV worldwide and more than 1 million living in the United States. Thus, in addition to the need for population-based strategies to combat HIV/AIDS, individual-based interventions would also be useful in facilitating harm reduction (primary prevention) strategies in HIV-infected communities and in serving those infected with chronic disease. Similarly, individual-based interventions with substance abusers, people infected with HIV, and violent offenders can complement population-based community strategies.

The design of intervention approaches is central to the role of behavioral–social sciences research into public health problems. Effort therefore needs to be expended in determining how to move from basic research to efficacy trials and when and how to move from efficacy to effectiveness trials. Decisions about whether to use a group-randomized controlled clinical trial or a quasi-experimental design have to be made with full knowledge of the advantages and drawbacks of each. Ideally, quasi-experimental designs should be carried out at multiple sites so that conclusions are not based on a single comparison. Comparisons across multiple sites minimize the likelihood that secular trends, unforeseen happenings, or overlooked variables may contaminate results.

In the application of behavioral and psychosocial interventions to public health problems, theories and models can help inform the design of the intervention and its implementation. Among the many theoretical formulations that have informed such research, this chapter has reviewed the health belief, social–cognitive, cognitive–behavioral, planned behavior, transtheoretical, and social action theory models. These models generally are directed toward understanding how and when behavior change can be facilitated.

Once a behavior change strategy is adopted, the issue becomes how to get the strategy to be used to benefit the health of a substantial portion of a population. Both the communication–behavior change model of McGuire (1981) and the diffusion of innovations model of Rogers (1983) provide useful insights concerning the transmission of behavior change messages into communities. The PRECEDE–PROCEED model of Green and Kreuter (1991) provides a useful guide for designing and evaluating health promotion programs.

As we look toward the future, the interdisciplinary, multilevel strategies described in this volume will become increasingly important. Whereas public health initiatives during the second half of the 20th century tended to focus on the identification of public health risk factors, strategies during the 21st century are likely to focus increasingly on problems that require behavioral change. Whereas the gradient relating socioeconomic status and health has grown steeper within the United States during the past quarter century, studies by Lynch (chapter 3) and others have shown that this gradient can change across the life span. Thus, although scientists may not be able to deal directly with the distribution of national wealth per se, they may well be able to facilitate behavioral changes that help those at the lower end of the gradient improve their health. New improvements in technology including computer-based communication systems and increased potential for tailoring messages for the general population may be of some help. Increasingly the population of the United States will also become more diverse. Therefore, studies relating behavioral change to improved public health will have to become increasingly sensitive to cultural issues. As we explore the new millennium, improved knowledge of behavior change and sociocultural issues will be increasingly important as we design public health interventions. It is noteworthy that both the National Institutes of Health and the CDC have become increasingly attuned to these issues and are spearheading research into public health interventions that are culturally sensitive and use behavior change strategies.

A major challenge to the formulation of public health interventions is how to coordinate such interventions across multiple levels. It has become apparent that many interventions at the intrapersonal and interpersonal level need to be reinforced at the organizational and societal level if they are to succeed. Similarly, it is unlikely that many organizational and societal campaigns will be fully effective unless reinforced by behavior change strategies directed at the individual and interpersonal level. The challenge of integrating the behavioral and social sciences with public health in the 21st century rests on the use of transdisciplinary approaches to solve both clinical, high-risk and population-based public health problems.

REFERENCES

Ajzen, I. (1988). *Attitudes, personality and behavior*. Chicago: Dorsey Press.

Ajzen, I., & Fishbein, M. (1980). *Understanding attitudes and predicting social behavior*. Englewood Cliffs, NJ: Prentice-Hall.

American Cancer Society. (1994). Cancer facts and figures. Atlanta, GA: American Cancer Society.

American Heart Association. (1996). *Heart and stroke facts* [Brochure]. Dallas, TX.

Auerbach, J. D., Wypijewska, C., & Brodie, H. K. H. (Eds.). (1994). *AIDS and behavior: An integrated approach*. Washington, DC: National Academy Press.

Baker, S. P., O'Neill, B., Ginsberg, M. J., & Li, G. (1992). *The injury fact book*. New York: Oxford University Press.

Bandura, A. (1986). *Social foundations of thought and action*. Englewood Cliffs, NJ: Prentice-Hall.

Bartlett, E. E. (1983). Educational self-help approaches in childhood asthma. *Journal of Allergy and Clinical Immunology, 72*, 545–554.

Beck, A. T. (1976). *Cognitive therapy and the emotional disorders*. New York: International Universities Press.

Becker, M. H. (Ed.). (1974). The health belief model and personal health behavior. *Health Education Monographs, 2,* 324–473.

Campbell, D., & Stanley, J. (1966). *Experimental and quasi-experimental designs for research.* Chicago: Rand McNally.

Carter, W. B. (1990). Health behavior as a rational process: Theory of reasoned action and multiattribute utility theory. In K. Glanz, F. M. Lewis, & B. K. Rimer (Eds.), *Health behavior and health education: Theory, research, and practice* (pp. 63–91). San Francisco: Jossey-Bass.

Centers for Disease Control. (1990). Homicide among young black males—United States, 1978–1987. *Morbidity and Mortality Weekly Report, 39,* 869–873.

Centers for Disease Control and Prevention. (1993). Deaths and hospitalizations from chronic liver disease and cirrhosis—United States, 1980–1989. *Morbidity and Mortality Weekly Report, 41,* 969–973.

Centers for Disease Control and Prevention. (1996). Atlas of United States mortality (DHHS Publication No. PHS-97-1015). Hyattsville, MD: Author.

Condiotte, M. M., & Lichtenstein, E. (1981). Self-efficacy and relapse in smoking cessation programs. *Journal of Consulting and Clinical Psychology, 49,* 648–658.

Cook, T., & Campbell, D. (1979). *Quasi-experimentation: Designs and analysis issues for field settings.* Chicago: Rand McNally.

Cummings, K., Jette, A., Brock, B., & Haefner, D. (1979). Psychosocial determinants of immunization behavior in a swine influenza campaign. *Medical Care, 17,* 639–649.

Dawber, T., Meadors, G., & Moore, F. (1991). Epidemiological approaches to heart disease: The Framingham Study. *American Journal of Public Health, 41,* 279–286.

DeClemente, C. C., & Hughes, S. O. (1990). Stages of change profiles in outpatient alcoholism treatment. *Journal of Substance Abuse, 2,* 217–235.

DiClemente, R. J., Prochaska, J. O., Fairhurst, S. K., Velicer, W. F., Velasquez, M. M., & Rossi, J. S. (1991). The process of smoking cessation: An analysis of precontemplation, contemplation, and preparation stages of change. *Journal of Consulting and Clinical Psychology, 59,* 295–304.

Donowitz, G. R., & Mandell, G. L. (1995). Acute pneumonia. In G. L. Mandell, J. E. Bennett, & R. Dolin (Eds.), *Principles and practice of infectious diseases* (pp. 619–636). New York: Churchill Livingstone.

Dubos, R. (1959). *The mirage of health.* New York: Harper.

Eaton, R. M. (Ed.). (1927). *Selections of René Descartes.* New York: Charles Scribner & Sons.

Engel, G. (1981). The clinical application of the biopsychosocial model. *Journal of Medicine and Philosophy, 6,* 128–135.

Esterling, B. A., Antoni, M. H., Schneiderman, N., Carver, C. S., LaPerriere, A., Ironson, G., Klimas, N., & Fletcher, M. A. (1992). Psychosocial modulation of antibody to Epstein-Barr viral capsid antigen and human herpes virus type-6 in HIV-1-infected and at-risk gay men. *Psychosomatic Medicine, 54,* 354–371.

Ewart, C. K. (1991). Social action theory for a public health psychology. *American Psychologist, 46*, 931–946.

Fawzy, F. I., Fawzy, N. W., Hyun, C. S., Guthrie, D., Fahey, J. L., & Morton, D. L. (1993). Malignant melanoma: Effects of an early structured psychiatric intervention, coping, and affective state on recurrence and survival 6 years later. *Archives of General Psychiatry, 50*, 681–689.

Flay, B. R. (1985). Psychosocial approaches to smoking prevention: A review of findings. *Health Psychology, 4*, 449–488.

Flay, B. R. (1986). Efficacy and effectiveness trials (and other phases of research) in the development of health promotion programs. *Prevention Medicine, 15*, 451–474.

Friedman, M., Thoresen, C. E., Gill, J., Ulmer, D., Powell, L. H., Price, V. A., Brown, B., Thompson, L., Rabin, D. D., Breall, W. S., Bourg, W., Levy, R., & Dixon, T. (1986). Alteration of Type A behavior and its effects on cardiac recurrences in post-myocardial infarction patients: Summary results of the Recurrent Coronary Prevention Project. *American Heart Journal, 112*, 653–665.

Ginsberg, R. J., Kris, M. G., & Armstrong, J. G. (1993). Cancer of the lung. In V. T. DeVita, Jr., S. Hellman, & S. A. Rosenberg (Eds.), *Cancer: Principles and practice of oncology* (pp. 673–758). Philadelphia: Lippincott.

Glanz, K., Lewis, F. M., & Rimer, B. K. (1997). *Health behavior and health education: Theory, research, and practice.* San Francisco: Jossey-Bass.

Green, L. W., & Kreuter, M. W. (1991). *Health promotion planning: An educational and environmental approach.* Mountain View, CA: Mayfield.

Hjermann, I., Velve-Byre, K., & Holme, I. (1981). Effect of diet and smoking intervention on the incidence of coronary heart disease. Report from the Oslo Study Group of a randomized trial in healthy men. *Lancet, 2*, 1303–1310.

Howze, E. H., & Redman, L. J. (1992). The uses of theory in health advocacy: Policies and programs. *Health Education Quarterly, 19*, 369–383.

Jeffery, R. W. (1989). Risk behaviors and health: Contrasting individual and population perspectives. *American Psychologist, 44*, 1194–1202.

Jeffery, R. W. (1998). Prevention of obesity. In G. A Bray, C. Bouchard, & W. P. T. James (Eds.), *Handbook of obesity* (pp. 819–829). New York: Dekker.

Kannel, W., Dawber, T., Kagan, A., Revotskie, N., & Stokes, J. (1961). Factors of risk in the development of coronary heart disease—Six-year follow-up experience: The Framingham Study. *Annals of Internal Medicine, 55*, 33–49.

King, L. B. (1982). *Medical thinking: A historical preface.* Princeton, NJ: Princeton University Press.

Kosary, C. L., Ries, L. A. G., & Miller, B. A. (Eds.). (1996). *SEER cancer statistics review, 1973–1992: Tables and graphs, National Cancer Institute* (DHHS Publication No. NIH-96–2789). Washington, DC: U.S. Government Printing Office.

Last, J. M. (Ed.). (1988). *A dictionary of epidemiology.* New York: Oxford University Press.

Marcus, B. H., Selby, V. C., Niaura, R. S., & Rossi, J. S. (1992). Self-efficacy and the stages of exercise behavior change. *Research Quarterly for Exercise and Sport, 63*, 60–66.

McGuire, W. J. (1981). Theoretical foundations of campaigns. In R. E. Rice & W. J. Paisley (Eds.), *Public communications campaigns* (pp. 41–70). Beverly Hills, CA: Sage.

McKeown, T. (1976). *The role of medicine: Dream, mirage or nemesis.* London: Nuffield Provincial Hospitals Trust.

McKinlay, J., & McKinlay, S. (1997). The questionable contribution of medical measures to the decline of mortality in the United States in the twentieth century. *Milbank Memorial Fund Quarterly, 55*, 405–428.

Monk, M. (1987). Epidemiology of suicide. *Epi Reviews, 9*, 51–69.

Multiple Risk Factor Intervention Trial Research Group. (1982). Multiple risk factor intervention trial: Risk factor changes and mortality results. *Journal of the American Medical Association, 248*, 1465–1477.

National Heart, Lung, and Blood Institute. (1994). Morbidity and mortality: *Chartbook on cardiovascular, lung, and blood diseases* (pp. 36–42). Bethesda, MD: National Institutes of Health.

National Heart, Lung, and Blood Institute. (1998). *Report of the task force on behavioral research in cardiovascular, lung, and blood health and disease.* U.S. Department of Health and Human Services.

O'Connell, D. O., & Velicer, W. F. (1988). A decisional balance measure and the stages of change model for weight loss. *International Journal of the Addictions, 23*, 729–750.

Pareschi, P. L., & Tomasi, F. (1989). Epidemiology of diabetes mellitus. In M. Morsiani (Ed.), *Epidemiology and screening of diabetes* (pp. 77–114). Boca Raton, FL: CRC Press.

Parker, J. C., Smarr, K. L., Buescher, K. L., Phillips, L. R., Frank, R. G., Beck, N. C., Anderson, S. K., & Walker, S. E. (1989). Pain control and rational thinking. Implications for rheumatoid arthritis. *Arthritis and Rheumatism, 32*, 984–990.

Prochaska, J. O., & DiClemente, C. C. (1984). *The transtheoretical approach: Crossing traditional boundaries of therapy.* Homewood, IL: Dow Jones Irwin.

Puska, P. (1996). Community interventions in cardiovascular disease prevention. In K. Orth-Gomer, & N. Schneiderman (Eds.), *Behavioral medicine approaches to cardiovascular disease prevention* (pp. 237–262). Mahwah, NJ: Erlbaum.

Rakowski, W., Fulton, J. P., & Feldman, J. P. (1993). Stages-of-adoption and women's decision-making about mammography. *Health Psychology, 12*, 209–214.

Rice, R. E., & Atkin, C. K. (Eds.). (1989). *Public communication campaigns* (2nd edition). Newbury Park, CA: Sage.

Roccella, E. J., & Horan, M. J. (1988). The national high blood pressure education program: Measuring progress and assessing its impact. *Health Psychology, 7* (Suppl.), 297–303.

Rogers, E. (1983). *Diffusion of innovations.* New York: Free Press.

Rose, G. (1992). *The strategy of preventive medicine.* Oxford, England: Oxford University Press.

Rosenstock, I. M. (1966). Why people use health services. *Milbank Memorial Fund Quarterly, 44,* 94–127.

Sallis, J. F., Hovell, M. F., & Hofstetter, C. R. (1992). Predictors of adoption and maintenance of vigorous physical activity in men and women. *Preventive Medicine, 21,* 237–251.

Schneiderman, N. (1999). Behavioral medicine and the management of HIV/ AIDS. *International Journal of Behavioral Medicine, 6,* 3–12.

Schneiderman, N., & Orth-Gomér, K. (1996). Blending traditions: A concluding perspective on behavioral medicine approaches to coronary heart disease prevention. In K. Orth-Gomér & N. Schneiderman (Eds.), *Behavioral medicine approaches to cardiovascular disease prevention* (pp. 279–300). Mahwah, NJ: Erlbaum.

Strasser, T. (1978). Reflections on cardiovascular disease. *Interdisciplinary Science Review, 3,* 225–230.

Tuomilehto, J., Puska, P., Korhonen, H. J., Mustaniemi, H., Vartiainen, E., Nissinen, A., Kuulasmaa, K., Niemensives, H., & Salonen, J. T. (1989). Trends and determinants of ischaemic heart disease mortality in Finland: With special relevance to a possible levelling off in the early 1980s. *International Journal of Epidemiology, 18*(Suppl. 1), 109–117.

Turner, J. A. (1982). Comparison of group progressive relaxation training and cognitive–behavioral group therapy for chronic low back pain. *Journal of Consulting and Clinical Psychology, 50,* 757–765.

U.S. Surgeon General. (1990). *Healthy people 2000: National health promotion and disease prevention objectives* (DHHS Publication No. 91–50212). Washington, DC: U.S. Department of Health and Human Services.

II

APPLYING BEHAVIORAL AND SOCIAL SCIENCE APPROACHES TO SELECTED PUBLIC HEALTH PROBLEMS

2

CREATING SOCIAL AND PUBLIC HEALTH ENVIRONMENTS TO SUSTAIN BEHAVIOR CHANGE: LESSONS FROM OBESITY RESEARCH

MARGARET A. CHESNEY, REBECCA C. THURSTON, AND KATRINA A. THOMAS

Most interventions to change health behaviors emphasize various strategies derived from theories of behavior as it occurs at the level of the individual. The theories that have driven this approach are well known, including the health belief model (Hochbaum, 1958; Rosenstock, 1960, 1966, 1974), the theory of reasoned action (Fishbein & Ajzen, 1975), and the transtheoretical or "stages of change" model (Prochaska & DiClemente, 1983). Nonetheless, individual behavior is continuously influenced by factors from the biological, psychological, social, and environmental levels. New paradigms are needed that examine the practice of health behaviors from initiation, through change, and into maintenance of change that recognize these influences. Similarly, to effectively change behavior and maintain change, efforts should focus on all of these levels (Abrams, in press). This perspective would argue that efforts that fail to integrate across disciplines or that attempt to address behavior from only one level are less likely to be successful. A program encouraging an elderly individual to walk for exercise without addressing the availability of safe places to walk in the community, for example, likely will not achieve sustained exercise. The need for new paradigms has been recognized in the area of smoking research, where Abrams has called for a "new model emerging from a transdisciplinary synthesis of biological, psychological, and social science perspectives." The term *transdisciplinary* is used instead of *multidisciplinary* to convey approaches in which scientists with expertise in different disciplines and at various levels work collaboratively on a common problem, each contributing from his or her own discipline.

In this chapter, using obesity as an example, we point out how individual risk factors are influenced by multiple levels. The implication is that the success of previous efforts to address obesity has been limited because these have focused too heavily on the individual behavioral and psychological levels, examining eating patterns and psychological factors associated with habits and appetite. We review the influence of these, as well as the biological, social, and environmental levels, and propose that to be effective, obesity interventions require a transdisciplinary, multilevel perspective. A comprehensive, multilevel intervention for obesity would take into consideration biological factors such as genetic susceptibilities, psychological factors such as negative affect, social factors such as familial and group norms, and environmental factors such as the availability of healthy food alternatives in the environment.

OBESITY—A PUBLIC HEALTH PRIORITY

Obesity is described as an epidemic in North America. It presents a significant public health challenge because the number of affected people continues to grow each year.

The term *obesity* applies to individuals for whom excess weight presents serious health risks (Wickelgren, 1998). The clinical definition is a body mass index (BMI) of more than 30, which is calculated by dividing one's body weight in kilograms by the square of one's height in meters. The number of Americans who meet this criterion is staggering. More than half of Americans age 20 and older are considered overweight (BMI of 25 or more), whereas one quarter are designated as clinically obese (Wickelgren, 1998). The most recent National Health and Nutrition Examination Survey (NHANES–III) from 1988 to 1994 showed a large increase in obesity from NHANES–II (1976–1980), with rates of 14.5–22.5% in NHANES–III (Flegal, Carroll, Kuczmarski, & Johnson, 1998). This trend was seen in all ages, genders, and racial–ethnic groups, with a prevalence of class III obesity (BMI > 40) of more than 10% in non-Hispanic Black women between ages 40 and 59.

Obesity is associated with numerous physical and psychological health risks. Studies demonstrate an increased risk of heart disease, cancer, diabetes, hypertension, hyperlipidemia, and mortality in obese people (Flegal et al., 1998; Wickelgren, 1998). Nonetheless, it is debatable whether the risk is due to the weight itself or instead to what contributes to the weight, such as sedentary lifestyles and low socioeconomic status. Depression and low self-esteem, in addition to discrimination and social stigmatization, are among the psychological and social effects linked with obesity. As well as associated individual costs, obesity has serious societal ramifications. An estimated $70 billion is spent every year on health care and lost productivity due to weight-related issues (Wickelgren, 1998).

TRADITIONAL OBESITY INTERVENTIONS—INDIVIDUAL BEHAVIOR

Interventions for obesity have historically focused on individual behavior and attempted to achieve weight loss by reducing energy intake and increasing energy expenditure. More recent efforts have included energy expenditure through aerobic exercise. Most behavioral interventions, although successful at producing weight loss in the short term, have failed to maintain long-term weight loss. In the pursuit of improving treatment, these behavioral approaches to obesity have inspired a wealth of research surrounding the behavioral aspects of obesity.

The role of dietary factors and physical-activity levels in the etiology of most obesity cases is far from clear. Some epidemiological and behavioral studies cast some doubt on the central role of energy intake in the etiology of obesity. Specifically, although rates of obesity have progressively increased in the American population, the average consumption of both fat and total calories has decreased (Human Nutrition Information Service, 1993). In addition, research has indicated that obese individuals, on average, do not consume more daily calories than do nonobese individuals (Jeffery, 1998; Shah & Jeffery, 1991).

Researchers have cited a potential decrease in physical activity and energy expenditure as driving rising obesity rates in North America (Weinsier, Hunter, Heini, Goran, & Sell, 1998). Both obese and nonobese Americans are relatively inactive, however. Among American adults, 60% do not meet recommended levels of physical activity, and 25% are not active at all (U.S. Department of Health and Human Services [DHHS], 1996). Although obese people are generally less active than the nonobese people, adjustments for total body mass indicate that the total energy expenditure is similar in the normal-weight and obese populations (Jeffery, 1998). A severe limitation on these epidemiological lines of research is inadequate assessment of both diet and exercise habits in daily life. These dietary and physical-activity measures are highly inaccurate, with error variance within groups being large enough to mask differences between groups (Jeffery, 1998). In addition, the average American lifestyle differs markedly from other cultural lifestyles in the remarkably high fat consumption and lack of physical activity. Thus, behavioral factors are undoubtedly playing a role.

Although interventions such as pharmacotherapy, surgery, low-calorie diets, exercise prescriptions, and cognitive–behavioral therapy are available for weight loss, the safest and most highly utilized are any combination of behavioral approaches. In fact, the Expert Panel on the Identification, Evaluation, and Treatment of Overweight and Obesity (1998) called specifically for a behavioral component, including exercise and dietary interventions, and behavioral counseling. Dietary interventions primarily consist of controlled low-calorie diets (LCDs) or very-low-calorie diets (VLCDs) prescribed over an average period of 3–6 months. The Expert Panel recommends an LCD between 1,000 and 1,200 kcal/day for women and 1,200 and 1,500 kcal/day for men, with total fat restricted to 30% or less of total energy intake. Physical-activity interventions are recommended for use in conjunction with these dietary prescriptions. These interventions are usually based on American College of Sports Medicine (1990) guidelines, consisting of 30 minutes or more of moderate-intensity physical activity, such as walking, 5 or more days a week, or 25–60 minutes of vigorous physical activity at least 3 days a week (see also Expert Panel, 1998). Nonetheless, newer physical-activity interventions are utilizing shorter and more frequent bouts of home-based exercise, such as walking, with positive effects on long-term maintenance of weight loss (Jakicic, Polley, & Wing, 1998).

Finally, behavior counseling, often consisting of weekly meetings over a period of 3–6 months, is recommended for use in conjunction with diet, exercise, or both to aid weight loss (Expert Panel, 1998). These interventions utilize psychological approaches to target unhealthy lifestyle patterns, aid in adherence to diet and exercise prescriptions, manage stress, build social support, and teach other positive psychological tools to aid in weight loss. The counseling and specific diet and exercise interventions in the guidelines recommend tailoring to individual characteristics, concomitant risk factors, level of obesity, comorbid conditions, age, ethnicity, lifestyle, and preferences.

The efficacy of these behavioral approaches depends on the type of intervention used, adherence to the regimen, duration of treatment, and numerous other factors. Recent interventions have been successful in producing short-term weight loss, routinely showing losses of about 10% of body weight after a comprehensive diet, exercise, and behavior therapy program (Kramer, Jeffery, Forster, & Snell, 1989). These success rates reflect recent advances in the field and can be attributable to the lengthening of treatment duration and to the addition of behavioral counseling. Nonetheless, successful long-term weight loss, often defined as a reduction of 10% of body weight or more sustained over a period of 5 years or more, is rare (Jeffery, 1998). Although long-term weight loss is successful in some cases, as evidenced by a registry of more than 2,500 people who have sustained weight losses of 50 pounds or more for an average of 5 years (Klem, Wing, McGuire, Seagle, & Hill, 1997), the vast majority of obese individuals return to preintervention weight within a year of initial loss. Typically, participants will lose weight rapidly for the first several months of the intervention and then steadily regain the weight (Jeffery, 1998; Kramer et al., 1989). Maintenance of weight loss is an area to which behavioral researchers are now turning their attention.

Although numerous strategies for long-term weight loss have been attempted, such as the restriction of fat intake versus caloric intake, a focus on high-protein diet composition, the use of spousal and other social support, or the implementation of monetary incentives, consistent long-term weight loss has not been achieved (Jeffery, 1998; Jeffery et al., 1993; Wing & Jeffery, 1999; Yamashita, Sasahara, Pomery, Collier, & Nestel, 1998). The one strategy that is showing promise in aiding long-term maintenance of weight losses is the increased use of aerobic exercise. Several studies comparing dietary changes alone and combined diet and exercise intervention have shown that combination exercise–diet programs increase both short-term and long-term weight losses (Expert Panel, 1998; Jeffery, 1998; Pavlou, Krey, & Steffee, 1989; Silkand, Kondo, Foreyt, Jones, & Gotto, 1988; Weinsier et al., 1998). In one correlational study assessing women successful at weight loss and maintenance compared to women who had regained lost weight, only 34% of the regainers exercised regularly, and 90% of the maintainers participated in regular exercise (Kayman, Bruvold, & Stern, 1990). The most recent clinical guidelines for treating obesity advise that exercise is integral to sustaining weight losses induced by dietary therapy (Expert Panel, 1998).

Originally, exercise for weight loss was prescribed according to the American College of Sports Medicine (1990) guidelines of 30 minutes of moderate-intensity exercise 5 or more days a week or 30 minutes of vigorous exercise at least 3 days a week. Other exercise regimes may be beneficial to weight loss, however, particularly in the long term. In one 18-month study of a comprehensive diet, exercise, and behavioral weight management program, obese women participated in one of three exercise groups: long sessions, multiple daily short sessions, or multiple daily short sessions with home exercise equipment (Jakicic et al., 1998). At 6 months, all of the women averaged 150 minutes or more of exercise a week and had lost an average of 20 pounds. The only women who maintained their losses after a year, however, were those who continued to average at least 150 minutes per week of exercise. Long-term maintenance of this level of exercise is another concern.

Although significant strides in behavioral research have been achieved, only a subset of people with obesity seeks help. When help is sought, the effects are seen in only a subset of those who participate in programs, and among those, only a subset is able to sustain the effects. Thus, despite some success, effective behavior change that would affect the public health epidemic of obesity remains elusive.

TRADITIONAL INTERVENTIONS ADD PSYCHOLOGICAL PERSPECTIVES

Traditional efforts to understand obesity have attempted to identify an underlying psychological profile or psychopathology that renders a person vulnerable to obesity. These attempts failed to find that obesity is associated with a specific psychological profile (Klesges, 1984). In fact, the psychological heterogeneity of the obese population mirrors that of the normal-weight population (Leon & Roth, 1977). In addition, several findings reveal that in nonclinical samples, rates of psychopathology are not significantly higher in the obese population than in the normal-weight population (Fitzgibbon, Stolley, & Kirschenbaum, 1993; Stunkard & Wadden, 1992). Thus, the search for psychological underpinnings of obesity proved futile because of the psychological diversity of the obese population. This diversity is increasing as the rates of obesity continue to rise, with increasingly larger segments of the American population becoming obese.

Higher rates of psychopathology occur among obese people seeking treatment. Estimates of rates of Axis I psychological disorders, such as anxiety or depression, are as high as 57% (Berman, Berman, Heymsfeld, Fauci, & Ackerman, 1993; Fitzgibbon et al., 1993). Several key studies show elevated depression or distress symptom scores in overweight and non-treatment-seeking obese people relative to normal-weight people (Fitzgibbon et al., 1993; Klem, Wing, Simkin-Silverman, & Kuller, 1997). In these studies, obese participants seeking treatment were generally found to show more symptoms of depression, distress, and borderline personality than did the obese population not seeing treatment (Fitzgibbon et al., 1993). Importantly, obese populations show a higher prevalence of binge eating, and treatment-seeking obese people tend to show dramatically more binge eating and negative emotional eating than do nontreatment-seeking obese people (Fitzgibbon et al., 1993; Klem, Wing, Simkin-Silverman, et al., 1997). Binge eaters, both obese and not, show elevated rates of depression and other psychiatric disorders (O'Neil & Jarrell, 1992; Yanovski, Nelson, Dubbert, & Spitzer, 1993). Thus, some of the higher rates of psychopathology in treatment-seeking obese individuals may be related to binge-eating behavior. Finally, one subset of more severely obese women who have BMI measures greater than 36 kg/m^2 are more likely to report histories of rape, sexual molestation, and posttraumatic stress disorder than are mildly obese or normal-weight women (Williamson & O'Neil, 1998). Thus, although the majority of the obese population does not exhibit higher rates of clinical psychopathology than does the normal-weight population, notable subpopulations exist that are significantly distressed. The complexity of these findings reflects the heterogeneity of the obese population and the challenge of assessing the psychological correlates of obesity.

Although measures of prevalence of overall psychopathology in the obese population have, for the most part, shown no differences between the general obese and the normal-weight populations, measures of global self-esteem indicate that obesity is correlated with mildly depressed self-esteem. Specifically, obese adolescents and young adults tend to show lower self-esteem than their normal-weight counterparts (Freidman & Brownell, 1995; French, Story, & Perry, 1995). Among treatment-seekers, obesity is associated with distinctly impaired self-esteem (Kolotkin, Head, Hamilton, & Tse, 1995). Nonetheless, the directionality of this relationship is not yet clear. In two prospective studies, one of African American adolescent boys and girls and the other of White adolescent girls, self-esteem scores were associated with less weight gain over the next several years (French et al., 1995). Thus, low self-esteem may be a risk factor for the development of obesity, or obesity may lead to lower self-esteem. Further research needs to clarify this relationship.

The most striking psychological differences between obese and normal-weight populations are scores on eating or body-related variables (Williamson & O'Neil, 1998). Overall, obese people tend to exhibit more self-defeating, pessimistic, or perfectionistic thought patterns surrounding weight and eating than do normal-weight control participants (Williamson & O'Neil, 1998). In addition, obese individuals tend to react to perceived dietary transgressions with more absolutistic, perfectionistic self-statements than do normal-weight people (Williamson & O'Neil, 1998). These thought patterns are even more pronounced among obese individuals who binge eat (Williamson & O'Neil, 1998). Fitzgibbon et al. (1993) found that people showed more negative emotional eating, overeating, and difficulty resisting temptation than did normal-weight control participants and that treatment-seeking obese people scored significantly higher than non-treatment-seeking obese people. Studies of dietary restraint, or the tendency to cognitively impose limits on food consumption, suggest that "restrained eaters" are more common among the obese than the normal-weight populations (Klem, Wing, Simkin-Silverman, et al., 1997; Williamson & O'Neil, 1998). Among restrained eaters, overeating often results when imposed limits are exceeded or under other disinhibiting influences, such as stress, alcohol consumption, unplanned eating, or depressed mood (Mitchell & Epstein, 1995; Williamson & O'Neil, 1998). This disinhibition effect and subsequent eating is not observed among participants scoring low on dietary restraint (Mitchell & Epstein, 1995).

In addition to specific eating-related variables, obese people tend to score significantly differently on body image measures than do normal-weight individuals. Studies have shown that obese adults are less accurate than normal-weight adults in judging their own body size. Specifically, obese adults are three times more likely than normal-weight adults to over-estimate their body size, and their estimates are 6–12% larger than their actual sizes (Collins, Beaumont, Touyz, Krass, Thompson, & Philips, 1987; Counts & Adams, 1985). Normal-weight adults tend to estimate their body size 1–2% larger than their actual size. In addition, at all levels of obesity, significantly negative body esteem is found among adults (Williamson & O'Neil, 1998). This effect is particularly pronounced for women and for obese people seeking treatment (Williamson & O'Neil, 1998). Negative body esteem is found more often among obese children relative to normal-weight children (French et al., 1995). These patterns do not apply to all obese populations, however. For example, among the African American population, overweight and obese women possess a more positive body image than do their White counterparts (Kumanyika, Wilson, & Guilford-Davenport, 1993; Williamson & O'Neil, 1998). Although rates of obesity are higher in the African American population (Flegal et al., 1998), negative body image and dieting is less common than among White people (Kumanyika et al., 1993; Williamson & O'Neil, 1998). In sum, particularly among White people, body image distortion is more common and more severe in obese people, and overall body image and body esteem is more negative than among the normal-weight population.

Studies also have been conducted on overall quality of life in obese versus nonobese people. General scores on quality of life measures that assess physical, psychosocial, and professional functioning are lower among the obese than the normal-weight population (Kolotkin et al., 1995; Stunkard & Wadden, 1992). These scores are generally correlated with the severity of obesity. In addition, obese people may experience significant social discrimination. Specifically, research has documented discrimination toward obese people in both employment and educational settings (Gortmaker, Must, Perrin, Sobol, & Dietz, 1993). Negative attitudes toward obese people have been documented among a wide variety of groups, including health care workers (Price, Desmond, Krol, Snyder, & O'Connell, 1987). In fact, discrimination against obese people has been cited as one of the last acceptable forms of discrimination (Rothblum, 1994). Thus, social and cultural attitudes toward obesity can seriously impact the overall quality of life of individuals who are obese.

Treatment approaches on the psychological level for obesity are generally delivered in combination with other behavioral strategies. These combined approaches have had a positive impact on both short-term weight loss and long-term maintenance (Elmer et al., 1995; Expert Panel, 1998; Hypertension Prevention Trial Research Group, 1990). In addition, recent studies of the psychological impact of weight-loss interventions have found no negative impact of attempts at weight loss, including for those who are unsuccessful at losing weight (Expert Panel, 1998; French & Jeffery, 1994; Klem, Wing, Simkin-Silverman, et al., 1997; O'Neil & Jarrell, 1992). These findings stand in contrast to earlier reports that dieting had a negative psychological impact, including increasing depression, increasing anxiety, and reducing self-esteem (French & Jeffery, 1994). In fact, more recent studies report a neutral psychological impact at worst, and frequently positive psychological impact of low-calorie diets, surgery, and other behavioral interventions centered around weight loss (French & Jeffery, 1994; Klem, Wing, Simkin-Silverman, et al., 1997; O'Neil & Jarrell, 1992). One reason cited for this shift is the newer approaches to weight loss that often include psychological therapeutic components (French & Jeffery, 1994). One study compared the psychological impact of a very-low-calorie diet with and without behavioral therapy. Posttreatment and 1 year later, those who received the behavioral therapy showed significant reductions in depressive symptoms from baseline compared with those who did not (Wadden, Stunkard, & Liebschutz, 1988). Thus, the increasing use of psychological intervention has improved both the efficacy and psychological impact of weight-loss interventions.

Despite the increasing advances in weight-loss interventions, much is unknown about the psychological impact of attempts at weight reduction outside of formal programs. The majority of weight-loss attempts occur in nonclinical settings, and some estimates suggest that as much as 72% of all successful weight loss occurs outside of formal commercial or university-based weight-loss interventions (Brownell, 1993). Researchers note that published findings surrounding weight loss and its psychological impact are based primarily on university-based programs, and thus the generalizability of these findings may be limited (Brownell, 1993; French & Jeffery, 1994). One disturbing finding, as discussed previously, is that dieting can be associated with the development of eating disorders. For example, one prospective study that followed 1,000 adolescent girls showed that 21% of the dieters at baseline went on to develop eating disorders 1 year later (Patton, Johnson-Sabine, Wood, Mann, & Wakeling, 1990). Only 12% of the new eating-disorder cases at follow-up were not dieters at baseline. These data in concert with other research indicate that dieting behavior may be a risk factor for the development of eating disorders when it occurs in conjunction with other behavioral, social, psychological, and environmental risk factors (French & Jeffery, 1994). Additional prospective research is needed to fully clarify this relationship. In sum, psychological correlates or consequences of weight loss, although interesting, have not resulted in widespread, successful loss that is maintained.

MULTILEVEL PHENOMENON—THE BIOLOGICAL LEVEL

One area of research experiencing recent scientific advances is on the individual biological level, that is, the genetic determinants of human obesity. The single strongest predisposing factor to the development of obesity in a given individual is family history. Furthermore, the most influential aspect of the family history is believed to be shared genes rather than common environment; some studies estimate that 50% body fatness is due to genetic predisposition (Bouchard, 1994a; Jeffery, 1998). Obesity, an extremely complex condition, has multiple genetic components and is influenced by molecular biological, biological, and socio-environmental factors. Multiple genes interact with each other and the environment to result in an array of phenotypes that all characterize obesity. Multiple streams of genetic research, such as genetic epidemiology, research examining the interactive effects of genes and environment, and molecular genetics are converging to shed light on this complex condition. Nonetheless, even though major strides have been achieved in the genetics of human obesity, much more replication and research is needed.

Evidence for a genetic component of obesity is strong (Bouchard, 1994a; Bouchard, Perusse, Rice, & Rao, 1998; Jeffery, 1998). Genetic syndromes, often caused by the mutation of a single gene, that result in obesity illustrate that the complex phenomenon of obesity can be caused by one gene. One common condition is the Prader-Willi syndrome, most often the result of a deletion of 15q11.2–12 segment on the paternal chromosome. This type of obesity is not representative of the majority of cases, however (Bouchard et al., 1998). Recent research indicates that multiple genes influence obesity and that these genes interact with environmental conditions in critical ways. Research suggests that the genetic influence on obesity is stronger than that of the environment, although heritability estimates vary widely (Bouchard, 1994a; Jeffery, 1998). Heritability estimates of the BMI, the most common index of obesity, range from 10 to 80%. Most estimates fall in the range of 25–50% (Bouchard, 1994a). These figures are derived from adoption studies, twin studies, nuclear family studies, and studies that combine multiple approaches. Adding to the complexity of these findings is that the measurement of obesity is often imprecise (Bouchard et al., 1998). BMI is determined by muscle mass, skeletal mass, and other factors in addition to fat mass and does not lend itself to a simple genetic explanation. Other measures, such as waist-to-hip ratio, suffer from similar problems (Bouchard et al., 1998). Thus, it is hardly surprising that researchers are finding that multiple genes alone, even with no attention to environmental factors, come into play.

Four major patterns of obesity and fat distribution have been identified (Bouchard, 1994b). This indicates that obesity is not a homogeneous phenotype. Studies show that at least two sets of genes may be governing these various fat patterns, which run in families. Although obesity has multiple genetic components, the environment plays a critical role in the expression of phenotypes. Several streams of research have examined these interactions. For example, Claude Bouchard and colleagues have examined monozygotic twins in studies of the effects of short- and long-term positive and negative energy balance (Bouchard, Perusse, Leblanc, Tremblay, & Theriault, 1988; Bouchard et al., 1994; Poehlman et al., 1987). In one study examining body weight, fat mass, and fat-free mass after 100 days of overfeeding, three times more variance emerged between pairs of twins than within pairs of twins. Thus, with the environment carefully controlled, specific genotypes interacted with the overfeeding to produce widely different weight gain. Bouchard observed similar and significant patterns, although with weight losses, in studies of rigorous long-term exercise.

Finally, some of the most recent dramatic scientific advances in the genetics of obesity have been in the area of molecular genetics. Molecular genetic researchers utilize myriad methods to isolate single genes that may be contributing to obesity. Among molecular genetic research are linkage studies, association studies, Mendelian models, and transgenic and knock-out animal model studies. Because of a combination of these approaches, many genes potentially contributing to obesity have been identified on the human genome. Further research is under way to identify those that are definitively involved. In rodent models, several genes have been identified as leading to a specified physiological effect, such as the diabetes gene, the fat gene, the obese gene, and the adipose gene (Friedman, Leibel, & Bahary, 1991). The human genome does have genes corresponding to these rodent genes, and they have been identified, but they have not yet been found to have parallel effects in humans (Bouchard et al., 1998; Xu, Reed, Ding, & Price, 1995).

One recent dramatic discovery is the identification of a human gene clearly playing a role in certain forms of obesity. This gene is the Ob gene, and it produces the hormone leptin, which acts to suppress food intake and increase energy expenditure (Clement, 1999; Trayhurn, Hoggard, Mercer, & Rayner, 1999; Zhang et al., 1994). Leptin has been cited as one of the best biological markers of total body fat across a wide range of normal and obese BMIs and in numerous pathologies, such as non-insulin-dependent patients with diabetes mellitus and Prader-Willi children (Van Gaal, Waunters, Mertens, Considine, & De Leeuw, 1999). In rodent studies, leptin has been found to be significantly and dramatically higher in high-fat mouse strains than in leaner strains, thus indicating leptin resistance (Bunger, Nicolson, & Hill, 1999). Fasting serum leptin levels in humans are elevated in obese patients, often in proportion to the degree of obesity (Considine et al., 1996), and weight loss has been shown to reduce human leptin concentrations (Van Gaal et al., 1999). In three cases of morbid human obesity, mutations in the leptin or leptin-receptor genes have been discovered (Trayhurn et al., 1999). Thus, one key gene has been identified and mapped as instrumental to metabolic processes and energy balance. Leptin plays numerous physiological roles and is produced in several organs, however. For this reason, the leptin system is no longer considered a target for anti-obesity therapy (Trayhurn et al., 1999).

In summary, the empirical evidence indicates that genetic factors play a significant role in the etiology of human obesity. The magnitude of this role is yet to be fully determined and varies between individuals. Although recent advances in this area have been substantial, much research still needs to be undertaken. The multiple streams of genetic research, from the epidemiological to the molecular, have clearly shown obesity to be a strikingly complex condition, including several major types and involving numerous genes on the biological level alone.

The most common therapies for obesity that target the individual biological level are pharmacological therapy and surgical intervention. Pharmacological therapies include drugs that work on the monoamine neurotransmitter system, such as sibutramine, which influence neurotransmitters such as serotonin, norepinephrine, dopamine, and histamine (Leonhardt, Hrupka, & Langhans, 1999). These often act as appetite suppressants. Other pharmacological agents increase thermogenesis, whereas still others, such as orlistat, decrease fat absorption by inhibiting pancreatic lipase (Leonhardt et al., 1999). Newer drugs based on recent findings surrounding the mechanisms controlling body weight are under development and have promise. Nonetheless, the most recent clinical guidelines for the treatment of obesity clearly state that FDA-approved drugs should be used only in combination with behavioral intervention, such as controlled-energy diets, physical activity, and behavior therapy (Expert Panel, 1998). The panel states that pharmacotherapy is appropriate for patients with a BMI over 30 or those with a BMI over 27 with specified concomitant risk factors or diseases (Expert Panel, 1998). In addition, weight-loss surgery, such as gastric bypass, is deemed appropriate by the panel only in cases of extreme obesity. Surgery should only be undertaken with patients who have attempted medical and behavioral therapy and who are suffering the complications of severe obesity. As with the individual behavior approaches to obesity, the public health effect of these biological strategies on weight reduction, with or without behavioral counseling, has not been shown. The panel states that pharmacotherapy and surgery are not replacements for behavioral interventions and should only be used in severe cases in concert with diet, physical activity, and psychological therapies.

Obesity is a condition with several determinants at each of multiple levels, including the genetic, psychological, behavioral, proximal environmental, and distal environmental. Genetic research alone, although critical, will make significant strides only in combination with other approaches.

ENVIRONMENTAL LEVEL INFLUENCES

It has been proposed that the problem of obesity "is not in people, but rather in the environment" (Jeffery, 1998, p. 826). Modern environments promote obesity by modern transportation and conveniences, sedentary leisure-time activities, and abundance of high-calorie-dense foods. Technology has reduced the amount of physical ability and strength needed to survive in our current environment. The immediate social environmental level, characterized by the family home, school, or workplace, and the more macroenvironmental level, characterized by the media, both exert significant influences on behavior, which in turn can foster obesity.

The structural environment has reduced the need for physical activity in our everyday lives. In a culture that relies on computers and cars, elevators and television, the amount of time spent engaged in physical activity has decreased and the amount of time spent in sedentary pursuits has increased (Hill & Peters, 1998). As noted earlier, 60% of American adults are not meeting recommended levels of physical activity (DHHS, 1996). Television encourages sedentary behavior. Adults spend more than 4 hours a day watching television, and children spend about 3 hours at this activity (Nielsen, 1993). Computers also encourage sedentary behavior. The hours spent on computers at work, school, and in the home further decrease the amount of time engaged in physical activity. Indeed computers make it possible to communicate with friends and colleagues, shop, pay bills, and do research without moving from a chair. All of this sedentary activity reduces caloric needs. Unless dietary intake is similarly adjusted, weight gain will occur. In a cross-sectional study of 4,280 men and women between ages 23 and 35, those who watched more than 4 hours of television per day had a higher prevalence of obesity relative to those who watched less than 1 hour per day (Sidney et al., 1996).

Watching television is not only associated with sedentary behavior, it is a primary source of unhealthy food advertising (Jeffery, 1998). This advertising is effective as shown by studies linking the extent of television watching with the consumption of advertised food (Cotugna, 1988; Taras, Sallis, Patterson, Nader, & Nelson, 1989). Marketing of unhealthy food on television begins early with the high sugar and fat content foods that are advertised during children's shows (Cotugna, 1988).

Against this backdrop of Americans' sedentary lifestyles, the most common suggestion for weight-loss regimens is "eat healthy and exercise more." Through education and publicity, most Americans are aware of these recommendations but fail to adhere to them. There are economic barriers to increasing daily exercise and eating a healthier diet for many Americans. Many Americans do not live in environments where it is safe to exercise. Safe, convenient, well-lit areas away from automobiles are not available to many (Jeffery, 1998). There are few inexpensive indoor facilities available for exercise. Other barriers to exercise include long commutes, lack of social support, competing demands, and inclement weather (Dishman & Sallis, 1994).

Another environmental influence on obesity is the limited availability of healthy food in many areas. In a study by the Consumers Union (cited in Kaplan, 1995), it was found that the distribution and selection of available services were fewer in low-income neighborhoods compared with middle-income neighborhoods. More pharmacies, banks, restaurants, and specialty stores were found in the middle-income areas whereas there were more check-cashing stores, fast food restaurants, and liquor stores in the low-income neighborhoods. Produce was found to cost 22% more in the poor areas, and a typical market basket for four cost 15% more. The lower-income neighborhoods have a significant disadvantage when it comes to the availability of healthy foods.

SUGGESTIONS FOR CHANGE

Current interventions focusing on individual behavior are accomplishing little in the way of solving the problem of obesity in the population. These interventions may lead to weight reductions in some of those who access programs, but only a fraction of those who are obese avail themselves of them; among those who do, only a fraction lose weight. Among those who lose weight, only a fraction maintain the loss. In this chapter, we have outlined the extensive literature on the biological aspects of obesity, with attention to the gene and environmental interactions that play a causal role in weight gain for some. Similarly, we have noted the obvious role that the sociocultural environment plays in encouraging sedentary behavior and the intake of unhealthy food while presenting barriers to exercise and healthful eating, at least for many with limited means. We propose that successful obesity interventions need to take these factors into account.

Combined pharmacological and behavioral interventions may be necessary for people for whom obesity has a strong biological underpinning. Conducting this combined intervention in a sociocultural environment that is supportive of healthful eating and conducive to exercise would contribute significantly to the likelihood of sustained success.

The fact that there are individuals who are susceptible to weight gain and the evidence indicating how difficult it is to take weight off and keep it off point to prevention as a key to ending the epidemic. Such prevention efforts could be applied to the culture at large, with particular focus on those individuals who may be particularly susceptible receiving specialized assistance. One such program achieved long-term weight management in overweight preadolescent children by working with families to change the family environment to one that encouraged physical activity and healthy eating (Epstein, Valoski, Wing, & McCurley, 1994). Focusing on the youth community more broadly, the Child and Adolescent Trial of Cardiovascular Health demonstrated significantly greater levels of vigorous physical activity at schools that applied a curriculum for enhancing health behaviors, including physical activity, compared with control schools (Luepker et al., 1996). What was particularly impressive was that these gains were maintained 3 years after the intervention ended (Stone, McKenzie, Welk, & Booth, 1998).

Robert Jeffery (1998) suggested five possible environmental interventions that could be applied to change the current trends in weight gain. These interventions include improving the quality of the food supply; enhancing accessibility of physical activity; increasing advertising for healthy food alternatives and activity; providing economic incentives for healthy eating by taxing fat and sugar; and education about the importance of diet, exercise, and collective support of a healthy lifestyle. As was the case of tobacco, for which policies were implemented to discourage smoking (such as the creation of smoke-free settings and taxing tobacco), these recommendations will need to be addressed at a policy level.

Sustaining individual behavior change is impossible without addressing the influences on the behavior from the biological, social, and environmental levels. In this chapter, obesity has been used to illustrate the opportunities that are lost when these multiple levels of influence are overlooked. Conversely, interventions that are conducted across these levels of influence permit tailoring for those who are biologically susceptible and the designing of social and physical environments that will foster prevention of weight gain over time. They will also reinforce efforts by the obese to lose weight by promoting health and well-being.

REFERENCES

Abrams, D. B. (in press). Transdisciplinary paradigms for tobacco prevention research. *Nicotine and Tobacco Research.*

American College of Sports Medicine. (1990). American College of Sports Medicine Position Stand. The recommended quantity and quality of exercise for developing and maintaining cardiorespiratory and muscular fitness in healthy adults. *Medicine and Science in Sports and Exercise, 22*(2), 265–274.

Berman, W. H., Berman, E. R., Heymsfeld, S., Fauci, M., & Ackerman, S. (1993).

The effect of psychiatric disorders on weight loss in obesity clinic patients. *Behavioral Medicine, 18,* 167–172.

Bouchard, C. (1994a). Genetics of obesity: Overview and research directions. In C. Bouchard (Ed.), *The genetics of obesity* (pp. 223–234). Boca Raton, FL: CRC Press.

Bouchard, C. (1994b). Genetics of obesity: Introductory notes. In C. Bouchard (Ed.), *The genetics of obesity* (pp. 1–16). Boca Raton, FL: CRC Press.

Bouchard, C., Perusse, L., Leblanc, C., Tremblay, A., & Theriault, G. (1988). Inheritance of the amount and distribution of human body fat. *International Journal of Obesity, 12,* 205–215.

Bouchard, C., Perusse, L., Rice, T., & Rao, D. C. (1998). The genetics of human obesity. In G. A. Bray, C. Bouchard, & W. P. T. James (Eds.), *Handbook of obesity* (pp. 157–190). New York: Dekker.

Bouchard, C., Tremblay, A., Despres, J. P., Theriault, G., Nadeau, A., Lupien, P. J., Moorjani, S., Prudhomme, D., & Fournier, G. (1994). The response to exercise with constant energy intake in identical twins. *Obesity Research, 2,* 400–410.

Brownell, K. D. (1993). Whether obesity should be treated. *Health Psychology, 12,* 339–341.

Bunger, L., Nicolson, M., & Hill, W. G. (1999). Leptin levels in lines of mice developed by long-term divergent selection on fat content. *Genetical Research, 73,* 37–44.

Clement, K. (1999). Leptin and the genetics of obesity. *Acta Paediatrica, 88,* 51–57.

Collins, J. K., Beaumont, P. J. V., Touyz, S. W., Krass, J., Thompson, P., & Philips, T. (1987). Variability in body shape perception in anorexic, bulimic obese, and control subjects. *International Journal of Eating Disorders, 6,* 633–638.

Considine, R. V., Sinha, M. K., Heiman, M. L., Kriauciunas, A., Stephens, T. W., Nyce, M. R., Ohannesian, J. P., Marco, C. C., McKee, L. J., Bauer, T. L., & Caro, J. F. (1996). Serum immunoreactive-leptin concentrations in normal-weight and obese humans. *New England Journal of Medicine, 334,* 292–295.

Cotugna, N. (1988). TV ads on Saturday morning children's programming— What's new? *Journal of Nutrition Education, 20,* 125–127.

Counts, C. R., & Adams, H. E. (1985). Body image in bulimic, dieting, and normal females. *Journal of Psychopathology Behavior Assessment, 7,* 289–300.

Dishman, R. K., & Sallis, J. F. (1994). Determinants and interventions for physical activity and exercise. In C. Bouchard, R. J. Shephard, & T. Stephens (Eds.), *Physical activity, fitness, and health* (pp. 214–238). Champaign, IL: Human Kinetics.

Elmer, P. J., Grimm, R. J., Laing, B., Grandits, G., Svendsen, K., Van Heel, N., Betz, E., Raines, J., Link, M., Stamler, J., & Neaton, J. (1995). Lifestyle intervention: Results of the Treatment of Mild Hypertension Study (TOMHS). *Preventive Medicine, 24,* 378–388.

Epstein, L. H., Valoski, A., Wing, R. R., & McCurley, J. (1994). Ten-year outcomes of behavioral-family-based treatment for childhood obesity. *Health Psychology, 13,* 373–383.

Expert Panel on the Identification, Evaluation, and Treatment of Overweight and Obesity in Adults. (1998). Executive summary of the clinical guidelines on the identification, evaluation, and treatment of overweight and obesity in adults. *Archives of Internal Medicine, 158,* 1855–1867.

Fishbein, M., & Ajzen, I. (1975). *Belief, attitude, intention behavior: An introduction to theory and research.* Reading, MA: Addison-Wesley.

Fitzgibbon, M. L., Stolley, M. R., & Kirschenbaum, D. S. (1993). Obese people who seek treatment have different characteristics than those who do not seek treatment. *Health Psychology, 12,* 342–345.

Flegal, K. M., Carroll, M. D., Kuczmarski, R. J., & Johnson, C. L. (1998). Overweight and obesity in the United States: Prevalence and trends, 1960–1994. *International Journal of Obesity, 22,* 39–47.

Freidman, M. A., & Brownell, K. D. (1995). Psychological correlates of obesity: Moving to the next research generation. *Psychological Bulletin, 117,* 3–20.

French, S. A., & Jeffery, R. W. (1994). Consequences of dieting to lose weight: Effects on physical and mental health. *Health Psychology, 13,* 195–212.

French, S. A., Story, M., & Perry, C. L. (1995). Self-esteem and obesity in children and adolescents: A literature review. *Obesity Research, 3,* 479–490.

Friedman, J. M., Leibel, R. L., & Bahary, N. (1991). Molecular mapping of obesity genes. *Mammalian Genome, 1,* 130–144.

Gortmaker, S. L., Must, A., Perrin, J. M., Sobol, A. M., & Dietz, W. H. (1993). Social and economic consequences of overweight in adolescence and young adulthood. *New England Journal of Medicine, 329,* 1008–1012.

Hill, J. O., & Peters, J. C. (1998). Environmental contributions to the obesity epidemic. *Science, 280,* 1371–1374.

Hochbaum, G. M. (1958). *Public participation in medical screening programs: A sociopsychological study.* Public Health Service Publication no. 572. Washington, DC.

Human Nutrition Information Service. (1993). *Food and nutrient intakes by individuals in the United States, 1 day, 1987–1988* (Nationwide food consumption survey 1987–1988 87-I-1). Washington, DC: U.S. Department of Agriculture.

Hypertension Prevention Trial Research Group. (1990). The Hypertension Prevention Trial: Three-year effects of dietary changes on blood pressure. *Archives of Internal Medicine, 150,* 153–162.

Jakicic, J. M., Polley, B. A., & Wing, R. R. (1998). Accuracy of self-reported exercise and the relationship with weight loss in overweight women. *Medicine and Science in Sports and Exercise, 30,* 634–638.

Jeffery, R. W. (1998). Prevention of obesity. In G. A. Bray, C. Bouchard, & W. P. T. James (Eds.), *Handbook of obesity* (pp. 819–829). New York: Dekker.

Jeffery, R. W., Wing, R. R., Thorson, C., Burton, L. R., Raether, C., Harvey, J., & Mullen, M. (1993). Strengthening behavioral interventions for weight loss:

A randomized trial of food provision and monetary incentives. *Journal of Consulting & Clinical Psychology, 67,* 132–138.

Kaplan, G. A. (1995). Where do shared pathways lead? Some reflections on a research agenda. *Psychosomatic Medicine, 57,* 208–212.

Kayman, S., Bruvold, W., & Stern, J. S. (1990). Maintenance and relapse after weight loss in women: Behavioral aspects. *American Journal of Clinical Nutrition, 52,* 800–807.

Klem, M. L., Wing, R. R., McGuire, M. T., Seagle, H. M., & Hill, J. O. (1997). A descriptive study of individuals successful at long-term maintenance of substantial weight loss. *American Journal of Clinical Nutrition, 66,* 239–246.

Klem, M. L., Wing, R. R., Simkin-Silverman, L., & Kuller, L. H. (1997). The psychological consequences of weight gain prevention in healthy, premenopausal women. *International Journal of Eating Disorders, 21,* 167–174.

Klesges, R. C. (1984). Personality and obesity: Global versus specific measures. *Behavioral Therapy, 6,* 347–356.

Kolotkin, R. L., Head, S., Hamilton, M., & Tse, C.-K. J. (1995). Assessing the impact of weight on quality of life. *Obesity Research, 3,* 49–56.

Kramer, F. M., Jeffery, R. W., Forster, J. L., & Snell, M. K. (1989). Long-term follow-up of behavioral treatment for obesity: Patterns of weight regain among men and women. *International Journal of Obesity, 13,* 123–136.

Kumanyika, S., Wilson, J. F., & Guilford-Davenport, M. (1993). Weight-related attitudes and behaviors of black women. *Journal of the American Dietetic Association, 93,* 416–422.

Leon, G. R., & Roth, L. (1977). Obesity: Psychological causes, correlations, and speculations. *Psychological Bulletin, 84,* 117–139.

Leonhardt, M., Hrupka, B., & Langhans, W. (1999). New approaches in the pharmacological treatment of obesity. *European Journal of Nutrition, 38,* 1–13.

Luepker, R. V., Perry, C. J., McKinlay, S. M., Nader, P. R., Parcel, G. S., Stone, E. J., Webber, L. S., Elder, J. P., Feldman, H. A., Johnson, C. C., Kelder, S. H., & Wu, M. (1996). Outcomes of a field trial to improve children's dietary patterns and physical activity. The Child and Adolescent Trial for Cardiovascular Health (CATCH) Collaborative Group. *Journal of the American Medical Association, 275,* 768–776.

Mitchell, S. L., & Epstein, L. H. (1995). Changes in taste and satiety in dietary-restrained women following stress. *Physiology and Behavior, 60,* 495–499.

Nielsen. (1993). *Nielsen 1992–1993 report on television.* New York: Nielsen Media Research.

O'Neil, P. M., & Jarrell, M. P. (1992). Psychological aspects of obesity and dieting. In T. A. Wadden & T. B. VanItallie (Eds.), *Treatment of the seriously obese patient* (pp. 252–272). New York: Guilford Press.

Patton, G. C., Johnson-Sabine, E., Wood, K., Mann, A. H., & Wakeling, A. (1990). Abnormal eating attitudes in London schoolgirls—a prospective epidemiological study: Outcome at twelve month follow-up. *Psychological Medicine, 20,* 383–394.

Pavlou, K. N., Krey, S., & Steffee, W. P. (1989). Exercise as an adjunct to weight loss and maintenance in moderately obese subjects. *American Journal of Clinical Nutrition, 49*(Suppl. 5), 1115–1123.

Poehlman, E. T., Tremblay, A., Marcotte, M., Perusse, L., Theriault, G., & Bouchard, C. (1987). Heredity and changes in body composition and adipose tissue metabolism after short-term exercise-training. *European Journal of Applied Physiology & Occupational Physiology, 56*, 398–402.

Price, J. H., Desmond, S. M., Krol, R. A., Snyder, F. F., & O'Connell, J. K. (1987). Family practice physicians' beliefs, attitudes, and practices regarding obesity. *American Journal of Preventive Medicine, 3*, 339–345.

Prochaska, J. O., & DiClemente, C. C. (1983). Stages and processes of self-change of smoking: Toward an integrative model of change. *Journal of Consulting and Clinical Psychology, 51*, 390–395.

Rosenstock, I. M. (1960). What research in motivation suggests for public health. *American Journal of Public Health, 50*, 295–301.

Rosenstock, I. M. (1966). Why people use health services. *Milbank Memorial Fund Quarterly, 44*, 94–124.

Rosenstock, I. M. (1974). Historical origins of the Health Belief Model. *Health Education Monographs, 2*, 328–335.

Rothblum, E. D. (1994). "I'll die for the revolution but don't ask me not to diet": Feminism and the continuing stigmatization of obesity. In P. Fallon, M. A. Katzman, & S. C. Wooley (Eds.), *Feminist perspectives on eating disorders* (pp. 53–76). New York: Guilford Press.

Shah, M., & Jeffery, R. W. (1991). Is obesity due to overeating and inactivity, or to a defective metabolic rate? A review. *Annals of Behavioral Medicine, 13*(2), 73–81.

Sidney, S., Sternfeld, B., Haskell, W. L., Jacobs, D. R., Chesney, M. A., & Hulley, S. B. (1996). Television viewing and cardiovascular risk factors in young adults: The CARDIA study. *Annals of Epidemiology, 6*, 154–159.

Sikand, G., Kondo, A., Foreyt, J. P., Jones, P. H., & Gotto, A. M. (1988). Two-year follow-up of patients treated with a very-low-calorie diet and exercise training. *Journal of American Dietetic Association, 88*, 487–488.

Stone, E. J., McKenzie, T. L., Welk, G. J., & Booth, M. L. (1998). Effects of physical activity interventions in youth: Review and synthesis. *American Journal of Preventive Medicine, 15*, 298–315.

Stunkard, A. J., & Wadden, T. A. (1992). Psychological aspects of severe obesity. *American Journal of Clinical Nutrition, 55*, 5245–5325.

Taras, H. L., Sallis, J. F., Patterson, T. L., Nader, P. R., & Nelson, J. A. (1989). Television's influence on children's diet and physical activity. *Journal of Developmental and Behavioral Pediatrics, 10*, 176–180.

Trayhurn, P., Hoggard, N., Mercer, J. G., & Rayner, D. V. (1999). Leptin: Fundamental aspects. *International Journal of Obesity and Related Metabolic Disorders, 23*(Suppl. 1), 22–28.

U.S. Department of Health and Human Services. (1996). *Physical activity and health: A report of the Surgeon General.* Atlanta, GA: Centers for Disease Control and Prevention, National Center for Chronic Disease Prevention and Health Promotion.

Van Gaal, L. F., Waunters, M. A., Mertens, I. L., Considine, R. V., & De Leeuw, I. H. (1999). Clinical endocrinology of human leptin. *International Journal of Obesity and Related Metabolic Disorders, 23*(Suppl. 1), 29–36.

Wadden, T. A., Stunkard, A. J., & Liebschutz, J. (1988). Three-year follow-up of the treatment of obesity by very low calorie diet, behavior therapy, and their combination. *Journal of Consulting and Clinical Psychology, 56,* 925–928.

Weinsier, R. L., Hunter, G. R., Heini, A. F., Goran, M. I., & Sell, S. M. (1998). The etiology of obesity: Relative contribution of metabolic factors, diet, and physical activity. *American Journal of Medicine, 105,* 145–150.

Wickelgren, I. (1998). Obesity: How big a problem? *Science, 280,* 1364–1367.

Williamson, D. A., & O'Neil, P. M. (1998). Behavioral and psychological correlates of obesity. In G. A. Bray, C. Bouchard, & W. P. T. James (Eds.), *Handbook of obesity* (pp. 129–142). New York: Dekker.

Wing, R. R., & Jeffery, R. W. (1999). Benefits of recruiting participants with friends and increasing social support for weight loss and maintenance. *Journal of Consulting & Clinical Psychology, 67,* 132–138.

Xu, W., Reed, D. R., Ding, Y., & Price, R. A. (1995). Absence of linkage between human obesity and the mouse Agouti homologous region (20q11.2) or other markers spanning chromosome 20q. *Obesity Research, 3,* 559–562.

Yamashita, T., Sasahara, T., Pomeroy, S. E., Collier, G., & Nestel, P. J. (1998). Arterial compliance, blood pressure, plasma leptin, and plasma lipids in women are improved with weight reduction equally with a meat-based diet and a plant-based diet. *Metabolism: Clinical and Experimental, 47,* 1308–1314.

Yanovski, S. Z., Nelson, J. E., Dubbert, B. K., & Spitzer, R. L. (1993). Association of binge eating disorder and psychiatric comorbidity in obese subjects. *American Journal of Psychiatry, 150,* 1472–1479.

Zhang, Y., Proenca, R., Maffei, M., Barone, M., Leopold, L., & Friedman, J. M. (1994). Positional cloning of the mouse obese gene and its human homologue. *Nature, 372,* 425–432.

3

SOCIOECONOMIC FACTORS IN THE BEHAVIORAL AND PSYCHOSOCIAL EPIDEMIOLOGY OF CARDIOVASCULAR DISEASE

JOHN LYNCH

One of the aims of this book is to describe the contributions that the behavioral and social sciences have made and will continue to make to improve public health in the 21st century. Central to that mission is greater understanding of the pivotal role that socioeconomic factors play in determining levels of public health and influencing behavioral and psychosocial risk factors. Failure to deal with fundamental socioeconomic health determinants will be a major barrier to improving public health in the coming century, as indeed it has been throughout history.

BACKGROUND

The relationship between the socioeconomic position of individuals and populations and their health is well established. Almost invariably, those with greater socioeconomic disadvantage have worse health status regardless of the measures used. The negative association between socio-economic position, measured in various ways, and health status has been recognized for centuries (Antonovsky, 1967). In medieval Europe, Paracelsus (trans. 1941) noted unusually high rates of disease in miners. By the 19th century, Villermé (1840) was conducting systematic investigations in Paris into the relationship between rent levels and mortality. Virchow (1848/1988) reported on the relationship between poor living conditions and typhus in Upper Silesia. In England, Farr examined differences in mortality by occupation (Farr, 1864/1989; Rosen, 1958), whereas Engels (1848) deplored the impact of harsh working conditions on the health of the poor during the industrial revolution.

Differences in morbidity and mortality between socioeconomic groups have been observed in a large number of studies and are one of the strongest and most consistent findings in all epidemiological research (Davey Smith, Neaton, Wentworth, Stamler, & Stamler, 1996; Lynch, Kaplan, Cohen, Tuomilehto, & Salonen, 1996; Lynch, Kaplan, & Shema, 1997; Sorlie, Backlund, & Keller, 1995). This does not necessarily imply that poor people have a general susceptibility to poor health. Rather, this fact is better understood as reflecting how socioeconomic position structures the likelihood of certain exposures that are risk factors for particular diseases. Although poor people generally have higher risk for poor health outcomes, there are important exceptions. For instance, socioeconomically advantaged women tend to have higher incidence of breast cancer but a better survival rate (Heck & Pamuk, 1997). Why is this the case? Because the socioeconomic position of this segment of the population structures the exposure to the relevant risk factors for incidence and prognosis.

Although we do not often frame the issue this way, we should keep in mind that low socioeconomic position is as strong a risk factor for poor health outcomes as is smoking. In recent years, there has been an explosion of interest in socioeconomic inequalities in health (Kaplan & Lynch, 1997), and the evidence has been discussed in a number of places (Carroll, Davey Smith, & Bennett, 1996; Haan, Kaplan, & Syme, 1989; Kaplan & Keil, 1993; Lynch & Kaplan, 2000; Macintyre, 1997; Townsend & Davidson, 1982; Williams, 1990).

The primary purpose of this chapter is to discuss how socioeconomic factors influence important behavioral and psychosocial risk factors for cardiovascular disease (CVD). With that goal in mind, the first point of reference is to recognize that CVD itself is not randomly distributed among the population; it therefore should not be surprising that the important risk factors for CVD also are not randomly assigned. Greater awareness of socioeconomic differences in these behavioral and psychosocial risk factors is important because they are the focus of many public health intervention efforts. Conceptualizations of the psychosocial and behavioral correlates of low socioeconomic position can be located somewhere on a continuum, with one end defined by the view that these psychosocial and behavioral characteristics are essentially maladaptive phenomena that result from poor lifestyle management and as such are amenable to cognitive, emotional, and behavioral modification. The other end of the continuum is represented by the idea that although these psychosocial states and health behaviors may be maladaptive in terms of health and longevity, they must be viewed primarily as responses to adverse conditions imposed by broader social and economic structures acting over the entire life course (Evans, Barer, & Marmor, 1994; Lynch, Kaplan, & Salonen, 1997). These two approaches to understanding socioeconomic differences in health behaviors and psychosocial attributes have vastly different implications for intervention.

The recent "Socioeconomic Status and Health Chartbook" (National Center for Health Statistics [NCHS], 1998) shows strong income and education gradients in heart disease death rates. Men ages 25 to 64 with incomes less than $10,000 were at 2.5-fold risk of heart disease mortality compared with men with incomes greater than $25,000. These differences are even more striking for women. In a similar income comparison, the poorest women were 3.4 times more likely to die from heart disease (NCHS, 1998, pp. 92–93). Traditional risk factors for CVD also demonstrate strong associations with income and education. For instance, cigarette smoking is about twice as common in the poor population; low-income women have 60% higher levels of excessive weight and are much more likely to be sedentary. In addition, heavy alcohol use is more prevalent in those with less than 12 years of education, although this pattern differs by race and sex (NCHS, 1998, pp. 108–118). Although more complex patterns emerge for some risk factors than for others, the overall impression that emerges from this and other data sources suggests that those with lower socioeconomic position have poorer behavioral and psychosocial risk factor profiles (National Heart, Lung, and Blood Institute, 1995).

The reasons for these underlying differences in risk factor distribution across population subgroups have rarely been the object of study in their own right. The most common approach has been to statistically adjust for them as confounders of the association between measures of socioeconomic position and health. Although this approach may be potentially informative of *how* lower socioeconomic position is linked to poorer health, it reveals little about *why* lower socioeconomic groups have poorer risk factor profiles (see Figure 3.1; Lynch et al., 1996). The task of understanding the developmental processes that result in socioeconomic groups having different risk factor profiles is complicated and would involve long-term studies in natural population settings with assessments at multiple points over the life course. Although such comprehensive data are virtually nonexistent, clues about these processes can be gained from some prospective

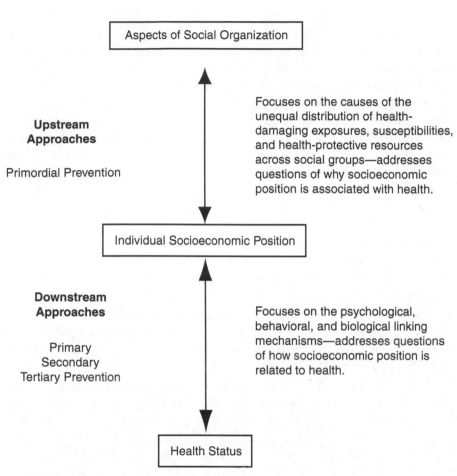

Figure 3.1. Upstream and downstream approaches to understanding socioeconomic inequalities in health.

population-based studies that do have information on socioeconomic circumstances at various stages of the life course.

A LIFE COURSE APPROACH TO UNDERSTANDING ADULT CARDIOVASCULAR DISEASE RISK

A life course approach to understanding socioeconomic differences in CVD stresses the idea that from conception to adulthood, social and biological factors are involved in complex, sometimes mutually reinforcing coevolution over time (Vågerö & Illsley, 1995). Exposures structured by socioeconomic circumstances may accumulate and ultimately increase the risk of adult disease (Davey Smith, Hart, Blane, Gillis, & Hawthorne, 1997; Davey Smith, Hart, Blane, & Hole, 1998; Lynch, Kaplan, & Salonen, 1997; Kuh & Ben Shlomo, 1997; Power, Hertzman, Mathews, & Manor, 1997). According to this view, different socioeconomic pathways through life might be associated with different accumulations of adult disease risk and indeed may be evidenced by systematic differences in health behaviors and psychosocial characteristics. Consider smoking as an example of an accumulation of risk over the life course: As a group, individuals who are born into more affluent homes are less likely to be exposed to tobacco metabolites in utero, are less likely to be exposed to second-hand smoke in childhood, are less likely to be exposed to tobacco advertising, are less likely to initiate the habit. If they do initiate, they are more likely to quit. In short, they are more likely to grow up, live, work, and play in environments that provide less encouragement for the development and maintenance of negative behavioral and psychosocial characteristics.

Figure 3.2 lays out a conceptual model of how socioeconomic disadvantage and other factors may come together to influence risk factors and health status at various stages of the life course. Such a model is important because it highlights the potential for social and economic factors to structure biological responses and vice versa. It is these interlacing chains of mutual influence that help define people's pathways through life and may ultimately affect their behavioral, psychosocial, and health profiles as adults. The figure starts with the idea that we all receive a genetic and social inheritance from our parents. Even in utero the biological environment provided by the mother for the fetus is influenced by social and economic factors through such mechanisms as maternal nutrition or exposure to toxins. As we age, we move through any number of important environments, including home, neighborhood, school, and work, and these environments all have exposure potential to influence levels of biological, behavioral, and psychosocial risk factors later in life. Although this idea is not new, research in this area has received a great deal of impetus from epidemiological evidence suggesting that adult CVD may be programmed by biological events in utero. In a series of studies since the mid-1980s, David Barker and colleagues have shown associations between anthropometric indicators (such as low birthweight) and cardiovascular disease outcomes (Barker & Martyn, 1992; Barker & Osmond, 1986; Barker, Osmond, Golding, Kuh, & Wadsworth, 1989). For CVD, Barker and colleagues have argued that maternal and consequently fetal undernutrition in mid-to-late gestation increases the risk of a low-weight, thin baby, and raises the risk of later CVD by programming of blood pressure, cholesterol metabolism, blood clotting, and hormonal control through such mechanisms as retarded organ development. Although some of the empirical evidence for biological programming has been questioned, the hypothesis is nevertheless provocative and may have potentially important implications for intervention (Joseph & Kramer, 1995).

Figure 3.2 goes on to indicate that during childhood, the socioeco-

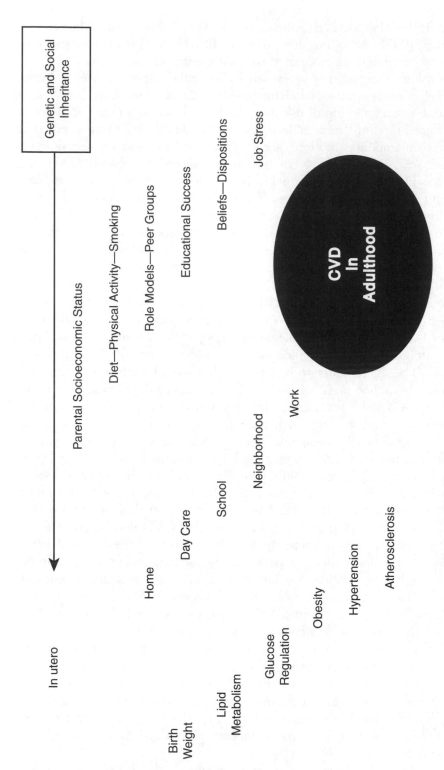

Figure 3.2. A life-course approach to cardiovascular disease.

nomic position of parents (income, type of housing, neighborhood) influence the types of environments in which children grow, learn, and begin to adopt a range of behaviors that can influence the early acquisition of risk factors. In adulthood, working conditions and income level affect job stress and have direct implications for the onset and progression of cardiovascular disease, whereas at older ages, income and assets impact the quality and availability of medical and support care. All of these processes may contribute to what is observed as adult socioeconomic differences in cardiovascular disease and its risk factors (Davey Smith et al., 1998; Lynch, Kaplan, & Salonen, 1997). This model has provided the conceptual basis for the construction of "socioeconomic life course pathways" that link early with later life socioeconomic circumstances (Lynch et al., 1994).

SOCIOECONOMIC PATHWAYS, HEALTH BEHAVIORS, PSYCHOSOCIAL, AND BIOLOGICAL CHARACTERISTICS

This section will present data that shows how adult behavioral, psychosocial, and biological risk factors for CVD are patterned by different life course socioeconomic pathways. These pathways are defined by socioeconomic position in childhood (based on father's occupation) and adult income level. Analyses presented in Table 3.1 show data from the Alameda County Study, a population-based prospective investigation of predictors of health and functioning in a representative sample of adults in Alameda County, California. The 1965 baseline sample comprised 6,982 men and women. This cohort has been followed for more than 30 years, and was surveyed in 1974, 1983, 1994, 1995, and again in 1999. The results presented here are based on the 1994 follow-up sample of 2,730 but limited to those with no missing information (n = 2,295). Details of the study sample and methods are available elsewhere (Lynch, Kaplan, & Shema, 1997).

Data on 1994 levels of smoking, sedentary behavior, body mass index (BMI), cynicism, lack of optimism, depression, and perceived health are presented according to the cross-classification of father's occupation (manual vs. nonmanual) and mean adult income in 1965–1974 (high 25% vs. middle 50% vs. low 25%). Thus, reading the table from left to right arrays a prospective temporal sequence from childhood socioeconomic conditions, to adult income in 1965–1974, to behavioral and psychosocial attributes in 1994. Results are based on general linear models and logistic regressions where those who were born into homes where the father was employed in nonmanual work and who went on to be in the top 25% of income earners as adults in 1965–1974 were considered the reference category for the calculation of odds ratios (OR). These results did not differ greatly when analyzed separately for women and men.

TABLE 3.1
Father's Occupation, Adult Income, and Selected Health Behaviors and Psychosocial Characteristics, Alameda County Study, 1965–1994

Father's occupation	Mean adult income 1965–1974 OR	Smoking pack-years[a] OR	Sedentary low 25% physical activity OR	High BMI high 25% OR	Cynicism high 25% OR	Lack of optimism high 25% OR	Depression DSM III-R Diagnosis OR	Perceived health fair-poor OR
Nonmanual								
High 25% n = 467		5,110	Reference	Reference	Reference	Reference	Reference	Reference
Middle 50% n = 400		5,110	1.1	1.2	1.2	1.1	1.2	1.8†
Low 25% n = 304		6,388[b]	1.7[b]	1.8[b]	1.9[b]	1.7[b]	1.3	1.9[b]
Manual								
High 25% n = 313		6,205	1.1	1.6[b]	1.4	1.4	0.90	1.5[b]
Middle 50% n = 368		6,205	1.3	1.9[b]	1.9[b]	1.4	1.4	1.5[b]
Low 25% n = 443		6,570[b]	1.6[b]	2.5[b]	2.1[b]	2.1[b]	1.8[b]	3.4[b]

Note. N = 2,295 men and women. BMI = body mass index. [a] Age-adjusted mean. [b] Significantly different from reference category; at least p < .05.

There are a number of noteworthy features of these results. In general, those who were born into poorer homes and who stayed poorer throughout their lives were also the most disadvantaged in terms of their health behaviors and psychosocial characteristics in 1994. For example, men and women whose fathers were in manual occupations and who were in the lowest 25% of income earners as adults had, on average, 6,570 pack-years of exposure to cigarette smoking, whereas those who were born into families with a father in a nonmanual occupation and had high levels of adult income had 5,110 pack-years of exposure. The differences observed here are even more striking when examined in younger age cohorts where smoking is now much less common in more advantaged socioeconomic groups than it was in the past. This same pattern of the highest accumulated risk associated with the most disadvantaged socioeconomic pathway is evident for lack of exercise, BMI, cynicism, lack of optimism, depression, and poor perceived health. In every case, those with the most advantaged socioeconomic pathway through life have the best behavioral and psychosocial risk factor profiles as adults.

This type of analysis also allows us to examine socioeconomic pathways through life that involved a degree of intergenerational socioeconomic mobility. There is a good deal of heterogeneity in adult risk factor profiles among the group with a poorer start in life (i.e., their father was in a manual occupation). In every case, upward mobility was associated with better adult risk factor profiles compared with those who stayed relatively poor throughout life. Nonetheless, the risk factor profiles for the group with greatest upward mobility were not as good as those with lifelong socioeconomic advantage. Men and women with the greatest upward mobility over the life course into the top 25% of income earners were at increased risk of elevated BMI (OR = 1.6, p = .01), fair or poor perceived health (OR = 1.5, p = .05), being cynical (OR = 1.4, p = .05), had higher pack-years of exposure to smoking, and were lacking optimism (although these were not statistically significant), but not for being sedentary (OR = 1.1, p = .71) or depressed (OR = 0.90, p = .70), compared with people who were born and stayed in advantaged circumstances throughout the life course. In other words, the upwardly mobile groups had risk factor profiles that were intermediate between the consistently most and least advantaged socioeconomic life course pathways. Interestingly, this group also had better adult risk factor profiles than the group of men and women who were downwardly mobile (i.e., they were born into homes where the father was in nonmanual work), but as adults they were in the lowest 25% of income earners. This group had statistically elevated rates of smoking, lack of exercise, high BMI, cynicism, lack of optimism, depression, and poor perceived health compared with the reference group. These rates were not as high as were those for individuals at lifelong socioeconomic disadvantage, however.

The data presented here demonstrate the heuristic value of conceptualizing and modeling the life course exposure to differing socioeconomic circumstances. In general, these data suggest two things. First, lifelong advantage and disadvantage are invariably associated with the best and worst adult behavioral and psychosocial risk factor profiles. Second, childhood socioeconomic conditions may have an enduring effect on adult patterns of behavioral and psychosocial risk factors.

The data in Tables 3.2 and 3.3 extend the results presented in Table 3.1 by showing results on the life course socioeconomic patterning of selected dietary and biological characteristics, albeit in a different population-based cohort. This data is based on information collected in the Kuopio Ischemic Heart Disease Risk Factor Study (KIHD), which was designed to investigate previously unestablished risk factors for ischemic heart disease, carotid atherosclerosis, and other related outcomes in a population-based sample of eastern Finnish men. It is one of the most comprehensive studies of biological, psychological, and social risk factors for CVD ever undertaken. The study population consisted of a 33% random sample of men who resided in the town of Kuopio or its six adjacent rural communities. The total sample was 2,682, but these analyses are based on 2,549 men who had no missing information on the variables of interest. Details of the study population and methods are available elsewhere (Lynch, Krause, Kaplan, Cohen, Salonen, & Salonen, 1997).

Information on selected dietary characteristics (Table 3.2) and biological parameters (Table 3.3) collected as part of the baseline exam are presented according to father's occupation (nonmanual and skilled manual vs. unskilled manual) and adult income levels at baseline. Table 3.2 shows somewhat different life course socioeconomic patterns in diet than do the behavioral and psychosocial risk factors displayed in Table 3.1. Men with the least advantaged life course socioeconomic position have the lowest levels of fruit and vegetable consumption and polyunsaturated to saturated fat ratio (P:S) and the highest levels of sodium consumption. They have more favorable dietary profiles for consumption of meat and whole grain products, however. It is likely that although these men have lower meat consumption overall, the meat they do eat is higher in fat. Their saturated fat intake is indicated by the lowest P:S ratio of 0.25, which is also influenced by higher consumption of butter and other dairy products. As was seen for the behavioral and psychosocial risk factors, the best dietary profiles were seen in men who remained socioeconomically advantaged over the life course, whereas the worst profiles were generally seen in men who were persistently disadvantaged. The effects of socioeconomic mobility were again evident.

It appears that the adult dietary habits of men who were the most upwardly mobile were closer to the dietary practices of those who were advantaged throughout the life course than to men who were consistently

TABLE 3.2
Father's Occupation, Adult Income, and Age-Adjusted Mean Levels of Selected Dietary Characteristics, Kuopio Ischemic Heart Disease Risk Factor Study, 1990

Father's occupation	Adult income	Meat gm/day	Vegetables gm/day	Fruit gm/day	Whole grain products gm/day	Sodium mg/day	P:S fat ratio[a]
Nonmanual and skilled manual	High 25% n = 466	161.2	98.0	206.7	132.9	3032	0.29
	Middle 50% n = 735	166.2	84.5[b]	173.0[†]	152.4[b]	3277[b]	0.27[b]
	Low 25% n = 343	154.1	72.0[b]	150.2[b]	145.8[b]	3236[b]	0.26[b]
Unskilled manual	High 25% n = 170	168.0	104.8	198.4	136.3	3111	0.29
	Middle 50% n = 531	165.4	79.6[b]	164.1[b]	154.1[b]	3397[b]	0.27[b]
	Low 25% n = 304	150.1[b]	65.3[b]	139.4[b]	151.8[b]	3451[b]	0.25[b]

Note. N = 2,549 men. [a]P:S ratio = polyunsaturated:saturated fat ratio. [b]Significantly different from reference category; at least p < .05.

TABLE 3.3
Father's Occupation, Adult Income, and Age-Adjusted Mean Levels of Selected Biological Characteristics, Kuopio Ischemic Heart Disease Risk Factor Study, 1989

Father's Occupation	Adult Income	Systolic Blood Pressure mmHg	LDL mmol/L	Total Cholesterol mmol/L	Fibrinogen g/L	Blood Leukocytes 10**9/L	Copper mg/L	Plasma Vit C mg/L	Mercury ug/gm
Nonmanual and skilled manual	High 25% n = 466	132.9	3.81	5.67	2.92	5.48	1.09	9.1	1.50
	Middle 50% n = 735	134.2	4.05[a]	5.91[a]	3.02[a]	5.70[a]	1.11[a]	8.2[a]	1.96[a]
	Low 25% n = 343	134.7	4.13[a]	6.04[a]	3.19[a]	6.10[a]	1.15[a]	7.5[a]	2.52[a]
Unskilled manual	High 25% n = 170	133.1	3.97[a]	5.81	2.92	5.57	1.09	9.1	1.80
	Middle 50% n = 531	133.4	4.10[a]	5.96[a]	2.99[a]	5.59	1.11[a]	8.0[a]	2.29[a]
	Low 25% n = 304	136.7[a]	4.13[a]	6.02[a]	3.17[a]	6.00[a]	1.14[a]	7.4[a]	2.59[a]

Note. LDL = low density lipoprotein. [a]Significantly different from reference category; at least $p < .05$.

disadvantaged. The pattern of downward socioeconomic mobility was again associated with a somewhat poorer dietary profile. It should be remembered that the socioeconomic pathways used here are relatively crude in that they only isolate two specific points in the life course and provide no information on the precise timing of socioeconomic mobility. For instance, it is impossible to distinguish between trajectories of upward mobility achieved through increased family affluence later in childhood that translated into better educational attainment, job prospects, and pay as an adult compared with relatively poor conditions throughout childhood, low educational attainment, but relatively highly paid adult employment. Health "habits" and psychosocial attributes develop in context, and the timing of the improvement in socioeconomic circumstances may have important implications for the potential to acquire and maintain certain behavioral and psychosocial characteristics. Nevertheless, these somewhat simplistic socioeconomic pathways help focus attention on the developmental interconnectedness of socioeconomic, behavioral, and psychosocial factors.

Finally, Table 3.3 shows data on particular biological parameters of the 2,549 men in the KIHD study according to their life course socioeconomic pathway. The life course socioeconomic patterns in biological risk factor profiles are broadly consistent with those observed for the behavioral, psychosocial, and dietary risk characteristics. Men who were socioeconomically advantaged over the entire life course had the most favorable levels for all the biological factors, whereas men at consistent disadvantage had the worst levels of systolic blood pressure, low density lipoprotein (LDL, associated with "bad" cholesterol), fibrinogen (related to blood clotting), and trace metals like copper and mercury that increase the oxidation of low density lipoproteins and may lead to accumulation of plaque in the arteries. Their levels of total cholesterol, leukocyte count (white blood cells), and plasma vitamin C levels were among the worst. Upwardly mobile men had biological risk factor profiles that were roughly comparable to the most consistently advantaged except for elevated LDL (3.97 mmol/L, $p = .05$) and mercury levels (1.80 ug/gm, $p = .10$). Although this is not an exhaustive list of relevant biological parameters, it does demonstrate that important differences exist in the patterning of biological risk factors for CVD by life course socioeconomic position. Nonetheless, it should also be noted that no differences were found for levels of high-density lipoprotein (HDL, associated with "good" cholesterol), blood glucose, or insulin.

The results presented in these tables suggest that adult levels of behavioral, psychosocial, dietary, and biological risk factors differ by life course socioeconomic pathway. There is evidence for the greatest accumulation of adverse risk factors among those who were born and remained socioeconomically disadvantaged over the entire life course. There is also evidence to support the idea that those who were upwardly mobile accumulated less risk, but this socioeconomic pathway through life did not completely obliterate the effects of poor childhood socioeconomic origins on higher adult levels of smoking, excessive weight, cynicism, lack of optimism, poor perceived health, LDL, and mercury. In addition, it is interesting to observe the consistently adverse behavioral, psychosocial, dietary, and biological risk factor profiles for those who began life in relative advantage but had low socioeconomic position as adults. It appears that childhood socioeconomic advantage does not confer much protection on risk factor profiles for people who have a low adult socioeconomic position. On the contrary, childhood disadvantage does appear to increase the likelihood of a poorer adult profile at least for some behavioral, psychosocial, and biological risk factors. The question is what happens to people who travel these different socioeconomic pathways through life? What day-to-day and cumulative experiences do they have that seem to influence the behavioral, psychosocial, and biological characteristics they possess as adults. These results raise more questions than they offer answers, but they serve to highlight the importance of future research that elucidates what happens to the development, maintenance, and extinction of particular levels of behavioral, psychosocial, and biological risk factors in response to socioeconomic circumstances. I am not suggesting that people are completely programmed, robotlike, by social and economic conditions. In fact, these results do not support such a conclusion. There are clearly dimensions of choice involved in how people act and behave, but we must equally recognize the social and economic constraints in which these choices are made. The data presented here suggest some fairly powerful and consistent effects of life course socioeconomic position on adult risk factor profiles. If we limit understanding of these risk factor patterns to the proximal time frame of adulthood, we miss an important part of the picture, a part that has significant implications for intervention and public health in the 21st century.

IMPLICATIONS FOR PREVENTION

In public health, we are all familiar with the concepts of primary, secondary, and tertiary prevention (Last, 1988). Primary prevention usually refers to measures taken to reduce the incidence of disease and for chronic diseases typically involves activities such as modifying risk factor profiles. Secondary prevention involves reducing the prevalence of disease by shortening its duration through measures such as early detection and prompt, effective treatment. Tertiary prevention is aimed at reducing the complications associated with the disease process to minimize disability and suffering. Figure 3.1 shows how these downstream approaches focus on the biological, behavioral, and psychosocial mechanisms that link socioeconomic position to health. The behavioral and social sciences make important contributions in all these domains. Indeed, much of our work in primary prevention to reduce the incidence of CVD has focused on changing behavioral and psychosocial risk factor profiles through individual behavior modification of such things as smoking, diet, and exercise. There is little doubt that such programs have benefits. Nonetheless, we cannot ignore the fact that the disappointing effects of the large community-based interventions such as those at Stanford, Minnesota, and Pawtucket are modest in comparison with the secular changes in risk factors (McKinlay & Marceau, 1999; Winkelby, 1994). By focussing on those most at risk, even direct attempts to engage socioeconomically "hard-to-reach" communities are unlikely to have a significant impact on average population levels of risk factors. In addition, the data presented here show the importance of thinking about behavioral and psychosocial risk factors from a life course perspective. Even the best designed and conducted primary prevention programs aimed at altering risk factors in one generation may do little to alter underlying socioeconomic and other forces that help produce the appearance of risk factors in the next generation. After all our efforts at tobacco control in youth, how are we to understand the disturbing increase in smoking among young white women (NCHS, 1998)?

In 1978, Strasser (1978) suggested that prevention of CVD should go beyond programs encompassed under the idea of primary prevention. He coined the term *primordial prevention* to mean activities that prevented the penetration of risk factors into populations. The basic idea is to intervene to stop the appearance of the risk factor in the population. In some sense, this is not dissimilar to traditional public health immunization efforts for infectious conditions, which aim to prevent the appearance of the risk factor or condition before it takes hold in the population. Although Strasser's idea of primordial prevention was originally concerned with controlling the penetration of risk factors such as smoking in developing countries, the concept has important implications for how we think about the relationship between life course socioeconomic circumstances and adult risk factors. Labarthe (1998) has argued that, "The additional possibility that societal conditions favoring risk factor development could be controlled or reversed, even once established, adds further importance to the concept of primordial prevention" (p. 501). Table 3.4 contrasts the ideas of primordial and primary prevention and suggests different targets for intervention, looking beyond individuals and groups of individuals to aspects of social organization that can influence risk factor development. There are potentially many levels of intervention that could be informed by the idea of primordial prevention. For instance, many of our schools have become corporatized outlets for fast food of often-dubious nutritional quality. If we are interested in the principles of primordial prevention and intercepting the appearance in the population of risk factors, such as hypertension, excessive weight, and elevated blood lipids, then we should be con-

TABLE 3.4
Contrasting Primordial and Primary Prevention for
Cardiovascular Disease

	Primordial Prevention	Primary Prevention
Idea	Prevent the appearance of the mediating risk factor in the population	Alter the mediating risk factor level after it appears in the population
Focus	Aspects of social organization	Individual, groups of individuals
Goal	Modify the conditions that generate and structure the unequal distribution of health-damaging exposures, susceptibilities, and health-protective resources among the population	Modify the individual-level behavioral, psychosocial, and biological mediators that lead to increased incidence

cerned about the effects of this potentially negative structuring of the food choices our children are able to make. A life course approach to primordial prevention forces us to ask whether it is better in the long run to ensure inexpensive healthy food and establish the development of desirable eating habits in school children rather than running dietary interventions when these individuals reach adulthood or controlling their lipid levels with the next generations of lipid lowering drugs. Primordial prevention in this setting would involve making sure that the food choices available to kids were structured to minimize the chance that the CVD risk factors associated with poor diet would appear in the population. Similarly, school-based programs of physical education and sport have been reduced because of financial pressures, but is it not likely that this may contribute to later sedentary behavior and obesity? There are not necessarily easy answers to these questions, but the idea of primordial prevention may help us ask the right questions. Policy actions that influence structural characteristics of the environment, such as food and alcohol availability, have behavioral and public health dividends to be reaped in the future. Surely this is the lesson of environmental smoking bans in public places. Children who grow up in an environment with few opportunities to smoke are less likely to adopt the behavior in the first place. Can we apply the same logic to other risk factors for cardiovascular and other chronic diseases?

If there is one message that emerges from the data discussed here, it is that remaining in relatively poor circumstances throughout the life course is associated with a range of negative biological, behavioral, and psychosocial characteristics. Social, economic, and political conditions that help keep some groups poor, no matter how hard they work and toil, have implications for those people's health, behavior, and psychosocial attributes. The question that a focus on primordial prevention forces us to ask is whether there is anything we can do, or perhaps more correctly, what are we willing to do to avoid having poor children be poor all their lives? Recent policy initiatives such as welfare reform threaten to plunge many more children into poverty. Behavioral and social scientists have much to offer in raising awareness of the potential public health implications that such policies are likely to yield in the future and are anathema to the principles of primordial prevention. Behavioral and social science research has a vital role to play in bringing these issues of life course development and primordial prevention to the forefront of our efforts to improve public health in the 21st century. The results presented here suggest it is time to seriously engage in a discussion of how we might mitigate the conditions that give rise to the appearance of particular risk factors in the population. This sort of discussion has vastly different implications for intervention than a discussion of how we reduce the incidence of the disease through primary prevention.

CONCLUSION

Socioeconomic conditions over the life course do influence adult risk factor profiles. The worst profiles are for those groups who start out relatively poor and stay poor. Contrast this with groups who start out poor but are upwardly mobile: Their risk factor profile is closer to those who were socioeconomically advantaged throughout life. Whatever happens to people on that upward path through life seems to improve their risk factor levels as adults. The goal that our social and economic structures should maximize the potential for upward mobility is not exactly novel, but is it time for the public health community to seriously embrace and advocate this idea as a viable intervention based on principles of primordial disease prevention? Maximizing structural opportunities for upward socioeconomic mobility is usually a topic for economists, but it also has important implications for future public health.

It may be an even more salient idea given the unprecedented increases in income inequality that have recently been documented in the United States, Great Britain, and other industrial countries (Gottschalk & Smeeding, 1997). Furthermore, we need to consider primordial prevention in light of the fact that these historically high levels of income inequality have forced ever-larger numbers of families with children into low socioeconomic groups. Child poverty levels in the United States have been hovering around 20% since 1981 (Federal Interagency Forum on Child and Family Statistics, 1998). Although we have done much to reduce poverty among elderly people, who are a powerful political constituency, we have not done as well for our children. In addition to placing them into socioeconomic conditions that may be detrimental to their immediate health status, greater income inequality may produce a negative behavioral and psychosocial health dividend to be reaped in the future. Are we creating economic conditions today that will force larger numbers of children into groups who have a poor start in life? The potential health impact of this socioeconomic inequality is even more frightening in light of reduced commitments to public education and welfare programs that could offer some opportunities for social advancement. In 1994, there were 38 million Americans in poverty; 15 million of these individuals were under age 18, and 6 million were preschoolers under age 6 (Corcoran & Chaudry, 1997). How many of these young people will stay poor throughout their lives? The sorts of behavioral, psychosocial, and biological risk factor profiles that they develop by adulthood are surely of major public health concern.

We cannot ignore the fact that CVD risk factors are influenced by the social, political, and economic organization of our society. The perspectives of behavioral and social science have a vital role to play in fostering understanding that

> these behaviors are plainly embedded in the social structure. When questions are asked not merely how people behave but why they behave as they do, "lifestyles" provide no release from the need to confront that structure—which also has many other effects on health. (Morris, 1990, p. 493)

The public health community should consider the potential for a broad array of social, educational, and economic policies as effective public health interventions to reduce the unequal distribution of risk factors and the unequal burden of disease. The concept of primordial prevention should be a focal point for efforts in the behavioral and social sciences as we strive to improve public health in the 21st century.

REFERENCES

Antonovsky, A. (1967). Social class, life expectancy and overall mortality. *Milbank Memorial Fund Quarterly, 45,* 31–73.

Barker, D. J. P., & Martyn, C. N. (1992). The maternal and fetal origins of cardiovascular disease. *Journal of Epidemiology and Community Health, 46,* 8–11.

Barker, D. J. P., & Osmond, C. (1986). Infant mortality, childhood nutrition, and ischaemic heart disease in England and Wales. *Lancet, 1,* 1077–1081.

Barker, D. J. P., Osmond, C., Golding, J., Kuh, D., & Wadsworth, M. E. J. (1989). Growth in utero, blood pressure in childhood and adult life, and mortality from cardiovascular disease. *British Medical Journal, 298,* 564–567.

Carroll, D., Davey Smith, G., & Bennett, P. (1996) Some observations on health and socioeconomic status. *Journal of Health Psychology, 1,* 23–39.

Corcoran, M. E., & Chaudry, A. (1997) The dynamics of children in poverty. *The Future of Children, 7,* 40–54.

Davey Smith, G., Hart C., Blane, D., Gillis C., & Hawthorne, V. (1997). Lifetime socioeconomic position and mortality: Prospective observational study. *British Medical Journal, 314,* 547–552.

Davey Smith, G., Hart C., Blane, D., & Hole, D. (1998). Adverse socioeconomic conditions in childhood and cause specific adult mortality: Prospective observational study. *British Medical Journal, 316,* 1631–1651.

Davey Smith, G., Neaton, J. D., Wentworth, D., Stamler, R., & Stamler, J. (1996). Socioeconomic differentials in mortality risk among men screened for the Multiple Risk Factor Intervention Trial: 1. White men. *American Journal of Public Health, 86,* 486–496.

Engels, F. (1848). *The condition of the working class in England* (O. W. Henderson & W. H. Chaloner, Trans., 1958). Stanford, CA: Stanford University Press.

Evans, R. G., Barer, M. L., & Marmor, T. R. (Eds.). (1994). *Why are some people healthy and others not?* New York: Aldine de Gruyter.

Farr, W. (1989). Report of the evidence to the Royal Commission of Mines. In C. Buck, A. Llopis, E. Najera, & M. Terris (Eds.), *The challenge of epidemiology* (pp. 67–72). Washington, DC: Pan American Health Organization. (Original work published 1864)

Federal Interagency Forum on Child and Family Statistics. (1998). *America's children: Key national indicators of well-being.* Washington, DC: Author.

Gottschalk, P., & Smeeding, T. M. (1997). Cross-national comparisons of earnings and income inequality. *Journal of Economic Literature, 35,* 633–686.

Haan, M. N., Kaplan, G. A., & Syme, S. L. (1989). Socioeconomic status and health: Old observations and new thoughts. In J. P. Bunker, D. S. Gomby, & B. H. Kehrer (Eds.), *Pathways to health: The role of social factors* (pp. 76–135). Menlo Park, CA: HJ Kaiser Family Foundation.

Heck, K. E., & Pamuk, E. R. (1997). Explaining the relation between education and postmenopausal breast cancer. *American Journal of Epidemiology, 145,* 366–372.

Joseph, K. S., & Kramer, M. S. (1995) Review of the evidence on fetal and early childhood antecedents of adult chronic disease. *Epidemiologic Reviews, 18,* 158–174.

Kaplan, G. A., & Keil, J. E. (1993). Socioeconomic factors and cardiovascular disease: A review of the literature. *Circulation, 88,* 1973–1998.

Kaplan, G. A., & Lynch, J. W. (1997) Whither studies on the socioeconomic foundations of population health [Editorial]. *American Journal of Public Health, 87,* 1409–1411.

Kuh, D., & Ben Shlomo, Y. (Eds.). (1997). *A lifecourse approach to chronic disease epidemiology.* Oxford, UK: Oxford University Press.

Labarthe, D. R. (1998). *Epidemiology and prevention of cardiovascular diseases.* Gaithersburg, MD: Aspen.

Last, J. M. (Ed.). (1988). *A dictionary of epidemiology.* New York: Oxford University Press.

Lynch, J. W., & Kaplan, G. A. (2000). Socioeconomic position. In L. F. Berkman

& I. Kawachi (Eds.), *Social epidemiology* (pp. 13–35). New York: Oxford University Press.

Lynch, J. W., Kaplan, G. A., Cohen, R. D., Kauhanen, J., Wilson, T. W., Smith, N. L., & Salonen, J. T. (1994). Childhood and adult socioeconomic status as predictors of mortality in Finland. *Lancet, 343,* 524–527.

Lynch, J. W., Kaplan, G. A., Cohen, R. D., Tuomilehto, J., & Salonen, J. T. (1996). Do cardiovascular risk factors explain the relation between socioeconomic status, risk of all-cause mortality, cardiovascular mortality and acute myocardial infarction? *American Journal of Epidemiology, 144,* 934–942.

Lynch, J. W., Kaplan, G. A., & Salonen, J. T. (1997). Why do poor people behave poorly? Variations in adult health behaviour and psychosocial characteristics, by stage of the socioeconomic lifecourse. *Social Science and Medicine, 44,* 809–820.

Lynch, J. W., Kaplan, G. A., & Shema, S. J. (1997). Cumulative impact of sustained economic hardship on physical, cognitive, psychological, and social functioning. *New England Journal of Medicine, 337,* 1889–1895.

Lynch, J. W., Krause, N., Kaplan, G. A., Cohen, R. D., Salonen, R., & Salonen, J. T. (1997). Workplace demands, economic reward and progression of carotid atherosclerosis. *Circulation, 96,* 302–308.

Macintyre, S. (1997). The Black report and beyond: What are the issues? *Social Science and Medicine, 44,* 723–746.

McKinlay, J. B., & Marceau, L. D. (1999). A tale of 3 tails. *American Journal of Public Health, 89,* 295–298.

Morris, J. (1990). Inequalities in health: Ten years and little further on. *Lancet, 336,* 491–493.

National Center for Health Statistics. (1998). *Health, United States, 1998 with socioeconomic status and health chartbook.* Hyattsville, MD: Author.

National Heart, Lung, and Blood Institute. (1995). *Chartbook of U.S. national data on socioeconomic status and cardiovascular health and disease.* Bethesda, MD: Author.

Paracelsus. (1941). On the miner's sickness and other miner's diseases. In H. E. Sigerist (Ed.), *Four treatises of Theophrastus von Hohenheim called Paracelsus* (pp. 56–61). Baltimore: Johns Hopkins Press.

Power, C., Hertzman C., Mathews, S., & Manor O. (1997). Social differences in health: Life-cycle effects between ages 23 and 33 in the 1958 British birth cohort. *American Journal of Public Health, 87,* 1499–1503.

Rosen, G. (1958). *A history of public health.* New York: MD Publications.

Sorlie, P. D., Backlund, E., & Keller, J. B. (1995). U.S. mortality by economic, demographic, and social characteristics: The national longitudinal mortality study. *American Journal of Public Health, 85,* 949–956.

Strasser, T. (1978). Reflections on cardiovascular diseases. *Interdisciplinary Science Review, 3,* 225–230.

Townsend, P., & Davidson, N. (Eds.). (1982). *Inequalities in health: The Black report.* Harmondsworth, UK: Penguin Books.

Vågerö, D., & Illsley, R. (1995). Explaining health inequalities: Beyond Black and Barker. *European Sociological Review, 11,* 219–241.

Villermé, L. R. (1840). *Tableau de l'etat physique et moral des ouvriers employés dans les manufactures de coton, de laine et de soie.* Paris: Jules Renouard et Cie Libraires.

Virchow R. (1988). Report on the typhus epidemic in Upper Silesia. In L. J. Rather (Ed.), *Rudolph Virchow: Collected essays on public health and epidemiology* (Vol. 1, pp. 205–220). Canton, MA: Science History Publications. (Original work published 1848)

Williams, D. R. (1990). Socioeconomic differentials in health: A review and redirection. *Social Psychology Quarterly, 53,* 81–99.

Winkelby, M. A. (1994). The future of community-based cardiovascular disease intervention studies [Editorial]. *American Journal of Public Health, 84,* 1369–1372.

4

COMMUNITY INTERVENTION IN CARDIOVASCULAR HEALTH PROMOTION: NORTH KARELIA, 1972–1999

PEKKA PUSKA AND ANTTI UUTELA

We begin this chapter with general principles of community intervention programs for cardiovascular disease prevention. We offer a survey of the literature to provide an epidemiological basis for developing community programs and to give credit to behavioral and social scientific theories, described elsewhere in the book, that are relevant for planning and evaluating these programs. Finally, we share our experience and results to substantiate the final recommendations concerning community programs as important tools of health promotion in various contexts.

THE RATIONALE

Atherosclerotic cardiovascular disease (CVD) is a global health problem that will continue to be a leading cause of death in the near future (World Health Organization [WHO], 1998). Much is known about the biomedical aspects of the disease, and present research in this area is promising. Epidemiological research has provided information about the risk factors of CVD, contributing to an understanding of disease processes in many of the world's populations. Smoking, elevated serum low-density lipoprotein cholesterol, and high blood pressure levels have been shown to have a strong effect on cardiovascular ischemic problems (WHO, 1973, 1982), and scientists are still learning about new risk factors.

A recent study from Finland indicated that lowering cholesterol levels was predictive of the decline in national ischemic heart disease mortality (Vartiainen, Puska, Pekkanen, Tuomilehto, & Jousilahti, 1994). Furthermore, concurrence of certain unhealthy behaviors (including smoking, high intake of dairy fat, and physical inactivity) potentiated the risk for cardiovascular mortality. The contribution of various risk factors appears to have varied across cultures and time periods (Luoto, Prättälä, Uutela, & Puska, 1998). Risk factor disparities can explain about a half of the differences between social classes with regard to CVD mortality rates (Pekkanen, Tuomilehto, Uutela, Vartiainen, & Nissinen, 1995).

Physicians are used to treating individuals, not populations, with health problems. As the notion of risk factors became widely accepted and the means to reduce the influence of these factors became available, physicians moved from treating patients to screening subpopulations to locate those people most at risk for acquiring health problems. Looking from an individual perspective, the poorer the risk factor profile, the higher the probability of developing disease. This provides a legitimate reason for the person identified as high risk to ask for treatment. From the point of view of public health, however, an individual-based solution alone may be neither the most effective nor the most egalitarian approach.

This chapter deals with community interventions that take advantage of available resources in communities to help their members improve their health. We use experiences derived from the first intervention of this kind, which was implemented in 1972 in the province of North Karelia in eastern Finland (Puska et al., 1981; Puska, 1996). The project was followed by others, some of them almost concurrently in the United States (e.g., Stanford Three-Community Study, Meyer, Nash, McAlister, Maccoby, & Faquhar, 1980; Stanford Five City Project, Farquhar et al., 1985; Minnesota Heart Health program, Carlaw, Mittelmark, Bracht, & Luepker, 1984), and then later in other countries (see Sorensen, Emmons, Hunt, & Johnston, 1998). We look at the theoretical basis, implementation, process, and evaluation of results for the North Karelia project to give an overall view of the strengths and weaknesses with respect to the present state of our knowledge.

Working with the medical problems of individuals with manifest illness or who are at high risk for future illness is common in health care. Although this continues to be necessary, one of the main tenets of modern public health is to target primary prevention, thereby including those people in the middle range of risk. It should also be noted that the context of public health has changed during the past 25 years. Whereas the emphasis in public health in the early 1970s focused on the reduction of risk factors, more contemporary approaches have focused on more comprehensive ideas of health promotion. Another new trend has been the growing interest of businesses to introduce health enhancement into their products and services.

Targets for Health Promotion Interventions

Examination of the risk factor distribution in the population indicates that the majority of disease cases occur among those individuals who exhibit only a slight elevation in risk factor levels. This suggests that the most substantial reduction of disease may be achieved when risk factor profiles among these individuals are lowered (WHO, 1986). A benefit of community interventions as a means to achieve such improvements in public health is that these interventions have proven to be both health effective and cost effective (Graham, Corso, Morris, Segui-Gomez, & Weinstein, 1998). Additionally, community-based interventions may be seen as vehicles of empowerment for members of the community, an important aspect of health promotion (Robertson & Minkler, 1994).

It is a common assumption that feelings of stress, together with inadequate coping mechanisms and unhealthy lifestyles, are partly responsible for the origination and development of chronic disease conditions, including CVD. Schneiderman and Orth-Gomér (1996) described a number of social and biobehavioral factors that appear to play a role in the development of CVD. Nonetheless, we must acknowledge that the biological pathways between stress and disease have not yet been proven conclusively (Kelly, Hertzman, & Daniels, 1997). The other route of risk increment, analytically separate but related to sociocultural and psychosocial factors, is that of health behavior, or lifestyle (WHO, 1973), which was the primary target of the community intervention in the North Karelia study and others.

Hypotheses that stress and lifestyle induced cardiovascular problems were circulating at the time the North Karelia project was launched in the beginning of the 1970s. That period saw not only a high level of coronary heart disease (CHD) in North Karelia, but also rapid social change. Migration took large numbers of young people to other parts of the country and to Sweden. The traditional occupations of the area, dairy farming and forestry were endangered because they no longer interested the youth. This rapid social change resulted in experiences of stress and perhaps anomie, which was met with both the coping processes of individuals and with a national policy of giving more resources to the remote and less modernized provinces (e.g., establishing provincial universities, including one in North Karelia). National measures such as these and the unique cultural identity of the people of North Karelia may have helped the population withstand the ill effects of stress and spurred them to change health behaviors.

Viewpoints on Health Behavior

Among the multiplicity of theories about health behaviors (see Research Unit in Health and Behavioral Change, 1993), the idea that health-damaging behaviors (e.g., smoking, consuming saturated fat) lead to life-threatening illnesses stands out as an important one. Individuals do not live in isolation, but are members of social organizations (Blaxter, 1998). The economic activity and social structures related to these social groups form the material basis of communities and influence individual lifestyles, including behaviors, attitudes, and even outlooks on life (Bruhn, 1988).

The determinants of a person's health behaviors are varied, giving rise to an abundance of theories concerning the resolution of health problems. A number of diverse, partially connected, or overlapping theoretical positions affected the North Karelia project. We feel that it is important to note the special role of behavioral and social science theories to community interventions. Kok, Schaalma, De Vries, Parcel, and Paulussen (1996) mentioned two possible uses for social and psychological theories in scientific research. With appropriate adaptations, these ideas could be applied to any behavioral or social science. First, Kok and colleagues described how theory-driven applications use hypotheses to help evaluate the (external) validity of research findings (e.g., generalizing research findings from a study conducted on university students to the population as a whole). Another approach is problem-driven applications. This refers to an attempt to contribute to practical problem solving using theories that can be instrumental to the task at hand. The latter application was well suited to the North Karelia project.

Our study involved a number of theories regarding either individuals or groups. Understanding research findings in terms of theories is essential for designing community programs. Otherwise, the mix of possible interventions used would be less than complete, and the positive health effects would not reach their potential. Multiple viewpoints are also needed for evaluation purposes.

A good starting point to begin this discussion is with theories focusing on behaviors at the individual level, for instance, those dealing with health behaviors as learned routines of the individuals. Theories such as the social–cognitive theory of Bandura (1986) and the health belief model of Rosenstock (1974) described elsewhere in this book deal with motives for health behavior maintenance and change. Prentice-Dunn and Rogers's

(1986) protection motivation theory may be used as a link between the health belief model and other cognitive models involving attitudes. The theory assumes that health-threatening messages may arise as a cognitive appraisal process that can lead to attitude change. In maladaptive cases, the threat is perceived as sizeable enough to prevent thinking about it, which decreases the chances for adaptive reactions (Rippetoe & Rogers, 1987).

The theory of reasoned action (Fishbein & Ajzen, 1975) and its development theory of planned behavior (Ajzen, 1985), as well as the attitudes-social-influence-self-efficacy (ASE) model of De Vries (Kok, Hospers, den Boer, & De Vries, 1996), deal with the cognitive control of the person from another perspective, that involving intentions. ASE replaced Fishbein's notion of subjective norms with the idea of social influence and prepared the way for using cognitive models in the field of health education (Kok, Hospers, et al., 1996). The ASE model also connected the trans-theoretical constructs (Prochaska & DiClemente, 1984) of precontemplation, contemplation, preparation, action, and maintenance to attitudinal theory (Lechner, 1998).

William J. McGuire (1986) postulated that behavior change based on communication requires exposure and attention to as well as comprehension of messages that would have the persuasive power to achieve and maintain action. These ideas were applied to health communication by Flay and colleagues (Flay, DiTecco, & Schlegel, 1980) and later by Donovan and Rossiter (Donovan, 1997). Their model added new elements in the cognitive stages preceding action that is useful for community interventions.

Moving on to group-level theories, community organization strategies are important to community programs (Bracht, 1990). Communities can be depicted as complex systems of interwoven social organizations, both official and unofficial, that partly determine people's functioning. Broad and long-lasting effects on individuals are best achieved when existing community structures can be utilized. External influences can be important, but communities must start a process of self-development in which they first detect health problems and then become organized to deal with them. The latter requirement sees to it that the control in community interventions remains in the hands of the citizens, empowering them to deal with their own health problems.

Lifestyle changes can also be thought of as innovations that find their way into the community through natural networks of communication in a community. Everett Rogers (1983) used the idea of two-step flow of ideation, first proposed by Katz and Lazarsfeld (1955), to describe the dissemination of innovations. According to this theory, the role of the mass media is to set an agenda and then influence the opinion leaders. Interpersonal channels are then effective in changing attitudes and behaviors of the general public. The community members may be viewed either as innovators; early, middle, and late adopters; or laggards. The norms of the social system exert strong effects on the diffusion of innovations. The principles of innovation diffusion theory are crucial to the success of community programs. Up to this point, we have been focusing on individual forms of behavior. In Finland, for example, it has been established that smoking and unhealthy food habits tend to co-occur, particularly in men (Prättälä, Laaksonen, & Rahkonen, 1998). Smoking seems to be particularly important in the forming of unhealthy lifestyles (Laaksonen, Rahkonen, & Prättälä, 1998). Nonetheless, the association is not powerful enough to provide a sum of unhealthy behaviors that equal the best predictor of mortality (Luoto, Prättälä, Uutela, & Puska, 1998). Blaxter (1998) has reported similar results from Great Britain.

EXPERIENCES FROM THE NORTH KARELIA PROJECT

In January 1971, the governor of the province, all North Karelian members of the Finnish Parliament, and several representatives of official and voluntary organizations signed a petition for national help concerning the epidemic of cardiovascular problems in North Karelia. This rural province of about 180,000 persons in eastern Finland reportedly had the highest CVD mortality in the world. A delegation led by the governor took the petition to the Finnish government and other relevant bodies in Helsinki, where the petition was met with sympathy. During the same period, two important national processes were introduced: the writing of the Public Health Law of 1972 and the establishment of the University of Kuopio in eastern Finland. The law was designed to strengthen preventive and primary health services by introducing local health centers; the creation of the university included the founding of a medical school to educate professionals about the needs of the people of eastern Finland (Puska et al., 1981).

In response to the North Karelian petition, the Finnish Heart Association formed a working group led by Professor Martti Karvonen to review the situation and to contact the national and international experts necessary for the preparation of an action plan. In the working group, the contention grew that no small-scale intervention could possibly reach the goals set for the project: to lower the CVD and other similar disease morbidity and mortality in the population. The working group also felt that existing social organizations had to be included in the intervention and that an evaluation plan would have to be developed.

In September 1971, a planning seminar for the intervention and evaluation was held involving several international and national experts, representatives of the North Karelia Province administration and the Finnish

Heart Association, and researchers from the University of Turku, who were then active in studying the east-west health differentials in Finland. At the end of the seminar, the participants recommended that a comprehensive community-based CVD control program should be set in motion in North Karelia. This recommendation led to the organization of a project group. In the autumn of 1971, the project's steering committee identified the need for four working groups, which would focus on the following areas: health education, stroke register, myocardial infarction, and hypertension control. To ensure a relatively untouched initial evaluation, the survey and clinical checkups were performed early in 1972. The intervention program and the formation of the registers were started in the following May.

Aims

The project aimed at carrying out a community health intervention to decrease cardiovascular morbidity and mortality, especially among the middle-aged male population in North Karelia, who were most at risk. Its intention was to create health care services and to study the health behaviors and risk factors of the population to influence disease outcomes and improve health in the community. A unique strength of the intervention plan was that it used contemporary behavioral and social sciences principles available at that time, including Lewin's (1951) field theory. The basic goals of the intervention were the following:

- to provide improved preventive services to identify risk factor status and give appropriate services
- to distribute information to make people aware of the effects of their behavior on their health
- to provide persuasive messages to motivate people to make the changes needed to improve health
- to establish training for skills in self-management, environmental control, and performing healthful activities
- to give social support to help maintain a healthful lifestyle
- to make changes in the environment to improve opportunities for healthy actions and eliminate unhealthy ones
- to use existing community organizations to promote wide-ranging changes, resulting in increased social support and favorable environmental modification to support new lifestyles in the community.

Accomplishing the Goals

The communication–behavior-change model by McGuire (1986) was used as a planning aid for implementation. The program used experts to facilitate the credibility of the messages, which were directed toward important group identification and provincial pride and were devised to fit the local culture and anticipate possible counterarguments. Practical cooking skills were dispersed through the housewives' organization Martta. Various activities were performed simultaneously to provide the social support and environmental conditions needed, such as the production of healthier foods and their introduction to local groceries.

Personal and mass communication were used to introduce new forms of behavior. In cooperation with the Finnish Broadcasting Company, educational television programs were planned to be helpful at various stages of the program (Puska et al., 1981, 1985, 1987).

Acquisition of new lifestyles requires the adoption of innovations. The innovation diffusion theory uses the idea of a two-step flow of ideas, first to the opinion leaders and then to the people. Opinion leaders can be identified either by their special expertise or position or by asking the people whom they would consider as role models. This latter technique is more useful to reveal informal opinion leaders. Time is an important element in the diffusion, but the spreading of innovation can be promoted using models of communication skillfully, provided that the community structure favors the diffusion.

In our project, community organization involved community self-development, but also external impetus by the North Karelia project group. For community development to be successful, a program must offer incentives for collaboration. Personal contacts with the mass media (newspapers, radio); health, social, and educational services personnel (administrators, physicians, nurses, teachers, social workers, school principals); business leaders (such as those involved in the production and distribution of foods); nongovernmental organization leaders (from heart, housewives', labor, and sports organizations); and local politicians (provincial and municipal leaders) were all important (see, for example, Milio, 1981).

Basic Rules for Conducting Community Programs

Based on the principles of Green and Kreuter (1991), the praxis of community programs can be understood through the sequence of diagnosis, planning, implementation, and evaluation. Each of these phases need to be repeated. In the diagnosis and project-planning phase, the North Karelia project (a) defined the objectives, (b) performed the initial community analysis, (c) established a project organization, and (d) made preparatory steps toward implementation of the intervention (i.e., administrative and policy diagnosis; Puska, 1996).

The most general level of objectives for community programs involves improvement of the quality of life in the community. They are established to conform to the perceived health needs of the population. The next objectives are based on medical or epidemiological information available regarding the determinants of the health problem. Practical objectives visible in the intervention are based on the behavioral–social sciences framework after a thorough analysis of the community situation has been performed and the role of the intermediate objective is understood in terms of the educational and organizational diagnosis.

The goal of the North Karelia Project was to systematically carry out the program as planned. Nonetheless, the implementation had to be flexible to respond to the reactions of the community. Much creative work usually happens within the community, but it is the duty of the project organization to provide the necessary support. The program activities should be relatively uncomplicated; otherwise they cannot be fully utilized. Keeping the program simple makes the training easier. Participation in preventive activities should be a part of the regular working schedule of the local health care professionals. Close, personal contacts between the project team and the health care personnel help with motivation and compliance. Using people from popular local organizations or other opinion leaders adds to the success of the project. The mass media can generate the population's interest and support to establish further activities.

The degree of success a project achieves can be measured by internal, formative, and summative evaluations. Internal evaluation is used within the program to give rapid feedback to the program workers and management. An overlapping notion is that of the formative evaluation, referring to the formulation of the program. A summative evaluation assesses the program's effects or consequences over time, and is usually done by a group of experts from outside the project. The evaluation procedures used within the North Karelia project can be categorized as follows: (a) feasibility or performance evaluation, (b) effects evaluation (impact and outcomes), (c) process evaluation, (d) costs evaluation, and (e) additional consequences evaluation (see Puska et al., 1981, for details).

Program feasibility evaluations assess the extent to which the planned activities can be implemented. This is related to the amount of resources, the efficacy of their use, and the acceptance of the measures by the target population. Feasibility assessments are based on records of activities, statistical data within the community, or on survey data gathered from the community.

Program effect evaluations include evaluation of both a program's impact on lifestyle and environment and its outcome in terms of health measures and quality of life (risk factor profiles, morbidity, mortality, etc.). Because programs target the whole community, evaluation information should be representative of it. Thus, independent cross-sectional random samples should be used to avoid influence on the results from prior measurements or from selective loss at follow-ups. Relatively large sample sizes are needed for analyses of subpopulations, as well as to detect small but significant risk factor changes for the population.

Because several years (i.e., 5 years in the case of the North Karelia project) pass between measurements, use of a similar community as a reference area is necessary to ensure sufficient internal validity of the quasi-experimental design (see Cook & Campbell, 1976). This reference area should be matched to that receiving the intervention, and a simultaneous measuring schedule should be used. One may have problems keeping the internal validity high, however, because people in the reference area may have opinions of their own about health concerns. If the intervention is successful, it will lead to the adoption of the proven interventions in the reference area as well as among study participants. Although this will threaten the validity of design, it also will result in health improvements in the reference area. (In the case of the North Karelia project, the establishment of a medical school in the reference area posed a clear validity problem that could not be eliminated by statistical means, because people in the reference area had easier access to health care.)

Process evaluations involve the changes observed among the predisposing, reinforcing, and enabling factors, as well as in lifestyle and the environment. Measures of these factors indicate how well the intermediate goals of the intervention have been achieved.

Cost evaluations are based on the total resource consumption of a project and on determining how resources were allocated. Efforts also can be made to assess the direct versus indirect costs to the community of gains achieved by the intervention. This latter task is obviously much more difficult to perform properly.

Additional consequences of a major national program also may be evaluated. A cardiovascular program may also influence the status of other diseases, for example. Side effects may appear. Finally, as the level of health is not the only target in modern health promotion, we should also analyze the results of community interventions from the viewpoint of health differentials. These should include, for example, gender, cohort, regional, ethnic, and socioeconomic status health differentials (e.g., Carroll & Davey Smith, 1997).

Community Programs as National Demonstration Projects

One advantage of a relatively small community intervention is that almost every member can be reached. Nonetheless, there are also disadvantages because many important decisions are made on a supracommunity level. This concerns such undertakings as the passage of laws or decisions made by private enterprises, such as producers of food products.

It would demand a great deal of resources to evaluate health interventions on a national level. Therefore, we may consider a community program such as the one in North Karelia as a demonstration or model activity for the nation. This role of the North Karelia project was officially recognized in 1982 when North Karelia became part of the WHO CINDI-framework (Countrywide Integrated Noncommunicable Diseases Intervention). We assume that program activities can be performed more easily in a restricted area than in the nation as a whole, but when such activities are done at both the demonstration and the national level, they can support each other. The demonstration areas are useful in providing a learning context that is inspiring for the national-level activities.

Visibility of demonstration projects is one of their assets. For this reason, they must be successfully planned, implemented, and evaluated to be worthy of the attention they receive. Furthermore, they should be backed up by national health authorities; this ensures that the knowledge derived from such projects will be brought to the attention of political decision makers and then disseminated to the nation's citizens.

INTERVENTIONS WITHIN THE NORTH KARELIA PROJECT

There were eight diverse programs used in the North Karelia project. These involved use of lay opinion leaders, television programs, smoking-cessation contests, youth and work-site projects, and collaboration with housewives' organizations, the food industry, and produce growers. Results given below from the programs may be taken as partial fulfillment of the process evaluation goal.

Lay Leader Program

In the 1970s, more than 800 opinion leaders were trained to promote healthy lifestyles in their environment. Several years later, the significance of this operation based on innovation-diffusion theory was tested, and it was learned that lay leaders were having a substantial contribution to the success of the project (Puska et al., 1986).

Television Programs

Since 1978, a number of major national television programs have been broadcast in collaboration between the North Karelia project and the Finnish Broadcasting Corporation's Channel 2 (Wiio, 1984). They have been developed using ideas from the communication–behavior change theory of McGuire (1986). Program series designed to aid in smoking cessation were shown in the years 1978, 1979, 1986, and 1989. Each of these series included seven to nine programs that were 30–45 minutes in length. A more general series called *Keys to Health* was shown in the years 1980,

1982, and 1984–1985, which included 10–15 programs. This form of intervention was proven to be feasible, and viewing rates were high, even among viewers in lower socioeconomic groups. The cost–benefit ratio of these types of interventions seems to be favorable.

"Quit and Win" Contests

In connection with the 1989 smoking-cessation television series, a general contest to promote smoking cessation, "Quit and Win," was held. The contest required 4 weeks of abstinence from smoking in May 1989. More than 16,000 Finnish smokers participated. The 6-month abstinence rate for the participants was approximately 20%. A second contest was organized in conjunction with Estonia (Korhonen, Puska, Lipand, & Kasmel, 1993). Many new versions of the idea were tried, and by May 2000, the contest was organized in 83 countries around the world.

Youth Projects

A major aim in health promotion involves children and adolescents. As a part of the general community intervention, schools in North Karelia were involved in multiple ways. Since 1978, two major youth projects have been carried out for more systematic and innovative interventions in grade classes in the province (Vartiainen, Tossavainen, Viri, Niskanen, & Puska, 1991). The short and long-term significance of the youth projects has been evaluated (Paavola, Vartiainen, & Puska, 1996).

Work-Site Interventions

Several work-site interventions were conducted in North Karelia as a part of the project. Begun on a small scale in the 1970s, the work culminated in large-scale interventions during the 1980s (Puska et al., 1989).

Collaboration With Martta

The housewives' organization Martta, which is active in rural and semirural areas, has been influential in the adoption of new cooking habits. The first special collaborative program was "Parties for Life" in the 1970s, followed by "The Happy Hearts' Evening" in the 1980s, and "Control Your Weight" in the 1990s. These programs have involved thousands of housewives and their family members (Puska, 1996).

Collaboration With the Food Industry and Supermarkets

In the 1970s, the focus of this collaboration was on the promotion of low-fat dairy products and low-fat sausage. By the end of the decade, it also focused on reducing salt in many food items. In the late 1980s, intensive activities were organized to promote lower cholesterol levels. In this phase, the focus was on the industry using products containing vegetable oil. A breakthrough was the initiation and promotion of domestic rapeseed oil (Puska, 1996). A recent, even international breakthrough was the development of sitostanol margarine, which was shown to have a great cholesterol-lowering effect in a carefully conducted trial in North Karelia (Miettinen, Puska, Gylling, Vanhanen, & Vartiainen, 1995).

Berry Project

In the 1980s, the project started a large collaborative program to promote the use of local berries, sponsored by the ministries of agriculture, the interior, and commerce and industry. The aim was to increase consumption of the healthy local berries and to support their farming (Kuusipalo, Mikkola, & Moisio, 1986).

Health Education Materials

The North Karelia project has produced and distributed health education materials (such as leaflets and posters) and produced material for local radio stations and newspapers. The mass media became increasingly important to the project's activities in the 1990s (Muuttoranta, Korpelainen, & Puska, 1995).

RESULTS OF THE NORTH KARELIA PROJECT

A sizeable change in health behavior, risk factors, and disease endpoints has taken place in North Karelia since the 1970s and also in the reference area and the rest of the country. We describe some changes observed in relation to the North Karelia project by comparing the North Karelian results to those found elsewhere in the country. Smoking was especially targeted in the evaluation because it has an obvious significance for health.

Did the Project Affect the Smoking-Cessation Process?

Although health professionals did not use every opportunity to remind patients who smoked about the importance of quitting, this advice was given more often to smokers in North Karelia than elsewhere in the country (Korhonen, Uutela, Korhonen, & Puska, 1998). The annual proportion of male smokers who reported having been advised to stop smoking during a visit to the physician varied from 28 to 34% during 1989–1996 in North Karelia and 22–25% elsewhere. The corresponding figures for female smokers were 18–24% in North Karelia and 18–19% elsewhere. Taking into consideration advice from other health professionals (e.g., public health nurses and dentists), the true figures are somewhat higher but are geographically consistent.

In a logistic regression analysis, it was discovered that North Karelian male smokers reported being advised to stop smoking by a health professional more often than did men elsewhere in the country. Appropriately enough, older, less educated male smokers with a poor health status most often received smoking-cessation advice. Among female smokers, North Karelians still received more recommendations to quit smoking than did their counterparts elsewhere in the country. A longer, heavier smoking history was associated with the reporting of more frequent cessation advice among the women.

Information provided by health professionals, trained lay persons, and the mass media all appeared to be helpful. Korhonen, Uutela, Korhonen, and Puska (1998, 1999) found that for male and female smokers, exposure to both mass media and lay-person smoking-cessation advice proved to be beneficial, especially if both were encountered repeatedly.

Quit and Win campaigns (Korhonen, Urjanheimo, et al., 1999), which involved contests to encourage smoking cessation for at least 4 weeks, gathered twice the amount of interest in North Karelia than in the rest of the country. The first contest managed to get 3.2% of North Karelian and 1.6% of smokers elsewhere in Finland to participate. Since that time, the motivation to participate has declined to some extent. In 1996, the smoking-cessation phases were thoroughly monitored. In North Karelia, 75% of smokers had heard about the campaign, whereas the corresponding figure elsewhere was 40%. About 9% of the North Karelian smokers indicated an intention to quit, compared with 6% elsewhere. About 2% of North Karelian smokers and 1% of smokers elsewhere made an actual attempt to quit. Finally, 0.3% of smokers in North Karelia and 0.1% of smokers elsewhere managed to maintain abstinence for at least 6 months, indicating better results in North Karelia at various stages of smoking cessation.

Did the Intervention Influence Risk Factors?

A survey of risk factors of CVD (excluding smoking) showed major changes in North Karelia during the first 10 years of interventions and a more modest change in the reference area (Puska et al., 1981). In the 1980s, the observed changes tended to be moderate, but since 1987, the development accelerated again. A major reduction in cholesterol level related to the intervention was observed among men in North Karelia between 1972 and 1977 (Puska, Vartiainen, Tuomilehto, Salomaa, & Nissinen, 1998). In 1972, the average cholesterol level of the average 30- to 59-year-old man in North Karelia was 6.9 mmol/L, but this was continuously reduced over the years to reach 5.6 mmol/L in 1997 (Vartiainen et al., 1998). The corresponding figures for women do not differ greatly: 6.8 mmol/L in 1972 and 5.5 mmol/L in 1997, even though no statistically significant difference in relation to the reference area was observed in any 5-year period examined.

Blood pressure levels have been lowered as well (Vartiainen et al., 1998). Several significant differences to the benefit of North Karelian residents have been observed in blood pressure development. In both men and women a reduction of both systolic and diastolic blood pressures were observed in the initial 5-year period, as well as in some of the subsequent periods. Thus, average systolic blood pressure decreased from 148 mmHg to 140 mmHg among men and from 153 mmHg to 133 mmHg among women in North Karelia. On the other hand, average male body mass index (BMI) increased from 26.0 kg/m^2 to 27.0 kg/m^2 but decreased slightly for women 26.8 kg/m^2 and 26.4 kg/m^2. Only one significant difference by region was observed in BMI. This was related to the BMI reduction between 1992 and 1997 that was substantial both in North Karelia and Southwest Finland, but not elsewhere in the country.

Did the Intervention Affect Disease and Health Outcomes?

There has been a remarkable decline in CVD and cancer mortality in the middle-aged male population of North Karelia after the intervention was started in 1972 (Puska, Vartiainen, Tuomilehto, Salomaa, & Nissinen, 1998). At present, North Karelia is no longer the province with highest national CHD figures. Comparison of the North Karelia (−2.9% annual average) decline of cardiovascular mortality in relation to that found in the rest of the country (−1.0% annual average) in the period 1969–1978 corroborates a more rapid decline in North Karelia during the initial 5-year period of the project. This decline can be attributed at least in part to the community intervention, although quasi-experiments do not provide conclusive evidence. There were also many cultural and structural changes in the society, including a growing economy and strengthening of the welfare system, until the start of the economic recession in the early 1990s. Such changes may have lowered the stress level of the population and affected the mortality rate.

Between 1979 and 1985, when the initial 5-year intervention stopped, the decline in CHD mortality leveled off in North Karelia but increased nationwide (annually −0.2% and −3.5, respectively). As the CINDI phase began, North Karelia witnessed a sharp decline of CHD again, starting in 1986 (−8.0% annually), as did the rest of the country (−6.5%).

Cancer mortality trends for men also show an improvement in North Karelia, compared with the rest of the country. Because it takes time to see the effects of health behavior changes (particularly with regard to smoking) on cancer (including lung cancer), the improvements first became visible in the 1980s. Between 1980 and 1995, the male lung cancer mortality declined −7.3% in North Karelia and −4.8% in the rest of the country.

The decline in CVD mortality has taken place much in the same way in both CHD and cerebrovascular disease (Puska et al., 1998). CVD mortality among women has shown the same general trend as it did of men. Women's cancer deaths, however, have not declined as they did among men because women have increased—not decreased—their smoking.

Were There Health Differences?

The North Karelia Project was originally established to better the situation of men showing high CHD mortality figures. This reflects the bearing of both regional and gender-related factors on health in Finland. Even at present, when the situation of the North Karelian men has improved, we can propose that regional and gender-related health differences exist in risk factors, morbidity, mortality, and quality of life.

Another angle, used often in recent years to view health differentials, is that of socioeconomic status (Ministry of Social Affairs and Health, 1998). We find that socioeconomic-status-based health differences prevail. In terms of health behavior, differences that are detrimental to the lower classes include smoking and obesity, and the disparity between social groups seems to be widening (Helakorpi, Uutela, Prättälä, & Puska, 1998). A similar trend has been reported for several other European populations (Cavelaars, Kunst, & Mackenbach, 1997). Nonetheless, when comparing both diet and exercise levels, socioeconomic status differences in Finland have diminished.

What has happened in North Karelia? Has the development been more equal because of the community intervention? Unfortunately, we cannot answer such questions with complete reliability given our present state of knowledge. Evaluation of the risk factor trends during the initial 5 years of the project in North Karelia indicated that the reduction of risk factors in lower socioeconomic groups was at least as great if not greater than it was among the high socioeconomic groups of the population (Puska et al., 1981). According to some previously unpublished data, we can observe certain trends. Looking at reports of exposure to health messages in North Karelia, we find that among both men and women, less educated individuals reported the highest exposure in relation to need, defined by daily smoking, use of butter on bread, heavy alcohol consumption, or sedentary lifestyle (see Table 4.1). Usually men in need of change reported having

TABLE 4.1
Reported Relative Exposure to Health Messages (Defined in Terms of Need) From Health Care Personnel in North Karelia by Length of Education

	Men				Women			
	Up to 9 years (%)	Index	10–12 years Index	From 13 years on Index	Up to 9 years (%)	Index	10–12 years Index	From 13 years on Index
Stop smoking	(29.8)	100.0	60.5	60.6	(14.2)	100.0	55.3	51.1
Reduce whole milk	(71.3)	100.0	63.7	69.9	(51.4)	100.0	61.0	52.4
Reduce butter on bread	(38.9)	100.0	63.7	69.9	(32.1)	100.0	61.0	52.4
Reduce alcohol consumption	(21.0)	100.0	32.4	29.3	(9.7)	100.0	14.7	3.1
Increase exercise	(77.8)	100.0	61.3	47.7	(65.8)	100.0	74.5	54.1
Reduce weight	(48.3)	100.0	89.2	67.1	(52.6)	100.0	119.4	109.5

Note. Percentage is given of those men and women with least education in need of advice who reported receiving it. Index numbers for other educational groups are relative to the least educated in that gender.

received health communication from a health professional more often than did women. The same goes for those with less education. The only case in which moderately and highly educated people reported receiving more advice than did their less educated counterparts was among overweight women. Weight reduction is the only topic in which women reported receiving advice more often than did men. This is yet another indication that weight-related cultural norms have a greater effect on women, and especially on well-educated women, than on men.

Of course, we cannot take these results as straight signs of positive intervention effects, especially with regard to the benefit of less educated individuals. We found the greatest differences in reports concerning exposure to advice to reduce alcohol consumption, a phenomenon that rarely occurred among well-educated men and even less frequently among well-educated women.

Differences with regard to socioeconomic status have not been evident in the Quit and Win contests. The contests have been useful for North Karelian smokers, but because of the data-gathering practices, no analysis of contest participation by educational status can be made. Looking at 1-year successful quitting rates, no difference by education was observed (Korhonen, Sun, Korhonen, Uutela, & Puska, 1997).

CONCLUSION AND RECOMMENDATIONS

Significant improvements have taken place in Finland during the past 25 years, both nationally and in the province of North Karelia. Men's tobacco smoking has decreased, and that of women has been kept under control. Use of saturated fat has been reduced considerably. Cardiovascular diseases and cancer have declined among the working-age population, as has mortality attributable to these factors. Although this cannot be attributed completely to the effects of health behavior changes, adoption of healthier lifestyles is a major contributory factor. There are good reasons to believe that the community intervention not only had an impact in North Karelia, but on the nation as a whole. The annual national health behavior surveys (Helakorpi et al., 1998) have indicated a steady improvement in health-related quality of life from the 1970s into the early 1990s; while subjective health has improved, feelings of stress have diminished.

All health behavior changes in recent decades have not been positive, however, either nationwide or in the province of North Karelia. One problematic development has been the increase in alcohol consumption (Luoto, Prättälä, Uutela, & Puska, 1998). Another is the increase in excess weight due to radical decreases in energy use without a reduction of energy intake. This in turn has been related to changes in activity level associated with both work and leisure pursuits. Evidence mentioned above also suggests that, particularly with regard to smoking, we are dealing with a health inequality problem. Challenges such as these, and others related to an aging population, need further investigation.

Certain unique features of the Finnish culture must be taken into consideration when examining the North Karelia Project results. We have already mentioned that the special identity of the population and improvements in the welfare system, with associated social and health care systems (see Roemer, 1993) were important contributing factors. Regardless of what province individuals may be from, the Finnish culture was—and largely still is—uniform. These factors obviously helped people adopt new lifestyles in various parts of the country. It is furthermore reasonable to suppose that when unhealthy behavior is common, it is relatively easy to find people capable of change when becoming informed about its significance. In addition, in the early 1970s, the Finnish government was more centralized than it is today, making it easy to control local changes. Mass media was concentrated too, and the audience had relatively few choices. In this peculiar environment, the will to improve health could be transformed into partnerships (e.g., Israel, Schulz, Parker, & Becker, 1998) and actions capable of producing change. At present, the situation has changed: Local governments have much more power, and a market economy has become more strongly established in Finland, a recent member of the European Union.

Preventive community programs or community health promotion programs should be considered long-lasting health promotional efforts that use all available resources within the society, not only those allocated for health improvement. The following recommendations based on the North Karelia Project may be helpful:

- Community health promotion programs should pay attention to the corroborated principles of program planning, implementation, and evaluation.
- The medical and epidemiological knowledge base should be used to select the intermediate targets of health promotion.
- Behavioral and social sciences theories should be used in devising, evaluating, and developing the programs.
- Good understanding of the situation in the community and close cooperation with local organizations, as well as the full participation of the general public, are prerequisites for successful interventions.
- The intervention programs should combine well-planned mass media messages with other community activities involving primary health care, voluntary organizations, the educational system, work sites, and private enterprise interested in making health their business.

- Health promotion activities need collaboration and support from the community decision makers and informal opinion leaders.
- Community members form an important source of social support to family members and others.
- Dedicated, persistent practical work is needed to make the theories a reality in the community.
- Major emphasis should be given to changing the context of the social and physical environment in an attempt to make the community more conducive to good health and healthier lifestyles.
- Major community health promotion programs can be used as national models. Thus, they should be properly evaluated, and the results of these evaluations should be widely publicized.

REFERENCES

Ajzen, I. (1985). From intentions to actions. A theory of planned behavior. In J. Kuhl & J. Beckman (Eds.), *Action control. From cognition to behavior* (pp. 11–39). Berlin: Springer Verlag.

Bandura, A. (1986). *Social foundations of thought and action. A social cognitive theory.* Englewood Cliffs, NJ: Prentice Hall.

Blaxter, M. (1998). *Health and lifestyles.* London: Tavistock & Routledge.

Bracht, N. (1990). *Community organization strategies for health promotion.* New York: Sage.

Bruhn, J. G. (1988). Life-style and health behavior. In D. S. Cochman (Ed.), *Health behavior: Emerging research perspectives* (pp. 71–86). New York: Plenum.

Carlaw, R. W., Mittelmark, M. B., Bracht, N., & Luepker, R. (1984). Organization for a community cardiovascular program: Experiences from the Minnesota heart health program. *Health Education Quarterly, 11*, 243–252.

Carroll, D., & Davey Smith, G. (Eds.). (1997). Health variations [Special issue]. *Journal of Health Psychology, 2*, 275–430.

Cavelaars, A. E. J. M., Kunst, A. E., & Mackenbach, J. P. (1997). Socio-economic differences in risk factors and mortality in the European Community: An international comparison. *Journal of Health Psychology 2*, 353–372.

Cook, T. D., & Campbell, D. T. (1976). The design and conduct of quasi-experiments and true experiments in field settings. In M. E. Dunnette (Ed.), *Handbook of industrial and organizational psychology* (pp. 223–326). Chicago: Rand McNally.

Donovan, R. J. (1997). *The effective use of mass media for tobacco control.* Proceedings of the 10th World Conference on Tobacco and Health, August 24–28, 1997, Beijing, p. 28.

Farquhar, J. W., Fortman, S. P., Maccoby, N., Haskell, W. L., Williams, P. T., et al. (1985). The Stanford Five City Project: Design and methods. In J. W. Gentry (Ed.), *Handbook of behavioral medicine* (pp. 437–478). New York: Guilford.

Fishbein, M., & Ajzen, I. (1975). *Belief, attitude, intention, and behavior. An introduction to theory and research.* Reading, MA: Addison-Wesley.

Flay, B. R, DiTecco, D., & Schlegel, R. P. (1980). Mass media in health promotion. *Health Education Quarterly, 7,* 127–143.

Graham, J. D., Corso, P. S., Morris, J. M., Segui-Gomez, M., & Weinstein, M. C. (1998). Evaluating the cost-effectiveness of clinical and public health measures. *Annual Review of Public Health, 19,* 125–152.

Green, L. W., & Kreuter, M. W. (1991). *Health promotion planning: An educational and environmental approach* (2nd ed.). Mountain View, CA: Mayfield.

Helakorpi, S., Uutela, A., Prättälä, R., & Puska, P. (1998). *Suomalaisen aikuisväestön terveyskäyttäytyminen, kevät 1998* [Health behavior among Finnish adult population, Spring 1998]. Helsinki: Publications of the National Public Health Institute (B10/1998).

Israel, B. A., Schulz, A. J., Parker, E. A., & Becker, A. B. (1998). Review of community-based research: Assessing partnership approaches to improve public health. *Annual Review of Public Health 19,* 173–202.

Katz, E., & Lazarsfeld, P. (1955). *Personal influence: The part played by people in the flow of mass communications.* New York: Free Press.

Kelly, S., Hertzman, C., & Daniels, M. (1997). Searching for the biological pathways between stress and health. *Annual Review of Public Health, 18,* 437–462.

Kok, G., Hospers, H. J., den Boer, D. J., & De Vries, H. (1996). Health education at the individual level. In K. Orth-Gomér & N. Schneiderman (Eds.), *Behavioral medicine approaches to cardiovascular disease prevention* (pp. 185–202). Mahwah, NJ: Erlbaum.

Kok, G., Schaalma, H., De Vries, H., Parcel, G., & Paulussen, T. (1996). Social psychology and health education. In W. Stroebe & M. Hewstone (Eds.), *European review of social psychology* (Vol. 7, pp. 241–282). Chichester, England: Wiley.

Korhonen, H. J., Puska, P., Lipand, A., & Kasmel, A. (1993). Combining mass media and contest in smoking cessation. An experience from a series of national activities in Finland. *Hygie, 12,* 15–18.

Korhonen, T., Sun, S., Korhonen, H. J., Uutela, A., & Puska, P. (1997). Evaluation of a national Quit and Win contest: Determinants of successful quitting. *Preventive Medicine, 26,* 556–564.

Korhonen, T., Urjanheimo, E-L., Mannonen, P., Korhonen, H. J., Uutela. A., & Puska, P. (1999). Quit and Win campaigns as a long-term anti-smoking intervention in North Karelia and other parts of Finland. *Tobacco Control, 8,* 175–181.

Korhonen, T., Uutela, A., Korhonen, H. J., & Puska, P. (1998) Impact of mass media and interpersonal health communication on smoking cessation attempts: A study in North Karelia 1989–1996. *Journal of Health Communication, 3,* 105–118.

Korhonen, T., Uutela, A., Korhonen, H. J., & Puska, P. (1999). Health professionals' smoking cessation advice: Process evaluation of a community-based program. *Patient Education and Counselling, 36,* 13–31.

Kuusipalo, J., Mikkola, M., Moisio S., et al. (1986). The East Finland Berry and Vegetable Project: A health-related structural intervention programme. *Health Promotion, 1,* 385–391.

Laaksonen, M., Rahkonen, O., & Prättälä, R. (1998). Smoking status and relative weight by educational level in Finland 1978–1995. *Preventive Medicine, 27,* 431–437.

Lechner, L. (1998). *Social-psychological determinants of health risk behaviors related to cancer and CVD. Applications and elaborations of the ASE model.* Unpublished thesis, University of Maastricht, The Netherlands.

Lewin, K. (1951). Field theory in social science. In D. Cartwright (Ed.), *Selected theoretical papers.* New York: Harper & Row.

Luoto, R., Prättälä, R., Uutela, A., & Puska, P. (1998). Impact of unhealthy behaviors on cardiovascular mortality in Finland, 1978–1993. *Preventive Medicine, 27,* 93–100.

McGuire, W. J. (1986). Attitudes and attitude change. In G. Lindzey & E. Aronson (Eds.), *Handbook of social psychology* (3rd ed.). New York: Random House.

Meyer, A., Nash, J., McAlister, A. L., Maccoby, N., & Farquhar, J. (1980). Skills training in a cardiovascular health education campaign. *Journal of Consulting and Clinical Psychology, 48,* 129–142.

Miettinen, T. A., Puska, P., Gylling, H, Vanhanen, H. T., & Vartiainen, E. (1995). Reduction of serum cholesterol with sitostanol-ester margarine in a mildly hypercholesterolaemic population. *New England Journal of Medicine, 333,* 1308–1312.

Milio, N. (1981). *Promoting health through public policy.* Philadelphia: F.A. Davis.

Ministry of Social Affairs and Health. (1998). *Third evaluation of the Progress Towards Health for All Finland* (Report 1998:2eng). Helsinki: Author.

Muuttoranta, A., Korpelainen, V., & Puska, P. (1995). The intervention in practice. In P. Puska, J. Tuomilehto, A. Nissinen, & E. Vartiainen (Eds.), *The North Karelia Project: 20 years results and experiences* (pp. 65–73). Helsinki: National Public Health Institute.

Paavola, M., Vartiainen, E., & Puska, P. (1996). Predicting adult smoking: The influence of smoking during adolescence and smoking among friends and family. *Health Education Research Theory & Practice 11,* 309–315.

Pekkanen, J., Tuomilehto, J., Uutela, A., Vartiainen, E., & Nissinen, A. (1995). Social class, health behavior, and mortality among men and women in Eastern Finland. *British Medical Journal, 311,* 589–593.

Prättälä, R., Laaksonen, M., & Rahkonen, O. (1998). Smoking and unhealthy food habits. How stable is the association? *European Journal of Public Health, 8,* 28–33.

Prentice-Dunn, S., & Rogers, R.W. (1986). Protective motivation theory and preventive health: Beyond the health belief model. *Health Education Research,* *1*, 153–161.

Prochaska, J. O., & DiClemente, C. C. (1984). *The transtheoretical approach: Crossing traditional boundaries of therapy.* Homewood, IL: Dow Jones Irwin.

Puska, P. (1996). Community interventions in cardiovascular disease prevention. In K. Orth-Gómer & N. Schneiderman (Eds.), *Behavioral medicine approaches to cardiovascular disease prevention* (pp. 327–362). Mahwah, NJ: Erlbaum.

Puska, P., Koskela, K., McAlister, A., Mäyränen, H, Smolander, A., Moisio, S., Viri, L., Korpelainen, V., & Rogers, E. M. (1986). Use of lay opinion leaders to promote diffusion of health innovations in a community programme: Lessons learned from the North Karelia Project. *WHO Bulletin, 64,* 437–446.

Puska, P., McAlister, A., Niemensivu, H., Piha, T., Wiio, J., & Koskela, K. (1987). Television format for national health promotion: Finland's "Keys to Health." *Public Health Reports, 102,* 263–269.

Puska, P., Tuomilehto, J., Nissinen, A., & Vartiainen, E. (Eds.). (1995). *The North Karelia Project: 20 year results and experiences.* Helsinki: National Public Health Institute.

Puska, P., Tuomilehto, J., Salonen, J. T., Nissinen, A., Virtamo, J., Björkqvist, S., Koskels, K., Neittaanmäki, L., Takalo, T., Kottke, T. E., Mäki, J., Sipilä, P., & Varvikko, P. (1981). *Community control of cardiovascular diseases. Evaluation of a comprehensive community programme for control of cardiovascular diseases in North Karelia, Finland 1972–1977.* Copenhagen: World Health Organization, Regional Office for Europe.

Puska, P., Vartiainen, E., Tuomilehto, J., Salomaa, V., & Nissinen, A. (1998). Changes in premature deaths in Finland: Successful long-term prevention of cardiovascular diseases. *Bulletin of the World Health Organization, 76,* 419–427.

Puska, P., Wiio, J., McAlister, A., Koskela, K, Smolander, A, Pekkola, J., & Maccoby, N. (1985). Planned use of mass media in a national health promotion: The "Keys to Health" TV-program in 1982 in Finland. *Canadian Journal of Public Health, 76,* 336–342.

Research Unit in Health and Behavioral Change, University of Edinburgh. (1993). *Changing the public health.* Chichester, England: Wiley.

Rippetoe, P. A., & Rogers, R. W. (1987). Effects of components of protection-motivation theory on adaptive and maladaptive coping with health threat. *Journal of Personality and Social Psychology, 52,* 596–604.

Robertson, A., & Minkler, M. (1994). New health promotion movement: A critical examination. *Health Education Quarterly, 21,* 295–312.

Roemer, M. I.. (1993). National health systems throughout the world. *Annual Review of Public Health, 14,* 335–353.

Rogers, E. (1983). *Diffusion of innovations.* New York: Free Press.

Rosenstock, I. M. (1974). Historical origins of the health belief model. *Health Education Monographs, 2,* 409–419.

Schneiderman, N., & Orth-Gomér, K. (1996). Blending traditions: A concluding perspective on behavioral medicine approaches to coronary heart disease prevention. In K. Orth-Gomér & N. Schneiderman (Eds.), *Behavioral medicine approaches to cardiovascular disease prevention* (pp. 279–300). Mahwah, NJ: Erlbaum.

Sorensen, G., Emmons, K., Hunt, M. K., & Johnston, D. (1998). Implications of the results of community intervention trials. *Annual Review of Public Health, 19,* 379–416.

Vartiainen, E., Jousilahti, P., Juolevi, A., Sundvall, J., Alftan, G., Salminen, I., & Puska, P. (1998). *Tutkimus kroonisten kansantautien riskitekijöistä, niihin liittyvistä elintavoista, oireista ja terveyspalveluiden käytöstä* [A study on risk factors and lifestyles related to chronic diseases, symptoms, and use of health services. Implementation and basic tables] (Publications of the National Public Health Institute B1/1998). Helsinki: National Public Health Institute.

Vartiainen, E., Puska, P., Pekkanen, J., Tuomilehto, J., & Jousilahti, P. (1994). Changes in risk factors explain changes in mortality from ischemic heart disease in Finland. *British Medical Journal, 309,* 23–27.

Vartiainen, E., Tossavainen, K., Viri, L., Niskanen, E., & Puska, P. (1991). The North Karelia Youth Programs. *Annals of New York Academy of Science, 623,* 32–349.

Wiio, J. (1984). *Televisio ja arkikäyttäytyminen* [Television and everyday behavior]. Espoo: Weilin & Göös.

World Heath Organization, Regional Office for Europe. (1973). *Methodology of multifactorial preventive trials in ischemic heart disease. Report of a working group* (Document EURO 8202[6]). Copenhagen: Author.

World Health Organization. (1982). *Prevention of coronary heart disease. Report of a WHO expert committee* (Technical Report Series 678). Geneva: Author.

World Health Organization. (1986). *Community prevention and control of cardiovascular diseases. Report of a WHO expert committee* (Technical Report Series 732). Geneva: Author.

World Health Organization. (1998). *The world health report 1998: Executive summary.* Geneva: Author.

5

EXPOSURE TO URBAN VIOLENCE: SHIFTING FROM AN INDIVIDUAL TO AN ECOLOGICAL PERSPECTIVE

RAYMOND P. LORION

As is echoed throughout this volume, the social and behavioral sciences generally, and psychology specifically, have much to gain from and to contribute to public health science and practice. Over the past decade, I have attempted to understand the complementarity of these disciplines and initiate dialogues to increase collaborations among their respective members (Lorion, 1991; Lorion & Iscoe, 1996). Consistent with those goals, this chapter focuses specifically on urban violence and its implications for public health and welfare. The salience of this issue for the population is confirmed almost daily in the media. The seemingly epidemic levels of the problem observed in the early 1990s appear to be tempering. Nevertheless, the issue remains a matter of serious public concern, and its consequences extend beyond the direct victims and perpetrators. As explained elsewhere (Lorion, 1998), the understanding of those consequences may increase if one focuses not on isolated individual acts but on violence as a characteristic of settings.

Viewing urban violence contextually can shift behavioral scientists toward recognition of and interest in public health's concern for the etiological and intervention significance of community-based pathogens. Traditionally, criminologists (e.g., Elliot, Williams, & Hamburg, 1998), sociologists (e.g., Levine & Rosich, 1996), psychologists (e.g., American Psychological Association, 1993), and other social scientists (e.g., Singer, Anglin, Song, & Lunghofer, 1995) have described community violence in terms of the occurrence of events or behaviors intended to cause injury, harm, or death to another. Summaries of such events are found in national and local crime statistics (e.g., *Uniform Crime Report* rates) and provide information about the characteristics (e.g., age, race, gender) of the victims and perpetrators of community violence. Other archival sources (e.g., emergency room and trauma center records) reflect associated levels of morbidity and mortality, whereas other data (e.g., local law enforcement, judiciary and corrections budgets and records) document the fiscal investments and demands related to responses to these problems.

Such records do not, however, convey the qualitative experience of those who encounter such events where they live, work, learn, and play. As a confirmed risk factor for engaging in antisocial behavior (Elliot, Williams, & Hamburg, 1998; Levine & Rosich, 1996), exposure to pervasive community violence has been likened to an environmental toxin that potentially contaminates intraindividual and interindividual functioning (Lorion, 1998; Lorion, Brodsky, & Cooley-Quille, 1998). This chapter argues that understanding the toxic influence of pervasive community violence presents both a challenge and an opportunity for the mental health and public health disciplines. Pervasive community violence represents a "public" issue insofar as it affects, directly or indirectly, broad segments of the population regardless of age, gender, ethnicity, and economic status. Its documented impact on the nation's morbidity and mortality makes it a "health" issue. As argued below, its affective and behavioral consequences justify its consideration jointly by the health, public health, social, and behavioral science disciplines.

DEFINITIONAL ISSUES

In this chapter, *violence* refers to the act and to the consequences of the use—or threat of the use—of force to cause intentional injury, harm, or death to another. The qualifier "intentional" excludes accidental injury or death. Systematic study will be necessary to define validly the perpetrator's intentions. The health and mental health consequences of violent acts refer to (a) the injuries or deaths of those directly victimized by a violent act or threat; (b) the emotional trauma or behavioral sequellae of being a bystander, witness, or loved one of someone victimized by a violent act or threat; and (c) the emotional trauma or behavioral sequellae experienced by those aware that violent acts or threats may occur within settings they occupy or might occupy.

Reported pervasive community violence levels confirm the application of Apfel and Simon's (1996) description of *communal violence* as referring to settings in "which every child has witnessed or expects to witness violence and has been or expects to be violated" (pp. 4–5) to many of the nation's urban and suburban settings. *Community violence*, therefore, locates acts and consequences within a geographic setting (e.g., a neighborhood or school), an identifiable social grouping (e.g., a grade cohort, gang, or nuclear or extended family), or both. *Pervasive community violence* refers to the chronic and widespread occurrence of violent acts or threats within such settings or groups. The qualifier "pervasive" applies when violent acts and their consequences are encountered by a substantial portion of a community's population within a single setting, across multiple settings, or over an extended period of time. Similar to "intentionality," the qualifiers "substantial," "multiple," and "extended" must be operationalized through systematic research. Epidemiological studies will also be needed to determine the nature and rate of violent acts within a community and risk factors for encounters with violent acts.

Conceptualizing pervasive community violence as an environmental characteristic implies that it has the potential to contaminate settings and the actions and interactions of at least some of their inhabitants. *Contamination* refers to the corrosive or pathogenic effect of exposure to the physical and psychological health of a community. As explained below, changes in individual assumptions about the threatening quality of others, the need to limit one's contact with others, and the urgency of responding aggressively to actual or anticipated attacks may occur gradually or suddenly following a traumatic event. Understanding the patterns and mechanisms through which contamination occurs within and across individuals is likely to provide important clues into the design of interventions to limit exposure and prevent or reduce its consequences. How such contamination occurs, over what period of time, and with what degree of specificity across diverse parameters of human functioning and individual characteristics need clarification. These merit the same attention and rigor applied by public health science to other pathogens.

HEALTH AND MENTAL HEALTH COSTS OF EXPOSURE

Hamburg (1998) estimated the impact of pervasive community violence on health care costs for the general population as follows:

> The total medical cost of all violence that occurred in the United States was $13.5 billion in 1992, including $10.5 billion that resulted from interpersonal violence such as murder, rape, assault, robbery,

drunk driving, and arson. To these figures we must add the costs of years of potential life lost and the psychological trauma that results from intentional injuries. The latter costs are impossible to calculate, especially for children and adolescents who witness or experience violence at the most critical developmental stages in their lives. Although the health burden of violence strikes minority youth disproportionately hard, high rates of death and injury from violence in all racial and ethnic groups ensure that violence has without question become the most serious health problem facing all of our country's young people. (p. 37)

As a most important setting in children's lives, the school was chosen to illustrate the contextual impact of pervasive community violence. Examining this setting reveals a disturbing picture of the capacity of violence to distress individuals and corrode environmental quality (Lorion, 1998). Within schools, acts of violence affect not only students, but faculty and administrators as well. Such acts can range from verbal hassling to abuse; from poking and pushing others as they move down a hallway to knocking them over; from verbal threats to acts of assault and even homicide; and from vandalism to robbery to sexual harassment to rape. As described by Beland (1996):

> In schools, teachers find themselves spending increasing amounts of time attending to students' disruptive and angry outbursts, interpersonal conflicts, and off-task behavior, or worse. Every day, approximately 100,000 children are assaulted at school, 5,000 teachers are threatened with physical assault, and 200 are actually attacked (Geiger, 1993). Although teachers are expected to concentrate on teaching academics, they are finding that student behavior prevents them from doing so; eventually it drives many of them from the teaching profession. (p. 209)

Addressing school-based pervasive community violence as a public health problem, the design and implementation of a setting-specific response depends on the capacity to assess the pathogen's presence, its consequences, and its variability across time and circumstances. Pervasive community violence exposure, for example, may impair the cognitive, emotional, behavioral, or biological status of those exposed. Measurable effects across these functional modalities may evolve simultaneously, sequentially, or synergistically.

As a contextual factor, pervasive community violence would affect, for example, not only the students within a school but also the adults (teachers, staff, administrators, etc.) working in those settings. Depending on its actual or presumed level, pervasive community violence also shapes the feelings and behaviors of those who visit (or choose to avoid) the building or pass through (or circumvent) its classrooms, hallways, restrooms, and offices. It is assumed to shape how people interact; who is able or chooses to learn, teach, or work there; how events are interpreted by its inhabitants; and how other systems (e.g., the board of education, the police) respond to those events.

Understanding the patterns and mechanisms by which pervasive community violence influences individuals singly and in interaction with others is an appropriate concern for public health investigators. As with other pathogens, what is learned about pervasive community violence should have significant heuristic import beyond its specific focus (i.e., violence). The resulting knowledge may, for example, provide important clues into what Sarason (1996) described as the "culture of schools." In his analysis, Sarason focused attention on linkages among environmental qualities, educational policies, and the attainment of academic goals. Examining pervasive community violence within schools may lead to new methodologies for studying environmental factors. It may also generate hypotheses about how setting characteristics influence the learning, instructional, and interpersonal environment of schools. Pervasive community violence exposure, for example, may reduce the quality of teachers' instructional effectiveness, consistency of enforcement of classroom rules, or sensitivity to student needs. Lorion and Saltzman (1993) linked pervasive community violence exposure with children's responsiveness to parent and teacher control and involvement in the distribution or use of substances. Recently collected data (Cooley-Quille & Lorion, 1999) have suggested that exposure relates to the affective status, physiological functioning, and relationship of parents and children. Presumably, such links also will be found for teachers and other school staff. Research will need to be carried out to determine how levels of physiological stress, interpersonal tension, fear, and aggression in one segment of those who live, work, study, or play in a setting influence the functioning and affective experience of others in that setting.

Consideration of pervasive community violence as a pathogen may also catalyze study of factors that limit, neutralize, or sustain environmental qualities such as a community's competence (Iscoe, 1974) or its members' positive (Macmillan, 1996) or negative (Brodsky, 1996) sense of community. At a minimum, study of the nature and mechanisms of pervasive community violence should stimulate reexamination of the knowledge bases available to the social sciences for understanding human behavior from an ecological and contextual frame of reference.

MEASURING THE IMPACT

Investigation of pervasive community violence's contextual influence requires methods to estimate its presence and effects. Much work has already occurred on that front. Various measures of pervasive community violence exposure (Lorion et al., 1998) share elements of the Survey of

Children's Exposure to Community Violence (Richters & Saltzman, 1990). Using a five-point Likert scale (from 0 = *never* to 4 = *a lot of the time*), respondents indicate how often they have been victimized by, heard about, or witnessed violent events or related activities (e.g., shooting, stabbing, mugging, seeing a dead body). Variations of this measure were applied by Martinez and Richters (1993) and Osofsky, Wewers, Hahn, & Fick (1993) in studies of mothers of elementary graders and by Richters and Martinez and Saltzman (1992) in their studies of fifth and sixth graders. A further variation of this measure was applied by Saltzman (1995) to examine the relevance of pervasive community violence exposure to adolescent involvement in antisocial and delinquent behaviors.

Building on these variations, Singer, Anglin, Song, and Lunghofer (1995) designed the Recent Exposure to Physical Violence and the Past Exposure to Violence surveys to obtain adolescent reports of exposure during the prior year and while growing up, not including the past year respectively. The acts surveyed by Singer et al. include threats, slapping, hitting, punching, beatings, knife attacks, and shootings. Adolescents provided separate reports for the occurrence of each item (other than knife attacks and shootings) at their home, school, and neighborhood. Respondents also were asked how often they had witnessed someone else victimized at each of these sites. Two additional items inquired about respondents having been made to do a sexual act or having witnessed someone else being made to do a sexual act. Using related measures, Jenkins and her colleagues (Bell, Hildreth, Jenkins, Levi, & Carter, 1988; Bell & Jenkins, 1993; Jenkins & Thompson, 1986) surveyed youth's exposure in terms of (a) knowing someone who was a victim of violence, (b) having witnessed real-life violent events, (c) having been a victim of a violent incident, and (d) having perpetrated a violent act. Comparable to the work mentioned above, information about such forms of exposure was obtained from students enrolled in grades 2 through 12.

The author and his colleagues have begun to examine the value of archival data as an alternative index of exposure. Specifically, we are associating self-reports of pervasive community violence exposure to records of police contacts and emergency vehicle calls for varying circumferences (6, 10, or 12 blocks) around respondents' home addresses. We hope the findings will independently validate self-reports and offer an inexpensive, efficient, and nonintrusive (reporting pervasive community violence exposure may be emotionally iatrogenic) index of exposure. Analyzing such archival records via geocoding may enable public health practitioners to depict relative levels of contamination or contagion potential across urban areas. Overlapping pervasive community violence estimates with prevalence estimates of selected emotional, behavioral, or physical outcomes can, we believe, facilitate needs assessment and intervention targeting, design, and evaluation.

Findings from studies of youth confirm the toxicity of pervasive community violence. Negative concomitants in preadolescents include heightened levels of (a) generalized emotional distress (Bell & Jenkins, 1993; Martinez & Richters, 1993; Osofsky et al., 1993; Richters & Martinez, 1993; Saltzman, 1992), (b) affective and vegetative signs of depression, and (c) indices of stress-related disorders. Also reported were decreases in self-esteem and social skills. Pervasive community violence exposure has been linked to levels of aggression, conduct disorder, and running away in large, ethnically diverse samples of urban and suburban youth (Saltzman, 1995; Singer et al., 1994, 1995). Rubinetti's (1996) findings suggest that levels of empathy, hopefulness, and self-esteem mediate the link between pervasive community violence exposure and involvement in violent activities.

Pilot findings (Cooley-Quille & Lorion, 1999) suggest links among pervasive community violence exposure, sleep patterns, and self-report and physiological indices of stress in both youth and adults. If replicated, these links would extend evidence that pervasive community violence exposure affects cognitive functions such as arousal, memory, attention, abstract reasoning, vigilance, and emotional reactivity (e.g., Pynoos & Nader, 1989). Pervasive community violence has also been linked to symptoms of post-traumatic stress disorder such as flashbacks, depersonalization, anhedonia, hypervigilance, exaggerated startle responses, and generalized irritability (Fitzpatrick & Boldizar, 1993; Jenkins, 1993; Raia, Pederson, & Dana, 1995).

CONTEXTUALIZING THE PATHOGEN

Evidence confirms the toxicity for individuals of pervasive community violence. Qualitative reports of violent communities (e.g., Garbarino, Kostelny, & Dubrow, 1991), however, argue for exploration of its potential as an environmental pathogen. It is argued that in some settings, individual acts of violence become so commonplace and attention to their actual or potential occurrence so widespread that pervasive community violence becomes a defining quality of the settings or situations. Similar to an airborne toxin, it may disrupt the emotional, physical, behavioral, and interpersonal functioning of those entering or approaching that environment. The consequences of the encounter appear to meet Wakefield's (1992, 1997) definition of *disorder* as "harmful dysfunction," where "harm" is judged by social values and "dysfunction" is the failure of a mental or physical mechanism to perform a function for which it was naturally selected.

Conceptualizing pervasive community violence as an environmental toxin can be understood in terms of Lewin's (1935) concept of "psychological ecology" as a perspective for inclusion of setting *and* individual characteristics and into predictions of human behavior. Building on Lewin's base, Barker and his colleagues (Barker, 1964, 1968; Barker & Wright, 1951; Shoggen, 1989) found that setting characteristics were better predictors of children's behavior than were individual characteristics. In effect, children acted more like each other within a given setting than like themselves across settings. Barker offered the concept of "behavior-setting" to describe how setting characteristics influence behaviors. Wicker (1979) explained this process as follows:

> Behavior settings are self-regulating, active systems. They impose their program of activities on the persons and objects within them. Essential persons and materials are drawn into settings, and disruptive components are modified or ejected. It's as if behavior settings were living systems intent on remaining alive and healthy, even at the expense of their individual components. (p. 12)

Wicker went on to summarize some of the essential features of behavior settings:

> Most of them can be presented in a single sentence: A behavior setting is a bounded, self-regulated and ordered system composed of replaceable human and nonhuman components that interact in a synchronized fashion to carry out an ordered sequence of events called the setting program. (p. 12)

Although the heuristic potential of Barker's work on setting characteristics has yet to be aggressively mined (readers are encouraged to review Levine & Perkins, 1997, Moos & Insel, 1974, and Wandersman & Hess, 1985, for illustrations of the potential richness of this perspective), it seems to offer a heuristic avenue for understanding and responding to the setting influences of pervasive community violence. It is hypothesized that high pervasive community violence settings are characterized by a setting program that "pulls" for aggressive and defensive behaviors generally and violent reactions specifically. Inhabitants of such settings presumably would be likely to interpret interpersonal ambiguity as threatening and respond aggressively and defensively. Systematic studies must determine whether the contextual influence of pervasive community violence is sufficient to alter initially and shape ultimately individual predispositions. We must also learn whether, how, and at what levels it changes the physical characteristics or the shared assumptions of settings such as schools, playgrounds, or homes.

If, as proposed, pervasive community violence represents a quality of settings (e.g., neighborhoods, schools, apartment buildings), it must be determined whether all who inhabit such settings are potentially (or equally) vulnerable to its contaminating effects on psychological and physical health. The extent of exposure to violence and its impact on adult emotional and behavioral functioning have yet to be systematically assessed. It seems reasonable to assume, however, that some parents, caregivers (e.g., teachers), and adults residing and working in affected communities are resistant to it. Which factors inoculate them needs to be determined. Estimation of the spread of pervasive community violence throughout a community's residents defines one aspect of the toxin's pervasiveness. Understanding that spread also seems necessary for targeting (e.g., should the focus be on youth or on their caregivers?) as well as for staffing an intervention. If, for example, teachers or parents are to buffer the effects of children's exposure, it may first be necessary to mitigate the effects of violence on their own functioning.

INITIAL STEPS IN PREVENTION AND TREATMENT

Interventions against violence have lacked clear linkages across service delivery systems, organizations, and service settings (Blum, 1994). Programs targeted to youth, for example, have developed within schools, mental health clinics, recreation centers, and juvenile justice settings. Little if any contact typically occurs across or within these systems. To remedy this, Blum encouraged identification of "common components" across programs. This step requires appreciation that the meaning of each intervention for those who provide and those who receive it is affected greatly by its host system.

If, as argued, pervasive community violence represents a contextual pathogen, then related interventions must cross setting boundaries. To respond to this pathogen, health and mental health professionals must communicate and be willing to work together to bring services into the communities. Schools and recreation centers, for example, may be ideal sites for providing universal preventive interventions. Examples of community centers sponsoring general violence prevention programs include the Police Athletic League centers and the South Baltimore Youth Center (Baker, Pollack, & Kohn, 1995). Schools provide educational services relevant to violence prevention. Additions to the curriculum provide students with health-related knowledge (e.g., medical and social consequences of aggressive behavior and substance use), strategies for conflict resolution, access to peer support, and upward social mobility through education (Walker, Goodwin, & Warren, 1992).

Health clinics may be involved in indicated interventions. Community efforts to reduce risks for lead poisoning fall within this category. This work is based on Needleman's (1990) hypothesis that "some of the disorder behaviors of those who commit violent crimes result from disordered brain function and that much of this disorder is provoked by lead exposure" (reported in Walker et al., 1992, p. 492). Such a preventive effort might include early lead screening and diagnostic evaluation of children.

Community mental health centers may provide violence prevention programs to reduce the negative effects of violence exposure in groups at increased risk (selected intervention), to short-circuit the traumatic consequences of exposure to a traumatically violent event, or to treat victims exposed to violence (indicated interventions). By contrast, because of the close association of adjudicated juvenile crime and violence (Tolan & Guerra, 1994), the juvenile justice system typically relies on indicated preventive strategies. The juvenile justice system has substantial contact with youth at high individual risk for engaging in violent acts (e.g., as members of a gang) or who have already acted violently and thus risk involvement in more serious and potentially lethal acts. This system relies on diversion programs for at-risk youth as an alternative to adjudication. Such efforts involve sponsored programs such as vocational training, education, counseling, casework, and clinical services.

Unfortunately, it does not appear that the problem can be solved by relying solely on the methods reviewed thus far. Their documented effects are limited (Tolan & Guerra, 1994). In his assessment of the effects of available preventive interventions on the nation's youth, Elias (1997) concluded (perhaps too pessimistically) that

> Little progress has been made across key areas such as alcohol, tobacco, and other drug use; mental health and mental disorders; violent and abusive behavior; sexually transmitted disease; and child protective and clinically preventive services. There is a trend toward more youth being caught in the grips of poverty and dangerous environments in their schools and communities. Leaders in the field continue to recognize that the impact of preventive mental health services on public policy and public health has not been substantial, yet must become so if the field is to be viable in the future (Lorion, 1993). (p. 253)

The number of youth still presenting problems is currently too high and seems likely to remain so in the near future. We must, however, balance our focus on the problems of urban[1] youth with a viewpoint that

> takes into consideration youth's positive behavior, which the bleak accounts tend to overlook. The overwhelming majority of U.S. youth claim to have close and respectful relationships with their parents ..., are seriously engaged in schoolwork and related activities ..., and say that religion is important in their lives. (Youniss & Yates, 1999, p. 2)

The presence of this "overwhelming majority" in communities represents not merely a target for preventive interventions seeking to avoid

---

[1]Although this chapter has focused on violence within urban settings, the unfortunate repetition of school-based violence in urban and suburban communities makes evident the national scope of the problem and the need for its solution.

further perpetrators of violence or a pool of potential victims to be protected. As an aggregate, they and their families represent a vital community resource whose involvement is essential to reducing pervasive violence. If families such as these, along with other positive segments of a community, can be mobilized, they hold a key to resolving the problem or at least reducing it to a manageable level. Although the point has yet to be systematically determined (and one may need to do so for each community), it is likely that below a given level, violence loses its environmental force and returns to an individual-level pathogen in a community.

STEPS BEYOND THE INDIVIDUAL

The interventions discussed thus far illustrate diverse paths for reducing the likelihood of individual involvement in pervasive community violence or for responding to the needs of its individual victims. Reliance on such efforts is limited in reach because it places the causes of violence and its consequences on individuals. That such a perspective leaves untouched the environmental quality of pervasive violence may explain the limited effectiveness of individual interventions in solving the problem. As argued in this chapter and elsewhere (Lorion, 1998), at some point in the escalation of community violence, the setting is altered and contributes to the likelihood of further violence and the vulnerability of its victims. If the hypothesized environmental toxicity is valid, alternative preventive approaches must be designed that reduce the source of contamination, that is, the factors that support pervasive community violence. Just as herd immunity explains how members of a population are protected by the resistance of a sufficient portion of the population, its counterpart (i.e., an increase in vulnerability) may follow from having some portion of the population engaged in violence or fearing its occurrence.

Were urban violence likened to secondhand tobacco smoke, the interventions described thus far would be similar to behavior change (e.g., convincing individual smokers to extinguish their cigarettes) and setting change (e.g., placing "No Smoking" signs on the walls; creating no-smoking sections). Some would be helped, but the components of the problem would remain present, and reductions in the prevalence of consequences of exposure would accrue slowly and only with continuing effort.

Unlike infectious diseases such as chicken pox, prior exposure to pervasive violence does not immunize one against further infection or remove one from "carrier" status (i.e., one who commits a violent act). Similarly, protection from one smoker in one setting does not carry over to other settings, nor is a smoker who agrees to extinguish a cigarette in one setting likely to cease smoking thereafter. Exposure to secondhand smoke has not been identified as a risk factor for smoking. By contrast, Singer et al. (1995) reported a significant link between prior exposure to urban violence and both future exposure and participation in subsequent violent acts.

Public health strategies for reducing environmental contamination range, for example, from killing mosquitoes that carry malaria, to draining the swamps in which they breed, to vaccinating and educating those exposed so that they neither acquire nor transmit the disease. By definition, pervasive community violence means that a substantial number of individuals in a community engage in violent behavior, and multilevel interventions are required to address this complex problem. To achieve the equivalent of "draining the swamp" in a neighborhood or community where violence is pervasive would require identifying and altering setting characteristics that encourage and sustain violent behavior, including the public's general acceptance of violence.

To control pervasive community violence requires that both its practices and their underlying assumptive bases change. In effect, passive tolerance of public acts of vandalism and violence would need to be replaced with organized and sustained resistance. Thus, the lessons of Alinski (1946, 1972) concerning community organization may need to be incorporated within preventive efforts. The "overwhelming majority" of youth and adults must refuse to stay inside, must act together in response to acts of violence, and must express and live the sentiment that aggression against any one of its members is aggression against all. As noted by Youniss and Yates (1999), that majority already tends to rely heavily on community organizations ranging from churches to formal and informal youth groups to neighborhood or tenant associations and to linkages with social systems. Joining individuals and social organizations within a community may enable expression of a community's health and thereby release its herd immunity.

The next generation of interventions to resist pervasive violence must therefore shift from an individual to a community level of effect. The agents of change must also be the intervention targets, that is, reduce the risk for involvement in or suffering from violent acts among the "overwhelming majority" through their participation in the community's resistance. In turn, reducing their sense of risk and increasing the community's sense of security can decontaminate the environment and thereby lessen the frequency that violence is used as a defense against anticipated violence. Combining elements such as Neighborhood Watch and community policing, adults and older adolescents share responsibility for protecting each other and their younger neighbors; this creates what Macmillan (1996) referred to as a "sense of community" and what I argue removes the medium essential for violence to breed, spread, and contaminate the setting.

CONCLUSION

In considering intervention alternatives, Blum (1994) noted that his review of services and programs makes evident the need for a clear definition of target problems and populations. This chapter has argued that pervasive community violence be reconceptualized as an environmental rather than an individual experience and that its contextual effects be determined and addressed programmatically. In effect, it is proposed that readers appreciate distinctions among forms of violence and how they are experienced cumulatively over time and circumstance. The proposed shift in understanding community violence is rooted in a public health appreciation of the reality of environmental factors whose effects are contagious, contaminating, and corrosive.

If this alternative is valid, distinctly different kinds of interventions will be needed. Such interventions will be targeted to and located within settings with high levels of pervasive community violence. To design and implement such interventions, new partnerships will need to be formed across the health, public health, social, and behavioral sciences disciplines. That violence must be a catalyst for the formation of such collaborations is, in one sense, unfortunate. The need for such partnerships has long been recognized and encouraged. Nevertheless, pervasive community violence may represent the crisis-defining opportunity that produces new systems of care with important positive consequences for the nation's long-term health and welfare.

Such interventions will merge the roles of provider and recipient. The residents of a community must become engaged directly in the reduction of their vulnerability. Program developers will actually be enablers whose role is to offer an alternative experience and to provide the information, the technical support, and perhaps the funding for programs that, if adopted by the community, empower its members against the pathogen. To work, those who are potential victims of violence and vulnerable to responding violently to the violence of their setting must become the source of resistance to infection and further contamination. Elements of such have been found in community-policing programs, in Neighborhood Watch, in programs in which all adults feel responsible for the well-being and proper behavior of local youth, and so forth. The antigen for pervasive community violence appears to lie within the community.

REFERENCES

Alinski, S. D. (1946). *Reveille for radicals*. Chicago: University of Chicago Press.
Alinski, S. D. (1972). *Rules for radicals*. New York: Aldine.
American Psychological Association Commission on Violence and Youth. (1993).

Violence and youth: psychology's response. Vol. I: Summary report of the American Psychological Association Commission on violence and youth. Washington, DC: Author.

Apfel, R. J., & Simon, B. (Eds.). (1996). *Minefields in their hearts.* New Haven, CT: Yale University Press.

Baker, K., Pollack, M., & Kohn, I. (1995). Violence prevention through informal socialization: An evaluation of the South Baltimore Youth Project. *Studies on Crime and Prevention, 4,* 61–85.

Barker, R. G. (1964). *Big school, small school: High school size and student behavior.* Stanford, CA: Stanford University Press.

Barker, R. G. (1968). *Ecological psychology.* Stanford, CA: Stanford University Press.

Barker, R. G., & Wright, R. F. (1951). *One boy's day.* New York: Harper & Row.

Beland, K. R. (1996). A schoolwide approach to violence prevention. In R. L. Hampton, P. Jenkins, & T. P. Gullota (Eds.), *Preventing violence in America* (pp. 209–232). Thousand Oaks, CA: Sage.

Bell, C. C., Hildreth, C. J., Jenkins, E. J., Levi, D., & Carter, C. (1988). The need for victimization screening in a poor, outpatient medical population. *Journal of the National Medical Association, 80,* 853–860.

Bell, C. C., & Jenkins, E. J. (1993). Community violence and children on Chicago's southside. *Psychiatry: Interpersonal and Biological Processes, 56,* 46–54.

Blum, A. (1994). *Innovation in service delivery and direct practice: A framework for analysis.* Unpublished manuscript, Center for Practice Innovations, Case Western Reserve University.

Brodsky, A. E. (1996). Resilient single mothers in risky neighborhoods: Negative psychological sense of community. *Journal of Community Psychology, 24,* 347–364.

Cooley-Quille, M., & Lorion, R. P. (1999). Exposure to violence: Preliminary evidence of psycho-physiological links for urban youth. *Journal of Community Psychology, 27,* 367–376.

Elias, M. J. (1997). Reinterpreting dissemination of prevention programs as widespread implementation with effectiveness and fidelity. In R. P. Weissberg, T. P. Gullotta, R. L. Hampton, B. A. Ryan, & G. R. Adams (Eds.), *Establishing preventive services* (pp. 253–289). Thousand Oaks, CA: Sage.

Elliott, D. S., Williams, K. R., & Hamburg, B. (Eds.). (1998). *Violence in American schools: A new perspective.* New York: Cambridge University Press.

Fitzpatrick, K., & Boldizar, J. (1993). The prevalence and consequences of exposure to violence among African American youth. *Journal of the American Academy of Child and Adolescent Psychiatry, 32,* 424–430.

Garbarino, J., Kostelny, K., & Dubrow, N. (1991) *No place to be a child: Growing up in a war zone.* Lexington, MA: Lexington Books.

Geiger, K. (1993, January 14). *Violence in the schools.* Statement presented at a news conference given by the president of the National Education Association, Washington, DC.

Hamburg, M. (1998). Violence as a public health problem for children and youth. In D. S. Elliott, K. R. Williams, & B. Hamburg (Eds.), *Violence in American schools: A new perspective* (pp. 31–54). New York: Cambridge University Press.

Iscoe, I. (1974). Community psychology and the competent community. *American Psychologist, 29,* 607–613.

Jenkins, E. (1993, March). Posttraumatic stress disorder symptoms of African American youth exposed to violence. Paper presented at the meeting of the American Association of Behavior Therapy, Atlanta, GA.

Jenkins, E. J., & Thompson, B. (1986, August). *Children talk about violence: Preliminary findings from a survey of Black elementary school children.* Presented at the Nineteenth Annual Convention of the Association of Black Psychologists, Oakland, CA.

Levine, M., & Perkins, D. V. (1997). *Principles of community psychology: Perspectives and applications* (2nd ed.). New York: Oxford University Press.

Levine, F. J., & Rosich, K. J. (1996). *Social causes of violence: Crafting a science agenda.* Washington, DC: American Sociological Association.

Lewin, K. (1935). *A dynamic theory of personality: Selected papers* (D. K. Adams, Trans.). New York: McGraw-Hill.

Lorion, R. P. (1991). Prevention and public health: Psychology's response to the nation's health care crisis. *American Psychologist, 46,* 516–519.

Lorion, R. P. (1993). Counting the stitches: Preventive intervention promises and public health. *American Journal of Community Psychology, 21,* 673–679.

Lorion, R. P. (1998). Exposure to urban violence: Contamination of the school environment. In D. S. Elliott, K. R. Williams, & B. Hamburg (Eds.), *Violence in American schools: A new perspective* (pp. 293–311). New York: Cambridge University Press.

Lorion, R. P., Brodsky, A. E., & Cooley-Quille, M. (1998). Exposure to pervasive community violence: Resisting the contaminating effects of risky settings. In D. E. Biegel & A. Blum (Eds.), *Innovations in practice and service delivery across the life span* (pp. 124–146). New York: Oxford University Press.

Lorion, R. P., & Iscoe, I. (1996). Introduction: Reshaping our views of the field. In R. P. Lorion, I. Iscoe, P. H. DeLeon, & G. R. VandenBos (Eds.), *Psychology and public policy: Balancing public service and professional need* (pp. 1–19). Washington, DC: American Psychological Association.

Lorion, R. P., & Saltzman, W. (1993). Children's exposure to community violence: Following a path from concern to research to action. *Psychiatry: Interpersonal and Biological Processes, 56,* 55–65.

Macmillan, D. W. (1996). Sense of community. *Journal of Community Psychology, 24,* 315–326.

Martinez, P., & Richters, J. E. (1993). The NIMH Community Violence Project: II. Children's distress symptoms associated with violence exposure. *Psychiatry: Interpersonal and Biological Processes, 56,* 22–35.

Moos, R. H., & Insel, P. M. (Eds.). (1974). *Issues in social ecology.* Palo Alto, CA: National Press Books.

Osofsky, J. D., Wewers, S., Hahn, D. M., & Fick, A. C. (1993). Chronic community violence: What is happening to our children? *Psychiatry: Interpersonal and Biological Processes, 56,* 36–45.

Pynoos, R. S., & Nader, K. (1989). Children's memory and proximity to violence. *Journal of the American Academy of Child and Adolescent Psychiatry, 28,* 236–241.

Raia, J., Pederson, L., & Dana, J. (1995, August). Community violence exposure and posttraumatic stress reactions. Paper presented at the annual convention of the American Psychological Association, New York.

Richters, J. E., & Martinez, P. (1993). The NIMH Community Violence Project: I. Children as victims of and witnesses to violence. *Psychiatry: Interpersonal and Biological Processes, 56,* 7–21.

Richters, J. E., & Saltzman, W. (1990). *Survey of Exposure to Community Violence —Parent Report Version.* Unpublished measure, Child and Adolescent Disorders Research, National Institute of Mental Health.

Rubinetti, F. (1996). *Empathy, self-esteem, hopelessness, and belief in the legitimacy of aggression in adolescents exposed to pervasive community violence.* Unpublished doctoral dissertation, University of Maryland, College Park.

Saltzman, W. R. (1992). *The effect of children's exposure to community violence.* Unpublished master's thesis, University of Maryland, College Park.

Saltzman, W. R. (1995). *Exposure to community violence and the prediction of violent antisocial behavior in a multi-ethnic sample of adolescents.* Unpublished doctoral dissertation, University of Maryland, College Park.

Sarason, S. B. (1996). *Revisiting the culture of the school and the problem of change.* New York: Teachers College Press.

Shoggen, P. (1989). *Behavior settings: A revision and extension of Roger G. Barker's Ecological Psychology.* Stanford CA: Stanford University Press.

Singer, M. I., Anglin, T. M., Song, L., & Lunghofer, L. (1994). *The mental health consequences of adolescents' exposure to violence.* Cleveland, OH: Case Western Reserve University.

Singer, M. I., Anglin, T. M., Song, L., & Lunghofer, L. (1995). Adolescents' exposure to violence and associated symptoms of psychological trauma. *Journal of the American Medical Association, 273,* 477–482.

Tolan, P. H., & Guerra, N. G. (1994). *What works in reducing adolescent violence: An empirical review of the field.* Boulder, CO: Center for the Study and Prevention of Violence.

Wakefield, J. C. (1992). The concept of mental disorder: On the boundary between biological facts and social values. *American Psychologist, 47,* 373–388.

Wakefield, J. C. (1997). When is development disordered? Developmental psychopathology and the harmful dysfunction analysis of mental disorder. *Development and Psychopathology, 9,* 269–290.

Walker, B., Goodwin, N. J., & Warren, R. C. (1992) Impact of violence on African-American children and adolescents: A public health challenge. *Journal of the National Medical Association, 84,* 490–496.

Wandersman, A., & Hess, R. (1985). *Beyond the individual: Environmental approaches and prevention*. New York: Haworth Press.

Wicker, A. W. (1979). *An introduction to ecological psychology*. Monterey, CA: Brooks/Cole.

Youniss, J., & Yates, M. (1999). Introduction: International perspectives on the roots of civic identity. In M. Yates & J. Youniss (Eds.), *Roots of civic identity: International perspectives on community service and activism in youth* (pp. 1–15). Cambridge, England: Cambridge University Press.

6

ACTION RESEARCH: INFORMING INTERVENTIONS IN MALE VIOLENCE AGAINST WOMEN

SARAH L. COOK AND MARY P. KOSS

In this chapter, we consider models of behavioral and social sciences that will best inform interventions and public policy pertaining to male violence against women. The behavioral and social sciences comprise a broad range of disciplines including psychology, sociology, anthropology, political science, public health, criminology and criminal justice, law, geography, and economics, and we focus on a question that is germane to all: Will traditional models of scientific research produce knowledge adequate to direct the development of effective interventions aimed at reducing the scope and consequences of male violence against women? To answer this question, we examine assumptions underlying the application of science to social problems generally and specifically. We also catalogue the critical needs and challenges for scientific intervention in male violence against women. We define intervention broadly to include preventive and treatment interventions and public policies that target behavioral regularities (Seidman, 1983) at the individual and group levels, as well as within settings. We conclude that strict adherence to traditional models of science are limiting. Progress will be fostered if social and behavioral sciences researchers transcend basic and applied science distinctions and adopt an action-research orientation (Lewin, 1951).

LANGUAGE AND DEFINITIONS

Language powerfully shapes and limits people's understanding of the world in which we live and the social problems that we experience (Hare-Mustin & Marecek, 1990). The phrase *male violence against women* reflects the predominant pattern of perpetration and victimization in domestic violence, rape and other forms of sexual assault, sexual harassment, and stalking. Women are six times more likely than men to experience violent victimization by an intimate (Bureau of Justice Statistics, 1995) and more likely than men to be victimized by someone whom they know (Bureau of Justice Statistics, 1997). Women are at greater risk of assault, including rape and homicide, by a husband, ex-husband, boyfriend, or ex-boyfriend than they are by an acquaintance or stranger (Browne & Williams, 1989; Bureau of Justice Statistics, 1997; Campbell, 1992; Finkelhor & Yllo, 1985; Frieze, 1983; Mahoney & Williams, 1998; Russell, 1990). Because stalking is strongly linked to intimate violence, women are also more likely than men to be stalked by a current or former partner (Tjaden & Thoennes, 1998). Estimates indicate that 18–53% of employed women have experienced sexual or gender harassment by male employers and coworkers (National Victims Center, 1992; U.S. Merit Systems Protection Board, 1987). Given these data, it is not surprising that women are also more likely than men to be victimized in private contexts such as their homes (Bureau of Justice Statistics, 1997; Craven, 1996; Greenfield et al., 1998). Even in the workplace, women are more likely than men to be victimized by an intimate (Warchol, 1998). Violence against girls or women perpetrated within same-sex relationships is not the focus of this chapter, but preliminary research has begun to describe its nature and consequences (Berrill, 1990; Garnets, Herek, & Levy, 1990; Kanuha, 1990; Lobel, 1986; Renzetti, 1990). Tragically, the rate of women's victimization may be increasing (Craven, 1996).

Male violence against women includes a range of behaviors that produce fear, physical injury, and even death (Brownmiller, 1975; Koss et al., 1994; Leidig, 1981; Muehlenhard, Powch, Phelps, & Giusti, 1992). Recognizing the complex definitional issues, the American Psychological Task Force on Male Violence Against Women defined *male violence against women* to encompass

> physical, visual, verbal, or sexual acts that are experienced by women or girls as a threat, invasion, or assault, and that have the effect of hurting or degrading her and/or taking away her ability to control contact (intimate and otherwise) with another individual. (adapted from Kelly, 1988, as cited in Koss et al., 1994, p. xvi)

Other professional organizations have adopted similar definitions. The American Medical Association (1992) characterized *partner violence* as "a pattern of coercive behaviors that may include repeated battering and injury, psychological abuse, sexual assault, progressive social isolation, deprivation, and intimidation" (p. 40). All of these manifestations of male violence against women occur in a gendered society that fails to sanction them actively and consistently and thus perpetuates the behavior (Browne, 1993; Koss & Cleveland, 1997; Yllo, 1993).

Male violence against women is one of the most prevalent and insidious threats to women's well-being. Extensive empirical literature documents the deleterious aftermath of male violence against women that ripples through the fabric of women's lives (for comprehensive reviews, see Crowell & Burgess, 1996; Koss et al., 1994). Immediate and long-term negative mental health and psychological outcomes include posttraumatic stress disorder, depression, anxiety, and changes in cognitive belief structures about safety, esteem, and trust (Koss et al., 1994). Physical health is affected directly by injuries (Abbot, Johnson, Koziol-McLain, & Lowenstein, 1995; Browne, 1996; Goodman, Koss, & Russo, 1993) and indirectly by increased symptoms of illness (Acierno, Resnick, & Kilpatrick, 1997; Dunn & Gilchrist, 1993; Koss & Heslet, 1992; Koss, Koss, & Woodruff, 1991; Lesserman & Drossman, 1995) and high levels of risky health behaviors (Felitti et al., 1998; Walker et al., 1999). Victims of male violence are likely to experience impairment in work roles (Resick, Calhoun, Atkeson, & Ellis, 1981) and interpersonal relationships (Crome & McCabe, 1995; Letourneau, Resnick, Kilpatrick, & Saunders, 1996). Economic impacts are expressed at the individual and macrosystems levels in terms of lost wages and medical and legal expenditures (Cohen & Miller, 1998; Miller, Cohen, & Rossman, 1993).

Given the nature of male violence against women, the intensity, persistence, and pervasiveness of these consequences are not surprising. What is surprising is the diffusion of these consequences to affect all women's lives. At the outermost level of an ecological framework is the ever-present threat of violence that creates a specific context, enveloping and limiting women's lives and opportunities (Gordon & Riger, 1991; Hickman & Muehlenhard, 1997; Kelly & DeKeseredy, 1994; Klodawsky & Lundy, 1994; Riger & Gordon, 1981; Warr, 1985; Weinrath & Gartrell, 1996). Men do not live under this particular burden.

ASSUMPTIONS REGARDING SCIENCE AND SOCIAL PROBLEM SOLVING

The central premise of this book is that scientific methods can be effectively applied to solve social problems. This claim is boldly optimistic, especially considering the history of social science's relationship to social problems (Harris & Nicholson, 1998; Kelly, 1990; Weiss, 1983). Today society has renewed but realistic expectations for science's ability to alleviate social problems (Schneider, 1996). The future of science (i.e., continued federal funding) will be determined by its ability to reduce threats to human welfare that originate from within society. Science's salvation therefore rests on a series of assumptions: (a) social problems are valid areas of scientific inquiry, (b) the enterprise of science is structured in a way that facilitates social problem solving, (c) science can arrive at valid analyses of social problems, and finally (d) science can formulate solutions that society will embrace and implement.

Science assumes that all problems are solvable, especially in our age of technological sophistication. If problems appear intractable, that is, "not-solvable-in-the-once-and-for-all-you-don't-have-to-solve-it-again-fashion," science claims that the problem was not formulated and attacked scientifically (Sarason, 1978). Sarason, a community psychologist, admonished,

> In science, problems may be extraordinarily difficult, but they can never be viewed as intractable, and if some fool says a problem is intractable it is because he or she is not posing the problem correctly or does not have the brain power to work through to the solution. In science, fools are people who say problems are intractable. In the realm of social action, fools are people who say all problems are tractable. (p. 378)

Asking whether male violence against women is intractable is premature because neither society nor science has tried very hard or very long to reduce its scope and ameliorate its consequences. The Battered Women's Movement and the Rape Crisis Movement identified rape and domestic violence as barriers to women's equality more than two decades ago, but only recently has society united behind violence against women as a significant social problem. Science validated it as a topic for scholarly inquiry relatively recently compared with other social problems (e.g., addiction research). Although literature across the behavioral and social sciences has grown exponentially within the past decade, only a minority describes preventive and treatment intervention efficacy or effectiveness or the impact of policy reforms. For example, in the psychological literature on domestic violence, only 18% of publications between 1990 and 1997 reported some type of intervention study (Salazar, 1997).

The process and structure of science creates obstacles to developing knowledge on social problems even though there is "almost universal agreement that multidisciplinary approaches are necessary to study contemporary scientific problems" (Schneider, 1996, p. 718). Most researchers approach their studies by investigating narrow questions. Segregated lines of scientific inquiry investigate those who are sexually assaulted and those who are battered without regard to the reality that these are often the same women. Moreover, researchers are as defined by the type of violence they study as they are by their respective disciplines, despite the large degree of overlap in theories and constructs studied across forms of violence. Separate professional societies, journals, and conferences promote this balkanization. Nelson (1977), a noted economist, asserted

> Analysts within each of the traditions have had a tendency to combine tunnel vision with intellectual imperialism. Members of the different traditions have had a tendency to be lulled by their imperialistic rhetoric. This has often led them to provide interpretations and prescriptions that the public, and the political apparatus, have rightly scoffed at. Failure to recognize the limitations of one's own perspective has made analysis of problems that require an integration of various perspectives very difficult. (as cited in Sarason, 1978, p. 377)

The publication of several multidisciplinary journals in the field, for example, *Violence Against Women*, *Journal of Interpersonal Violence*, and *Violence and Victims*, mitigates against these unproductive and entrenched traditions that will most likely dominate the way in which the field disseminates knowledge for some time to come.

Attempts at resolving social problems are shaped by the way they are formulated (Humphreys & Rappaport, 1993; Seidman, 1983; Watzlawick, Weakland, & Fisch, 1974). Society's—and therefore, science's—understanding of male violence against women evolved considerably throughout the 20th century and especially in the past two decades (Fagan, 1996; Loseke, 1991; Sanday, 1996). Early analyses of rape pursued theories of victim precipitation (Amir, 1971; Kanin, 1957; Selkin, 1978), social control (Burt, 1980; Field, 1978), and situational blame (Bart, 1981; Javorek, 1979). Quick and decisive individual action by women when confronted by an assailant was promoted as effective prevention (e.g., Kaufman, Rudeen, & Morgan; 1980; Storaska, 1975). Analyses of domestic violence focused on victim pathology as causal factors and often ignored perpetrator pathology and the social and cultural context (Rosewater, 1987; Walker, 1987). Nelson stated that, "a good portion of the reason why rational analysis of social problems hasn't gotten . . . very far lies in the *nature of the analyses* that have been done" (as cited in Sarason, 1978, p. 377, emphasis added). Contemporary conceptualizations are far more ecological and holistic (e.g., Dutton, 1985; Malamuth, Sockloskie, Koss, & Tanaka, 1991; Perilla, Bakeman, & Norris, 1994), but disagreement remains that blocks the emergence of an integrated perspective incorporating each vantage point (see Gelles & Loseke, 1993; Swisher, Wekesser, & Barbour, 1994).

It is unavoidable to acknowledge that solutions to social problems threaten the status quo. Society's reactions to solutions that follow from social and behavioral analyses frequently interfere with the implementation and evaluation of interventions. When male violence against women was posed as a criminal justice problem, implementation of mandatory and pro-arrest policies has been slow and inconsistent (Feder, 1997; Finn & Stalans, 1997; Martin, 1997). When male violence against women is conceptualized as a civil rights violation (Hallock, 1993; Maloney, 1996; McTaggart, 1998; Stellings, 1993) or in economic terms (Brownell, 1996; Farmer & Tiefenthaler, 1997; Raphael & Tolman, 1997; Tauchen, Witte, & Long, 1991), opposition can be extreme (Blair, 1995; Fein, 1993; Kaplan, 1993; Reske, 1995; Teepen, 1994). The Civil Rights Remedy of the Violence Against Women Act (42 U.S.C. § 13981) allowed women to pursue federal civil action if a crime committed against them was motivated by a gender animus (Goldscheid & Kraham, 1995). This provision cast violence against women as a civil rights violation and it rested on an economic analysis of male violence against women as a threat to interstate commerce (Hallock, 1993; McTaggart, 1998). The provision's constitutionality was rigorously challenged by claims that it violated the 14th amendment and the Commerce Clause of the U.S. Constitution. Although all federal circuit courts that reviewed the provision upheld the law (Trial, 1988), the U.S. Supreme Court rejected it (United States v. Morrison et al.).

These illustrations highlight problems that are endemic to the relationship between science and social problems. Some social problems may indeed be intractable. Science may not ever adopt some social problems as valid areas of inquiry. The demands of science and the structure of the academy pose formidable obstacles to adequate formulations of social problems that lead to effective solutions, solutions that society may reject in the end. At best, traditional models consider the extension of basic research to intervention research as the purview of practitioners; at worst, it is viewed as "dangerous and corrupting" (Sarason, 1974, p. 249). Before suggesting a model more appropriate for social problem solving related to male violence against women, it is important to consider critical questions facing the field.

CRITICAL QUESTIONS FOR THE FIELD: THE NATIONAL RESEARCH COUNCIL AGENDA

Despite numerous obstacles, science has accumulated knowledge about male violence against women at a tremendous rate across the social and behavioral sciences. The National Research Council highlighted the major social and behavioral sciences contributions to the field with respect to the scope of violence against women, its causes and consequences, and interventions for victims and male perpetrators (Crowell & Burgess, 1996). The resulting research agenda outlined critical questions to prevent violence against women, improve research methods, build knowledge about violence against women, and develop a supportive research infrastructure in service of these goals (Crowell & Burgess, 1996). Below, each recommendation is briefly summarized.

Encouraging Prevention Research

The panel encouraged future prevention research that incorporates longitudinal methods to compare developmental trajectories of violent behavior against women with those of other violent behaviors, rigorous evaluation of immediate and long-term effects of the range of sexual and intimate partner violence preventive interventions (media-based, educational, and legal), and examination of risk factors for perpetration across ecological levels of analysis. Particularly notable is the call for the inclusion of questions about male violence against women in etiologic studies of other violent behavior and in evaluations of interventions designed to prevent a range of related social problems, for example, delinquency, teenage pregnancy, and substance abuse.

Improving Research Methods

To improve comparison of data across diverse disciplines and fields, the panel asked researchers to define clearly the terms and constructs used and to develop and refine reliable and valid measurement instruments for use with diverse populations. The panel called on researchers to clarify the link between theory and expected outcomes in intervention and program evaluation; to use randomized, controlled outcome studies to identify technical and community characteristics of effective legal and social services interventions; and to incorporate qualitative and quantitative methods that capture the confluence of social and cultural contexts of women's experiences with violence.

Building Knowledge

The panel called for the expansion of knowledge on the scope of violence against women, particularly in ethnic minority populations. To achieve this goal, the panel recommended the inclusion of questions to detect violent experiences in current and future national and community surveys of women's mental and physical health and their social and economic well-being. The panel also encouraged research on the intergenerational and ecological consequences of male violence against women and on barriers and alternative approaches to the range of mental health, social, and legal and criminal justice services.

Developing a Research Infrastructure

To meet these research goals, the panel supported the development of a research infrastructure to encourage interdisciplinary efforts and the integration of those efforts into interventions and public policies. The panel specifically called for the development of a coordinated research strategy by government agencies and the establishment of research centers that focus on collaborative research, training, and integration of research findings into service provision.

MEETING NRC RECOMMENDATIONS

The agenda is praiseworthy in many respects. It is broad in scope yet specific enough to provide direction to a diverse field. It involves big questions that inevitably entail risk taking (Bevan, 1991; Schneider, 1996) and has already made an impact at the federal level. Several of the recommendations for further research and the establishment of additional violence against women research centers appear in draft language of the House and Senate versions of the Violence Against Women Act of 2000, currently pending congressional approval ensuring a continued federal response. Most important, the agenda elevates community-based approaches to preventive and treatment interventions, as well as epidemiological and causal models.

The crucial question that remains asks what model of science fits the scope and complexity of the agenda's recommendations. At the same time the agenda calls for interdisciplinary, collaborative, and community-based work, it tacitly suggests that researchers develop knowledge in one arena —the academy—and export it to another—the field—by calling for the integration of knowledge *into* services, interventions, and public policies. Research centers are expected to provide technical assistance *to* the field. This language encourages a traditional approach in which power and knowledge reside in the researcher and are bestowed on the participants. Assuming that knowledge cannot be gained by being in the midst of a social problem and that knowledge develops and flows in only one direction (Sarason, 1982) will impair progress. The point is subtle, but not trivial. If researchers use traditional models in community-based research, they are likely to rekindle the ineffective pattern of estrangement between science and those who work directly with social problems (Cohall, 1999). Especially in the area of male violence against women, already-strained relationships between researchers and advocates will be aggravated by disagreements over a broad range of issues (Gelles & Loseke, 1993; Swisher, Wekesser, & Barbour, 1994; Yllo, 1988). Some of these include the extent of men's versus women's use of violence within relationships (Dobash, Dobash, Wilson, & Daly, 1992; Straus, 1995), the appropriateness of various arrest policies (Berk, 1993; Buzawa & Buzawa, 1993; Miller & Krull, 1997), the role of alcohol in domestic violence (Flanzer, 1993; Gelles, 1993), the adequacy of court-mandated batterer intervention programs (Davis & Smith, 1995), and the most effective methods for sexual assault prevention (Lonsway, 1996; Rozee, Bateman, & Gilmore, 1991).

The Centers for Disease Control and the National Institute of Justice (but conspicuously not the National Institute of Mental Health) have responded by issuing requests for proposals (RFPs) to fund intervention development, implementation, and evaluation. Recent RFPs mandate drastic changes in the scientific process by requiring applicants to engage in collaboration, community partnerships, field-initiated research, program development and evaluation, and especially to examine questions in diverse and underserved populations (Gondolf, Yllo, & Campbell, 1997; Koss, 1998). Federal officials, however, question whether the field is sufficiently capable to respond to these proposals (Koss, 1998). To an extent, this concern is valid. Many of these terms and concepts are not familiar to the majority of traditionally trained scientists.

ACTION RESEARCH

Action research best serves the requirements of community-based etiological, epidemiological, and intervention research. Lewin, an early proponent of problem-oriented social science, first proposed the concept of action research in his enduring work *Field Theory in Social Science* (Lewin, 1951, 1997). Questioning the notion that science should be conducted without regard for practical and social consequences, Lewin believed that science should focus exclusively on social problem solving. Few are familiar with the totality of Lewin's legacy, even within his own discipline of psychology (see Bargal, Gold, & Lewin, 1992, for contemporary perspectives). As Reppucci (1984) pointed out,

> Though Lewin was well ahead of his time, few have heeded his call. One of Lewin's most famous comments is, "nothing is so practical as a good theory," but the context in which it was stated is usually forgotten: "[Close cooperation between theoretical and applied psychology] can be accomplished . . . if the theorist does not look toward applied problems with highbrow aversion or with a fear of social problems, and if the applied psychologist realizes that there is nothing so practical as a good theory." (p. 133)

Lewin defined *action research* as "comparative research on the conditions and effects of various forms of social action, and research leading to social action" (Lewin, 1997, p. 144). He believed that it was critical to discover *knowledge of laws*, or theory, through basic research to guide interventions, but that it was also imperative to understand the *specific character of the situation*, contemporarily referred to as the ecology of a problem. In action research, understanding the ecology of a social problem is not relegated to secondary status relative to basic research because both are viewed as essential.

Lewin influenced a number of scientists interested in social problems. Piecemeal social engineering, experimental social innovation, systematic experimentation, and social experimentation (see Argyris, 1993, and the following as cited in Doyle, Wilcox, & Reppucci, 1983: Fairweather, 1974; Popper, 1957; Riecken, 1974; Rivlin, 1971) and more recently participatory action research (Brydon-Miller, 1997) are based on or contain tenets of action research. Despite the infusion of action research into a variety of disciplines and subdisciplines, relatively few social and behavioral sciences regularly use it. Exceptions include community psychology and some subdisciplines of public health such as community health and health education, each of which focus on ecology, prevention, and well-being; building individual and community capacities; and linking existing resources (Levine & Perkins, 1987; Leviton, 1996).

In practice, action research transcends a simple combination of basic and applied research. As a method, it generates knowledge through the study of change, resting on the following maxim: "if you really want to understand how something works, try to change it" (Sarason, 1974). Action research does not wait for, nor does it require, basic theory and knowledge to become fully realized before proceeding to intervention. In contrast to traditional models, action research *depends* on the process of change to produce knowledge, assuming that interventions illuminate processes or consequences that would otherwise remain unobserved through basic research (Sarason, 1974). Instead of theory informing action, theory and action mutually inform one another (Argyris, 1993; Elias, 1994; Schneider, 1996). By its nature, action research is an upwardly spiraling process in which each turn produces a more ecologically valid conceptualization of the problem and what is required to change it (Elias, 1994).

Action research entails more than theory development and its application to a social problem (Argyris, Putnam, & Smith, 1985). For example, community-based research extends beyond intervention development and implementation (Center for Substance Abuse Prevention, 1998; Reppucci, Britner, & Woolard, 1997) and process and outcome evaluation research (Guba & Lincoln, 1989; Wholey, Hatry, & Newcomer, 1994) to include ecological assessment (Moos & Lemke, 1983; Shinn, 1996), and the development of technology transfer systems to ensure fidelity (Bauman, Stein, & Ireys, 1991; Lane, 1999; Rappaport, Seidman, & Davidson, 1979), diffusion (Rogers, 1995), sustainability (Altman, 1995; Shediac-Rizkallah & Bone, 1998), and dissemination (Steckler, Goodman, McLeroy, Davis, & Koch, 1992). In the process, researchers are asked to fulfill multiple roles including those of translator, advocate, consultant, and collaborator (Gondolf et al., 1997; Reppucci, 1984; White, 1994). The number and variety of components crucial to community-based research can quickly overwhelm the researcher who is accustomed to independent, laboratory, or clinic-based research. Multiple roles contribute to role strain when difficult decisions have to be made that have differential effects on the interventions, stakeholders, and communities and when results are unexpected (DeLeon & Williams, 1997; Guba & Lincoln, 1989; Weinstein et al., 1991). Researchers must also become participant conceptualizers and praxis explicators: those who work within settings to understand and help conceptualize change processes, to reflect on theory and processes that are a part of the setting, and to share relevant lessons from the intervention process (Elias, 1994; see also Stanley, 1990; Stanley & Wise, 1993). Elias, a community psychologist, stated that praxis explicators could

> identify the elusive, dynamic processes of multifaceted, multisystemic interrelationships that are the essence of change (Fullan, 1993; Sarason, 1983) . . . and [the] complex patterns through which change has proceeded in various contexts and offer guidelines for navigating the avowedly uncertain future course an intervention may take. Although luck plays a role in the natural history of change efforts, participant conceptualizers and praxis explicators can play a significant role in helping to react to unforeseen events in a way that fosters the goals of a change effort. (p. 302)

Action research exacts high demands on scientists. Researchers must move outside the safe and easily controlled confines of the university laboratory and into settings where problems reside. As a result, the action researcher must be creative in overcoming internal and external threats to the validity of design and method posed by community-based research (Boruch & Shadish, 1983; Davidson, Redner, & Saul, 1983). A partial list includes mismatched levels of intervention and outcome measures, history, maturation, testing, instrumentation, selection, attrition, differential, and compensatory interventions, as well as the intervention diffusion and imitation (Cook & Campbell, 1979; Linney & Reppucci, 1982; Tolan, Keys, Chertok, & Jason, 1990). Furthermore, issues related to cultural appropriateness, language and literacy, definitions of central constructs, and lack of validated measurement instruments pose unique challenges. The action researcher must also be well trained in the use of multiple methods of design and comfortable with the quantitative and qualitative data collection and statistical techniques at all levels of analysis (see Miller & Banyard, 1998).

Action research necessitates effective collaboration with stakeholders (including advocates and service providers) and clients. Guidelines for embarking on collaborative relationships exist, but there are no guaranteed roadmaps to success (Baker, Homan, Schonhoff, & Kreuter, 1999; Gondolf et al., 1997; Jorgenson, 1989; Lorentz & Sarason, 1997; McCall, 1990). Collaboration often is viewed as inefficient because it extends all phases of research including framing of the issues, planning, implementation, data collection, evaluation, and dissemination. It requires considerable effort to build the relationships that enable the process to begin and to endure (Browne, 1996; Cross, 1999; Elias, 1994; Jorgenson, 1989). Researchers also find that they may need to engage in capacity building before their organization is able to collaborate (Poole, 1997; Rutledge & Donaldson, 1995).

Several research programs demonstrate action research. For example, in community psychology, Campbell developed an innovative research program using multiple methodologies and data analytic techniques to investigate community-level factors that influence recovery from rape (Campbell, 1998; Campbell, Baker, & Mazurek, 1998; Campbell & Johnson, 1997) and the evolution of rape crisis centers as part of an ecological model of rape recovery. Goodman and colleagues have assessed the needs of women engaged in civil and criminal domestic violence cases (Goodman, Bennett, & Dutton, in press) and have begun an intervention through the criminal court system (Goodman, personal communication, 1998). In criminology, extensive attention has been paid to understanding the dynamics of arrest policies as criminal justice interventions and using empirical data to refine theories of deterrence specific to male violence against women (Berk, 1993; Sherman, Smith, Schmidt, & Rogan, 1992).

Perhaps the most exemplary action research program related to violence against women has been executed in East Lansing, Michigan. Sullivan and colleagues have developed, implemented, and evaluated an advocacy intervention program for women in domestic violence shelters (Sullivan, Basta, Rumptz, & Davidson, 1992; Sullivan, Campbell, Angelique, Eby, & Davidson, 1994; Sullivan & Davidson, 1991; Sullivan & Rumptz, 1994; Sullivan, Tan, Basta, Rumptz, & Davidson, 1992). Through a long-term collaborative relationship with a local domestic violence shelter, they were able to assess the needs of women leaving the shelter and then design a 10-week experimental intervention. The program trained undergraduate students over a 10-week period to serve as advocates by providing social support to women in shelters as they attempted to navigate various systems (e.g., criminal justice, housing, health care). Initial results indicated that women who worked with advocates reported higher levels of social support, overall quality of life, and effective experiences of accessing resources than women who did not work with advocates. Significant differences in social support between control and experimental groups did not persist, underscoring the effectiveness of advocacy services through the end of the intervention period. Data from the 6-month follow-up showed that both groups of women reported increased social support, quality of life, and sense of personal power and less depression and emotional attachment to their assailants. Overall quality of life continued to be significantly higher for women who received advocacy services due to either a sense of empowerment gained through advocacy or simply to the knowledge that someone expressed interest in their welfare on exiting the shelter.

Two policy implications emerge. First, time-limited advocacy appears to be an inexpensive and effective strategy for short-term positive results. Sullivan and colleagues suggested that providing advocacy services on an ongoing, "as-needed" basis may increase effectiveness. Second, advocacy services will be limited in value as long as they operate in the contexts that are unresponsive to abused women, for example, the criminal and civil justice systems. Advocates could not rectify a lack of affordable housing or criminal justice systems that ignore orders of protection. Therefore, advocacy services would be most effective if they occur in tandem with system-level change. By training undergraduates who will become the future leaders and gatekeepers of community institutions and systems, Sullivan and colleagues have begun that process.

Equally valuable are the research team's findings regarding women's experiences once they leave the shelter, irrespective of whether they worked with advocates. Few studies have tracked and described the ecology of women's lives as they establish themselves in new homes, schools, and communities. As a result, the field holds a static view of these women's lives when in fact women continue to adapt and change and are quite resilient despite numerous challenges. At 6 months after a shelter stay, 88% of the women leaving the shelter were no longer involved with the men who had originally abused them, a finding that Sullivan and colleagues asserted is higher than previously estimated. Women continued to report experiences of further abuse from their assailants even though they were physically separated from their abusers. Among those no longer involved with their assailants, 28% reported having been physically abused. Police intervention had minimal utility. Of the total sample, 63% called the police at least one time, resulting in arrests for 21% of the batterers. Only two of the batterers were convicted, providing further evidence of the limits of individual advocacy without system change.

Economic factors were paramount in women's ability to remain safe from their assailants. Financial dependence on assailants made leaving difficult. Of those no longer involved with their assailants, nearly 80% were financially independent compared with 57% of those whose assailants were main sources of support. The proportion of women employed, attending school, and with regular access to a car increased modestly by 13%, even though the majority reported difficulty in obtaining employment and child care, and most found it necessary to move at least once. Contrary to public perception, battered women are generally resourceful individuals who, given appropriate levels of tangible assistance and social support, are able to leave an abusive situation.

Sullivan and colleagues have also provided the research community with a significant methodological advance for conducting longitudinal community-based research. The comprehensive protocol use in the advocacy study reviewed above reduced attrition, allowing a 97% retention rate at the 24-month follow-up period (Sullivan, Rumptz, Campbell, Eby, & Davidson, 1996). Included in the protocol are specific instructions to ensure women's safety. The protocol is quickly becoming a standard in community-based violence against women research.

These research programs illustrate principles of action research through the development, implementation, and evaluation of theoretically and ecologically derived interventions in community settings. Most important, proximate outcomes focus on intervention in individual women's lives, and distal outcomes focus on system and social change through interaction with institutions and systems that profoundly influence women's safety.

CONCLUSION

Action research is the best model of science by which the National Research Council's recommendations can be achieved. Currently, federal funding patterns create a climate in which collaborative work between scientists, advocates, and policymakers is not only preferred, but is imperative. The ultimate goal of reducing the scope and consequences of violence against women depends on the buy-in of current and future community-based programs to the national research agenda and on the mutual development and transfer of information and technology in formats that they can use in maintaining efficacious and effective interventions.

Institutional changes are warranted, however, if social and behavioral scientists are to adopt action research. Current training focuses too heavily on producing scientists trained to ask small questions, focus on narrowly defined problems, and communicate only with peers (Schneider, 1996) at the expense of scientists trained to think about the significance of their work outside the research setting. Graduate programs need to evaluate the appropriateness of their training and mentoring for new and current scientists in action-research methods (Doyle et al., 1983; Schneider, 1996). Editorial boards must consider strategies to encourage authors to include descriptions of the process through which essential components of action research (e.g., collaboration) were developed and maintained (Felner, Phillips, Dubois, & Lease, 1991). These processes can be incorporated into theories of intervention and change (Trickett, 1991). Federal funding agencies can facilitate these processes by utilizing funding mechanisms that already exist to encourage action-oriented research, by considering inducements to scientists to enter these types of collaborative relationships, and by developing additional funding mechanisms specifically engineered to nurture collaborative relationships between researchers and community-based advocates and service providers. Although the relationship between science and social problems has at times been estranged, there is every reason to believe that social and behavioral sciences are poised to make significant contributions toward reducing male violence against women if action-oriented research is embraced.

REFERENCES

Abbot, J., Johnson, R., Koziol-McLain, J., & Lowenstein, S. R. (1995). Domestic violence against women: Incidence and prevalence in an emergency department population. *Journal of the American Medical Association, 273,* 1763–1767.

Acierno, R., Resnick, H. S., & Kilpatrick, G. D. (1997). Health impact of interpersonal violence: Section I: Prevalence rates, case identification, and risk factors for sexual assault, physical assault, and domestic violence in men and women. *Behavior Medicine, 23,* 53–64.

Altman, D. G. (1995). Sustaining interventions in community systems: On the relationship between researchers and communities. *Health Psychology, 14,* 526–536.

American Medical Association. (1992). Diagnostic and treatment guidelines on domestic violence. *Archives of Family Medicine, 1,* 39–47.

Amir, M. (1971). *Patterns in forcible rape.* Chicago: University of Chicago Press.

Argyris, C. (1993). *Knowledge for action: A guide for overcoming barriers to organizational change.* San Francisco: Jossey-Bass.

Argyris, C., Putnam, R., & Smith, D. M. (1985). *Action science: Concepts, methods and skills for research and intervention.* San Francisco: Jossey-Bass.

Baker, E. A., Homan, S., Schonhoff, R., & Kreuter, M. (1999). Principles of practice for academic/practice/community research partnerships. *American Journal of Preventive Medicine, 16,* 86–93.

Bargal, D., Gold, M., & Lewin, M. (1992). The heritage of Kurt Lewin: Theory, research, and practice. *Journal of Social Issues, 48,* 3–187.

Bart, P. B. (1981). A study of women who both were raped and avoided rape. *Journal of Social Issues, 37,* 123–137.

Bauman, L. J., Stein, R. E., & Ireys, H. T. (1991). Reinventing fidelity: The transfer of social technology among settings. *American Journal of Community Psychology, 19,* 619–639.

Berk, R. D. (1993). What the scientific evidence shows: On the average, we can do no better than arrest. In R. J. Gelles & D. R. Loseke (Eds.), *Current controversies in family violence* (pp. 323–336). Newbury Park, CA: Sage.

Berrill, K. T. (1990). Anti-gay violence and victimization in the United States: An overview. *Journal of Interpersonal Violence, 5,* 274–294.

Bevan, W. (1991). Contemporary psychology: A tour inside the onion. *American Psychologist, 46*, 475–883.

Blair, A. K. (1995, July 25). Bad problem, wrong solution. *New York Times*, p. A15.

Boruch, R. F., & Shadish, W. R. (1983). Design issues in community intervention research. In E. Seidman (Ed.), *Handbook of social Intervention* (pp. 73–98). Beverly Hills, CA: Sage.

Browne, A. (1993). Violence against women by male partners. *American Psychologist, 48*, 1077–1087.

Browne, A., & Williams, K. R. (1989). Exploring the effect of resource availability and the likelihood of female-perpetrated homicide. *Law and Society Review, 23*, 75–94.

Browne, D. (1996, November). *Working with communities in effectiveness trials.* Paper presented at the 5th National Conference on Prevention Research, McLean, VA.

Brownell, P. (1996). Domestic violence in the workplace: An emergent issue. *Crisis Intervention, 3*, 129–141.

Brownmiller, S. (1975). *Against our will: Men, women and rape.* New York: Simon & Schuster.

Brydon-Miller, M. (1997). Participatory action research: Psychology and social change. *Journal of Social Issues, 53*, 657–666.

Bureau of Justice Statistics. (1995). *Violence against women: Estimates from the redesigned survey.* Washington, DC: U.S. Department of Justice.

Bureau of Justice Statistics. (1997). *Sex differences in violent victimization, 1994.* Washington, DC: U.S. Department of Justice.

Burt, M. R. (1980). Cultural myths and supports for rape. *Journal of Personality and Social Psychology, 38*, 217–229.

Buzawa, E. S., & Buzawa, C. G. (1993). The scientific evidence is not conclusive: Arrest is no panacea. In R. J. Gelles & D. R. Loseke (Eds.), *Current controversies on family violence* (pp. 337–356). Newbury Park, CA: Sage.

Campbell, J. C. (1992). "If I can't have you, no one can": Power and control in homicide of female partners. In J. Radford & D. E. H. Russell (Eds.), *Femicide: The politics of woman killing* (pp. 99–113). New York: Twayne.

Campbell, R. (1998). The community response to rape: Victim's experiences with the legal, medical, and mental health systems. *American Journal of Community Psychology, 26*, 355–379.

Campbell, R., Baker, C. K., & Mazurek, T. L. (1998). Remaining radical? Organizational predictors of rape crisis centers' social change initiatives. *American Journal of Community Psychology, 26*, 457–483.

Campbell, R., & Johnson, C. R. (1997). Police officers' perceptions of rape: Is there consistency between state law and individual beliefs? *Journal of Interpersonal Violence, 12*, 255–274.

Center for Substance Abuse Prevention. (1998). *A guide for evaluating prevention effectiveness*. Washington, DC: U.S. Department of Health and Human Services.

Cohall, A. (1999). Applied prevention research: Challenges of working with urban communities. *American Journal of Preventive Medicine, 16*, 16–17.

Cohen, M. A., & Miller, T. R. (1998). The cost of mental health care for victims of crime. *Journal of Interpersonal Violence, 13*, 93–110.

Cook, T. D., & Campbell, D. T. (1979). *Quasi-experimentation: Design and analysis issues for field settings*. Chicago: Rand-McNally.

Craven, D. (1996). *Female victims of violent crime*. Washington, DC: U.S. Department of Justice.

Crome, S., & McCabe, M. P. (1995). The impact of rape on individual, interpersonal, and family functioning. *Journal of Family Studies, 1*, 58–70.

Cross, A. W. (1999). Bridging the gap between academia and practice in public health. *American Journal of Preventive Medicine, 16*, 14–15.

Crowell, N. A., & Burgess, A. W. (1996). *Understanding violence against women*. Washington, DC: National Academy of Sciences.

Davidson, W. S., Redner, R., & Saul, J. A. (1983). Research modes in social and community change. In E. Seidman (Ed.), *Handbook of social intervention* (pp. 99–118). Beverly Hills, CA: Sage.

Davis, R. C., & Smith, B. (1995). Domestic violence reforms: Empty promises or fulfilled expectations? *Crime & Delinquency, 41*, 541–552.

DeLeon, P. H., & Williams, J. G. (1997). Evaluation research and public policy formulation: Are psychologists collectively willing to accept unpopular findings? *American Psychologist, 52*, 551–552.

Dobash, R. P., Dobash, R. E., Wilson, M., & Daly, M. (1992). The myth of sexual symmetry in marital violence. *Social Problems, 39*, 71–91.

Doyle, E. L., Wilcox, B., & Reppucci, N. D. (1983). Training for social and community change. In E. Seidman (Ed.), *Handbook of social intervention* (pp. 615–638). Beverly Hills, CA: Sage.

Dunn, S. P., & Gilchrist, V. J. (1993). Sexual assault. *Primary Care, 20*, 3184–4169.

Dutton, D. G. (1985). An ecologically nested theory of male violence toward intimates. *International Journal of Women's Studies, 8*, 404–413.

Elias, M. J. (1994). Capturing excellence in applied settings: A participant conceptualizer and praxis explicator role for community psychologists. *American Journal of Community Psychology, 22*, 293–318.

Fagan, J. (1996). *The criminalization of domestic violence: Promises and limits*. Washington, DC: U.S. National Institute of Justice.

Farmer, A., & Tiefenthaler, J. (1997). An economic analysis of domestic violence. *Review of Social Economy, 55*, 337–358.

Feder, L. (1997). Domestic violence and police response in a pro-arrest jurisdiction. *Women and Criminal Justice, 8*, 79–98.

Fein, B. (1993, June 3). Reject this legal mischief. *USA Today*, p. A12.

Felitti, V. J., Anda, R. F., Nordenberg, D., Williamson, D. F., Spritz, A. M., Edwards, V., Marks, J. S., & Koss, M. P. (1998). Adverse childhood environments and health problems from adolescence to adulthood. *American Journal of Preventive Medicine, 14,* 245–258.

Felner, R. D., Phillips, R. S. C., Dubois, D., & Lease, M. (1991). Ecological interventions and the process of change for prevention: Wedding theory and research to implementation in real world settings. *American Journal of Community Psychology, 19,* 379–387.

Field, H. S. (1978). Attitudes toward rape: A comparative analysis of police, rapists, crisis counselors, and citizens. *Journal of Personality and Social Psychology, 36,* 156–179.

Finkelhor, D., & Yllo, K. (1985). *License to rape: Sexual abuse of wives.* New York: Rinehart.

Finn, M. A., & Stalans, L. J. (1997). The influence of gender and mental state on police decisions in domestic assault cases. *Criminal Justice and Behavior, 24,* 157–176.

Flanzer, J. P. (1993). Alcohol and other drugs are key causal agents of violence. In R. J. Gelles & D. R. Loseke (Eds.), *Current controversies on family violence* (pp. 171–181). Newbury Park, CA: Sage.

Frieze, I. H. (1983). Investigating the causes and consequences of marital rape. *Signs: Journal of Women in Culture and Society, 8,* 532–553.

Garnets, L., Herek, G. M., & Levy, B. (1990). Violence and victimizations of lesbians and gay men: Mental health consequences. *Journal of Interpersonal Violence, 5,* 366–383.

Gelles, R. J. (1993). Alcohol and other drugs are associated with violence—they are not its cause. In R. J. Gelles & D. R. Loseke (Eds.), *Current controversies on family violence* (pp. 182–196). Newbury Park, CA: Sage.

Gelles, R. J., & Loseke, D. R. (Eds.). (1993). *Current controversies in family violence.* Newbury Park, CA: Sage.

Goldscheid, J., & Kraham, S. (1995). The civil rights remedy of the Violence Against Women Act. *Clearinghouse Review, August-September,* 505–527.

Gondolf, E. W., Yllo, K., & Campbell, J. (1997). Collaboration between researchers and advocates. In G. K. Kantor & J. L. Jasinski (Eds.), *Out of the darkness: Contemporary perspectives on family violence* (pp. 255–267). Thousand Oaks, CA: Sage.

Goodman, L., Bennett, L., & Dutton, M. A. (in press). Systemic obstacles women face in cooperating with the prosecution of their batterers: A victim perspective. *Journal of Interpersonal Violence.*

Goodman, L. A., Koss, M. P., & Russo, N. F. (1993). Violence against women: Physical and mental health effects. Part I. Research findings. *Applied and Preventive Psychology, 2,* 79–89.

Gordon, M. T., & Riger, S. (1991). *The female fear: The social cost of rape.* Urbana: University of Illinois Press.

Greenfield, L. A., Rand, M. R., Craven, D., Klaus, P. A., Ringel, C., Warchol, G.,

Maston, C., & Fox, J. A. (1998). *Violence by Intimates*. Washington, DC: U.S. Department of Justice.

Guba, E. G., & Lincoln, Y. S. (1989). *Fourth generation evaluation*. Newbury Park, CA: Sage.

Hallock, W. H. (1993). The Violence Against Women Act: Civil rights for sexual assault victims. *Indiana Law Journal, 68*, 577–617.

Hare-Mustin, R. T., & Marecek, J. (1990). *Making a difference: Psychology and the construction of gender*. New Haven, CT: Yale University Press.

Harris, B., & Nicholson, I. A. M. (1998). Experts in the service of social reform: SPSSI, psychology, and society, 1936–1996. *Journal of Social Issues, 54*, 1–235.

Hickman, S. E., & Muehlenhard, C. L. (1997). College women's fears and precautionary behaviors relating to acquaintance rape and stranger rape. *Psychology of Women Quarterly, 21*, 527–547.

Humphreys, K., & Rappaport, J. (1993). From the community mental health movement to the war on drugs: A study in the definition of social problems. *American Psychologist, 48*, 892–901.

Javorek, F. J. (1979). *When rape is not inevitable: Discriminating between completed and attempted rape cases for non sleeping targets*. Denver, CO: Violence Research Unit.

Jorgenson, D. L. (1989). Developing and sustaining field relationships. In D. L. Jorgenson (Ed.), *Participant observation: A method for human studies* (Vol. 15, pp. 69–81). Newbury Park, CA: Sage.

Kanin, E. J. (1957). Male aggression in dating-courtship relations. *American Journal of Sociology, 63*, 197–204.

Kanuha, V. (1990). Compounding triple jeopardy: Battering in lesbian of color relationships. *Women and Therapy, 9*, 169–184.

Kaplan, D. (1993, July 8). Federal rape bill may be harmful. *Houston Post*, p. D1.

Kaufman, D., Rudeen, R., & Morgan, C. (1980). *Safe within yourself: A woman's guide to rape prevention and self-defense*. Alexandria, VA: Visage Press.

Kelly, J. G., (1990). Changing contexts and the field of community psychology. *American Journal of Community Psychology, 18*, 769–792.

Kelly, K. D., & DeKeseredy, W. S. (1994). Women's fear of crime and abuse in college and university dating relationships. *Violence and Victims, 9*, 17–30.

Kelly, L. (1988). *Surviving sexual violence*. Minneapolis: University of Minnesota Press.

Klodawsky, F., & Lundy, C. (1994). Women's safety in the university environment. *Journal of Architectural and Planning Research, 11*, 128–136.

Koss, M. P. (1998, August). *Does feminist rape research stand up to attack?* Paper presented at the annual meeting of the American Psychological Association, San Francisco, CA.

Koss, M. P., & Cleveland, H. H. (1997). Stepping on toes: Social roots of date rape lead to intractability and politicization. In M. D. Schwartz (Ed.), *Re-*

searching sexual violence against women: Methodological and personal perspectives (pp. 4–21). Thousand Oaks, CA: Sage.

Koss, M. P., Goodman, L. M., Browne, A., Fitzgerald, L. F., Keita, G. P., & Russo, N. F. (1994). *No safe haven: Male violence against women at home, at work, and in the community.* Washington, DC: American Psychological Association.

Koss, M. P., & Heslet, L. (1992). The somatic consequences of violence against women. *Archives of Family Medicine, 1,* 53–59.

Koss, M. P., Koss, P. G., & Woodruff, J. W. (1991). Deleterious effects of criminal victimization on women's health and medical utilization. *Archives of Internal Medicine, 151,* 342–347.

Lane, D. S. (1999). Research linkages between academia and public health practice: Building a prevention research agenda. *American Journal of Preventive Medicine, 16,* 7–9.

Leidig, M. W. (1981). Violence against women: A feminist-psychological approach. In S. Cox (Ed.), *Female psychology* (2nd ed., pp. 190–205). New York: St. Martin's Press.

Lesserman, J., & Drossman, D. A. (1995). Sexual and physical abuse history and medical practice. *General Hospital Psychiatry, 17,* 71–74.

Letourneau, E. J., Resnick, H. S., Kilpatrick, D. G., & Saunders, B. E. (1996). Comorbidity of sexual problems and posttraumatic stress disorder in female crime victims. *Behavior-Therapy, 27,* 321–336.

Levine, M., & Perkins, D. (1987). *Principles of community psychology: Perspectives and applications.* New York: Oxford University Press.

Leviton, L. C. (1996). Integrating psychology and public health: Challenges and opportunities. *American Psychologist, 51,* 42–51.

Lewin, K. (1951). *Field theory in social science.* New York: Harper & Brothers.

Lewin, K. (1997). *Resolving social conflicts and Field theory in social science.* Washington, DC: American Psychological Association.

Linney, J. A., & Reppucci, N. D. (1982). Research design and methods in community psychology. In P. Kendal & J. Butcher (Eds.), *Handbook of research methods in clinical psychology* (pp. 535–566). New York: Wiley.

Lobel, K. (1986). *Naming the violence: Speaking out about lesbian battering.* Seattle, WA: Seal Press.

Lonsway, K. A. (1996). Preventing acquaintance rape through education: What do we know? *Psychology of Women Quarterly, 20,* 229–266.

Lorentz, E. M., & Sarason, S. B. (1997). *Crossing boundaries: Collaboration, coordination, and the redefinition of resources.* San Francisco: Jossey-Bass.

Loseke, D. R. (1991). Changing the boundaries of crime: The battered women's social movement and the definition of wife abuse as criminal activity. *Criminal Justice Review, 16,* 249–262.

Mahoney, P., & Williams, L. M. (1998). *Sexual assault in marriage: Prevalence, consequences, and treatment of wife rape.* Thousand Oaks, CA: Sage.

Malamuth, N. M., Sockloskie, R. J., Koss, M. P., & Tanaka, J. S. (1991). Characteristics of aggressors against women: Testing a model using a national sample of college students. *Journal of Consulting and Clinical Psychology, 59,* 670–681.

Maloney, K. E. (1996). Gender-motivated violence and the commerce clause: The civil rights provision of the Violence Against Women Act after Lopez. *Columbia Law Review, 96,* 1876–1939.

Martin, M. E. (1997). Double your trouble: Dual arrest in family violence. *Journal of Family Violence, 12,* 139–157.

McCall, R. B. (1990). Promoting interdisciplinary and faculty-service-providers. *American Psychologist, 45,* 1319–1324.

McTaggart, K. C. (1998). The Violence Against Women Act: Recognizing a federal civil right to be free from violence. *Georgetown Law Journal, 86,* 1123–1151.

Miller, J. L., & Krull, A. C. (1997). Controlling domestic violence: Victim resources and police intervention. In G. K. Kantor & J. L. Jasinski (Eds.), *Out of the darkness: Contemporary perspectives on family violence* (pp. 235–254). Thousand Oaks, CA: Sage.

Miller, K. E., & Banyard, V. L. (1998). Qualitative research in community psychology. *American Journal of Community Psychology, 26,* 485–696.

Miller, T. R., Cohen, M. A., & Rossman, S. B. (1993). Victim costs of violent crime and resulting injuries. *Health Affairs, 12,* 186–197.

Moos, R. H., & Lemke, S. (1983). Assessing and improving social-ecological settings. In E. Seidman (Ed.), *Handbook of social intervention* (pp. 143–162). Beverly Hills, CA: Sage.

Muehlenhard, C. L., Powch, I. G., Phelps, J. L., & Giusti, L. M. (1992). Definitions of rape: Scientific and political implications. *Journal of Social Issues, 48,* 23–44.

National Victims Center. (1992). *Rape in America: A report to the nation.* Arlington, VA: National Victim Center and Crime Victims Research and Treatment Center.

Perilla, J. L., Bakeman, R., & Norris, F. H. (1994). Culture and domestic violence: The ecology of abused Latinas. *Violence and Victims, 9,* 325–339.

Poole, D. L. (1997). Building community capacity to promote social and public health: Challenges for universities [Editorial]. *Health & Social Work, 22,* 163–170.

Raphael, J., & Tolman, R. M. (1997). *Trapped by poverty, trapped by abuse: New evidence documenting the relationship between domestic violence and welfare.* Chicago: Taylor Institute.

Rappaport, J., Seidman, E., & Davidson, W. S. (1979). Demonstration research and manifest vs. true adoption: The natural history of a research project to divert adolescents from the legal system. In R. F. Munoz, L. R. Snowden, & J. G. Kelly (Eds.), *Social and psychological research in community settings* (pp. 101–144). San Francisco: Jossey-Bass.

Renzetti, C. (1990). *Violent betrayal: Partner abuse in lesbian relationships*. Newbury Park, CA: Sage.

Reppucci, N. D. (1984). Psychology in the public interest. In A. M. Rogers & C. J. Scheirer (Eds.), *The G. Stanley Hall Lecture Series* (Vol. 5, pp. 123–156). Washington, DC: American Psychological Association.

Reppucci, N. D., Britner, P. A., & Woolard, J. L. (1997). *Preventing child abuse and neglect through parent education*. Baltimore: Paul H. Brookes.

Resick, P. A., Calhoun, K. S., Atkeson, B. M., & Ellis, E. M. (1981). Social adjustment in victims of sexual assault. *Journal of Consulting and Clinical Psychology, 49*, 705–712.

Reske, H. J. (1995). An untested remedy for abused women: Some say new law will burden federal courts, provide divorce bargaining chip. *American Bar Association Journal, 81*, 20–21.

Riger, S., & Gordon, M. T. (1981). The fear of rape: A study in social control. *Journal of Social Issues, 37*, 71–92.

Rogers, E. M. (1995). *Diffusion of innovations* (4th ed.). New York: Free Press.

Rosewater, L. B. (1987). A critical analysis of the proposed self-defeating personality disorder. *Journal of Personality Disorders, 1*, 190–195.

Rozee, P. D., Bateman, P., & Gilmore, T. (1991). The personal perspective of acquaintance rape prevention: A three tier approach. In A. Parrot & L. Bechhofer (Eds.), *Acquaintance rape: The hidden crime* (pp. 337–354). New York: John Wiley.

Russell, D. E. H. (1990). *Rape in marriage*. Bloomington: Indiana University Press.

Rutledge, D. N., & Donaldson, N. E. (1995). Building organizational capacity to engage in research utilization. *Journal of Nursing Administration, 25*, 12–16.

Salazar, L. F. (1997). *All work and no change: A content analysis of articles pertaining to violence against women*. Unpublished manuscript, Georgia State University, Atlanta.

Sanday, P. R. (1996). *A woman scorned: Acquaintance rape on trial*. New York: Doubleday.

Sarason, S. B. (1974). *The psychological sense of community: Prospects for a community psychology*. San Francisco: Jossey-Bass.

Sarason, S. B. (1978). The nature of problem solving in social action. *American Psychologist, 33*, 370–380.

Sarason, S. B. (1982). *Psychology and social action: Selected papers*. New York: Praeger.

Schneider, S. F. (1996). Random thoughts on leaving the fray. *American Psychologist, 51*, 715–721.

Seidman, E. (1983). Unexamined premises of social problem solving. In E. Seidman (Ed.), *Handbook of social intervention* (pp. 48–67). Beverly Hills, CA: Sage.

Selkin, J. (1978). Protecting personal space: Victim and resister reactions to assaultive rape. *Journal of Community Psychology, 6*, 263–268.

Shediac-Rizkallah, M. C., & Bone, L. R. (1998). Planning for the sustainability of community-based health programs: Conceptual frameworks and future directions for research, practice, and policy. *Health Education Research, 13*, 87–108.

Sherman, L. W., Smith, D. A., Schmidt, J. D., & Rogan, D. P. (1992). Crime, punishment, and stake in conformity: Legal and informal control of domestic violence. *American Sociological Review, 57*, 680–690.

Shinn, M. (1996). Ecological assessment: Introduction to the special issue. *American Journal of Community Psychology, 24*, 1–3.

Stanley, L. (1990). Feminist praxis and the academic mode of production: An editorial introduction. In L. Stanley (Ed.), *Feminist praxis* (pp. 3–19). London: Routledge.

Stanley, L., & Wise, S. (1993). Method, methodology, and epistemology. In L. Stanley (Ed.), *Feminist praxis* (pp. 20–47). London: Routledge.

Steckler, A., Goodman, R. M., McLeroy, K. R., Davis, S., & Koch, G. (1992). Measuring the diffusion of innovative health promotion programs. *American Journal of Health Promotion, 6*, 214–223.

Stellings, B. (1993). The public harm of private violence: Rape, sex discrimination, and citizenship. *Harvard Civil Rights Civil Liberties Law Review, 28*, 185–216.

Storaska, F. (1975). *How to say no to a rapist and survive.* New York: Random House.

Straus, M. A. (1995). The Conflict Tactics Scales and its critics: An evaluation and new data on validity and reliability. In M. A. Straus & R. J. Gelles (Eds.), *Physical violence in American families: Risk factors and adaptations to violence in 8,145 families* (pp. 49–73). New Brunswick, NJ: Transaction.

Sullivan, C. M., Basta, J., Rumptz, M., & Davidson, W. S. (1992). After the crisis: A needs assessment of women leaving a domestic violence shelter. *Violence and Victims, 7*, 271–280.

Sullivan, C. M., Campbell, R., Angelique, H., Eby, K. K., & Davidson, W. S. (1994). An advocacy intervention program for women with abusive partners: Six-month follow-up. *American Journal of Community Psychology, 22*, 101–122.

Sullivan, C. M., & Davidson, W. S. (1991). The provision of advocacy services to women leaving abusive partners: An examination of short-term effects. *American Journal of Community Psychology, 19*, 953–960.

Sullivan, C. M., & Rumptz, M. H. (1994). Adjustment needs of African-American women who utilized a domestic violence shelter. *Violence and Victims, 9*, 275–286.

Sullivan, C. M., Rumptz, M. H., Campbell, R., Eby, K. K., & Davidson, W. S. (1996). Retaining participants in longitudinal community research: A comprehensive protocol. *Journal of Applied Behavioral Science, 32*, 262–276.

Sullivan, C. M., Tan, C., Basta, J., Rumptz, M., & Davidson, W. S. (1992). An advocacy intervention for women with abusive partners: Initial evaluation. *American Journal of Community Psychology, 20*, 309–332.

Swisher, K. L., Wekesser, C., & Barbour, W. (1994). *Violence against women*. San Diego, CA: Greenhaven Press.

Tauchen, H. V., Witte, A. D., & Long, S. K. (1991). Domestic violence: A non-random affair. *International Economic Review, 32,* 491–511.

Teepen, T. (1994, April 17). A crime bill we can do without. *Atlanta Journal Constitution,* p. G7.

Tjaden, P., & Thoennes, N. (1998). *Stalking in America: Findings from the National Violence Against Women Survey.* Washington, DC: U.S. Department of Justice.

Tolan, P., Keys, C., Chertok, F., & Jason, L. (Eds.). (1990). *Researching community psychology: Issues of theory and methods.* Washington, DC: American Psychological Association.

Trial. (1988, April). Violence Against Women Act withstands constitutional attack. *Trial,* p. 109.

Trickett, E. J. (1991). Paradigms and the research report: Making what actually happens a heuristic for theory. *American Journal of Community Psychology, 19,* 365–370.

U.S. Merit Systems Protection Board. (1987). *Sexual harassment of federal workers: An update.* Washington, DC: U.S. Government Printing Office.

Violence Against Women Act of 1994, P.L. 103–322, 48 Stat. 503.

Walker, E. A., Gelfand, A., Katon, W., Koss, M. P., Von Korff, M., & Bernstein, D. (1999). Adult health status of women with histories of childhood abuse and neglect. *American Journal of Medicine, 107,* 332–339.

Walker, L. E. (1987). Inadequacies of the masochistic personality diagnosis for women. *Journal of Personality Disorders, 1,* 182–189.

Warchol, G. (1998). *Workplace violence, 1992–1996.* Washington, DC: U.S. Department of Justice.

Warr, M. (1985). Fear of rape among urban women. *Journal of Social Issues, 32,* 239–250.

Watzlawick, P., Weakland, J. H., & Fisch, R. (1974). *Change: Principles of problem formation and problem resolution.* New York: Norton.

Weinrath, M., & Gartrell, J. (1996). Victimization and fear of crime. *Violence and victims, 11,* 187–197.

Weinstein, R. S., Soule, C. R., Collins, F., Cone, J., Mehlhorn, M., & Simontacci, K. (1991). Expectations and high school change: Teacher-researcher collaboration to prevent school failure. *American Journal of Community Psychology, 19,* 333–363.

Weiss, C. H. (1983). Ideology, interests, and information: The basis of policy positions. In D. Callahan & B. Jennings (Eds.), *Ethics, the social sciences, and policy analysis* (pp. 213–272). New York: Plenum.

White, J. W. (1994, August). *Understanding violence against women: The interface of theory and method.* Paper presented at the annual meeting of the American Psychological Association, Los Angeles, CA.

Wholey, J. S., Hatry, H. P., & Newcomer, K. E. (1994). *Handbook of practical program evaluation*. San Francisco: Jossey-Bass.

Yllo, K. (1988). Political and methodological debates in wife abuse research. In K. Yllo & M. Bograd (Eds.), *Feminist perspectives on wife abuse* (pp. 28–50). Newbury Park, CA: Sage.

Yllo, K. A. (1993). Through a feminist lens: Gender, power and violence. In R. J. Gelles & D. R. Loseke (Eds.), *Current controversies on family violence* (pp. 47–62). Newbury Park, CA: Sage.

7

STRATEGIES FOR PREVENTING HIV INFECTION AMONG INJECTING DRUG USERS: TAKING INTERVENTIONS TO THE PEOPLE

DON C. DES JARLAIS AND SAMUEL R. FRIEDMAN

The multiperson use ("sharing") of the equipment used in illicit drug injection is a relatively efficient method for transmitting HIV and other blood-borne pathogens (hepatitis C virus is another notable example). The HIV/AIDS epidemic among injecting drug users (IDUs) has been an international public health catastrophe and a tragedy for literally millions of drug injectors, their sexual partners, and their children. An epidemic of this magnitude has also presented new opportunities for research into human behavior and new opportunities to use expertise in psychology to literally "save lives." We have had the opportunity to examine fundamental conflicting forces in the determination of human behaviors, that is, potential conflict between the seeking of basic pleasures (drug induced and sexual) and the preservation of life. Fortunately, the data have clearly demonstrated the capability of the great majority of drug users to modify their

This chapter is adapted from an address given at the American Association for Applied and Prevention Psychology in May 1997. Preparation was supported by grant RO1 DA 03574.

behavior to protect against becoming infected with HIV and other pathogens.

Study of the politics of HIV prevention for drug users has also shown the power of belief systems about psychoactive drug use. These belief systems can be maintained despite large amounts of contradictory scientific data and despite the cost in human lives of not implementing effective HIV prevention programs.

The HIV epidemic is not likely to disappear in the near future, and we also are apt to see many newly emerging infectious diseases to which IDUs are susceptible. There is clearly still much for people with training in psychology to do with respect to the HIV/AIDS epidemic, the international epidemic of psychoactive drug abuse, and emerging infectious diseases. In contemplating the work that has been accomplished to date and the work yet to be done, it is important to remember that these efforts are likely to be successful only to the extent that the drug users themselves are considered respected partners in the work.

HIV infection and AIDS have been reported among IDUs in 129 countries (Ball, Rana, & Dehne, 1998). In some countries, such as Italy and Spain, IDUs have long been the largest group of people with AIDS. The most recent estimate of HIV infections in the United States indicates that approximately half of all new HIV infections are occurring among IDUs (Holmberg, 1996). At the level of viral transmission, the relationship between injecting drug use and HIV/AIDS is direct and easy to understand. Before someone injects a psychoactive drug intravenously, he or she typically pulls back on the plunger of the syringe. Blood entering into the barrel of the syringe signals that a vein has been properly located. After the drug solution has been injected, a small amount of blood is left in the needle and syringe. If another person then uses the needle and syringe for a second injection, some of the blood left in the needle and syringe will then be injected into the vein of the second injector. These microtransfusions are a relatively effective method for transmitting blood-borne pathogens.

At the behavioral and social level, however, there are many complex aspects of HIV infection among IDUs. We now have more than 15 years of research on HIV and AIDS among IDUs. This research has shown surprising findings regarding the worldwide threat of blood-borne pathogens among IDUs, the ability of IDUs to change risk behaviors, and the often-difficult politics of public health regarding the issues of AIDS and injecting drug use, areas in which health psychologists can make key contributions.

THE GLOBAL DIFFUSION OF INJECTING DRUG USE

During the first half of the 20th century, the illicit injection of psychoactive drugs was sufficiently concentrated in the United States that it was called the "American disease" (Musto, 1973). After World War II, there was an increase in injecting drug use in the nation that led to epidemic levels of use during the late 1960s and early 1970s. During the middle and late 1970s, drug injection spread to many countries in Western Europe, and by the late 1980s, it was reported in 80 countries (Des Jarlais & Friedman, 1989). There were an estimated 5 million persons throughout the world who injected illicit drugs by 1992 (Mann, Tarantola, & Netter, 1992). This number is probably growing rapidly, and drug injection has now been reported in 129 countries (Ball et al., 1998). Although there is still much to be learned about the international diffusion of illicit drug injection, the following factors appear to be important:

- *International growth in the use of "licit" psychoactive drugs.* Use of nicotine and alcohol has spread to many areas of the world where these psychoactive drugs are not part of the traditional culture (Ambler, 1991; Mackay, 1994; Peto, 1994). Nonmedical psychoactive drug use as a whole, and not simply illicit psychoactive drug use, has been increasing over the past several decades.
- *The globalization of the world economy.* Improvements in communication and transportation and reductions in trade barriers have led to great increases in international trade. These same developments also facilitate illicit international trade in psychoactive drugs.
- *Economies of scale in illicit drug production.* The large profit margins possible in the illicit sale of psychoactive substances means that substantial profits can be made selling these drugs, even to "poor" people. The profit margins from selling illicit drugs in industrialized countries can be used to underwrite the development of new markets in developing countries. The economics of the illicit international distribution of drugs particularly facilitate the development of domestic drug markets in producing and transit countries.
- *Injecting produces a strong drug effect because of the rapid increase in the concentration of the drug in the brain.* Injecting is also highly cost efficient in that almost all of the drug is actually delivered to the brain. On these grounds, intravenous injection can be considered a technologically superior method of psychoactive drug administration. Inexpensive technological advances tend to disperse widely and are very difficult (although not impossible) to reverse (Rogers, 1982).

Although it is probably possible to improve current efforts to reduce the illicit supplies of psychoactive drugs, the effectiveness of such efforts is likely to vary across time and place. Given the recent spread of injecting drug use, elimination of this form of psychoactive drug use would not appear to be a realistic goal for the near future. Public health officials should plan for further worldwide increases in illicit psychoactive drug injection, with the potential for severe public health consequences that include transmission of blood-borne pathogens such as HIV and hepatitis B and C.

THE GLOBAL DIFFUSION OF HIV AMONG IDUS

Before the study of HIV infection among IDUs, it was assumed that drug users generally stayed close to home because all of their discretionary income was spent on drugs, and they could not risk being far from their sources of drug supply. Thus, health problems such as blood-borne infectious diseases were likely to be confined to local populations of IDUs.

The global diffusion of HIV and of hepatitis B and hepatitis C has shown the opposite. HIV has now been reported among IDUs in 103 countries (Ball et al., 1998). Hepatitis B and hepatitis C infections have been observed in all populations of drug injectors that have been studied (Hagan, 1994; Levine, Vlahov, & Nelsen, 1994). A substantial number of IDUs do travel and inject drugs in different locations (Ball et al., 1994). Stimson (1994) has provided an excellent reconstruction of the diffusion of HIV among drug injectors in southeast Asia. Although these travel patterns are not yet well understood, some of this travel can be considered "drug tourism," in which drug users travel to locations where higher quality drugs can be purchased for lower prices (Simons, 1994). The travel often occurs along drug distribution routes.

Travel by drug injectors has important implications for the study of emerging infectious diseases (Des Jarlais, Stimson, et al., 1996). Injecting drug users may form an important ecological niche for blood-borne infectious agents with relatively long "latency periods" (where there is a long time between infection and the development of serious illness). Travel among IDUs can lead to worldwide diffusion of such emerging infectious diseases. Coping with the problems of emerging infectious diseases among IDUs will require an international perspective. It will not be possible to successfully address these problems if one assumes that illicit drug use is a problem that is confined within national boundaries.

POTENTIAL RAPID SPREAD OF HIV AMONG IDUS

In many areas, HIV has spread extremely rapidly among IDUs, with the HIV seroprevalence rate (the percentage of IDUs infected with HIV) increasing from less than 10% to 40% or greater within 1–2 years. Rapid transmission has occurred in both industrialized nations (e.g., in Scotland and the United States) and in developing countries (e.g., Thailand and India; Des Jarlais, Friedman, Choopanya, Vanichseni, & Ward, 1992). Several factors have been associated with extremely rapid transmission of HIV among IDUs: (a) lack of awareness of HIV/AIDS as a local threat, (b) restrictions on the availability and use of new injection equipment, and (c) mechanisms for rapid and efficient mixing within the local IDU population. Without an awareness of AIDS as a local threat, IDUs are likely to use each other's equipment frequently. Indeed, before one is aware of HIV/AIDS, providing previously used equipment to another IDU is likely to be seen as an act of solidarity or as a service for which one may legitimately charge a small fee.

There are various types of legal restrictions that can reduce the availability of sterile injection equipment and thus lead to increased multiperson use (sharing) of drug injection equipment. In some jurisdictions, medical prescriptions are required for the purchase of needles and syringes. Possession of needles and syringes can also be criminalized through laws against possession of "drug paraphernalia," putting users at risk of arrest if needles and syringes are found in their possession (for a discussion of U.S. laws, see Gostin, Lazzarini, Jones, & Flaherty, 1997). In some jurisdictions, drug users have also been prosecuted for possession of drugs based on the minute quantities of drugs that remain in a needle and syringe after it has been used to inject drugs. The possible legal restrictions on the availability of sterile injection equipment and the actual practices of pharmacists and police can create additional limits. Even if laws permit sales of needles and syringes without prescriptions, pharmacists may choose not to sell without prescriptions or not to sell to anyone who "looks like a drug user." Similarly, police may harass drug users found carrying injection equipment even if there are no laws criminalizing the possession of drug paraphernalia.

"Shooting galleries" (places where IDUs can rent injection equipment, which is then returned to the gallery owner for rental to other IDUs), "dealer's works" (injection equipment kept by a drug seller that can be lent to successive drug purchasers), and injecting in prisons are all examples of situations that provide rapid, efficient mixing among an IDU population. The mixing is rapid in that many IDUs may use the injection equipment from the shooting gallery, the drug dealer, or a fellow inmate within short periods of time. Several studies have indicated that the infectiousness of HIV is many times greater in the 2- to 3-month period after initial infection compared with the long "latency" period between initial infection and the development of severe immunosuppression (Jacquez, Koopman, Simon, & Longini, 1994). Thus, the concentration of new infections in these settings may synergistically interact with continued mixing and lead to highly infectious IDUs transmitting HIV to large numbers of other drug injectors. *Efficient mixing*, the sharing of drug injection equipment or drug solutions with few restrictions on who shares with whom, serves to spread HIV across potential social boundaries, such as friendship groups, which otherwise might have served to limit transmission.

Although the general processes involved in extremely rapid spread have now been identified, we still do not have a detailed understanding of these processes and, given the potential for rapid spread in many populations of IDUs throughout the world, additional research is urgently needed.

HEALTH PSYCHOLOGY INTERVENTIONS TO REDUCE RISK AMONG IDUS

Before research on AIDS among IDUs, there was a common stereotype that these individuals are not at all concerned about health and that they would not change their behavior because of AIDS. In sharp contrast to these expectations, reductions in risk behavior were observed among IDU participants in a wide variety of early prevention programs, including outreach and bleach distribution (Thompson, Jones, Cahill, & Medina, 1990; Wiebel, Chene, & Johnson, 1990), "education only" (Jackson & Rotkiewicz, 1987; Ostrow, 1989), drug abuse treatment (Blix & Gronbladh, 1988), syringe exchange (Buning, Hartgers, Verster, van Santen, & Coutinho, 1988), increased over-the-counter sales of injection equipment (Espinoza, Bouchard, Ballian, & Polo DeVoto, 1988; Goldberg et al., 1988), and HIV counseling and testing (Cartter, Petersen, Savage, & Donagher, 1990; Higgins et al., 1991). These interventions were designed, implemented, and evaluated by people from a wide variety of disciplines, including epidemiologists, anthropologists, sociologists, and psychologists. The multidisciplinary nature of this intervention work undoubtedly contributed to the success of the interventions in reducing HIV risk behavior. The contributions of psychologists were often critical with respect to the theories of behavior change and the measurement of risk behaviors.

It is also important to note that there is evidence that IDUs will reduce HIV risk behavior in the absence of any specific prevention program. IDUs in New York City reported risk reduction before the implementation of any formal HIV prevention programs (Friedman et al., 1987; Selwyn, Feiner, Cox, Lipshutz, & Cohen, 1987). IDUs had learned about AIDS through the mass media and the oral-communication networks within the drug-injecting community, and the illicit market in sterile injection equipment had expanded to provide additional equipment (Des Jarlais, Friedman, & Hopkins, 1985).

These early reports of behavior change among IDUs were questioned on both methodological and epidemiological grounds. Methodologically, there is the question of social desirability effects: Did the risk reduction reported by IDUs reflect "real" changes in behavior or merely that research participants learned what they were expected to say to the researchers? Even if the risk reduction did reflect actual changes in behavior, were these of sufficient magnitude that they would correspond to meaningful changes in the rate of new HIV infections among IDUs? More recent studies have been able to use actual HIV infections as an outcome measure for HIV risk reduction among IDUs. Reported risk reduction and lower rates of new HIV infections have been observed in association with street outreach (Wiebel, Jimenez, Johnson, Ouellet, Murray, & O'Brien, 1993), methadone maintenance treatment (Metzger et al., 1993), and syringe exchange (Des Jarlais, Marmor, et al., 1996).

The relationship between self-reported AIDS behavior change and avoiding HIV infection was examined in the World Health Organization (WHO) Multi-Centre Study of AIDS and Injecting Drug Use. In this study, more than 4,400 IDUs were recruited from Athens, Bangkok, Berlin, Glasgow, London, Madrid, New York City, Rio de Janeiro, Santos (Brazil), Sydney, and Toronto (Des Jarlais, Friedmann, Hagan, & Friedman, 1996). The participants were recruited from drug abuse treatment programs and from nontreatment sources in each city. A standardized questionnaire and HIV counseling and testing were administered. Participants were permitted to define (and asked to describe) their own "change in behavior to avoid getting AIDS" since they had first learned about AIDS. Among these participants, 82% reported that they had changed their behavior in response to AIDS, with reduced sharing of drug injection equipment the most commonly reported type of behavior change. Participants who reported having changed their behavior in response to AIDS were significantly less likely to have been infected with HIV (20%) compared with those who reported that they had not changed their behavior since learning about AIDS (34% infected with HIV, protective odds ratio for self-reported behavior change = .50, $p > .001$).

Contrary to beliefs at the beginning of the HIV/AIDS epidemic, IDUs have shown that they are capable of changing their behavior in response to AIDS, of accurately reporting on the behavior change, and of making changes of sufficient magnitude to provide meaningful reduction in the chances of becoming infected with HIV.

Although there has been unexpected success in reducing risk behavior among IDUs, no single intervention or set of interventions has led to risk elimination in a population of IDUs. (In fact, no interventions have led to risk elimination in any other population at risk for HIV infection.) *Residual risk behavior*—risk behavior occurring after implementation of "standard" interventions—can lead to unacceptably high rates of new HIV infections in areas of high HIV prevalence (Holmberg, 1996). This problem is a major challenge for psychologists and others working in HIV prevention.

Community-Level Prevention

Although it is critical to show that AIDS risk reduction "works" at the level of the individual IDU, this does not answer the larger question of protecting populations of IDUs from HIV infection. Prevention programs that protected only a small minority (perhaps those "most motivated to change") and prevention programs that slowed transmission (so that the same number of persons became infected, but over a longer time period) would have at most modest value. Whether it is possible to avert epidemics of HIV transmission requires studying populations at risk rather than simply studying individuals at risk.

As part of the WHO Multi-Centre Study, we identified five cities with "stable low" HIV seroprevalence among IDUs (Des Jarlais et al., 1995). Stable low seroprevalence in a population implies a very low rate of new HIV infections, although not necessarily a rate of zero. It is incompatible with the rapid transmission of HIV discussed above. Stable, low HIV seroprevalence was operationally defined as having (a) at least 5 consecutive years of data on HIV seroprevalence from a local population of IDUs, including data from drug abuse treatment and nontreatment samples; (b) a minimum HIV seroprevalence of 1% (indicating that the virus had entered the local IDU population); and (b) seroprevalence that had remained less than 5%, with no trend toward increasing seroprevalence over time. A literature search identified five cities that met these criteria: Glasgow, Scotland; Lund, Sweden; Sydney, Australia; Tacoma, Washington; and Toronto, Canada.

We then compared HIV prevention activities and HIV risk behavior among IDUs in these five cities. There were three common components of prevention activities: (a) prevention activities were begun early, usually in the middle to late 1980s, when HIV seroprevalence was low in each of the cities; (b) outreach to develop trusting communication between health workers and IDUs was implemented; and (c) good access to sterile injection equipment was provided through legal pharmacy sales, syringe exchange, or both. A large majority—70% or greater—of the IDUs in each city reported having changed their behavior to reduce their risk of developing AIDS. Interestingly, this risk reduction was far from risk elimination. Substantial percentages—from 30% to 58%—of the IDUs in each city reported that they had engaged in sharing needles and syringes in the 6 months before the interviews. Rapid, efficient-mixing risk behavior, such as sharing in shooting galleries, was rare in all of the cities.

Studies of additional cities will be needed to further specify the conditions of stable, low HIV seroprevalence among populations of IDUs and how prevention programs can facilitate those conditions. Recent data from Vancouver provide a cautionary note. Despite active prevention programs, including a syringe exchange program, a rapid outbreak of HIV infection occurred among local IDUs, with HIV seroprevalence rising from under 5% to more than 20% within a period of a few years (Strathdee et al., 1997). Exactly what went "wrong" in Vancouver has not been determined. It appears that the introduction of cocaine injection into the local IDU population led to large increases in the frequency of injection and that the supply of sterile injection equipment was not sufficient for this increase in injection frequency. It also appears that hotel rooms in the downtown area came to function similarly to shooting galleries in that they provided settings for rapid, efficient mixing of the IDU population.

At present, we do not have good methods for distinguishing the extent of residual risk behavior that is compatible with maintaining low HIV seroprevalence versus the extent of residual risk behavior that will lead to a rapid outbreak of HIV transmission as that which occurred in Vancouver. Developing methods for measuring these differences is a formidable challenge for psychologists, sociologists, epidemiologists, and mathematical modelers.

Syringe Exchange Programs

Syringe exchange programs have been an important component of HIV prevention for IDUs in almost all industrialized countries and in some developing countries. Syringe exchange has remained relatively controversial in the United States, however, and to date there is no federal funding of syringe exchange programs in the country (although many cities and several states do fund syringe exchange programs).

Part of the controversy over syringe exchange revolves around two empirical questions: (a) whether syringe exchange programs lead to increased illicit drug use and (b) whether syringe exchange programs actually reduce HIV transmission among IDUs. It is an interesting aspect of the controversy that since 1988, federal law has prohibited federal funding of syringe exchange until it has been shown to be "safe" (i.e., that it does not lead to increased drug use) and "effective" (i.e., that it does reduce HIV transmission; Normand, Vlahov, & Moses, 1995). It is unusual, in the midst of a large-scale epidemic, to require evidence that a program works before any federal funding can be used to support even demonstration programs. These criteria have not been applied to any other type of AIDS prevention program in the United States or in any other country.

There have now been several hundred studies of syringe exchange throughout the world and a series of reviews of this research literature (Des Jarlais & Friedman, 1992; Lurie, Reingold, & Bowser, 1993; National Commission on AIDS, 1991; Normand et al., 1995; U.S. Government Accounting Office, 1993). All of these reviews have supported syringe exchange. In the most recent report (Normand et al., 1995), 17 studies were identified on the question of whether syringe exchange programs lead to increased drug use. Six studies examined community-level drug use, using indicators such as drug-related emergency room visits or the mean age of the local IDU population. All studies failed to show any increase in drug use after the implementation of syringe exchange programs. Normand and colleagues identified 11 studies in which individual-level drug use was examined; these were primarily comparisons of the frequency of injection before and after the participants began using a syringe exchange program. Among these 11 studies, five showed decreases in drug injection frequency, five showed no change in drug injection frequency, and only one showed an increase in injection frequency.

There are clearly many factors other than syringe exchange programs that might affect injecting drug use in a community or among individuals. If implementation of syringe exchange programs was leading to increased drug injection, however, we would expect that the majority of studies would show increases in drug injection after syringe exchange programs were implemented. Instead, the preponderant majority of studies show either no change or decreases in drug injection.

There are now a sufficient number of studies of HIV incidence among participants in syringe exchange programs that it is possible to assess the association between participation in an exchange and the likelihood of becoming infected with HIV. Table 7.1 presents HIV incidence data among participants in syringe exchange programs.

First, HIV incidence is generally low among syringe exchange participants in areas with low background HIV prevalence. Studies of HIV incidence among IDUs who do not use syringe exchange in several of these areas (including Lund, Tacoma, Portland, Sydney, England, and Wales) also show low incidence. These areas are probably best considered as examples of successful community-level HIV prevention (discussed above), of which syringe exchange is one important component.

IDUs from the Montreal and Vancouver exchanges have an HIV incidence rate notably above that of the other cities in Table 7.1. The Montreal and Vancouver programs appear to attract a subgroup of IDUs with extremely high initial risk levels (Hankins, Gendron, & Tran, 1994; Lamothe et al., 1994; Strathdee et al., 1997), including high rates of cocaine injection, high levels of unprotected commercial sex work, and homelessness (which may make it difficult to have clean needles available at the time of drug injection). Still, additional data are needed to fully explain the Montreal and Vancouver incidence rates, and researchers are presently initiating new studies are in these cities.

The HIV incidence data from three United States cities with high HIV seroprevalence (New Haven, Chicago, and New York) that have syringe exchange programs must be considered extremely encouraging with respect to reducing HIV transmission in high seroprevalence areas. The data from New Haven are generally consistent with the previously devel-

TABLE 7.1
Recent Studies of HIV Incidence Among Syringe Exchange Participants

City	HIV prevalence[a]	Measured HIV seroconversions[b]	Estimated HIV seroconversions[c]	Reference
Lund	low	0		(Ljungberg et al., 1991)
Glasgow	low		0–1 (2)	(Ball et al., 1994)
Sydney	low		0–1 (2)	(Ball et al., 1994)
Toronto	low		1–2 (1)	(Ball et al., 1994)
England and Wales (except London)	low		0–1 (1)	(Stimson, 1995)
Kathmandu	low	0		(Maharjan, Peak, Rana, & Crofts, 1994)
Tacoma, WA	low	<1		(Hagan, Des Jarlais, Purchase, Reid, & Friedman, 1991)
Portland, OR	low	<1		(Oliver, Maynard, Friedman, & Des Jarlais, 1994)
Montreal	moderate	5–13		(Hankins, Gendron, & Tran, 1994)
London	moderate			(Stimson, 1995)
Vancouver, BC	moderate	18	1–2 (3)	(Strathdee et al., 1997)
Amsterdam	high	4		Van den Hoek (personal communication, October 1998)
Chicago	high	3		Wiebel (personal communication, October 1999)
New York	very high	1.5		(Des Jarlais, Marmor, et al., 1996)
New Haven, CT	very high		3 (4)	(Kaplan & Heimer, 1994)

Note. [a]low = 0–5%; moderate = 6–20%; high = 21–40%; very high = 41% or more. [b]Cohort study, repeated testing of participants, or both in per 100 person-years at risk. [c]Estimated from (a) stable, very low <2% seroprevalence in area; (b) self-reports of previous seronegative test and a current HIV blood or saliva test; (c) stable or declining seroprevalence; (d) from HIV testing of syringes collected at exchange per 100 person-years at risk.

oped mathematical model to assess the effectiveness of the New Haven syringe exchange program (O'Keefe, Kaplan, & Khoshnood, 1991).

A major difficulty in interpreting the HIV incidence studies of syringe exchange participants is the lack of meaningful comparison groups. In almost all of the areas (e.g., United Kingdom, Sydney, Amsterdam, Montreal, Vancouver), IDUs who do not use the syringe exchanges purchase sterile injection equipment from pharmacies. In the New York City study, however, only the IDUs who used the syringe exchanges had legal access to sterile injection equipment because New York has a prescription law requirement. The New York City study did show a significantly higher HIV incidence rate among IDUs who did not use the syringe exchanges: 5.3/100 person-years at risk (Des Jarlais, Marmor, et al., 1996). The New York City study was the first to show a difference in HIV incidence between IDUs who had full legal access to sterile injection equipment for injecting illicit drugs versus those who used illegal sources for obtaining their injection equipment.

Because of the difficulties in constructing precisely equivalent comparison groups, the HIV seroincidence data in Table 7.1 cannot be considered "experimental proof" of the effectiveness of syringe exchange programs in reducing transmission of blood-borne viruses. Nevertheless, these data clearly indicate that IDUs will use syringe exchange programs, and in the great majority of programs, they will successfully protect themselves against infection with blood-borne viruses.

Research on syringe exchange programs has answered the "first-generation" questions (syringe exchange programs do lead to reductions in HIV risk behavior, syringe exchange programs do not lead to increased drug use); it is now time to consider the "second-generation" research questions. Prominent among these are, Why are some exchanges more effective than others? and What other services for drug users should be integrated into syringe exchange programs? These questions offer continuing research opportunities, particularly for psychologists with interests in health services delivery research.

DEVELOPING A PUBLIC HEALTH PERSPECTIVE ON PSYCHOACTIVE DRUG USE AND HIV/AIDS

Much has been learned in the past 15 years of research on preventing HIV infection among IDUs. During that time, however, injecting drug use has become the most common factor in new HIV infections in the United States (Holmberg, 1996). Programs to prevent HIV infection among IDUs in the United States often have been controversial and have been implemented only on a fragmentary basis across the country. Syringe exchange programs undoubtedly have been the most controversial, but methadone maintenance treatment for heroin dependence also remains controversial. At one point, Congress even voted to revoke funding from bleach distribution programs. One major component of the controversy has been the perceived incompatibility of many HIV prevention programs with the official policy of conducting a "War on Drugs." The War on Drugs rhetoric requires that official actions be seen as "fighting drugs" and "tough on drugs," even if this means failing to prevent further transmission of a deadly virus among drug users, their sexual partners, and their children. The public health crisis of the AIDS epidemic among injecting drug users has led to efforts to formulate alternatives to the War on Drugs policy framework.

HIV and AIDS have dramatically increased the adverse health consequences of injecting drug use and thus have led to seeing psychoactive drug use as more of a health problem and not just a criminal justice problem. At the same time, HIV infection can be prevented without requiring the cessation of injecting drug use. This potential separation of one severe adverse consequence of drug use from the drug use itself has encouraged analysis of other areas in which adverse consequences of drug use might be reduced without requiring cessation of drug use. The ability of many IDUs to modify their behavior to reduce the chances of HIV infection has also led to consideration of drug users as both concerned about their health and as capable of acting on that concern (without denying the compulsive nature of drug dependence).

These ideas have formed much of the basis for what has been termed the "harm reduction" perspective on psychoactive drug use (Brettle, 1991; Des Jarlais, 1995; Des Jarlais, Friedman, & Ward, 1993; Heather, Wodak, Nadelmann, & O'Hare, 1993). This perspective emphasizes the pragmatic need to reduce harmful consequences of psychoactive drug use while acknowledging that eliminating psychoactive drug use and drug misuse is not likely to be feasible in the near future. Harm reduction must not be confused with "legalization" of currently illicit drugs. Unrestricted legal opportunities to exploit the commercial possibilities of psychoactive drugs can lead to immense drug-related harm, as the example of nicotine cigarettes clearly shows. Three of the major strengths of the harm reduction perspective are that (a) it requires programs effective in reducing specified drug-related harm, rather than programs simply appearing to be "tough on drugs"; (b) it is applicable to both licit drug use (alcohol, nicotine) as well as illicit drug use; and (c) it can readily incorporate findings from scientific research.

Psychologists have the opportunity to make critical contributions to reformulating public policies on psychoactive drug use. These opportunities include developing a better scientific understanding of drug-related behaviors (including why relatively large numbers of drug users are able to control their drug use), developing and evaluating programs to reduce the adverse consequences of psychoactive drug use, and translating scientific findings into public policy.

Since AIDS was first noted among IDUs in 1981, both the problem of injecting drug use and the problem of HIV infection among IDUs have grown to become true pandemics. In contrast to the original stereotype of drug users being too "self-destructive" to change their HIV risk behavior, we have seen large-scale reductions of such behavior among IDUs. Preventing HIV infection in this population is a realistic public health goal but often requires behavior change among political leaders, not only among the IDUs. Unfortunately, changing the AIDS-related behavior of political leaders is often more difficult than changing the AIDS-related behavior of IDUs.

SUMMARY

The spread of HIV among IDUs and their sexual partners has been a global public health catastrophe. Research conducted by psychologists, sociologists, anthropologists, and epidemiologists has unequivocally demonstrated that the great majority of drug users will change their behavior to reduce their risks of HIV infection. This research has led to a reformulation of some basic concepts about drug use and drug dependence and, in particular, to a better understanding of which aspects of drug behavior can readily be changed (the use of clean versus contaminated syringes) and which aspects are exceedingly difficult to change (complete cessation of drug use). The HIV epidemic continues among drug users throughout the world. There is also a growing recognition of the need to extend risk reduction efforts to other blood-borne pathogens such as hepatitis B and C. This will create many additional opportunities for psychologists to make contributions to our basic scientific understanding of drug-related behaviors, to developing and evaluating programs that literally "save lives," and to formulating scientifically based public policies on psychoactive drug use.

REFERENCES

Ambler, C. H. (1991). Drunks, brewers and chiefs: Alcohol regulation in colonial Kenya 1900–1939. In S. Barrow & R. Room (Eds.), *Drinking behaviour and belief in modern history* (pp. 57–73). Berkeley: University of California Press.

Ball, A., Des Jarlais, D. C., Donoghoe, M., Friedman, S. R., Goldberg, D., Hunter, G. M., Stimson, G. V., & Wodak, A. (1994). *Multi-Centre Study on Drug Injecting and Risk of HIV Infection* (Programme on Substance Abuse). Geneva: World Health Organization.

Ball, A. L., Rana, S., & Dehne, K. (1998). HIV prevention among injecting drug users: Responses in developing and transitional countries. *Public Health Reports, 113*(Suppl. 1), 170–181.

Blix, O., & Gronbladh, L. (1988, June). AIDS and IV heroin addicts: The preventive effect of methadone maintenance in Sweden. Paper presented at the Fourth International Conference on AIDS, Stockholm, Sweden.

Brettle, R. P. (1991). HIV and harm reduction for injection drug users. *AIDS, 5,* 125–136.

Buning, E. C., Hartgers, C., Verster, A. D., van Santen, G. W., & Coutinho, R. A. (1988, June). The evaluation of the needle/syringe exchange in Amsterdam. Paper presented at the Fourth International Conference on AIDS. Stockholm, Sweden.

Cartter, M. L., Petersen, L. R., Savage, R. B., & Donagher, J. (1990). Providing HIV counseling and testing services in methadone maintenance programs. *AIDS, 4,* 463–465.

Des Jarlais, D. C. (1995). Harm reduction—A framework for incorporating science into drug policy [Editorial]. *American Journal of Public Health, 85,* 10–12.

Des Jarlais, D. C., & Friedman, S. R. (1989). AIDS and IV drug use. *Science, 245,* 578–579.

Des Jarlais, D. C., & Friedman, S. R. (1992). AIDS and legal access to sterile drug injection equipment. *Annals of the American Academy of Political and Social Science, 521,* 42–65.

Des Jarlais, D. C., Friedman, S. R., Choopanya, K., Vanichseni, S., & Ward, T. P. (1992). International epidemiology of HIV and AIDS among injecting drug users. *AIDS, 6,* 1053–1068.

Des Jarlais, D. C., Friedman, S. R., & Hopkins, W. (1985). Risk reduction for the acquired immunodeficiency syndrome among intravenous drug users. *Annals of Internal Medicine, 103,* 755–759.

Des Jarlais, D. C., Friedman, S. R., & Ward, T. P. (1993). Harm reduction: A public health response to the AIDS epidemic among injecting drug users. *Annual Review of Public Health, 14,* 413–450.

Des Jarlais, D. C., Friedmann, P., Hagan, H., & Friedman, S. R. (1996). The protective effect of AIDS-related behavioral change among injection drug users: A cross-national study. *American Journal of Public Health, 86,* 1780–1785.

Des Jarlais, D. C., Hagan, H. H., Friedman, S. R., Friedman, P., Goldberg, D., Frischer, M., Green, S., Tunving, K., Ljungberg, B., Wodak, A., Ross, M., Purchase, D., Millson, M. E., & Myers, T. (1995). Maintaining low HIV seroprevalence in populations of injecting drug users. *JAMA, 274,* 1226–1231.

Des Jarlais, D. C., Marmor, M., Paone, D., Titus, S., Shi, Q., Perlis, T., Jose, B., & Friedman, S. R. (1996). HIV incidence among injecting drug users in New York City syringe-exchange programmes. *Lancet, 348,* 987–991.

Des Jarlais, D. C., Stimson, G. V., Hagan, H., Perlman, D., Choopanya, K., Bastos, F. I., & Friedman, S. R. (1996). Emerging infectious diseases and the injection of illicit psychoactive drugs. *Current Issues in Public Health, 2,* 102–137.

Espinoza, P., Bouchard, I., Ballian, P., & Polo DeVoto, J. (1988, June). Has the open sale of syringes modified the syringe exchanging habits of drug addicts? Paper presented at the Fourth International Conference on AIDS, Stockholm, Sweden.

Friedman, S. R., Des Jarlais, D. C., Sotheran, J. L., Garber, J., Cohen, H., & Smith, D. (1987). AIDS and self-organization among intravenous drug users. *International Journal of the Addictions, 22,* 201–219.

Goldberg, D., Watson, H., Stuart, F., Miller, M., Gruer, L., & Follett, E. (1988, June). Pharmacy supply of needles and syringes—The effect on spread of HIV in intravenous drug misusers. Paper presented at the Fourth International Conference on AIDS, Stockholm, Sweden.

Gostin, L. O., Lazzarini, Z., Jones, T. S., & Flaherty, K. (1997). Prevention of HIV/ AIDS and other blood-borne diseases among injection drug users: A national survey on the regulation of syringes and needles. *Journal of the American Medical Association. 277,* 53–62.

Hagan, H. (1994). *The use of hepatitis as an outcome measure for evaluation of syringe exchange and bleach distribution programs for the prevention of HIV infection among injecting drug users.* Washington, DC: National Research Council/ Institute of Medicine.

Hagan, H., Des Jarlais, D. C., Purchase, D., Reid, T., & Friedman, S. R. (1991). The Tacoma Syringe Exchange. *Journal of Addictive Diseases, 10,* 81–88.

Hankins, C., Gendron, S., & Tran, T. (1994, August). Montreal needle exchange attenders versus non-attenders: What's the difference? Paper presented at the *Tenth International Conference on AIDS,* Yokohama, Japan.

Heather, N., Wodak, A., Nadelmann, E., & O'Hare, P. (Eds.). (1993). *Psychoactive drugs and harm reduction: From faith to science.* London: Whurr.

Higgins, D. L., Galavotti, C., O'Reilly, K. R., Schnell, D. J., Moore, M., Rugg, D. L., & Johnson, R. (1991). Evidence for the effects of HIV antibody counseling and testing on risk behaviors. *Journal of the American Medical Association, 266,* 2419–2429.

Holmberg, S. (1996). The estimated prevalence and incidence of HIV in 96 large US metropolitan areas. *American Journal of Public Health, 86,* 642–654.

Jackson, J., & Rotkiewicz, L. (1987, June). A coupon program: AIDS education and drug treatment. Paper presented at the *Third International Conference on AIDS,* Washington, DC.

Jacquez, J., Koopman, J., Simon, C., & Longini, I. (1994). Role of the primary infection in epidemic HIV infection of gay cohorts. *Journal of the Acquired Immunodeficiency Syndromes, 7,* 1169–1184.

Kaplan, E. H., & Heimer, R. (1994). HIV incidence among needle exchange participants: Estimates from syringe tracking and testing data. *Journal of AIDS, 7,* 182–189.

Lamothe, F., Bruneau, J., Soto, J., Lachance, N., Franco, E., Vincelette, J., & Fauvel, M. (1994, August). Risk factors for HIV seroconversion among injecting drug users in Montreal: The Saint-Luc cohort experience. Paper presented at the Tenth International Conference on AIDS, Yokohama, Japan.

Levine, O. S., Vlahov, D., & Nelsen, K. E. (1994). Epidemiology of hepatitis B virus infection among injection drug users: Seroprevalence, risk factors, and viral interactions. *American Journal of Epidemiology. 16*, 418–436.

Ljungberg, B., Christensson, B., Tunving, K., Anderson, B., Landvall, B., Lundberg, M., & Zall-Friberg, A. C. (1991). HIV prevention among injecting drug users: Three years of experience from a syringe exchange program in Sweden. *Journal of AIDS, 4*, 890–895.

Lurie, P., Reingold, A. L., & Bowser, B. (Eds.). (1993). *The public health impact of needle-exchange programs in the United States and abroad: Volume 1.* Atlanta, GA: Centers for Disease Control and Prevention.

Mackay, J. L. (1994). The fight against tobacco in developing countries. *Tubercle and Lung Disease, 75*, 8–24.

Maharjan, S. H., Peak, A., Rana, S., & Crofts, N. (1994, August). Declining risk for HIV among IDUs in Kathmandu: Impact of a harm reduction programme. Paper presented at the *Tenth International Conference on AIDS*, Yokohama, Japan.

Mann, J., Tarantola, J., & Netter, T. (1992). *AIDS in the world.* Cambridge, MA: Harvard University Press.

Metzger, D., Woody, G., McLellan, A., O'Brien, C., Druley, P., Navaline, H., DePhilippis, D., Stolley, P., & Abrutyn, E. (1993). Human immunodeficiency virus seroconversion among in- and out-of-treatment drug users: An 18 month prospective follow-up. *Journal of the Acquired Immune Deficiency Syndromes, 6*, 1049–1056.

Musto, D. (1973). *The American disease: Origins of narcotic control.* New Haven, CT: Yale University Press.

National Commission on AIDS. (1991). *The twin epidemics of substance use and HIV.* Washington, DC: Author.

Normand, J., Vlahov, D., & Moses, L. E. (Eds.). (1995). *Preventing HIV transmission: The role of sterile needles and bleach.* Washington, DC: National Academy Press/National Research Council/Institute of Medicine.

O'Keefe, E., Kaplan, E., & Khoshnood, K. (1991). *Preliminary report: City of New Haven Needle Exchange Program.* New Haven, CT: Office of Mayor John C. Daniels.

Oliver, K., Maynard, H., Friedman, S. R., & Des Jarlais, D. C. (Eds.). (1994). *Behavioral and community impact of the Portland syringe exchange program.* Washington, DC: National Academy of Sciences.

Ostrow, D. G. (1989). AIDS prevention through effective education. *Daedalus, 118*, 229–254.

Peto, R. (1994). Smoking and death: The past 40 years and the next 40. *British Medical Journal, 309*, 937–939.

Rogers, E. (1982). *Diffusion of innovations*. New York: Free Press.

Selwyn, P., Feiner, C., Cox, C., Lipshutz, C., & Cohen, R. (1987). Knowledge about AIDS and high-risk behavior among intravenous drug abusers in New York City. *AIDS, 1*, 247–254.

Simons, M. (1994, April 20). Drug tourism in Europe. *New York Times*, p. A8.

Stimson, G. (1994). Reconstruction of sub-regional diffusion of HIV infection among injecting drug users in South-East Asia: Implications for prevention. *AIDS, 8*, 1630–1632.

Stimson, G. V. (1995). AIDS and injecting drug use in the United Kingdom, 1987–1993: The policy response and the prevention of the epidemic. *Social Science and Medicine, 41*, 699–716.

Strathdee, S., Patrick, D., Currie, S., Cornelisse, P. G., Rekart, M. L., Montaner, J. S., Schechter, M. T., & O'Shaughnessy, M. V. (1997). Needle exchange is not enough: Lessons from the Vancouver injection drug use study. *AIDS, 11*, F59–F65.

Thompson, P. I., Jones, T. S., Cahill, K., & Medina, V. (1990, June). Promoting HIV prevention outreach activities via community-based organizations. Paper presented at the Sixth International Conference on AIDS, San Francisco.

U.S. Government Accounting Office. (1993). *Needle exchange programs: Research suggests promise as an AIDS prevention strategy. Report to the Chairman, Select Committee on Narcotics Abuse and Control, House of Representatives.* Washington, DC: U.S. House of Representatives.

Wiebel, W., Chene, D., & Johnson, W. (1990, June). Adoption of bleach use in a cohort of street intravenous drug users in Chicago. Paper presented at the Sixth International Conference on AIDS, San Francisco.

Wiebel, W., Jimenez, A., Johnson, W., Ouellet, L., Murray, J., & O'Brien, M. (1993, June). Positive effect on HIV seroconversion of street outreach intervention with IDU in Chicago, 1988–1992. Paper presented at the Ninth International Conference on AIDS, Berlin.

8

COMMUNITY INVOLVEMENT IN HIV/AIDS PREVENTION

SETH C. KALICHMAN, ANTON SOMLAI, AND KATHLEEN SIKKEMA

AIDS is among the greatest threats to global public health, with an estimated 31 million persons infected with HIV, the virus that causes AIDS, and more than 10 million people diagnosed with AIDS have died (World Health Organization, 1999). In the United States, AIDS is one of the leading causes of death among young people. By the middle of 1999, there were more than 700,000 cases of AIDS reported in the United States, and more than 1 million persons are believed to have HIV infection (CDC, 1999). Whereas it took a decade for the first 100,000 cases of AIDS to accumulate, the second 100,000 cases were diagnosed within 2 years, and an additional 400,000 cases were diagnosed shortly thereafter (see Figure 8.1). There are multiple subepidemics of HIV, with most of the early cases in North America occurring among men who had male sex partners and among injection drug users (IDUs). The second wave of the North American AIDS crisis occurred among female sex partners of bisexual men and male drug injectors, as well as other heterosexually active people. HIV/AIDS has therefore amplified faster than any previous disease, surpassing

National Institute of Mental Health Grant R01 MH57624 and Center Grant P30 MH52776 supported the preparation of this chapter.

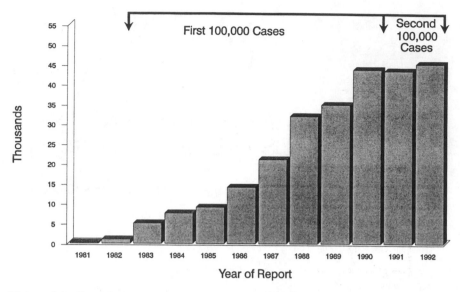

Figure 8.1. Cumulative cases of AIDS showing the first 100,000 in the first decade of the epidemic with rapid increases in cases shortly thereafter (CDC, 1999).

other leading causes of morbidity that have remained relatively stable for the most part (see Figure 8.2).

HIV infection causes impairment of the human immune system. Over the course of years, HIV ultimately disables a person's immune defenses against what would otherwise be benign diseases (for reviews of how HIV causes AIDS, see Kalichman, 1998b, or Schoub, 1993). Although treatments for HIV infection have effectively extended the lives of people infected with HIV, there is no cure for HIV/AIDS. One of the few positive aspects of AIDS, however, is that HIV is only transmitted through a few very specific behaviors that afford the virus direct access to susceptible cells. Thus, to a greater degree than most any other lethal illness, HIV infection can be completely prevented by altering those behavioral practices that lead to infection. Unfortunately, HIV is transmitted by behaviors that are linked to addictive injection drug use and anal and vaginal intercourse, behaviors that pose difficult challenges for behavior change. HIV/AIDS prevention also is complicated by the intersection of AIDS with poverty, which directly and indirectly ties AIDS to numerous other social ills. Further complicating prevention are societal perceptions of the subpopulations most afflicted by the epidemic: men who have sex with men, racial and ethnic minorities, the inner-city poor, substance abusers, homeless people, people with mental illness, and other socially disconnected populations. Thus, AIDS prevention has been as much a social movement for the underserved as it has been a public health campaign.

Indeed, preventing AIDS grew out of community-based, grassroots

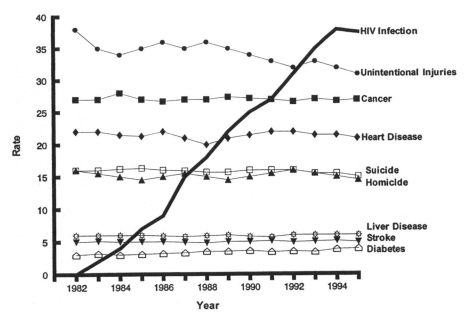

Figure 8.2. Growth of AIDS in young people (ages 25–44) relative to the stable patterns of other leading causes of death (CDC, 1990).

advocacy. The federal government was in the process of withdrawing public support for health and social services in the early days of AIDS (Freudenberg & Zimmerman, 1995). In many cases, government responses to AIDS lagged behind the urgent needs of the epidemic because of public denial, homophobia, racial discrimination, social conservatism, underdeveloped public health policies, and other social factors. For these reasons, grassroots community involvement played a crucial role in initial efforts to prevent the spread of HIV, and communities have remained an important force in AIDS prevention.

In this chapter, we review the landscape of community strategies aimed at preventing the spread of HIV infection. Our review gives special attention to the role that communities have played in preventing AIDS. For our purposes, we define *community* as any collection of persons linked together by a common agenda, in this case preventing AIDS, and unaffiliated to federal, state, or local governmental agencies, academic institutions, or medical establishments. First, we describe the history of HIV prevention, highlighting the role of community groups in early AIDS prevention efforts. Following our review of prevention strategies, we briefly describe three catalysts that have fueled community involvement in HIV prevention: social activism, federal research funding agencies, and the HIV Prevention Community Planning initiative of the Centers for Disease Control and Prevention (CDC). We conclude by discussing the challenges of implementing HIV prevention interventions in schools, inner-city neighborhoods, and community-based agencies, as well as by considering emerging issues for HIV prevention in community settings.

HISTORY OF AIDS PREVENTION

Most epidemiologists and virologists now conclude that AIDS was an unrecognized cause of death in the developing world as early as the 1950s. Nonetheless, AIDS was first identified in 1981 among a few young men living in Los Angeles, California (CDC, 1981). At first a mystery, the disease became associated with homosexual men, leading to such labels as "Gay Cancer," the "Gay Plague," and "Gay-Related Immune Disorder." The new disease was subsequently defined as AIDS, and its cause was determined to be a human retrovirus that requires direct contact with blood or blood-derived body fluids for transmission. Although the disease was soon identified in men and women who share equipment to inject drugs, as well as in other subpopulations, the first attempts to prevent AIDS can be traced to gay communities in New York City, San Francisco, and Los Angeles.

Gay activism emerged out of the civil rights movement that was at its peak in the late 1970s and early 1980s. Gay men's health also gained attention as gay physicians became more visible, particularly addressing epidemics of sexually transmitted diseases (STDs) in gay communities. As gay and lesbian health issues were pushed forward by gay rights advocates, diseases such as rectal and pharyngeal gonorrhea, herpes simplex virus infections, and hepatitis B virus came to the attention of public health agencies. In 1979, for example, the National Coalition of Gay STD Services was formed, which served to foreshadow the first AIDS forum in 1982 organized by the National Gay Task Force, the National Gay Health Education Foundation, and the National Gay Health Coalition (Ostrow, Sandholzer, & Felman, 1983). Gay men therefore appeared well positioned to address an emerging social health crisis. By the early 1980s, however, the political pendulum had swung toward social conservatism, with homophobia and antigay political agendas quickly on the rise. It is therefore no surprise that as gay men fell ill to AIDS, gay communities organized and initiated their own widespread education and prevention efforts (Shilts, 1987). The following is a sampling of self-stated purposes of some of the oldest and largest AIDS prevention organizations.

- The San Francisco AIDS Foundation was founded in 1982 in the Castro district as an emergency response to a quickly emerging health crisis. Its primary purpose was simply to assemble and disseminate critical information to gay men who were being diagnosed with a rare and frightening cancer. As the health crisis grew to epidemic proportions and spread into new populations, the San Francisco AIDS Foundation correspondingly grew and responded to new challenges. Building on its original mission to educate, the foundation added comprehensive services for people living with HIV disease and AIDS and an aggressive public policy component to compel federal and state governments to address the growing epidemic (San Francisco AIDS Foundation, 2000).

- The Gay Men's Health Crisis (GMHC), founded in 1981, is a model for AIDS care, education, and advocacy worldwide. Its mission is to provide compassionate care to New Yorkers with AIDS, to educate to keep people healthy, and to advocate for fair and effective public policies. The GMHC has more than 7,400 clients annually, more than 6,600 volunteers, and more than 169 staff. It has a $28.9 million yearly budget, with 60% from private donors and 26% from government. Volunteers offer services valued at $1.85 million annually. (GMHC, 2000)

- Since its birth in March 1987 in the Lesbian and Gay Community Services Center in downtown Manhattan, the AIDS Coalition to Unleash Power (ACT-UP) has grown to have thousands of members in more than 70 chapters in the United States and worldwide. ACT-UP's nonviolent direct action, often using vocal demonstrations and dramatic acts of civil disobedience, focuses attention on the crucial issues of the AIDS crisis. (ACT-UP, 2000; http://www.actupny.org/documents/capsule-home.html)

AIDS prevention was therefore born from gay activism, with governmental initiatives following the lead of communities to target drug users and adolescents. Thus, as the AIDS epidemic expanded to other populations, so, too, did prevention initiatives.

Looking back, the first generation of AIDS prevention was geared toward raising consciousness and increasing public awareness. Even before sound epidemiology concluded that the new disease was sexually transmitted, gay community organizations were founded to warn men of potential dangers of specific sex acts, with the quality and clarity of information changing as facts became known. The first AIDS prevention interventions primarily consisted of public information forums, educational flyers and brochures, and other attempts to inform large numbers of men in gay communities about the new alarming health condition. Although increasing numbers of men were falling ill each day, no one could imagine how devastating AIDS would become. It was also unknown what was causing the disease. Nonetheless, homosexuality was the common characteristic linking many of the first AIDS cases, so gay communities became widely informed about its threat. The linkages formed among concerned leaders in gay communities often composed the foundation for AIDS organizations and other channels for transmitting new information to communities.

For many gay men, information was sufficient to reduce their practice of unprotected sex. Many were able to make informed decisions as more information became available about what was causing death in their communities. In addition, information about AIDS invoked a sense of fear in many men, therefore motivating behavior change. The virus that causes AIDS was identified 3 years after the first cases of AIDS were diagnosed, paving the way for the second generation of AIDS prevention efforts that hinged on the development of the HIV antibody test. Once available, HIV antibody testing resulted in two dramatic breakthroughs in preventing the spread of AIDS: The test was used to screen blood supplies for HIV contaminated blood, and testing allowed people to know whether they were infected with HIV. Regardless of whether a person tested positive or negative for HIV antibodies, the test seemed to motivate some individuals to reduce their risks for transmitting or contracting the virus. For example, McKusick, Horstman, and Coates (1985) observed reductions in numbers of male sex partners, anal intercourse, and oral intercourse from late 1984 to early 1985 in San Francisco. Rates of rectal gonorrhea in gay men also declined sharply between 1983 and 1984. Several other researchers reported similar reductions in anal intercourse and related markers for sexual transmission risks for HIV infection (CDC, 1985; McCusker, Stoddard, Mayer, Zapka, Morrison, & Saltzman, 1988). Marked changes in sexual risk for HIV transmission in gay communities can, therefore, only be attributed to information, fear, shifts in community norms, and other motivating factors. Such agencies as the San Francisco AIDS Foundation, GMHC, the Los Angeles Gay and Lesbian Center, and the San Diego AIDS Foundation quickly responded by gathering and disseminating information about AIDS.

Of course, not every gay man changed his behavior in response to information and motivational messages. Significant numbers of gay and bisexual men remained at risk for HIV infection. For some men, risk was associated with relationships and perceptions of partners. For others, substance abuse was closely associated with HIV risk behaviors. In addition, gay men and the communities in which they live are not static entities. Younger men who came of age in the era of AIDS were likely affected differently by the prevention messages of the early 1980s than were men who were now 6–10 years their seniors. New models were therefore necessary to affect the behavior of men who either did not reduce their risks for HIV/AIDS or relapsed to unsafe sex following previously successful risk reduction efforts (Kelly, Kalichman, et al., 1991; Kelly, St. Lawrence, & Brasfield, 1991).

Following informational and motivational campaigns, the third generation of HIV prevention interventions focused on building behavioral skills for managing risk-producing situations. Behavioral-skills-building strategies again originated from communities, where public forums were transformed into small group workshops that gathered men together to learn better ways to practice safer sex. For example, the GMHC in New York City, considered the world's first nongovernmental organization committed to AIDS education and research, initiated a series of workshops for men to explore safer sex options for preventing HIV transmission. Similarly, the STOP AIDS Project (1995) was founded in San Francisco and developed innovative workshops for men to learn about AIDS and safer sex options. STOP AIDS groups met in men's homes and were facilitated by community volunteers. These programs included role-play exercises that clearly gave men the opportunity to practice initiating safer sex, negotiating safer sex with partners, and exploring safer sex options. Thus, it was within these intensive, small-group prevention interventions that individuals explored their behavioral options and gained new skills for practicing safer sex (Kalichman, Belcher, Cherry, & Williams, 1997). In addition, guidelines for counseling people who were tested for HIV also centered on assessing personal risks and acquiring risk reduction skills. Thus, HIV prevention efforts that started by informing the masses and motivating changes in attitudes and social norms evolved to include behavioral skills building for individuals who were at greatest risk for HIV infection and those most resistant to changing their risk behaviors.

A similar sequence of prevention programming was seen in the emergence of AIDS in IDUs. The first prevention strategies aimed at IDUs were information based, focusing on the health hazards of using contaminated drugs and needles. Information was widely disseminated through flyers and brochures placed in drug treatment centers and inner-city health clinics. These messages evolved into outreach efforts that relied more on direct communication with drug users to motivate treatment seeking and needle hygiene. After the peak of outreach information efforts, bleach and condom distribution programs were initiated that included skills instruction. Thus, similar to gay, community-based AIDS prevention efforts, prevention for IDUs began with broad-based information campaigns that stimulated motivational preventive messages, leading to the provision of prevention resources, and finally focusing on skills training for specific target behaviors. Unlike the early days of AIDS prevention among gay men, however, prevention for IDUs was supported by government and public health agencies.

As new populations continued to emerge in the AIDS epidemic, a similar progression can be seen in providing information, motivating behavioral changes, providing prevention resources, and building skills for preventive behavior change. The evolution of HIV prevention in communities therefore has reflected the essential elements of successful inter-

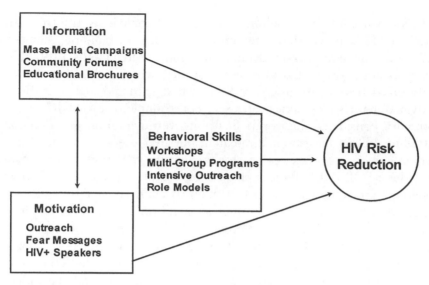

Figure 8.3. The Information–Motivation–Behavioral Skills Model with component features of prevention over the course of the HIV epidemic.

ventions to reduce risk behavior. Fisher and Fisher (1992) formulated a model of HIV prevention based on the notion that information, motivation, and behavioral skills building are necessary elements for effective HIV prevention efforts. The model was rationally derived through a content analysis of behavioral interventions. Figure 8.3 presents a representation of the information–motivation–behavioral skills (IMB) model (Fisher & Fisher, 1992), annotated with examples of community-born prevention strategies. Fisher and Fisher noted that information alone is sufficient for some people to evoke certain types of preventive behaviors. For example, information about HIV testing may be sufficient to prompt some persons to get tested. Also, knowing that a celebrity whom one identifies with has contracted the virus motivates individuals to seek HIV antibody testing (Kalichman, 1994; Kalichman & Hunter, 1992). In addition, some people who have the requisite skills may only need adequate resources and sufficient motivation to enact the use of condoms with specific partners. Nonetheless, regardless of how much people know about AIDS or the degree to which they are motivated to change, individuals who lack risk reduction skills will require skills building to effectively change certain behaviors. Thus, information and motivation work through behavioral skills associated with reducing HIV transmission risk behaviors. Community-initiated HIV prevention efforts therefore captured the essential elements of the IMB model and did so over time as the nature of the AIDS epidemic changed.

The expected outcomes of HIV risk reduction interventions match the needs of target populations at various points in the HIV epidemic.

Prevention goals change as the HIV epidemic evolves. At first, there was a need to educate the masses about AIDS—what it is, how it is transmitted, and who is at greatest risk. Motivational interventions aimed at promoting risk reduction practices and seeking HIV antibody testing were developed and targeted to those people at greatest risk. Third, individuals who remained at risk, whether because they were resistant to change or because they required assistance to change, were targeted for risk reduction behavioral-skills-building interventions. The history of AIDS shows that communities have been involved at every level of prevention throughout its course.

CATALYSTS FOR INVOLVING COMMUNITIES IN HIV/AIDS PREVENTION

As AIDS became a greater threat to the public health, grassroots organizations that were previously established in AIDS-afflicted communities spawned informational, then motivational, and then skills-based prevention oriented responses. Stimulating many early HIV prevention efforts were sociopolitical organizations, such as gay rights activists groups, drug treatment advocates, and inner-city health initiatives. Social activism therefore played key roles in some of the first responses to AIDS. Governmental responses to AIDS have been criticized for lagging behind community-based prevention efforts (Burkett, 1995; Shilts, 1987). Although there are many examples of government agencies that have addressed AIDS prevention, two initiatives provide the clearest involvement of communities at their outset. First, the research agenda set forth by the National Institutes of Health (NIH) incorporated community advocacy in its early inception. Second, community involvement is mandatory in the CDC's HIV prevention efforts, particularly activities included under its HIV Prevention Community Planning process. Social activism, federal research initiatives, and CDC community planning therefore represent three catalysts for involving communities in HIV/AIDS prevention.

Social Activism

Community activists became better organized and more sophisticated as AIDS epidemics have grown. The first financial support to a community agency in San Francisco for AIDS prevention was awarded in 1982 from the San Francisco Department of Health (Amory, 1990). The first well-organized AIDS prevention programs were developed in the early 1980s, just a few years into the AIDS crisis. STOP AIDS, for example, was founded in San Francisco in 1985 based on an innovative approach to bringing gay men together to learn about AIDS. Based on a model akin to the "Tupperware Party," gatherings were held in the homes of volunteers who hosted peer-facilitated groups. The STOP AIDS model focuses on the impact that AIDS has on each individual and calls on community members to take action by answering the question "What will you do to stop AIDS?" (STOP AIDS Project, 1995).

Safer sex workshops were innovated in New York City in the early 1980s. The GMHC (1982) was the first to organize education programs that emphasized techniques for eroticizing safer sex practices. Among the earliest of such workshops was "Hot, Horny, and Healthy," which was a peer-led program delivered in community settings. Group discussions focused on how AIDS was affecting gay men and how men could maintain sensual and erotic sex lives while remaining safe. These first safer sex workshops blended the dissemination of basic information about sexual transmission risks with personal, expressive, and emotionally cathartic discussions of homophobia, sex roles, relationships, and values. Thus, at the heart of the first community-based AIDS prevention initiatives were efforts to educate and motivate behavior change.

The goals of educating gay men about AIDS and raising their AIDS consciousness were achieved by reaching thousands of men who participated in community forums, small media campaigns, and workshops. The messages diffused across gay communities with men subsequently sharing their experiences with friends and sex partners. Men also enrolled in more intensive skills development programs, signaling the shift in focus toward men most resistant to changing HIV risk behaviors. The same lineage of AIDS prevention interventions can be seen in substance abuse populations. Drug treatment advocacy groups in large cities founded outreach teams to inform IDUs of the potential risks. People who shared injection equipment were provided with resources to clean syringes, such as bleach and instructions, and messages were crafted to motivate needle hygiene behaviors. For those who persisted in sharing injection equipment, behavioral skills interventions were developed to further enhance capacities to reduce HIV transmission risks.

The roles of advocacy in community responses to AIDS were not unique to large cities in the United States. As AIDS became a growing problem in Central and East Africa and as AIDS spread in Europe, Australia, Mexico, and Thailand, similar grassroots prevention efforts emerged. For example, the AIDS Service Organization in Uganda was formed to address AIDS in Africa, demonstrating the same level of commitment and action seen in U.S. gay communities (Altman, 1994). More recently, community-based AIDS prevention has been driven by small groups of concerned community members in Russia and other areas of Eastern Europe. For example, one of the first Russian nongovernmental organizations committed to AIDS is An Effective Shield of Prevention (AESOP) Center, a private, nongovernmental, nonprofit agency that supports initiatives in sexual health, including sexuality and sex education, HIV/STD prevention, drug use, family planning, reproductive health, gender issues, antiviolence, and human rights (AESOP Center, 2000). Its mission is to promote the right of every person to receive accurate and up-to-date information about sexual health and related issues—especially the prevention and treatment of HIV/AIDS and other STDs—regardless of nationality, race, ethnicity, religion, creed, language, culture, class, profession, gender, sexual orientation, or age. Thus, as in the United States and elsewhere, nongovernmental organizations were intervening to prevent HIV in Russia before the government was equipped to provide any such response.

Government Research Agencies

Prompted by community advocates and the increasingly serious threat to public health posed by AIDS, federal research agencies, primarily the NIH and the CDC, began stimulating AIDS prevention research. In 1983, for example, the National Institute of Mental Health (NIMH) committed $200,000 to fund AIDS behavioral research, increasing to $76.2 million in 1992 (Auerbach, Wypijewska, & Brodie, 1994). The NIMH focused on funding biomedical research to address behavioral prevention of HIV transmission, as well as psychosocial research concerning people living with HIV/AIDS. The NIMH has been a leader in involving communities in setting research agendas from its earliest days. Of particular importance has been the involvement of communities in setting research priorities, identifying gaps in the prevention literature, and addressing issues of transferring research technologies to community providers. The director of the NIMH has described their AIDS research efforts as follows:

> Our AIDS behavior prevention program—indeed our entire AIDS program, which has been built from the ground up and continues to be run by Dr. Ellen Stover—offers an extraordinary example of how, through the efforts of talented and dedicated individuals, one institute can succeed, can make a difference, and can change policy at the national level, even when working at the crossroads of many stigmas. Our portfolio has had an immense impact on understanding the importance of AIDS behavior prevention. More critically, the scientific yield of this research program is working its way through the highest levels of scientific and policy review and is having dramatic impact on changing national policy. A NIH Consensus Development Conference in 1997 demonstrated convincingly that our HIV risk reduction research portfolio, complemented by research conducted by the National Institute of Drug Abuse [NIDA], other NIH institutes, and the CDC, is absolutely integral to the public health of our nation. (Hyman, 1998, p. 39)

Similar to the NIMH, the NIDA launched its AIDS prevention portfolio in 1983. The NIDA program also grew quickly, allocating $125.3 million in 1992 to AIDS behavioral research compared with $314,000 in 1983. NIDA's AIDS budget increased 31% between 1983 and 1993. NIDA states in its mission that it "supports biomedical research to investigate the interrelationships among HIV infection and effects of drugs of abuse on the immune, endocrine, and central nervous systems" (Auerbach et al., 1994, p. 209). Among NIDA's most visible activities have been the National AIDS Demonstration Research projects that ran from 1987 to 1992 and the Cooperative Agreement for AIDS Community-Based Outreach/ Intervention Research conducted in the early 1990s, both aimed at out-of-treatment substance abusers. In both cases, intervention development and study implementation were conducted in close collaboration with community members. In addition, both NIDA and NIMH fund research centers that require inclusion of community advisory boards in their organizational structures and specific units dedicated to disseminating information to communities. Involving communities in NIH research planning and priority setting has surely improved the applicability of research findings to community settings and has helped to inform researchers of emerging problems in need of study.

There is, however, little evidence that behavioral-sciences-based prevention technologies are used by community services providers. Behavioral-sciences-based prevention is typically disseminated in the form of articles and books, media that are not easily translated for program development. Behavioral science research also is made available to communities through presentations and workshops. Nonetheless, unless sufficiently intensive to allow for acquiring new skills, these forums will not likely result in programmatic changes. That numerous barriers exist in transferring science-based interventions to frontline practice is widely known and not unique to HIV/AIDS prevention (see Beutler, Williams, Wakefield, & Entwistle, 1995; Kalichman, 1998a). Given the long history of discrimination and prejudice toward communities that are also most affected by AIDS it is not surprising that community-based HIV prevention providers meet science-based public health interventions with skepticism. Thus, communities that are involved in HIV/AIDS prevention have not always benefited from prevention research findings either because of typical barriers in technology transfer, community resistance to new technologies, or a poor fit between science-based prevention and community needs.

Prevention Community Planning

The CDC community planning process offers the most direct route for involving communities in HIV prevention. Community involvement is at the heart of its HIV Prevention Community Planning program, as shown in the language of the Comprehensive HIV Prevention Act of 1993, which stated that local and regional groups should be empowered to establish community-based prevention programming (Valdiserri, Aultman, & Curran, 1995). Since 1994, the CDC has worked with state and territorial health departments to restructure federally sponsored HIV prevention practices. HIV Prevention Community Planning requires that priorities be set for intervention strategies based on documented need, science, consumer preferences, and local circumstances (Valdiserri et al., 1995). Community planning was initiated in the 1994 federal budget by including an additional $45 million above the 1993 funding level, allocated specifically for community planning. The process is locally driven by a planning council or planning group, which CDC requires to include community members from demographic groups that represent the populations most affected by AIDS in each jurisdiction, including people who are HIV positive. In addition, a community representative, as well as a representative from local and state health departments, must cochair community planning groups. These groups consider the state's epidemiological data, conduct targeted needs assessments, identify interventions effective for their identified at-risk populations, and set priorities for HIV prevention funding. Key community representatives therefore serve as the advisory group to health departments through the community planning process. Community planning groups are the conduits through which HIV prevention priorities flow from community representatives to both prevention funding agencies and community-based prevention service providers. The explicit goals of HIV Prevention Community Planning are therefore to empower communities in taking leadership roles in HIV prevention and to improve the fit between local needs and the allocation of prevention resources (Franks, Blum, Coates, Morales, & Gibson, 1990). The idea of community planning embodies the value that prevention will be most effective when it comes from inside target communities rather than from outside. As stated by Freudenberg and Zimmerman (1995), "successful community health interventions, particularly those for stigmatized or marginalized groups, should be controlled by organizations that are within the target population's social environment" (p. 186).

Valdiserri et al. (1995) identified the following seven steps as necessary for HIV prevention community planning: (a) assessing the extent and distribution of HIV infection in specific populations, (b) assessing existing community resources for HIV prevention, (c) identifying unmet prevention needs, (d) defining the potential impact of specific strategies and interventions to prevent HIV infections in specific populations, (e) prioritizing HIV prevention needs by specific populations and specific intervention strategies, (f) developing a comprehensive HIV prevention plan, and (g) evaluating the effectiveness of the prevention planning process. In achieving the goals of HIV prevention planning, Valdiserri et al. explicitly noted that community planning must be an inclusive process with representatives who reflect the characteristics of groups affected by the local epidemic. The diversity of people who compose community planning groups surely represents some of the greatest strengths of HIV prevention planning, but by design, the diversity also is intended to create conflict. The open dialogue of differences and the resolution of conflicts between segments of AIDS-affected communities therefore is intended to promote fairness in the allocation of HIV prevention resources. Only through community involvement can these ideals be achieved.

BARRIERS TO COMMUNITY INVOLVEMENT

Community involvement is essential to successful HIV/AIDS prevention. Indeed, the majority of programs designed to reduce HIV risk behaviors have stemmed from grassroots efforts in the communities most affected by AIDS. In light of the many successes in HIV/AIDS prevention, there are many challenges to mobilizing communities to become involved in AIDS prevention. Below we briefly discuss four key barriers to involving communities in AIDS prevention.

Projecting the Trajectories of Epidemics

It is not accurate to discuss a single HIV/AIDS epidemic because there are actually multiple epidemics that vary in geography, genetic diversity, and modes of viral transmission. The complex mosaic of HIV infection complicates prevention planning and therefore requires the involvement of community partnerships in prevention. Local HIV surveillance is an essential step toward community involvement because it provides communities with the most relevant information about their local epidemics. Communicating local surveillance data to community leaders and community-based prevention service providers, through both community planning and direct dissemination channels, can therefore help mobilize communities in AIDS prevention.

Pressing Organizational Capacity and Infrastructure

Community-based HIV/AIDS prevention organizations often lack adequate prevention resources for delivering the most effective interventions. Short staffing, lack of training, inability to reach people at greatest risk, and inadequate tools for evaluating programs are among the barriers that community-based organizations face in launching prevention programs. Funding must therefore be targeted to build organizational capacity rather than for programming alone.

Diminishing Prevention Sources

Health promotion and disease prevention dollars are vulnerable to budget cuts, particularly when there is insufficient evidence for program effectiveness. Of most concern are grassroots agencies, which are closest to the community and therefore offer the most promise for success. Unfortunately, grassroots organizations often have the least resources and the weakest organizational capacity for supporting intensive prevention programs. Shrinking prevention budgets pose the greatest threat to community involvement in AIDS prevention at the local level.

Integrating Prevention With Care

Early in the AIDS crisis, preventing HIV in uninfected people was distinct from services for people living with HIV/AIDS. Nonetheless, care-related services and funding have begun to integrate prevention-related services. Examples of the melding of HIV/AIDS care and prevention include reconceptualizing HIV antibody testing as a diagnostic evaluation rather than a prevention activity, including prevention counseling in case management services for people living with HIV/AIDS and the use of medical treatments for preventing the onset of HIV infection (e.g., post-exposure prophylaxis). Although bringing care and prevention services together will likely increase prevention resources and enhance some prevention-related activities, these benefits will surely come at the expense of community involvement. Thus, communities must meet the ongoing challenge of redefining their roles in the ever-changing landscape of HIV prevention.

CONCLUSION

The greatest successes in HIV/AIDS prevention have occurred through collaborative partnerships between communities affected by AIDS, public health services, and behavioral scientists. The complex social conditions that cultivate HIV epidemics require multiple prevention strategies that embrace community standards and are implemented at multiple levels. Efforts must be concentrated on building capacity of community-based organizations to implement effective behavioral interventions and to build collaborative partnerships between prevention scientists and prevention service providers. Only through such collaborations will sound prevention programs reach those people at greatest risk for HIV/AIDS.

REFERENCES

ACT-UP. (2000, April). [On-line]. Available http://www.actupny.org/documents/capsule-home.html

AESOP Center. (2000, April). *Aesop profile* [On-line]. Available http://www.openweb.ru/windows/aesop/eng/profile.html

Altman, D. (1994). *Power and community: Organizational and cultural responses to AIDS*. London: Taylor & Francis.

Amory, J. W. (1990). A city responds to crisis: Creating new approaches. In S. Petrow (Ed.), *Ending the HIV epidemic* (pp. 65–79). Santa Cruz, CA: Network.

Auerbach, J., Wypijewska, C., & Brodie, K. H. (1994). *AIDS and behavior: An integrated approach*. Washington, DC: National Academy of Medicine.

Beutler, L., Williams, R., Wakefield, P., & Entwistle, S. (1995). Bridging scientist and practitioner perspectives in clinical psychology. *American Psychologist, 50*, 984–994.

Burkett, E. (1995). *The gravest show on earth: America in the age of AIDS*. New York: Houghton Mifflin.

Centers for Disease Control and Prevention. (1981). Pneumocystis pneumonia—Los Angeles. *Morbidity and Mortality Weekly Report, 30*, 250–252.

Centers for Disease Control and Prevention. (1985). Self-reported behavioral change among gay and bisexual men—San Francisco. *Morbidity and Mortality Weekly Report, 34*, 334–339.

Centers for Disease Control and Prevention. (1999). HIV/AIDS Surveillance Report—1999 Mid-Year Edition, Vol. 11, No. 1. Atlanta, GA: Author.

Fisher, J. D., & Fisher, W. A. (1992). Changing AIDS-risk behavior. *Psychological Bulletin, 111*, 455–474.

Franks, P., Blum, H. L., Coates, T. J., Morales, E., & Gibson, P. (1990). Planning and implementing community strategies. In S. Petrow (Ed.), *Ending the HIV epidemic* (pp. 113–130). Santa Cruz, CA: Network.

Freudenberg, N., & Zimmerman, M. (1995). The role of community organizations in public health practice: The lessons from AIDS prevention. In N. Freudenberg & M. Zimmerman (Eds.), *AIDS Prevention in the Community* (pp. 183–198). Washington, DC: American Public Health Association.

Gay Men's Health Crisis. (1982, November). *GMHC Newsletter*. New York: Author.

Gay Men's Health Crisis, (2000, April). GMHC at a glance: Departments and mission [On-line]. Available http://www.gmhc.org

Hyman, S. E. (1998). NIMH during the tenure of Director Steven E. Hyman, M.D. 1996–present: The now and the future of NIMH. *American Journal of Psychiatry, 155*(Suppl. 9), 36–40.

Kalichman, S. C. (1994). Magic Johnson and public attitudes towards AIDS: A review of empirical findings. *AIDS Education and Prevention, 6*, 542–557.

Kalichman, S. C. (1998a). *Preventing AIDS: A sourcebook for behavioral interventions.* Hillsdale, NJ: Erlbaum.

Kalichman, S. C. (1998b). *Understanding AIDS: Advances in treatment and research* (2nd ed.). Washington, DC: American Psychological Association.

Kalichman, S. C., Belcher, L., Cherry, C., & Williams, E. (1997). Primary prevention of sexually transmitted HIV infections: Transferring behavioral research to community programs. *Journal of Primary Prevention, 18,* 149–172.

Kalichman, S. C., & Hunter, T. (1992). Disclosure of celebrity HIV infection: Effects on public attitudes. *American Journal of Public Health, 82,* 1374–1376.

Kelly, J. A., Kalichman, S., Kauth, M., Kilgore, H., Hood, H., Campos, P., Rao, S., Brasfield, T., & St. Lawrence, J. (1991). Situational factors associated with AIDS risk behavior lapses and coping strategies used by gay men who successfully avoid lapses. *American Journal of Public Health, 81,* 1335–1338.

Kelly, J. A., St. Lawrence, J. S., & Brasfield, T. L. (1991). Predictors of vulnerability to AIDS risk behavior relapse. *Journal of Consulting and Clinical Psychology, 59,* 163–166.

McCusker, J., Stoddard, A. M., Mayer, K. H., Zapka, J., Morrison, C., & Saltzman, S. P. (1988). Effects of HIV antibody test knowledge on subsequent sexual behaviors in a cohort of homosexually active men. *American Journal of Public Health, 78,* 462–467.

McKusick, L., Horstman, W., & Coates, T. J. (1985). AIDS and sexual behavior reported by gay men in San Francisco. *American Journal of Public Health, 75,* 493–496.

Ostrow, D. G., Sandholzer, T. A., & Felman, Y. (1983). *Sexually transmitted diseases in homosexual men: Diagnosis, treatment, and research.* New York: Plenum Press.

San Francisco AIDS Foundation. (2000, April). *About SFAF* [On-line]. Available http://www.sfaf.org/history/about.html

Schoub, B. D. (1993). *AIDS and HIV in perspective.* New York: Cambridge University Press.

Shilts, R. (1987). *And the band played on: Politics, people, and the AIDS epidemic.* New York: Penguin.

STOP AIDS Project. (1995). Facilitator training manual. (Available from STOP AIDS San Francisco, 201 Sanchez Street, San Francisco, CA 94114)

Valdiserri, R. O., Aultman, T., & Curran, J. (1995). Community planning: A national strategy to improve HIV prevention programs. *Journal of Community Health, 20,* 87–100.

World Health Organization. (1999). Report on the Global HIV/AIDS Pandemic. New York: UNAIDS and the World Health Organization.

9

SOCIAL AND BEHAVIORAL INTERVENTIONS TO INCREASE BREAST CANCER SCREENING

BARBARA K. RIMER, HELEN MEISSNER, NANCY BREEN,
JULIE LEGLER, AND CATHY A. COYNE

Over the past 10 years, breast cancer screening has increased greatly among women in the United States. Among women ages 50 and older, more than 56% reported having received a clinical breast exam and mammogram (X-ray images of the breast) in the 2 years preceding the 1994 National Health Interview Survey (NHIS), compared with 25% in 1987 (U.S. Department of Health and Human Services [DHHS], 1990). Mammography rates doubled or tripled for most ethnic groups over that period.

In the past decade, the progress that has been made in breast cancer screening is striking. Although it may be impossible to demonstrate a causal relationship, the increase in screening rates surely is a result of a concerted effort by researchers, clinicians, and practitioners. The investments made by the National Institutes of Health (NIH), the Centers for Disease Control and Prevention, the American Cancer Society, and other organizations to conduct research, promote screening, and deliver services have played an important role in the increase in breast cancer screening.

In this review, we examine briefly, and with more emphasis on breadth than depth, the efforts undertaken and chronicled in a decade of published research on breast cancer screening, with an emphasis on mammography use. First, we provide a brief summary of the barriers to mammography use. Then we focus on intervention research, highlighting the behavioral and social sciences theories that have informed interventions. We end with a discussion of the findings and issues. This broad overview is designed to allow researchers and practitioners the opportunity to examine systematically the body of published intervention research in terms of types of interventions, where they were implemented, efforts at translation, and related information. By doing so, we provide a look at where we have been and what opportunities exist for new research. Some excellent meta-analyses are available for readers who want more detailed quantitative data on study and intervention outcomes (Snell & Buck, 1996; Wagner, 1998).

Mammography is the focus of our review of intervention research for several reasons. First, mammography has a particularly solid research base and a history of successful interventions (Rimer, 1994). Much of the research is grounded in the behavioral and social sciences. These interventions have provided the basis for a dramatic increase in the use of mammography over the past decade. Second, practitioners and those in the public health sector need to know where research interventions already have occurred and what types of interventions have been implemented and their impact, to determine where and what kinds of new interventions are needed. Third, research designed to increase adherence to regular mammography has helped increase its use dramatically over the past decade. It is also one of the best examples of the behavioral and social sciences' valuable contributions to health. Behavioral and social scientists have been on the front line of this research by identifying the barriers to mammography use and then developing theory-informed interventions to overcome these barriers. In compiling this review, we aimed to answer the following questions:

- How much research occurred in the past decade?
- Where did the research occur?
- What types of interventions were conducted?
- What behavioral and social sciences theories informed the results?
- Who did the interventions target?
- What can be said about the results of the interventions?
- How have the results been disseminated?

BACKGROUND

This review is limited to breast cancer screening interventions that were conducted in the United States and published from 1988 through

1998. Our major interest was in research designed to encourage use of mammography. The search procedure for identifying articles and abstracting information has been reported previously (Meissner et al., 1998). Briefly, in the detailed section on intervention research, we included articles published from 1987 to 1998 that reported outcomes of interventions designed to increase utilization of mammography in asymptomatic populations. Needs assessments, pilot or feasibility studies for an intervention, and reports of preliminary findings without measures of intervention impact were excluded. Additionally, only reports of intervention studies that used experimental or quasi-experimental research designs were included. These studies are the foundation of evidence-based decision making in cancer control. We identified 51 studies meeting these criteria. In addition to the 51 studies reporting outcomes, we also examined selected articles that described barriers to mammography use. For the examination of barriers, we did not exclude descriptive research.

Rimer's (1994) typology was used to categorize seven mammography intervention strategies: (a) individual directed, (b) system or provider directed, (c) community education, (d) access enhancing, (e) media campaign, (f) social network, and (g) policy level. Some programs used mul tiple strategies, and we highlight these as well. We discuss these categories in more detail later in the chapter.

The mammography research trials have included many target groups, including older women, rural women, and ethnic minorities. We used five different Healthy People 2000 (Healthy People 2000 progress review, 1998; DHHS, 1990) special population targets (slightly modified) for cancer screening (or, in the case of age, modified) to define the following underserved populations: Hispanic, Black, and Native American racial and ethnic groups; those with an annual family income of less than $10,000; those with less than high school education; and those ages 65 and older. We also examined whether investigators reported any cost analysis or efforts to institutionalize their interventions.

BARRIERS TO MAMMOGRAPHY

The first studies of mammography use focused on identifying the barriers to use (Howard, 1987). This work was, and continues to be, important, although the emphasis should evolve to focus on specific groups who are currently underusers. Interventions must overcome women's individual barriers to mammography to be effective. Fox, Roetzheim, and Velt (1997) reviewed the following barriers to mammography: sociodemographic characteristics, factors related to patient–doctor communication, knowledge gaps, physicians or patients' knowledge or attitudes about some aspect of breast cancer screening, and insufficient clinical or community support for education and reminders about screening. Other studies have shown that previous use of the test, number of persons in the household, race, age, income, level of education, and health insurance are important predictors of use (Breen, Kessler, & Brown, 1996; Gaudette, Ahmayer, Nobrega, & Lee, 1996; Harris et al., 1991; Mah & Bryant, 1997; Mandelblatt et al., 1993; Rakowski, Pearlman, Rimer, & Ehrich, 1995; Rakowski, Rimer, & Bryant, 1993; Rimer et al., 1996).

Researchers have documented general barriers to mammography and barriers in specific subgroups of women, such as poor, immigrant, and some minority groups (Dawson & Thompson, 1990; Gaudette et al., 1996; Harris et al., 1991; Lacey et al., 1993; Mayer et al., 1993; McPhee, Stewart, Brock, Jenkins, & Pham, 1997; Suarez, Roche, Nichols, & Simpson, 1997). Although there are differences among these subgroups of women, certain themes predominate. Being a recent immigrant, not having a regular physician, lacking health insurance, and having lower levels of education have been related negatively to breast and cervical screening (Camirand, Potvin, & Beland, 1995; Carney, Dietrich, & Freeman, 1992; MMWR, 1990). Knowledge barriers are important and, for some groups of women, so are access barriers and concerns about pain and radiation (Rimer, 1994). Lack of health insurance may be a significant barrier, particularly in the United States, where a universal health insurance system does not exist. One of the most important barriers to screening is the lack of physician recommendations (Dawson & Thompson, 1990; Harris et al., 1991; Lane, Caplan, & Grimson, 1996; Marchant & Sutton, 1990). There is some evidence that Black women are less likely than other groups of women to be advised by their doctors to get mammograms (Glanz, Resch, Lerman, & Rimer, 1996), even with similar use of primary care (Burns et al., 1996). Conversely, the most important facilitator of mammography is a physician's recommendation (Dawson & Thompson, 1990; Fox et al., 1997; Paskett et al., 1998; Rimer, Keintz, Kessler, Engstrom, & Rosan, 1989).

The general barriers to mammography have been well documented, and there is substantial consistency from one study to another. At this point, neither science nor practice will benefit from additional studies that attempt to identify barriers to mammography in the general population. Surveillance of general population barriers is needed to monitor trends, however. There also may be a need to identify barriers in specific population groups, particularly those who are not being screened on schedule.

TYPES OF INTERVENTIONS

This review is based on research studies of interventions that are designed to increase mammography use. The interventions evolved from earlier descriptive research that identified the barriers to women's use of mammography (Dawson & Thompson, 1990). These interventions have made a major contribution to behavioral intervention research over the past decade. Most of the research teams conducting breast cancer screening interventions have included at least one person with a behavioral sciences background, and many interventions have been grounded in behavioral theories and models, as discussed in a section below.

As noted earlier, we used the typology Rimer (1994) created to categorize mammography interventions, which represent the major strategies used for interventions. We defined seven types of interventions and provide representative examples of studies that used them.

1. Individual-directed interventions have included strategies such as mailed letters and reminders and in-person or telephone counseling (Rimer, 1994). Telephone counseling is an extension of the clinical encounter, a face-to-face occurrence that, at its best, is tailored to the needs of the individual patient. The benefits of telephone counseling have been demonstrated for a large number of topics and with a wide range of populations (McBride & Rimer, 1999). These interventions have been shown to double or triple the odds that women will have mammograms (Snell & Buck, 1996; Wagner, 1998) and, in some cases, are cost effective (King, Rimer, Seay, Balshem, & Engstrom, 1994). Telephone counseling, particularly barrier-specific telephone counseling, has significantly increased the proportion of women who get mammograms (Calle, Flanders, Thus, & Martin, 1993; Champion & Huster, 1995; Davis, Lewis, Rimer, & Harvey, 1997; Janz et al., 1997; King et al., 1994). Although most protocols use humans to deliver the interventions, some use computer-controlled, digitized human voices (Friedman, 1998).

   More recently, tailored letters and other print materials have been used to deliver personalized messages, and they have shown promising results (Drossaert, Boer, & Seydel, 1996; Rakowski, 1999; Rimer et al., 1999; Skinner, Strecher, & Hospers, 1994). Rakowski et al. (1998) found significant increases in mammography use when interventions were both tailored and matched to a woman's stage of readiness to adopt mammography.

   The individual-directed interventions have been informed by such models as the theory of reasoned action, the health belief model (HBM), and the stages of change model (see chapters 1–4 in Glanz, Lewis, & Rimer, 1997).

2. System-directed or provider-directed interventions have been based on the assumption that providers may fail to recom-

mend mammography, not because of a lack of support or commitment, but because they forget. Thus, strategies such as computerized and manual-prompting systems are designed to cue, reinforce, and remind health providers. Systemwide interventions can alter the practice environment to make it more supportive of cancer screening (Burack et al., 1994). The provider-directed strategies have been informed by a number of theories, including the HBM, social learning theory (SLT) and, recently, the stages of change model (Rakowski, 1999).

3. Community education focuses on mammography within the community where women live. In Flynn et al.'s (1997) highly successful intervention study among rural women, a combination of community interventions, including a mobile van and reduced-cost mammograms, resulted in about a 10% difference reported in recent mammography use between the control and comparison communities.

4. Access-enhancing strategies are designed to reduce the impediments to mammography. Such interventions include attempts to lower the costs of mammograms and to make mammograms more accessible, for example, through the use of mobile vans as reported by Rimer et al. (1992). Some of these approaches have been based on the HBM (Strecher & Rosenstock, 1997) and the recognition that women's access barriers may keep them from getting mammograms.

Several studies have reported the efficacy of vouchers and other mechanisms to reduce or remove the cost barrier to screening, increase access, or both. The results are encouraging. When vouchers for free mammograms were added to the usual health instruction in migrant health clinics, women who received the vouchers were found to be 47 times more likely to have had mammograms than women in the control group (Skaer, Robison, Sclar, & Harding, 1996). In an inner-city public hospital clinic, Kiefe, McKay, Halevy, and Brody, (1994) used vouchers to increase mammography use and found that they resulted in about a sevenfold increase in use. Stoner et al. (1998) concluded that a vouchering program, with limited resources, may be more efficient if it focuses on women who are currently out of compliance and women who are financially vulnerable, rather than women who are already getting screened routinely.

5. Media campaigns rely on the use of mass media, alone or in combination with other strategies, to increase mammography use (Rimer, 1994). Mayer et al. (1992) showed that mass

media could increase awareness and heighten intentions about mammography. The A Su Salud project (Ramirez & McAlister, 1988) used more specialized, local media to reach ethnic minorities with messages about mammography. The media campaigns have been based on several theoretical models. To date, SLT (Bandura, 1995) has been the most widely used model.

6. Social network interventions have included the use of peer and lay health advisors who, based on SLT, model the desired behavior while also seeking to overcome women's barriers. Peer leaders and community organization techniques can change social norms regarding breast cancer screening (Eng, 1993; Israel, 1985). For example, the Save Our Sisters Program was designed to increase breast cancer screening among low-income Black women in North Carolina by using Black women to reach others from their community (Eng, 1993). In the A Su Salud program, volunteers reinforced media campaigns (Amezcua, McAlister, Ramirez, & Espinoza, 1990; Ramirez & McAlister, 1988). Senior health advocates were used in Chicago to reach older, low-income women (List, Lacey, Hopkins, & Burton, 1994). Peer leaders may be an important vehicle for reaching underserved women.

    Recently, results of several studies were published that assessed the effectiveness of peer- or lay-led interventions. These strategies have shown mixed results (Suarez, Roche, Pulley, et al., 1997; Sung et al., 1997).

7. Policy level interventions, such as changes in payment for mammography under Medicare, can be an important part of a strategy to overcome cost barriers. There is some evidence that, although these interventions are important and sometimes even necessary for behavior change, they are not sufficient (Rimer et al., 1992).

Multistrategy interventions have been used by a number of investigators. They include continuing medical education and prompting systems; cost reductions; access-enhancing interventions; and interventions aimed at physicians and other providers, individual women, the community, or a combination thereof (Costanza et al., 1992; Fletcher et al., 1993; Trock et al., 1993; Zapka, Chasan, Barth, Mas, & Costanza, 1992; Zapka, Costanza, et al., 1993). In many cases, a combination of interventions is better than one, because multiple levels of intervention can be used to target different groups who can facilitate and reinforce the behavior (e.g., women, providers, and the health care systems).

Generally, more interventions are better than fewer interventions

(Snell & Buck, 1996). Several authors have shown that multistrategy interventions were effective in increasing mammography use within community health centers (Ansell et al., 1994; Rimer, 1994; Zapka et al., 1992). As Fox et al. (1997) concluded, well-structured interventions have increased screening rates in an impressive variety of patient care settings and for patients of varied ethnicities and socioeconomic status. Most of the successful programs around the world have used mailed letters or reminders, targeted outreach, free or reduced-price screening, inreach techniques to facilitate mammograms among women already enrolled at a health care facility, professional education, or some subset of these interventions.

CHARACTERISTICS OF THE MAMMOGRAPHY LITERATURE

In the following sections, we discuss several key features of mammography intervention studies. These include factors such as where the research was conducted, what types of interventions were used and their frequency in the literature, target populations, year of publication, and whether or not there was any discussion of cost effectiveness or attempts to disseminate the intervention. This information provides a picture of the intervention research landscape at the time this analysis was performed.

Location of Interventions

Figure 9.1 shows the interventions that were reported in more than one third of the United States, largely in densely populated states and localities. Many publications reported the state's name only with no other detail. There was one national study, which is not reflected in the map (Anderson, Duffy, Hallett, & Marcus, 1992). Two studies (Grady, Lemkau, Lee, & Caddell, 1997; King et al., 1998) that were implemented in two states are recorded in both states in Figure 9.1.

Frequency of Intervention Types and Target Populations

Rimer's (1994) seven intervention categories were used to group the reported intervention strategies in Table 9.1. We indicated where multiple strategies were used. Table 9.2 shows the study locations and the number of studies targeting underserved populations. It also summarizes interventions according to the combination of strategies used because many studies used more than one approach. Of the 51 studies, 19 targeted underserved populations. Individual-directed strategies, alone or in combination with system- or provider-directed interventions, were used most frequently to target underserved populations.

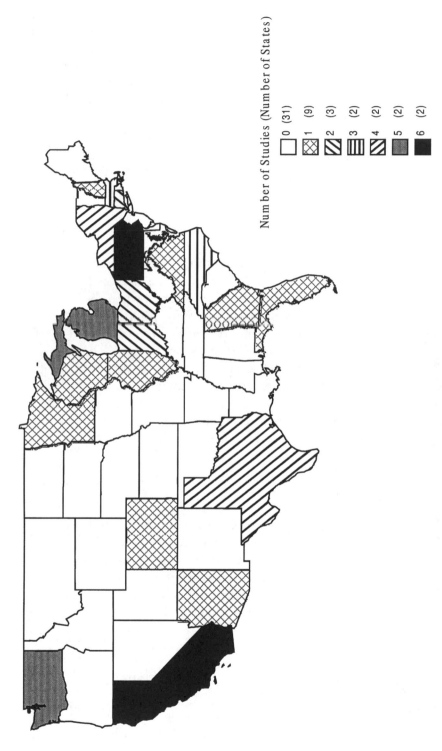

Figure 9.1. Where mammography screening interventions were reported (1988–1998). One national study is not reflected in this map. Two studies were implemented in two states.

Number of Studies (Number of States)

0	(31)
1	(9)
2	(3)
3	(2)
4	(2)
5	(2)
6	(2)

TABLE 9.1
Breast Cancer Screening Intervention Types, 1988–1998

Intervention type	Frequency
Individual directed	27
System or provider directed	26
Community education	10
Access enhancing	8
Media campaign	4
Social network	4
Policy level	0

Note. Multiple intervention types were reported for some studies.

Year of Publication

Scientific information is disseminated through peer-reviewed publications, among other routes. Figure 9.2 displays a time line of the chronological order of publications from studies that reported when the interventions occurred. Fifteen studies reported no intervention dates. The first published mammography screening interventions were conducted in the mid-1980s. The most recently reported study began in 1994. The time line also shows the publication date for each study and the dates of duration; publication occurs about 2.9 years after study completion. The time line therefore represents the accumulated published knowledge about breast cancer interventions for the past decade and indicates that, on average, almost 3 years elapse before a study becomes part of the scientific literature.

Cost Effectiveness and Institutionalization

Information about cost effectiveness and the process of institutionalization is critical to ensure that research results are disseminated into public practice. Documentation of costs is particularly important in a managed care environment in which costs may be scrutinized as closely as is efficacy. Although only seven studies reported either costs or cost effectiveness, recent intervention studies are more likely to include some measure of costs. None of the publications included a discussion of institutionalization. It is possible that such discussion was delayed for other articles.

THEORIES USED TO INFORM RESEARCH

A major contribution to the study of mammography by the behavioral and social sciences has been the application of theory to inform both research and practice (Glanz et al., 1997). This is a critical contribution,

TABLE 9.2
Populations Targeted and Location of Types of Intervention Reported

Intervention type	No. of studies	No. of studies targeting underserved	Study locations
Access enhancing	2	2	MN, WA
Individual directed	15	4	CT, NH, NY, MI, CA, WA, GA, NC, PA, TX, IN
Community education	2		CT, AZ
Individual directed, access enhancing	1	1	TX
Individual directed, community education	1	0	CA
Individual directed, system or provider directed	6	3	MI, WI, PA, OH
Individual directed, system or provider directed, access enhancing	1	1	IL
Individual directed, system or provider directed, access enhancing, community education	1	1	NY
Individual directed, system/provider directed, community education	1	0	WA
Media campaign, individual directed, social network	1	1	TX
Media campaign, social network, community education	1	1	TX
Media campaign, system/provider directed, access enhancing, community education	1	1	NC
Media campaign, system/provider directed, community education	1	0	MA
Social network, community education	1	1	CA
Social network, community education, access enhancing	1	1	NC, PA
System or provider directed	14	1	OH, CO, WA, FL, PA, NY, VA, MI, IN, CA, MA
System or provider directed, access enhancing	1	1	MI

because theory-informed interventions are more likely to be effective. As shown in Table 9.3, a variety of theoretical models have been used in the study of mammography. Some investigators have used different models for different levels of planning and evaluation. This review does not permit an analysis of the utility of the models, and 28 articles did not report any theory. In the literature reported here, the most frequently used theories and models were the HBM, the transtheoretical model, SLT, the theory of reasoned action, prospect theory, and the PRECEDE–PROCEED model.

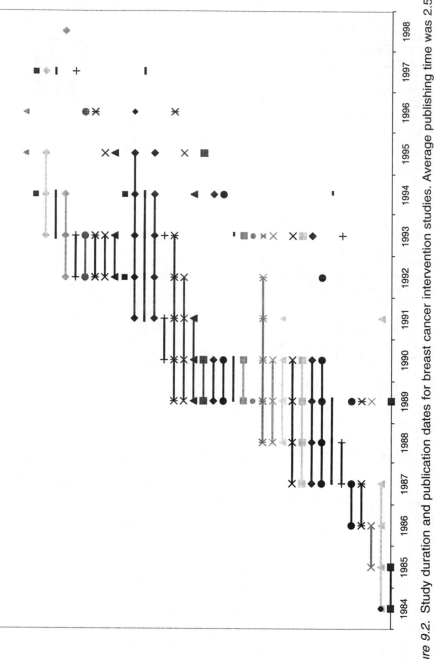

Figure 9.2. Study duration and publication dates for breast cancer intervention studies. Average publishing time was 2.5 years.

TABLE 9.3

Reported Theoretical Basis for Breast Cancer Screening Interventions by Type of Intervention Strategy, 1988–1998

Intervention type	Theory						
	HBM	Trans	Social	Reason	Pros/mess	PRECEDE	Diffusion
Individual directed	6	3	2	1	1	2	1
System/provider directed	4	0	1	0	0	6	1
Community education	2	0	3	0	1	5	1
Access enhancing	0	0	1	0	0	3	0
Media campaign	1	0	2	0	0	2	0
Social network	0	0	3	0	0	1	0

Note. Multiple intervention types and multiple theories were reported for some studies. Dual-task performance theory was cited in one study (Litzelman, Dittus, Miller, & Tierney, 1993) and is not reflected in the table. HBM = health belief model. Trans = transtheoretical model/stages of change. Social = social learning theory. Reason = theory of reasoned action. Pros/mess = prospect and message framing theories. PRECEDE = PRECEDE framework. Diffusion = diffusion of innovations.

In the past few years, researchers have expanded the theoretical basis on which interventions were developed. Rakowski, Fulton, and Feldman (1993) were among the first to extend the transtheoretical or stages of change model to the study of mammography, which is now one of the most widely used because of its application in designing stage and stage-matched interventions (Green & Kreuter, 1989; Rakowski, Fulton, & Feldman; Rakowski et al., 1998; Skinner et al., 1994). Other models, such as Weinstein's (1989) precaution adoption model, are appropriate when response to a risk is a major concern. The best approach to theory is probably an ecological one that uses different theories for different levels of intervention (McLeroy, Steckler, Goodman, & Burdine, 1991).

An examination of Table 9.3 suggests that the theories have been selected in a deliberative manner. For example, although individual-directed interventions have used all the theories, community education interventions have relied more appropriately on SLT and the PRECEDE–PROCEED model (Morisky, Fox, Murata, & Stein, 1989). Social network interventions have been based most often on SLT, again with some logic. At a macro level, there does not seem to be any real mismatch between theories and intervention types. There are a large number of reports that omit any mention of theory, however. Although the social psychological theories used to date are valid and appropriate for many problems and populations, it is appropriate to broaden the theoretical basis as the focus of interventions shifts. For example, theories of organizational change may be useful for studying provider behavior. Similarly, diffusion theories may be helpful in examining the trajectory of mammography behavior at a given point in time (see Glanz et al., 1997, for a fuller discussion of these theories). In addition, theories from other disciplines, such as marketing, sociology, and economics, also may be informative in applying tested intervention strategies to public health practice.

DISCUSSION

Our review of a decade of social and behavioral interventions to improve mammography suggests opportunities for future research. Mammography intervention research has not been distributed evenly or widely across the United States. No published intervention research was reported in 31 states. There are vast areas where no research has been conducted, which should provide a rationale to encourage partnerships between researchers and health care delivery units from different areas. Such research is needed to establish the external validity of interventions. In addition, only about one third of the reported intervention studies focused on underserved populations. This reflects a critical problem, because underuse of mammography increasingly is concentrated in these groups. Moreover, researchers are starting to experience ceiling effects in research that is conducted among more mainstream groups.

Most mammography interventions that were reviewed for this chapter drew from several strategies and their combinations: individual-directed, system- or provider-directed, community education, and access-enhancing interventions. There is now strong documentation suggesting the efficacy of patient reminders, letters, and other provider-directed and patient-directed interventions (Stoner et al., 1998). As intervention research increasingly targets underserved populations, researchers should draw on a wider range of research strategies or different combinations of research strategies, and should focus on populations and geographic areas where intervention research is lacking.

Over the last decade of the 20th century, thousands of women were enrolled in studies designed to increase mammography use. Rates increased dramatically from 1987 through 1996. Yet, there remain many unanswered questions. For example, how intensive or extensive must interventions be to promote mammography (or other cancer screening) effectively and to ensure routine use over time? How can intervention effects be sustained and measured? Here, reports have been mixed (Burack & Gimotty, 1997; Foley, D'Amico, & Merenstein, 1995; Mandelblatt & Kanetsky, 1995), but there are no widely replicated strategies for assuring maintenance. Nonetheless, there is substantial evidence that many women will respond to simple prompts, such as letter reminders (King et al., 1994; Snell & Buck, 1996; Taplin, Anderman, Grothaus, Curry, & Montano, 1994; Wagner, 1998). Reminders should become usual care. In addition, more attention should be paid to maintenance of mammography. Interventions that are effective in motivating initial use or encouraging mammography among nonadherent women may be different from those that are needed to sustain the behavior over time. The preponderance of research has focused on initial mammography use rather than maintenance of mammography over time.

How can we diffuse effective strategies for initiation and maintenance at a population level? How can higher technology interventions, such as tailored communications and computer-based prompting systems, be adapted for public health? Some of the most effective interventions may be too complex and costly to be integrated without adaptation into public health practice. What mechanisms are needed to translate research interventions so that they can be used in public health settings? Future cancer control research should aim to promote both initiation of cancer screening and maintenance over time to have a lasting impact on public health. To be effective, mammography interventions may have to be packaged with other screening or risk factor interventions.

Researchers should address the topics of cost, institutionalization, and dissemination in their publications. There was no mention of institutionalization in the studies that we reviewed. Intervention scientists can help meet the challenges of dissemination by designing studies to evaluate how effective intervention strategies can be used in public health settings. Successful interventions that are never institutionalized represent a long-term loss on research investment. Funding is needed to permit researchers to move research into practice. Clinicians must be provided with useful syntheses and tools that can help them use efficacious interventions, as Scott, Wong, and Rimer (1999) demonstrated. Successful translation of research also demands that, although the public health sector encourages innovative practices, it must base practice on evidence. The lack of cost analyses makes it difficult for health plans and other organizations to determine whether they can adopt a promising strategy.

It has become increasingly clear from research reports that most studies have recruited women who have had prior mammograms. Even researchers who intend to recruit nonadherent women may find that their studies have a disproportionate number of women who have had prior mammograms. This results in both an attenuation of statistical power and a failure to reach the women who could most benefit from intervention. The adherent women should not be ignored, but they are likely to respond to minimal interventions (King et al., 1994). Intensive interventions should be reserved for the women who require them.

One of the greatest challenges for future research will be to reach the women who will benefit most from intervention, especially women who have not adopted mammography—the women referred to in stage models as precontemplators. Among these individuals are those who may have contemplated mammography and decided not to have it and those who are referred to as relapsers, that is, they have had at least one mammogram but are off schedule (Rakowski et al., 1995). Thus, future interventions must focus increasingly on women who are not regular users of the health care system, immigrants, older women, and those with lower levels of education. Strategies such as same-day screening, offered in conjunction with an acute care visit, may increase the likelihood that women will have mammograms (Dolan, McDermott, Morrow, Venta, & Martin, 1999). In addition, several community health center studies have shown the success of combinations of inreach and outreach strategies in promoting mammography (Paskett et al., 1998; Zapka, Costanza, et al., 1993; Zapka, Harris, et al., 1993). The potency of such interventions might be enhanced through the use of tailored print communications (Rimer & Glassman, 1998) and tailored interactive communications (Strecher, Greenwood, & Wang, 1999). Other electronic media, such as culturally sensitive videos played in health center waiting rooms, also have shown promise in reaching underserved women (Yancey, Tanjasiri, Klein, & Tunder, 1995). Increasingly sophisticated techniques are being developed to guide both researchers and investigators in developing theory and evidence-based health education programs (Bartholomew, Parcel, & Kok, 1998). We recommend that these techniques be adopted.

With national surveys showing that 60% or more women ages 50–65 report having mammograms, researchers need to understand what is keeping nonadherent women from getting them. As the focus on research is narrowed to the women who are not getting regular mammograms, new (or revised) theories and interventions may be needed. An Institute of Medicine (1999) report on quality of cancer care stressed the need to understand barriers in these women. There is much to learn about the people whose health we are trying to influence, including what inhibits their use of mammography and how we, as researchers, can encourage breast cancer screening through culturally sensitive, effective interventions that are consistent with women's lives, economic circumstances, and values. The impact of peer leaders and vouchers, in conjunction with community interventions, may be strengthened by combining them with individual- and provider-directed interventions. This would be a promising direction for the next generation of cancer-screening research conducted among underserved populations.

As researchers attempt to motivate nonadherent women to get mammograms by using multiple strategies grounded in communities, the work will be labor intensive, and the effects may be smaller than those found in the earlier mammography studies. Those studies had much less "noise" with which to contend. A growing number of mammography providers and programs can be found in communities throughout the United States. Some of the nonsignificant results that researchers (Suarez, Roche, Pulley, et al., 1997) have found are undoubtedly a result of the "contamination" of control sites. What is good for public health poses new challenges for research.

REFERENCES

References marked with an asterisk indicate studies included in the analyses discussed in the Characteristics of the Mammography Literature section.

*Aiken, L. S., West, S. G., Woodward, C. K., Reno, R. R., & Reynolds, K. D. (1994). Increasing screening mammography in asymptomatic women: Evaluation of a second-generation, theory based program. *Health Psychology, 13,* 526–538.

Amezcua, C., McAlister, A., Ramirez, A., & Espinoza, R. (1990). A Su Salud: Health promotion in a Mexican-American border community. In N. Bracht (Ed.), *Health promotion at the community level* (pp. 257–277). London: Sage.

*Anderson, D. M., Duffy, K., Hallett, C. D., & Marcus, A. C. (1992). Cancer prevention counseling on telephone helplines. *Public Health Reports, 107,* 278–283.

*Ansell, D., Lacey, L., Whitman, S., Chen, E., & Phillips, C. (1994). A nurse-delivered intervention to reduce barriers to breast and cervical cancer screening in Chicago inner city clinics. *Public Health Reports, 109,* 104–111.

Bandura, A. (1995). *Self efficacy in changing societies.* New York: University Press.

*Banks, S. M., Salovey, P., Greener, S., Rothman, A. J., Moyer, A., Beauvais, J., & Epel, E. (1995). The effects of message framing on mammography utilization. *Health Psychology, 14,* 178–184.

Bartholomew, L. K., Parcel, G. S., & Kok, G. (1998). Intervention mapping: A process for developing theory- and evidence-based health education programs. *Health, Education & Behavior, 25,* 545–563.

*Bastani, R., Marcus, A. C., Maxwell, A. E., Das, I. P., & Yan, K. X. (1994). Evaluation of an intervention to increase mammography screening in Los Angeles. *Preventive Medicine, 23,* 83–90.

*Becker, D. M., Gomez, E. B., Kaiser, D. L., Yoshihasi, A., & Hodge, R. H. (1989). Improving preventive care at a medical clinic: How can the patient help? *American Journal of Preventive Medicine, 5,* 353–359.

Breen, N., Kessler, L., & Brown, M. (1996). Breast cancer control among the underserved—An overview. *Breast Cancer Research and Treatment, 40,* 105–115.

Burack, R. C., & Gimotty, P. A. (1997). Promoting screening mammography in inner-city settings. The sustained effectiveness of computerized reminders in a randomized controlled trial. *Medical Care, 35,* 921–931.

*Burack, R. C., Gimotty, P. A., George, J., Simon, M. S., Dews, P., & Moncrease, A. (1996). The effect of patient and physician reminders on use of screening mammography in a health maintenance organization. Results of a randomized controlled trial. *Cancer, 78,* 1708–1721.

*Burack, R. C., Gimotty, P. A., George, J., Stengle, W., Warbasse, L., & Moncrease, A. (1994). Promoting screening mammography in inner-city settings: A randomized controlled trial of computerized reminders as a component of a program to facilitate mammography. *Medical Care, 32,* 609–624.

Burns, R. B., McCarthy E. P., Freund, K. M., Marwill, S. L., Shwartz, M., Ash, A., & Moskowitz, M. A. (1996). Black women receive less mammography even with similar use of primary care. *Annals of Internal M⌐˙ ᵔine, 125*(3), 173–182.

Calle, E. E., Flanders, W. D., Thus, M. J., & Martin, L. M. (1993). ᴜemographic predictors of mammography and pap smear screening in U.S. women. *American Journal of Public Health, 33,* 51–60.

Camirand, J., Potvin, L., & Beland, F. (1995). Pap recency: Modeling women's characteristics and their patterns of medical care use. *Preventive Medicine, 24,* 259–269.

Carney, P., Dietrich, A. J., & Freeman, D. H., Jr. (1992). Improving future preventive care through educational efforts at a women's community screening program. *Journal of Community Health, 17,* 167–174.

*Chambers, C. V., Balaban, D. J., Carlson, B. L., Ungemack, J. A., & Grasberger,

D. M. (1989). Improving the compliance of primary care physicians with mammography screening guidelines. *Journal of Family Practice, 29,* 273–280.

*Champion, V., & Huster, G. (1995). Effect of interventions on stage of mammography adoption. *Journal of Behavioral Medicine, 18,* 169–187.

*Costanza, M. E., Zapka, J. G., Harris, D. R., Hosmer, D., Barth, R., Gaw, V. P., Greene, H. L., & Stoddard, A. M. (1992). Impact of a physician intervention program to increase breast cancer screening. *Cancer Epidemiology, Biomarkers and Prevention, 1,* 581–589.

*Curry, S. J., Taplin, S. H., Anderman, C., Barlow, W. E., & McBride, C. (1993). A randomized trial of the impact of risk assessment and feedback on participation in mammography screening. *Preventive Medicine, 22,* 350–360.

*Davis, N. A., Lewis, M. J., Rimer, B. K., & Harvey, C. M. (1997). Evaluation of a phone intervention to promote mammography in a managed care plan. *American Journal of Health Promotion, 11,* 247–249.

*Davis, N. A., Nash, E., Bailey, C., Lewis, M. J., Rimer, B. K., & Koplan, J. P. (1997). Evaluation of three methods for improving mammography rates in a managed care plan. *American Journal of Preventive Medicine 13,* 298–302.

Dawson, D. A., & Thompson, G. B. (1990). *Breast cancer risk factors and screening: United States, 1987* (DHHS Publication No. PHS 90–1500, pp. 1–33). Hyattsville, MD: U.S. Department of Health and Human Services.

*Dietrich, A. J., & Duhamel, M. (1989). Improving geriatric preventive care through a patient-held checklist. *Family Medicine, 21,* 195–198.

Dolan, N. C., McDermott, M. M., Morrow, M., Venta, L., & Martin, G. J. (1999). Impact of same-day screening mammography availability. *Archives of Internal Medicine, 159,* 393–398.

Drossaert, C. H. C., Boer, H., & Seydel, E. R. (1996). Health education to improve repeat participation in the Dutch breast cancer screening programme: Evaluation of a leaflet tailored to previous participants. *Patient Education Counseling, 28,* 121–131.

Eng, E. (1993). The Save Our Sisters Project: A social network strategy for reaching rural Black women. *Cancer, 72,* 1071–1077.

*Fletcher, S. W., Harris, R. P., Gonzalez, J. J., Degnan, D., Lannin, D. R., Strecher, V. J., Pilgrim, C., Quade, D., Earp, J. A., & Clark, R. L. (1993). Increasing mammography utilization: A controlled study. *Journal of the National Cancer Institute, 85,* 112–120.

*Flynn, B. S., Gavin, P., Worden, J. K., Ashikaga, T., Gautarn, S., & Carpenter, J. (1997). Community education programs to promote mammography participation in rural New York State. *Preventive Medicine, 26,* 102–108.

Foley, E. C., D'Amico, F., & Merenstein, J. H. (1995). Five-year follow-up of a nurse-initiated intervention to improve mammography recommendations. *Journal of the American Board of Family Practitioners, 8,* 452–456.

Fox, S. A., Roetzheim, R., & Velt, C.T. (1997). Barriers to breast cancer screening and strategies to overcome them. In I. Jatoi (Ed.), *Breast cancer screening* (pp. 135–153). Austin, TX: Landes Bioscience.

Friedman, R. H. (1998). Automated telephone conversations to assess health behavior and deliver behavioral intentions. *Journal of Medical Systems, 22,* 95.

*Gardiner, J. C., Mullan, P. B., Rosenman, K. D., Zhu, Z., & Swanson, G. M. (1995). Mammography usage and knowledge about breast cancer in a Michigan farm population before and after an educational intervention. *Journal of Cancer Education, 10,* 155–162.

Gaudette, L. A., Ahmayer, C. A., Nobrega, K. M., & Lee, J. (1996). Trends in mammography screening 1981–1994. *Health Reports, 8,* 17–27.

Glanz, K., Lewis, F. M., & Rimer, B. K. (1997). *Health behavior and health education: Theory, research, and practice.* San Francisco: Jossey-Bass.

Glanz, K., Resch, N., Lerman, C., & Rimer, B. K. (1996). Black-white differences in factors influencing mammography use among employed female health maintenance organization members. *Ethnicity and Health, 1,* 207–220.

*Grady, K. E., Lemkau, J. P., Lee, N. R., & Caddell, C. (1997). Enhancing mammography referral in primary care. *Preventive Medicine, 26,* 791–800.

Green, L., & Kreuter, K. (1989). *Health promotion planning.* Palo Alto, CA: Mayfield.

Harris, R. P., Fletcher, S. W., Gonzales, J. J., Lannin, D. R., Degnan, D., Earp, J. A., & Clark, R. (1991). Mammography and age: Are we targeting the wrong women? A community survey of women and physicians. *Cancer, 67,* 2010–2014.

Healthy People 2000. (1998). Progress Review: Women's Health. Available http://odphp.osophs.dhhs.gov/pubs/hp2000/

*Herman, C. J., Speroff, T., & Cebul, R. D. (1995). Improving compliance with breast cancer screening in older women. Results of a randomized controlled trial. *Archives of Internal Medicine, 155,* 717–722.

*Houts, P., Wojtkowiak, S. L., Simmonds, M. A., Weinberg, G. B., & Heitjan, D. F. (1991). Using a state cancer registry to increase screening behaviors of sisters and daughters of breast cancer patients. *American Journal of Public Health, 81,* 386–388.

Howard, J. (1987). Using mammography for cancer control: An unrealized potential. *CA: A Cancer Journal for Clinicians, 37,* 33–48.

Institute of Medicine and Commission on Life Sciences National Research Council. (1999). *Ensuring quality cancer care.* Washington, DC: Institute of Medicine.

Israel, B. A. (1985). Social networks and cancer screening among older Black Americans. *Health Education Quarterly, 12,* 65–80.

*Janz, N. K., Schottenfeld, D., Doerr, K. M., Selig, S. M., Dunn, R. L., Strawderman, M., & Levine, P. A. (1997). A two-step intervention to increase mammography among women aged 65 and older. *American Journal of Public Health, 87,* 1683–1686.

*Kiefe, C. L., McKay, S. V., Halevy, A., & Brody, B. A. (1994). Is cost a barrier to screening mammography for low-income women receiving Medicare benefits? A randomized trial. *Archives of Internal Medicine, 154,* 1217–1224.

*King, E., Rimer, B. K., Benincasa, T., Harrop, C., Amfoh, K., Bonney, G., Kornguth, P., Denmark-Wahnefried, W., Strigo, T., & Engstrom, P. (1998). Strategies to encourage mammography use among women in senior citizen's housing facilities. *Journal of Cancer Education, 13,* 108–115.

King, E., Rimer, B. K., Seay, J., Balshem, A., & Engstrom, P. F. (1994). Promoting mammography use through progressive interventions: Is it effective? *American Journal of Public Health, 84,* 104–106.

Lacey, L., Whitfield, J., DeWhite, W., Ansell, D., Whitman, S., Chen, E., & Phillips, C. (1993). Referral adherence in an inner city breast and cervical cancer screening program. *Cancer, 72,* 950–955.

Lane, D. S., Caplan, L. S., & Grimson, R. (1996). Trends in mammography use and their relation to physician and other factors. *Cancer Detection and Prevention, 20,* 332–341.

*Lane, D. S., Polednak, A. P., & Burg, M. A. (1991). Effect of continuing medical education and cost reduction on physician compliance with mammography screening guidelines. *Journal of Family Practice, 33,* 359–368.

*Lantz, P. M., Stencil, D., Lippert, M. T., Beversdof, S., Jaros, L., & Remington, P. L. (1995). Breast and cervical cancer screening in a low-income managed care sample: The efficacy of physician letters and phone calls. *American Journal of Public Health, 85,* 834–836.

List, M. A., Lacey, L., Hopkins, E., & Burton, D. (1994). The involvement of low literate elderly women in the development and distribution of cancer screening materials. *Family and Community Health, 17,* 42–55.

*Litzelman, D. K., Dittus, R. S., Miller, M. E., & Tierney, W. M. (1993). Requiring physicians to respond to computerized reminders improves their compliance with preventive care protocols. *Journal of General Medicine, 8,* 311–317.

Mah, Z., & Bryant, H. E. (1997). The role of past mammography and future intentions in screening mammography usage. *Cancer Detection and Prevention, 21,* 213–220.

Mandelblatt, J., & Kanetsky, P. A. (1995). Effectiveness of interventions to enhance physician screening for breast cancer. *Journal of Family Practice, 40,* 162–171.

Mandelblatt, J., Traxler, M., Lakin, P., Kanetsky, P., Thomas, L., Chauhan, P., Matseoane, S., Ramsey, E., & the Harlem Study Team. (1993). Breast and cervical cancer screening of poor, elderly, black women: Clinical results and implications. *American Journal of Preventive Medicine, 9,* 133–138.

*Mandelblatt, J., Traxler, M., Lakin, P., Thomas, L., Chauhan, P., Matseoane, S., & Kanetsky, P. (1993). A nurse practitioner intervention to increase breast and cervical cancer screening for poor, elderly black women. *Journal of General Internal Medicine, 8,* 173–178.

Marchant, D. J., & Sutton, S. M. (1990). Use of mammography—United States. *Morbidity and Mortality Weekly Report, 30,* 621–630.

*Marcus, A. C., Bastani, R., & Reardon, K. (1993). Proactive screening mammography counseling within the Cancer Information Service: Results from a randomized trial. *NCI Monographs, 14,* 119–129.

*Margolis, K. L., & Menart, T. C. (1996). A test of two interventions to improve compliance with scheduled mammography appointments. *Journal of General Internal Medicine, 11,* 539–541.

*Mayer, J. A., Jones, J. A., Eckhardt, L. E., Haliday, J., Bartholomew, S., Slymen, D. J., & Hovell, M. F. (1993). Evaluation of a worksite mammography program. *American Journal of Preventive Medicine, 9,* 244–249.

Mayer, J. A., Kossman, M. K., Miller, L. C., Crooks, C. E., Slymen, D. J., & Lee, C. D., Jr. (1992). Evaluation of a media-based mammography program. *American Journal of Preventive Medicine, 8,* 23–29.

*McAlister, A. L., Fernandez-Esquer, M. E., Ramirez, A. G., Trevino, F., Gallion, K. J., Villareal, R., Pulley, L. V., Hu, S., Torres, I., & Zhang, Q. (1995). Community level cancer control in a Texas barrio: Part II—Baseline and preliminary outcome findings. *Journal of the National Cancer Institute Monographs, 18,* 123–126.

McBride, C. M., & Rimer, B. K. (1999). Using the telephone to improve health behavior and health services delivery. *Patient Education and Counseling, 37*(1), 3–18.

*McCarthy, B. D., Yood, M. U., Bolton, M. B., Boohaker, E. A., Macwilliam, C. H., & Young, M. J. (1997). Redesigning primary care processes to improve the offering of mammography. The use of clinic protocols by nonphysicians. *Journal of General Internal Medicine, 12,* 357–363.

McLeroy, K., Steckler, A., Goodman, R., & Burdine, J. (1991). Theory and practice—Future directions. *Health Education Research, 7,* 1–9.

*McPhee, S. J., Bird, J. A., Fordham, D., Rodnick, J. E., & Osborn, E. H. (1991). Promoting cancer prevention activities by primary care physicians. *Journal of the American Medical Association, 266,* 538–544.

*McPhee, S. J., Bird, J. A., Jenkins, C. N. H., & Fordham, D. (1989). Promoting cancer screening: A randomized controlled trial of three interventions. *Archives of Internal Medicine, 149,* 1866–1872.

McPhee, S. J., Stewart, S., Brock, K. C., Jenkins, C. N. H., & Pham, C. Q. (1997). Factors associated with breast and cervical cancer screening practices among Vietnamese American women. *Cancer Detection and Prevention, 21,* 510–521.

Meissner, H. I., Breen, N., Coyne, C., Legler, J. M., Green, D. T., & Edwards, B. K. (1998). Breast and cervical cancer screening interventions: An assessment of the literature. *Cancer Epidemiology, Biomarkers and Prevention, 7,* 951–961.

MMWR. (Ed.). (1990). Use of mammography—United States, 1990 [Editorial note]. *Morbidity and Mortality Weekly Report, 39,* 621–630.

*Mohler, P. J. (1995). Enhancing compliance with screening mammography recommendations: A clinical trial in primary care office. *Family Medicine, 27,* 117–121.

Morisky, D. E., Fox, S. A., Murata, P. J., & Stein, J. A. (1989). The role of needs assessment in designing a community-based mammography education program for urban women. *Health Education Research, 4,* 469–478.

*Navarro, A. M., Senn, K. L., McNicholas, L. J., Kaplan, R. M., Roppe, B., & Campo, M. C. (1998). Por la vida model intervention enhances use of cancer screening tests among latinas. *American Journal of Preventive Medicine, 15,* 32–41.

Paskett, E. D., McMahon, K., Tatum, C., Velez, R., Shelton, B., Case, L. D., Wofford, J., Moran, W., & Wymer, A. (1998). Clinic-based interventions to promote breast and cervical cancer screening. *Preventive Medicine, 27,* 120–128.

Rakowski, W. (1999). The potential variances of tailoring in health behavior interventions. *Annals of Behavioral Medicine, 21*(4), 284–289.

Rakowski, W., Ehrich, B., Goldstein, M. G., Rimer, B. K., Pearlman, D. N., Clark, M. A., Velicer, W. R., & Woolverton, H. (1998). Increasing mammography among women aged 40–74 by use of a stage-matched, tailored intervention. *Preventive Medicine, 27,* 748–756.

Rakowski, W., Fulton, J. P., & Feldman, J. P. (1993). Stages-of-adoption and women's decision-making about mammography. *Health Psychology, 12,* 209–214.

Rakowski, W., Pearlman, D., Rimer, B. K., & Ehrich, B. (1995). Correlates of mammography among women with low and high socioeconomic resources. *Preventive Medicine, 24,* 149–158.

Rakowski, W., Rimer, B. K., & Bryant, S. A. (1993). Integrating behavior and intention for the study of mammography data from the 1990 supplement to the National Health Interview Survey. *Public Health Reports, 108,* 605–624.

Ramirez, A. G., & McAlister, A. L. (1988). Mass media campaign—A Su Salud. *Preventive Medicine, 17,* 608–621.

Rimer, B. K. (1994). Mammography use in the U.S.: Trends and the impact of interventions. *Annals of Behavioral Medicine, 16,* 317–326.

Rimer, B. K., Conaway, M., Lyna, P., Glassman, B., Yarnall, K. S. H., Lipkus, I., & Barber, L. T. (1999). The impact of tailored interventions on a community health center population. *Patient Education and Counseling, 37*(2), 125–140.

Rimer, B. K., Conaway, M. R., Lyna, P. R., Rakowski, W., Woods-Powell, C. T., Tessaro, I., Yarnall, K., & Barber, L. T. (1996). Cancer screening practices among women in a community health center population. *American Journal of Preventive Medicine, 12,* 351–357.

Rimer, B. K., & Glassman, B. (1998). Tailoring communications for primary care settings. *Methods of Information in Medicine, 37,* 1610–1611.

Rimer, B. K., Keintz, M. K., Kessler, H. B., Engstrom, P. F., & Rosan, J. R. (1989). Why women resist screening mammography: Patient-related barriers. *Radiology, 172,* 243–246.

Rimer, B. K., Resch, N., King, E., Ross, E., Lerman, C., Boyce, A., Kessler, H., & Engstrom, P. F. (1992). Multistrategy health education program to increase mammography use among women ages 65 and older. *Public Health Reports, 107,* 369–380.

*Rimer, B. K., Ross, E., Balshem, A., & Engstrom, P. F. (1993). The effect of a comprehensive breast screening program on self-reported mammography use by primary care physicians and women in a health maintenance organization. *Journal of the American Board of Family Practice, 6,* 443–451.

*Rothman, A. J., Salovey, P., Turvey, C., Fishkin, S. A. (1993). Attributions of responsibility and persuasion: Increasing mammography utilization among women over 40 with an internally oriented message. *Health Psychology, 12,* 39–47.

*Schapira, D. V., Kumar, N. B., Clark, R. A., & Yag, C. (1992). Mammography screening credit card and compliance. *Cancer, 70,* 509–513.

Scott, T. L., Wong, F. L., & Rimer, B. K. (1999, February). Disease management: Dissemination of an evidence-based intervention manual to improve managed care mammography rates. *Managed Care Interface,* 83–90.

*Skaer, T. L., Robison, L. M., Sclar, D. A., & Harding, G. H. (1996). Financial incentives and the use of mammography among Hispanic migrants to the United States. *Health Care for Women International, 17,* 281–291.

*Skinner, C. S., Strecher, V. J., & Hospers, H. (1994). Physician recommendations for mammography: Do tailored messages make a difference? *American Journal of Public Health, 84,* 43–49.

Snell, J. L., & Buck, E. L. (1996). Increasing cancer screening: A meta-analysis. *Preventive Medicine, 25,* 702–707.

*Stoner, T. J., Dowd, B., Carr, W. P., Maldonado, G., Church, T. R., & Mandel, J. (1998). Do vouchers improve breast cancer screening rates? Results from a randomized trial. *Health Services Research, 33,* 11–28.

Strecher, V. J., Greenwood, T., & Wang, C. (1999). Interactive multimedia and risk communication. *Journal of the National Cancer Institute Monographs, 25,* 134–139.

Strecher, V., & Rosenstock, I. (1997). The health belief model. In K. Glanz, F. M. Lewis, & B. K. Rimer (Eds.), *Health behavior and health education: Theory, research, and practice* (pp. 39–62). San Francisco: Jossey-Bass.

Suarez, L., Roche, R. A., Nichols, D., & Simpson, D. M. (1997). Knowledge, behavior, and fears concerning breast and cervical cancer among older low-income Mexican-American women. *American Journal of Preventive Medicine, 113,* 137–142.

*Suarez, L., Roche, R. A., Pulley, L., Weiss, N. S., Goldman, D., & Simpson, D. M. (1997). Why a peer intervention program for Mexican-American women failed to modify the secular trend in cancer screening. *American Journal of Preventive Medicine, 13,* 411–417.

*Sung, J. F. C., Blumenthal, D. S., Coates, R. J., Williams, J. E., Alema-Mensah, E., & Liff, J. M. (1997). Effect of a cancer screening intervention conducted by lay health workers among inner-city women. *American Journal of Preventive Medicine, 13,* 51–57.

*Taplin, S. H., Anderman, C., Grothaus, L., Curry, S., & Montano, D. (1994). Using physician correspondence and postcard reminders to promote mammography use. *American Journal of Public Health, 84,* 571–574.

*Taylor, V. M., Robison, L. M., Sclar, D. A., & Harding, G. H. (1996). Community organization to promote breast cancer screening ordering by primary care physicians. *Journal of Community Health, 21,* 277–291.

Trock, B., Rimer, B. K., King, E., Balshem, A., Cristinzio, C. S., & Engstrom, R. F. (1993). Impact of an HMO-based intervention to increase mammography utilization. *Cancer Epidemiology, Biomarkers and Prevention, 2,* 151–156.

*Urban, N., Taplin, S. H., Taylor, V. M., Peacock, S., Anderson, G., Conrad, D., Etzioni, R., White, E., Montano, D. E., Mahloch, J., & Majer, K. (1995). Community organization to promote breast cancer screening among women ages 50–75. *Preventive Medicine, 24,* 477–484.

U.S. Department of Health and Human Services. (1990). *Healthy People 2000. National health promotion and disease prevention objectives.* (DHHS Publication No. PHS 91–50212). Washington, DC: U.S. Government Printing Office. (Also available http://www.health.gov/healthypeople/)

*Vietri, V., Poskitt, S., & Slaninka, S. C. (1997). Enhancing breast cancer screening in the university setting. *Cancer Nursing, 20,* 323–329.

Wagner, T. H. (1998). The effectiveness of mailed patient reminders on mammography screening: A meta-analysis. *American Journal of Preventive Medicine, 14,* 64–70.

*Weber, B. E., & Reilly, B. M. (1997). Enhancing mammography use in the inner city. A randomized trial of intensive case management. *Archives of Internal Medicine, 157,* 2345–2349.

*Weinstein, N. (1989). Optimistic biases about personal risks. *Science, 246,* 1232–1233.

Yancey, A. K., Tanjasiri, S. P., Klein, M., & Tunder, J. (1995). Increased cancer screening behavior in women of color by culturally sensitive video exposure. *Preventive Medicine, 24,* 142–148.

Zapka, J. G., Chasan, L., Barth, R., Mas, E., & Costanza, M. E. (1992). Emphasizing screening activities in a community health center: A case study of a breast cancer screening project. *Journal of Ambulatory Care Management, 15,* 38–47.

*Zapka, J. G., Costanza, M. E., Harris, D. R., Hosmer, D., Stoddard, A., Barth, R., & Gaw, V. (1993). Impact of a breast cancer screening community intervention. *Preventive Medicine, 22,* 34–53.

Zapka, J. G., Harris, D. R., Hosmer, D., Costanza, M. E., Mas, E., & Barth, R. (1993). Effect of a community health center intervention on breast cancer screening among Hispanic American women. *Health Services Research, 28,* 223–235.

10

INTEGRATING PERSPECTIVES ON THE PREVENTION OF UNINTENTIONAL INJURIES

ANDREA CARLSON GIELEN AND DEBORAH C. GIRASEK

Injuries were responsible for 2.6 million hospital discharges and more than 36 million emergency department visits in 1995 (CDC, 1997). Societal costs of injury-related morbidity and mortality are enormous: an estimated $260 billion in 1995 (Institute of Medicine, 1999). Moreover, an estimated 30% of all years of life lost before age 75 are due to injuries— more than those lost to cancer, heart disease, and stroke (Institute of Medicine, 1999). The epidemiology of fatal injuries has been well described (Baker, O'Neill, Ginsburg, & Li, 1992). We know, for example, that injury death rates vary by age and gender (Figure 10.1). The most frequent mechanisms or causes of these deaths are motor vehicles (29%), firearms (24%), poisoning (11%), falls (8%), and suffocation (7%); drowning, fires and burns, and being cut account for another 9% of deaths (Fingerhut & Warner, 1997). In addition to this classification of injuries by mechanism, injuries are also classified by intent; for example, 98% of the motor vehicle

The authors gratefully acknowledge helpful comments made by Dr. David Sleet on the previous version of this chapter.

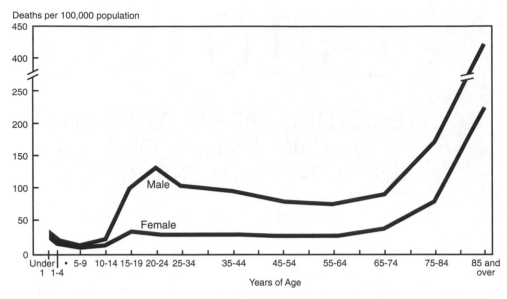

Deaths per 100,000 population

Figure 10.1. Injury death rates by age and gender: U.S., 1995. *Note.* Excludes international classification of disease (Vol. 9, WHO) codes E870–E879 and E930–E949. From *Injury Chartbook, Health, United States 1996–97* (p. 19), by L. A. Fingerhut and M. Warner, 1997.

deaths were unintentional, whereas 97% of all firearm deaths were intentional (Fingerhut & Warner, 1997). The focus of this chapter is on unintentional injuries, which continue to exact a huge toll on society and represent the leading cause of death among individuals from ages 1 to 34 (National Center for Injury Prevention and Control, 1997).

Reducing the burden of injury in this country is a national public health goal and one that requires interdisciplinary perspectives and action. The aim of this chapter is to provide examples of ways in which integrating behavioral sciences and epidemiological approaches can contribute to achieving this goal. First, we present brief historical overviews of advances in the injury control and health promotion fields. We then discuss the integration of behavioral and social sciences within an epidemiological approach to injury control, highlighting selected examples and future research needs.

ADVANCES IN INJURY CONTROL

John Gordon is credited with having observed 50 years ago that injuries could be studied like infectious diseases (Kraus & Robertson, 1992). In 1961, James Gibson advanced this line of reasoning by identifying that the agent of injury, rather than a bacteria or virus, could be thought of as

TABLE 10.1
The Haddon Matrix

	Host (Human)	Vector (Vehicle)	Environment (Physical and Social)
Precrash	Driver vision	Jackknife tendency	Road curvature
Crash	Safety belt use	Vehicle size	Safety belt use laws
Postcrash	Age of occupants	Fuel system integrity	Emergency medical training

Note. Adapted from National Committee for Injury Prevention and Control (1989).

energy (e.g., mechanical, electrical, thermal). William Haddon, Jr., illustrated the ease with which epidemiological approaches could be applied to injury by developing the now widely used Haddon Matrix. The example illustrated in Table 10.1 (only partially developed) demonstrates how the matrix can be applied to injuries related to motor vehicle crashes. Note that the left column relates to the chronological phase of an injury event, which is an important legacy from this era of injury prevention pioneers. They realized that in addition to taking steps to prevent accidents (i.e., injury-producing events), it was possible to prevent injury or death even when such events occur. This reconceptualization of the injury problem greatly expanded options for intervention. Previously, inanimate objects involved in injury causation were viewed as "innocent" and individuals at risk for injury as potentially "guilty." Injury control professionals argued that even if human behavior was the most proximal cause of an injury, it did not necessarily follow that the most efficient or effective preventive strategy was to change behavior (Baker & Teret, 1981; Robertson et al., 1975). Hugh DeHaven was one of the first to note that product design was linked to injury severity (DeHaven, 1942/2000), and as a result considerable effort was spent identifying engineering solutions to injury problems. This work eventually led to the availability of restraints in automobiles, guards on machinery, smoke alarms, and other important technologic innovations for safety.

PASSIVE VERSUS ACTIVE STRATEGIES FOR INJURY CONTROL

With this new understanding of injury causation and countermeasures came arguments over whether the limited injury prevention resources were being wasted on persuasive rather than *passive* strategies (Robertson et al., 1975). Passive strategies are those that require no action on the part of the at-risk individual and include manufacturing all cars with automatic restraint systems and airbags (Haddon & Baker, 1981). Conversely, active strategies require the cooperation of the person to be protected, such as by putting on a life jacket. The advantages of passive systems seem obvious and have resulted in notable injury reductions (e.g., child-resistant packaging of poisons, pedestrian overpasses, etc.).

CONTROVERSIES OVER BEHAVIORAL STRATEGIES IN INJURY CONTROL

The intuitive appeal and successes of passive strategies were bolstered by the absence of behavioral strategies with demonstrated effectiveness. When the concept of accident proneness—originally conceived of as an inherent personality trait that put individuals at special risk for multiple injuries—fell out of favor, behavioral science again lost some currency in injury circles (Matheny, 1987). Calls for "structural approaches" to injury control, which are "not primarily directed toward changing people" were frequently found in the literature (Wilson & Baker, 1987).

The effectiveness of education for behavior change has been described as "one of the most hotly debated issues among . . . safety professionals . . . both in absolute terms and relative to the other types of indirect measures available and *competing for the same countermeasure dollar*" (Johnston, 1992; emphasis added). One of the premises of this chapter is that virtually no change—in structure, design, or environment—is achievable without changing people's behavior. Nichols (1994) argued that education was an important first step in changing public behavior with regard to drunk driving, auto restraint use, and motorcycle helmets. He noted that education of the public and the role of advocacy groups have been effective in promoting passage and enforcement of safety legislation fostering behavior change. Another rationale for a combined behavioral and environmental approach was articulated by Tolsma (1984):

> There seems to be a curious and unproductive debate in certain public health circles. Some advocate bioengineering approaches, others argue for education approaches. The debate is pernicious because it rests on a false premise that we must choose between these strategies, as though they are mutually exclusive. Consider an analogy . . . should we choose to fluoridate water . . . or should we teach families to brush and floss their teeth. Obviously the answer is both. (p. 135)

As Sleet noted at the height of the airbag controversy, even this passive strategy requires the use of an active strategy (i.e., safety belts) for maximum protection (Sleet, 1984).

There is growing recognition among public health professionals and policy makers of the need to invest in the behavioral sciences for future advances in injury control. First, in 1989, the National Committee for Injury Prevention and Control commented that "The limited success of education/behavior change interventions in modifying injury prevention behavior to date may be a result in part of the failure to understand the behavioral causes of injuries and properly apply what is known to develop effective interventions." More recently Runyan (1993) reiterated the need for a "deeper understanding of the role of behavior in injury occurrence and control" to guide decisions about the proper balance between behavioral and environmental interventions. This sentiment has been echoed most recently by the Institute of Medicine's Committee on Injury Prevention and Control (1999),

> Future success of the injury field depends on its ability to broaden its base—by recruiting researchers and collaborators from the behavioral and social sciences—and to incorporate and integrate different ideas and perspectives, while preserving its intellectual bearings and distinct grounding in public health. (p. viii)

ADVANCES IN HEALTH PROMOTION

Parallel with the advances in the scientific understanding of injury as a public health problem were advances in the application of social and behavioral sciences in the field of health education, the mission of which has long been to facilitate healthful behaviors. In this section, we describe briefly the emergence of the field of health promotion from its health education roots, then review the early health education efforts in injury prevention. Finally, we provide examples of how advances in behavioral and social sciences have helped shape contemporary health promotion approaches to injury prevention.

From Health Education to Health Promotion

As early as 1975, there was a growing consensus that health education needed to go beyond simply imparting information and that to intervene successfully to promote health requires attending to "the parameters of social, psychological, cultural, economic and political power" (Richards, 1975, p. 144). Populations at risk could no longer be treated as "empty vessels" to be filled with professional wisdom, and it became clear that understanding a target audience's beliefs, values, desires, and life experiences was essential to designing effective health education programs (Green & Kreuter, 1991). In recognition of the complex determinants of health behavior and health status, the term *health promotion* was coined and defined as "any combination of health education and related organizational, political, and economic interventions designed to facilitate behavioral and environmental changes conducive to health" (Green & Kreuter, 1991, p. 14). This multilevel perspective on health problems and their solutions is reflected in contemporary models of health behavior labeled "ecological" (Green, Richard, & Potvin, 1996; McElroy, Bibeau, Steckler, & Glanz, 1988; Sallis & Owen, 1996; Simons-Morton et al., 1989). Readers interested in more information on specific health behavior theories are referred to Glanz, Lewis, and Rimer (1995).

Applications in Injury Control

Early behavior change efforts in injury control were limited to educational methods that included simply telling people what to do or expecting them to "know better" than to do something dangerous (Berger, 1981; Gielen, 1992). Injury prevention campaigns were characterized as "accident prevention," and consisted almost entirely of "safety education" that frequently relied on fear tactics and victim blaming. One example, from 1919, portrays a man lying in a hospital bed with a bandaged leg stump. The headline reads "Lost his foot through carelessness" (National Safety Council, 1919). An effort in the 1970s aimed at measuring the effects of a series of public service announcements (PSAs) found that they had no impact on observed safety belt use (Robertson et al., 1974). Despite formative research that found perceptions of comfort and convenience were strongly associated with safety belt use, the PSAs utilized the same appeals (e.g., fear, guilt, and stigmatization of the injured) that unsuccessful safety education campaigns had used for decades. In one, a teenage girl is shown sitting in a rocking chair. She says that since the crash, she goes out only on walks with her father, after dark to avoid stares. She then turns to reveal a severely scarred face, while an off-camera announcer pronounces "Car crashes kill two ways: right away and little by little. Wear your safety belts and live." Robertson's well-designed evaluation found no effect of the PSAs on seat belt use. Much of what is known today about the application of communications theory to public health campaigns would have predicted this negative outcome; public service announcements used in isolation are not sufficient for achieving behavior change (Rice & Atkin, 1989).

A recent example from the Netherlands illustrates the notion that achieving positive health behavior change "is difficult and unlikely to be successful when many forces in the social, cultural and physical environments conspire against such change" (Syme, 1992, p. 688). Children were asked to wear bicycle helmets for 6 weeks and then complete questionnaires about their experiences (Seijts, Kok, Bouter, & Klip, 1995). Although participants believed that helmets protected them from brain injury, 97% of children had stopped wearing their helmets three months after the study had ended. Why? Wearers reported they were teased, that their helmets were uncomfortable, and that they had nowhere to store them when they got to their destination. To address such barriers requires more than the education of bicycle riders.

Information targeted to individuals at risk—while usually necessary —is rarely powerful enough to overcome environments that discourage compliance. As one recent health promotion textbook stated, "the importance of using a mix of strategies to prevent and control injuries cannot be overemphasized" (Sleet & Gielen, 1998, p. 259). Results from the bicycle helmet survey suggest that in that case, an effective mix of strategies might be outreach to peers, manufacturers, and retailers, as well as to school and community leaders. Another classic injury prevention program, Children Can't Fly, involved police, emergency room staff, community organizations, and media with the installation of safety devices. It incorporated multiple levels and strategies and dramatically reduced the number of fatal falls from windows among children in New York City (Spiegel & Lindaman, 1977).

The health promotion field has benefited from substantial advances in behavioral and social sciences, which have helped shed light on the determinants of risk behaviors, including injury, and the means by which safety behaviors can be effectively encouraged (Geller et al., 1990; Sleet, 1984; Sleet et al., 1986; Towner, 1995). Research on theories of behavior change, such as social learning theory (also known as social–cognitive theory), have demonstrated the importance of incentives and deterrence, concepts of particular relevance to injury control (Institute of Medicine, 1999; McAlister, 1987). Financial incentives and other rewards for safety behaviors have demonstrated successes, for example, in programs promoting safety belt use. The threat of legal sanctions or punishment has also been found to be effective in areas such as drunk driving, safety belt use, and child restraint devices (Institute of Medicine, 1999). Laws have been characterized as "statements by society of new standards of acceptable behavior," and thus legislation is a means of formalizing societal norms (Hingson & Howland, 1989, p. 64). The sustained deterrence effects of legislation have, in fact, been attributed to "an accumulation of awareness developing into a moral and social commitment to the law" (Rogers & Schoenig, 1994, p. 75).

There are a growing number of examples of the utility of applying a health promotion framework to planning comprehensive injury prevention programs. As early as 1983, the PRECEDE framework (Green & Kreuter, 1991) was used to develop Maryland's statewide child passenger protection program, which combined elements of educating parents about the need to use car safety seats with community organizing to make lower cost seats available and to promote passage of a child restraint law (Eriksen & Gielen, 1983). This health promotion approach to planning injury prevention programs was recommended for wider adoption by Sleet (1987) and in the classic report *Injury Prevention: Meeting the Challenge* (National Committee for Injury Prevention and Control, 1989). The PRECEDE framework has also been used to study adolescent suicide risk (Clarke, Frankish, & Green, 1997) and the use of bicycle helmets (Hendrickson & Becker, 1998). A more detailed description of this approach and its application to an injury prevention program can be found in Gielen and McDonald (1996).

INTEGRATING HEALTH PROMOTION AND INJURY CONTROL

Behavioral and social sciences have and will continue to make meaningful contributions to acheiving injury prevention goals. In this section, we first build a rationale for increasing the attention paid to the role of behavioral sciences. Using the epidemiological framework as a guide, we describe specific roles for behavior change interventions and identify potentially fruitful behavioral science research needs for the future.

Need for Behavioral Sciences

The rationale for a new emphasis on applying behavioral sciences to injury is grounded in several aspects of current injury control problems. First, legislative strategies, a mainstay of much of injury control, often require behavioral compliance by those who are to be protected (e.g., auto restraint use and helmet use). Second, for some injury problems, passive protection is not absolute and requires behavioral adaptation of those who are to be protected. Even when products are designed to provide passive protection, existing unsafe products will still be in circulation (e.g., older cribs), and public education is required. Airbag-related deaths to children in the front seat and the need to transport children in the back seat provides another example: Airbags will continue to provide passive protection in crashes, *"provided that vehicle occupants practice the necessary safe behaviors"* (McLoughlin, 1997, p. 245, emphasis added). Such situations require what has been termed "an active approach to passive protection" (David Sleet, personal communication, November 1999). Finally, for some injury problems, technological or engineering solutions are not readily available (e.g., the multitude of choking hazards for children) or are unacceptable to the public (e.g., four-sided pool fencing) (Shield, 1997; Wintemute & Wright, 1990). Leaders in the injury control field have noted, "When manufacturers resist change . . . skill in dealing with political, social and economic issues is often required" (Kraus & Robertson, 1992, p. 1030). These barriers may in fact represent opportunities for behavioral and social science contributions to injury control.

Roles for Behavior Change Strategies

The widely used epidemiological framework for injury control can be used to identify areas in which behavioral scientists and health promotion professionals can contribute to addressing the host, agent, and environmental determinants of injury risk (Table 10.2). Each of these areas will be briefly described below, with illustrative examples provided and research needs highlighted.

Host

The individuals at risk for injury are typically considered the primary target audience for injury prevention, and messages have focused on their personal risk behaviors. These behaviors can include using personal protective devices, avoiding risky situations, or taking action to modify their own environment. The literature is replete with examples of efforts to educate, persuade, and mandate individual adoption of safer behaviors, such as drinking and driving (Hingson et al., 1996), having working smoke detectors (McLoughlin, Vince, Lee, & Crawford, 1982; Mallonee et al., 1996), and wearing bicycle helmets (Abularrage, DeLuca, & Abularrage, 1997; Dannenberg, Gielen, Beilenson, Wilson, & Joffe, 1993). For reviews of many such interventions, interested readers are referred to Towner (1995) and Gielen and Collins (1993).

Modifying Personal Risk Behaviors. Bicycle helmet use and seat belt use are two examples of addressing host factors. Rivara and colleagues (DiGuiseppi, Rivara, Koepsell, & Polissar, 1993; Rivara et al., 1994) demonstrated that even in the absence of legislation, bicycle helmet use could be significantly increased and head trauma decreased by working with a community coalition to implement a campaign that included educational materials, promotional community events, discount helmet coupons, and school programs. As a result, helmet use increased from 5% to 40% in 5 years, and bike-related head injuries decreased by two thirds. A recent evaluation study in New York reported that public campaigns are essential to reaping the benefits of legislating helmet use (Abularrage et al., 1997).

Nationally, seat belt use rates have increased from 11% in 1980 to 68% in 1996, which has been the result of laws and campaigns (National Safety Council, 1997, 1998). Nichols (1994) contrasted the relative ineffectiveness of early campaigns that promoted voluntary seat belt use with the effectiveness of using both strategies today. As noted previously, the ineffectiveness of early educational efforts may in part be due to the absence of behavior change theory applied to message construction. Today's more sophisticated understanding of social marketing and behavior change theories could well improve educational approaches to individual behavior change efforts, whether these behaviors are voluntary or mandated by law.

TABLE 10.2
Integrating Behavior Change Within the Epidemiological Framework for Injury Control

	Host	Agent/Vehicle	Environment
Target audience for behavior change	At-risk individuals, public at large	Manufacturers, engineers, business leaders	Policy makers, law enforcement officials, engineers, media, health care providers
Behavior change goals	Modify personal risk behaviors Advocate for change in products, environments, and laws	Make safer products Make products easier to use safely Make safety products more accessible	Make safer environments Support and enforce safety legislation Promote public awareness and safety-enhancing social norms
Examples	Auto restraint use, drunk driving, use of safety products	Safer vehicles, child-resistant containers, smoke detectors	Safer highways, auto restraint legislation, helmet legislation, media portrayals of injuries and risk behaviors
Behavioral sciences research needs	Behavior change in groups at highest risk for injury Public perceptions of and support for changes in the agent and environmental determinants of injury	Determinants of decision making regarding safer products	Interventions to influence decision making regarding safety legislation Determinants of successful implementation of laws Influence of media portrayals on social norms and safety behaviors

Even in the context of mandated behavior, however, there is evidence that those at highest risk for injury are least likely to comply with existing laws. For example, auto restraint use among fatally injured drivers is much lower in intoxicated drivers (18%) than in sober drivers (46%) (National Safety Council, 1998). Important areas for future research thus include how to design more effective persuasive campaigns to promote voluntary as well as mandated safety behaviors and how to achieve behavior change in those most at-risk or hard-to-reach segments of society.

Behavioral and social sciences research can contribute by helping to identify the relevant cognitive, attitudinal, perceptual, and psychosocial factors associated with safety behaviors and injury risk, as well as to determine the extent to which they are modifiable. Examples of such factors include risk perceptions and health beliefs (Gielen, Joffe, Dannenberg, Wilson, & Beilenson, 1994; Gielen, Wilson, Faden, Wissow, & Harvilchuck, 1995; Glik, Kroenfeld, & Jackson, 1991; Peterson, Farmer, & Kashani, 1990); the impact of stress under conditions of low social support and coping skills (Smith & Smoll, 1991); overactive, emotionally reactive, and inattentive children, whose parents may be experiencing difficulty managing them (Irwin, Cataldo, Matheny, & Peterson, 1992; Matheny, 1987). The role of parental supervision to reduce children's injury risks is poorly understood and particularly important, given the numerous injury hazards children face that are not amenable to passive intervention (Peterson, Ewigman, & Kilvahan, 1993). A recent Institute of Medicine (1999) report highlighted psychosocial research as one of three promising areas for the injury field and recommended intensified research into "differences in risk perception, risk taking, and behavioral responses to safety improvements among different segments of the population, particularly among those groups at highest risk of injury" (p. 6).

Transforming Hosts Into Advocates for Change. Another approach at the level of modifying the host is to think of individuals as potential allies or agents for change in the other determinants of the injury problem. In this case, the host would be targeted to advocate for changes in the products and environments that increase injury risk. An example of this approach is the history of child passenger safety. Early efforts to increase the use of child safety seats in Maryland included work by health and safety professionals to actively seek out community advocates to establish local child passenger safety associations throughout the state (Eriksen & Gielen, 1983). These partners provided local public education on the importance of child restraints and ultimately were successful in generating widespread support for child restraint legislation, thus changing the social environment to support child passenger safety.

There are many other examples in which individual efforts have led to governmental actions on behalf of safer environments and products. Mothers Against Drunk Driving and more recently established parent-sponsored groups have focused public attention and support for improved drunk driving legislation and for the development of child-friendly airbags. Public health professionals should capitalize on the successes of such approaches and more actively seek out opportunities to facilitate such partnerships with civic and community organizations.

This approach in part depends on having an accurate understanding of what the Institute of Medicine (1999) report described as the "interaction of attitudes toward prevention and personal responsibility in an overall injury prevention strategy" (p. 84). Injury professionals often know little about the public's perceptions of injury or the prevention strategies they advocate. For example, the use of the word *accident* has been eschewed by professionals (and banned in some settings) because of concerns that it suggests to the public that injuries are not preventable; however, a recent national survey found that a majority of adults do associate the notion of preventability with the word (Girasek, 1999). A few studies have shown that public support for an injury countermeasure is directly related to beliefs about its efficacy (Hingson & Howland, 1989; Schenk, Runyan, & Earp, 1985; Wintemute & Wright, 1990). For most injury problems, however, we have no clear sense of what the public knows and believes about alternatives to safe behavior as an injury prevention strategy. Additional behavioral and social science research is needed to better understand the public's perceptions of injury risk, countermeasure effectiveness, and support for product and environmental modifications.

Agent

Many of the leading causes of unintentional injury death in the United States are the outcome of interactions between humans and products. Motor vehicle crash injuries may be the most obvious example of this phenomenon, but falls (e.g., ladders, baby walkers), drowning (e.g., swimming pools, bathtubs), fires and burns (e.g., cigarettes, children's sleepwear, water heaters), poisoning (e.g., cleaning products, medications, lead paint), and choking (e.g., toys, foods) can also be the result of interactions with commercial products. Thus, the behavior of manufacturers, engineers, and business leaders becomes relevant to achieving the goal of safer products. Understanding the factors that influence these behaviors and how to promote safety-enhancing decisions in these target audiences has the potential to prevent many product-related injuries.

Making Products Safer. Successes in this arena are notable (e.g., child-resistant packaging), although we in the injury prevention field tend to have limited knowledge of the process by which they have occurred and, furthermore, how they can be facilitated in the future. That this process is not easily understood is amply demonstrated by the lengthy history of how automobiles were modified with airbags, a process that was influenced by politics, public sentiment, engineering innovations, litigation, and manufacturers' power in the economic arena. Other consumer products come under the purview of the Consumer Product Safety Commission, which can be an important ally in efforts to modify manufacturer behavior. Their 1995 conference "Safety Sells" was an attempt to reach manufacturers with the message that profitability and safety could be mutually obtainable objectives. Another example particularly relevant to behavioral scientists and health educators is toy labeling to reduce choking hazards from small parts. Research that demonstrated how parents' understanding of various warning labels influenced their intentions to purchase a particular toy was used by the study investigators to educate legislators and regulators about the need to change the labeling requirements for small parts (Langlois et al., 1991). Today there are clear warnings about choking hazards, and parents can make better-informed decisions about toy purchases. Arguably, such formative research should be conducted when warning labels are initially devised; nevertheless, this type of research and advocacy after the fact can be a powerful tool for injury prevention.

More adversarial approaches to influencing those who control the extent to which people are exposed to hazardous products are exemplified by strategies such as boycotts and litigation. One study of boycotts aimed at changing corporations' environmental or animal rights policies found that advocates' efforts met with limited success. The authors noted, however, that boycotts were more "media- than market-oriented" (Friedman, 1997), suggesting that this strategy may be more appropriate for raising public awareness and beginning to generate public pressure for change. Another study of how firms respond to pressures to design safer products suggested that in some circumstances lawsuits may be more "motivating" to corporations than is federal regulation (Eads & Reuter, 1983). There is a growing body of literature on litigation as a tool for modifying hazardous products, and interested readers are referred to Christoffel and Teret (1993).

Facilitating the Use of Safety Products. Also widespread in the marketplace are safety products designed specifically to provide protection (e.g., car seats, smoke alarms, security systems, safety gates). Manufacturers and retailers of these products should represent natural allies of injury prevention advocates. Efforts by car seat manufacturers to design seats that are easier to use correctly and by auto manufacturers to make auto restraint systems more accommodating to seats are examples of ways in which the transportation safety, public health, and industry sectors are collaborating to facilitate the availability and use of safety products. Retailers who distribute products also have a role to play in facilitating their safe use. There is little in the literature on the role of retailers in injury prevention, however, and what exists is not encouraging. Personnel who sell children's nightwear and bicycle helmets have been found to possess inadequate knowledge for assisting consumers in making safer purchases (McLoughlin, Langley, Laing, 1986; Plumridge, McCool, & Chetwynd, 1996).

Because products—both hazardous and safety-enhancing—are such important components of injury prevention efforts, it is essential that injury control professionals become educated about the processes by which modifications in their manufacture, distribution, and promotion occur. Case study research methods might be particularly appropriate for improving understanding of some of these issues. Behavioral scientists can contribute to these efforts, for example, by helping to explicate the product-related factors that influence consumer behavior or to design and evaluate consumer education programs for retailers.

Environment

Modifications of the physical and social environment are frequently applied solutions to a variety of injury problems. Examples include modifying roadways to reduce the risk of motor vehicle crashes and pedestrian injuries, legislating the use of safety devices (e.g., auto restraints, smoke alarms, pool fencing), and portrayals in the media of various aspects of the injury problem (e.g., risk-taking behaviors, descriptions of injury events, and coverage of safety-related legislation).

Modifying the Physical Environment. Legal requirements and standards in the construction of roadways, homes, and pools are examples of means to modify the physical environment in support of safety. Identifying such issues and working with the appropriate authorities are challenges that typically require interdisciplinary collaboration. A model for facilitating such collaboration was the Centers for Disease Control and Prevention (CDC) Panel to Prevent Pedestrian Injuries Conference, which brought together public health and transportation safety professionals, educators and psychologists, law enforcement professionals, engineers, and community advocates (CDC, 1998). The utility of modifying the physical environment to promote "walkability" was emphasized as a strategy to enhance pedestrian safety, as was the role of public education as a means to facilitate these changes and promote new social norms. Even in the absence of legislation and regulation, injury control advocates have been successful in modifying the physical environment of playgrounds to make them safer by using community-organizing strategies (Consumer Federation of America Foundation, n.d.). Behavioral scientists and health promotion professionals can contribute to physical environment modifications by careful examination of how pedestrians and children actually behave in the risky environments, how changes in these environments affect risk behaviors, and the process by which coalitions function to effectively implement environmental changes.

Legislation to Promote Environmental Change. Injury control professionals have called for health care providers to play an active role as advocates for legislative changes that promote safety, and in fact they frequently have been the successful initiators of social change (Smith, 1990; Wilson, Baker, Teret, Shock, & Garbarina, 1991). For example, a pediatrician in Tennessee, Dr. Robert Sanders, was the driving force behind the first child restraint law in the United States (National Committee for Injury Prevention and Control, 1989). The child safety seat movement in this country has been influenced greatly by health care providers and their professional organizations, such as the Physicians for Automotive Safety and the American Academy of Pediatrics.

There is a considerable body of knowledge about how best to use the political system to promote change in the physical and social environment and what influences political decision making. For example, politicians have become increasingly sensitive to public opinion in recent years (Jacobs, 1992), and perceived public support has been positively associated with pro-safety votes. In a study of legislators considering a child passenger restraint bill, Jason and Rose (1984) randomly selected half of the legislators to receive a letter containing information on current use patterns, public support for the measure, injury statistics, related economic costs, and another state's experience. Legislators who received the letters were significantly more likely to vote for the bill, a finding that suggests that traditional health education techniques may have the power to influence political leaders. Researchers in Colorado found that the factors that were most strongly associated with supporting safety belt legislation included believing that constituents favored the law, believing that mandatory seat belt laws save lives, and attaching extreme importance to individual freedoms (a negative association) (Lowenstein, Koziol-McLain, Satterfield, & Orleans, 1993). The authors concluded that although valid data is a prerequisite for successful passage of injury control legislation, elected officials interpret such data within "personal, social and political contexts" (p. 791).

It is important to remember that many elected officials join citizens in opposing injury prevention legislation because they "believe strongly in unbridled freedom" (Christoffel & Teret, 1993). In Norway, a form of needs assessment was conducted among public officials who were responsible for transportation policy in that country. Interviewed officials explained that, "no one is praised for the lasting effects of . . . the 'aggregation' of accidents that do not occur" (Koltzow, 1993, p. 654). They also acknowledged the impotence of restricting their prevention activities to changing attitudes, but saw such measures as an honorable way out when charged with protecting public mobility and safety simultaneously (Koltzow, 1993). A related and potentially uncomfortable issue for injury control advocates is the political necessity of compromise; in fact, safety legislation failures have been blamed on advocates' refusal to adopt an incrementalist approach (Carey, Chapman, & Gaffney, 1994).

An obstacle frequently encountered by advocates of passive solutions is the notion of "individual responsibility." American culture appears to place a particularly high value on this notion (Wallack, Dorfman, Jernigan, & Themba, 1993). Little empirical research has been carried out with regard to how political ideology that interferes with the acceptance of injury prevention legislation is formed or can be modified. A thoughtful analysis of the gulf that often separates safety proponents from their opponents can be found in Carey and colleagues' (1994) description of why pool fencing legislation was repealed in New South Wales, Australia. Those interested in using the political process to control injuries should refer to Abraham Bergman's *Political Approaches to Injury Control at the State Level* (1992).

Once passed, legislation must be adequately enforced to be effective. Visible enforcement of safety laws can increase perceptions that punishment is likely to result from noncompliance. Unfortunately, many laws with life-saving potential are not enforced consistently. A study of police and state alcohol control agents attempted to shed light on why public officials were not adequately enforcing purchasing age laws for alcohol. Researchers found that the participants did not perceive strong social norms against underage drinking. They also cited personnel and resource shortages as barriers, as well as dissatisfaction with the penalties imposed by courts (Insurance Institute for Highway Safety, 1996). The literature suggests that law enforcement personnel exercise considerable latitude in choosing among the laws they will enforce (Frank, Fagan, & Ayers, 1987; Pontell, Granite, Keenan, & Geis, 1985; Worden, 1989). Fortunately, however, behaviorally based programs have been successful in increasing the enforcement of public safety laws (Insurance Institute for Highway Safety, 1994), particularly when paired with public education and community support (Lavelle, Hovell, West, & Wahlgreen, 1992). Although we are not aware of evaluated interventions aimed at judges, Mothers Against Drunk Driving does offer its chapters a guide to "court monitoring." Anecdotal reports suggest that advocacy on this level has had a positive effect on how the judicial system responds to drunk driving.

Mass Media as Agents for Social Change. The mass media have many critical roles to play in facilitating changes in the social environment, changes that are relevant to both voluntary and legislated safety behaviors. There have been calls for the mass media to present injury prevention messages through public service announcements, via the news and in risk-related portrayals in the entertainment media (Wilson et al., 1991). The media have been criticized, however, for focusing on individual-level rather than policy-level causes and interventions (Wallack & DeJong, 1995). This approach may reduce public support for people who suffer injuries, and limit media's facilitation of the most powerful prevention strategies.

If the media portrayed public policy initiatives as both contributors to and remedies for America's injury problem, public awareness and involvement might be raised. The natural evolution of many safety laws has been described as one that includes a period in which public education is used to induce a level of voluntary behavior change after which legislation to mandate the behavior becomes politically viable (Johnston, 1992). It also has been pointed out that simply putting a law on the books will not necessarily change behavior or reduce injuries. To be optimally effective, legislation must be accompanied by sustained public information and enforcement (Johnston, 1992; Mock, Maier, Boyle, Pilcher, & Rivara, 1995). The impact of successful legal interventions also should be more widely communicated to the public (Girasek, Gielen, & Smith, 1998), perhaps priming them to support subsequent legislation or resist repeal efforts.

The role of the media in contributing to evolving social norms about risk behaviors is not well understood and merits further study. American society for example seems to now accept drunk driving as a criminal act, while turning a blind eye to speeding. This is evidenced by the glamorization of speed that appears in our automobile advertisements (such ads are outlawed in some European countries) and movies, the legality of radar detectors in many states, and the availability of vehicles that drive in excess of 100 miles per hour. The process by which risk behaviors fall in and out of favor is difficult to measure; it is undoubtedly multifactorial, and it can take years or decades. A better understanding of how social norms about risk behaviors occur, and in particular the role of the media, may allow the acceleration of a movement toward safety and reduced risk.

Using educational strategies to raise consciousness about injury issues has been called, "creating a climate of concern" (Johnston, 1992, p. 376). The potential for using the mass media to direct public attention away from the host (i.e., behavior) and toward the role of the agent and the environment is uncharted territory. Combining the science of injury control with that of health communications could be a powerful force for change in the public's perceptions and support for injury prevention countermeasures. Strategies for utilizing the media to advance political ends and change social conditions can be found in *Media Advocacy and Public Health: Power for Prevention* (Wallack et al., 1993).

Social sciences research can help injury control professionals understand when and how communities or the public will support safety legislation. In addition to the progress made, research is needed on the determinants of successful implementation of safety legislation. There is also a need for behavioral sciences and health communications research to advance the understanding of how to influence both the news and entertainment media's portrayals of injury risks and prevention strategies, as well as the impact of their coverage on such outcomes as personal safety behaviors, social norms, and policy makers.

CONCLUSION

In this chapter, we have attempted to acquaint the reader with the magnitude of the injury problem in the United States and to provide a brief review of progress and challenges in dealing with this major public health problem. As public health professionals consider the nation's health goals for reducing injuries in a new century, the need for an interdisciplinary approach is clear and supported by contemporary injury control literature (Kraus, Peek, & Vimalachandra, 1998). It is encouraging to observe the nexus that has developed between the fields of health behavior and injury control: "those involved in health education should not expect a very brief exposure to a single educational approach to change behavior" (Ferguson, 1998); and "limiting injury prevention strategies to any single aspect of the many causes of injuries is an ineffective and narrow approach" (Kraus et al., 1998, p. 1217).

The interaction of host, agent, and environment suggests a multilevel or ecological model in which the behavior of private citizens, manufacturers, engineers, business leaders, legislators and other policy makers, health care providers, and the media influence the collective perception of injury risk. In injury control, perhaps more so than with other health problems, prevention requires that action be taken by influential individuals in addition to those persons at risk. The behaviors of these key audiences should become a focus for interventionists and researchers alike. The degree to which products and environments can be modified to reduce injury risk depends not just on technology, but equally on the will of the public. It is in this regard that professionals should consider the public as the "center of gravity" for injury prevention programs, providing the balance in government intervention and individual freedom that is required (Green & Kreuter, 1991). For the public to make informed decisions requires that they be enlisted as full partners in finding and implementing solutions. Principles of health promotion practice and behavioral sciences theories can be used effectively to guide these efforts (Sleet & Gielen, 1998; Sleet & Hopkins, in press).

More than 20 years ago social scientists interested in health problems were encouraged to venture into the "strange territory of corporate boardrooms, legislative bodies, and the labyrinthine bureaucracies of governmental regulatory agencies" (Robertson et al., 1975, p. 169). Fifteen years later, health psychology's potential for influencing policy makers was still being described as "untapped" and "striking" (Winett, King, & Altman, 1989). Why the lack of progress? In part, training programs for behavioral scientists may still reflect an *intra*-individual approach that clashes with public health's multilevel perspective. Even within schools of public health, behavioral science training programs may often lack faculty with expertise in economics or political science. Courses in the science of injury control and in advocacy are the exception in academic training programs.

The scientific study of injury, grounded in the well-established principles of epidemiology, has provided direction for future training, research, and policy development. Much is known about the interaction of the host, agent, and environment in producing injury. Public health and transportation safety professionals can claim noteworthy successes in modifying this interaction to reduce injury. Progress in social and behavioral sciences theories and methods has paralleled the advances in injury control. The contribution of these advances to reducing the burden of injury is just beginning to be realized. Future research can help explain the processes of change at the individual and societal levels so that effective injury prevention policies and programs can be widely disseminated.

REFERENCES

Abularrage, J. J., DeLuca, A. J., & Abularrage, C. J. (1997). Effect of education and legislation on bicycle helmet use in a multi-racial population. *Archives of Pediatrics and Adolescent Medicine, 151,* 41–44.

Baker, S. P., O'Neill, B., Ginsburg, M. J., & Li, G. (1992). *The injury fact book* (2nd ed.). New York: Oxford University Press.

Baker, S. P., & Teret, S. P. (1981). Freedom and protection: A balancing of interests. *American Journal of Public Health, 71,* 295–297.

Berger, L. R. (1981). Child injuries: Recognition and prevention. *Current Problems in Pediatrics, 12,* 1–59.

Bergman, A. B. (1992). *Political approaches to injury control at the state level.* Seattle: University of Washington Press.

Carey, V., Chapman, S., & Gaffney, D. (1994). Children's lives or garden aesthetics? A case study in public health advocacy. *Australian Journal of Public Health, 18,* 25–32.

Centers for Disease Control and Prevention. (1997). *Health United States, 1996–1997 and injury chartbook.* Hyattsville, MD: National Center for Health Statistics.

Centers for Disease Control and Prevention. (1998). Conference Binder: Panel to Prevent Pedestrian Injuries Conference. Atlanta, GA: National Center for Injury Prevention and Control.

Christoffel, T., & Teret, S. P. (1993). *Protecting the public: Legal issues in injury prevention.* New York: Oxford University Press.

Clarke, V. A., Frankish, C. J., & Green, L. W. (1997). Understanding suicide among indigenous adolescents: A review using the PRECEDE model. *Injury Prevention, 3,* 126–134.

Consumer Federation of America Foundation. (No date). *Fun and safe, A playground guide for parents.* Washington, DC: Author.

Dannenberg, A. L., Gielen, A., Beilenson, P. L., Wilson, M. H., & Joffe, A. (1993). Bicycle helmet laws and educational campaigns: An evaluation of strategies to increase helmet use by children. *American Journal of Public Health, 83*, 667–674.

DeHaven, H. (2000). Mechanical analysis of survival in falls from heights of fifty to one hundred and fifty feet. *Injury Prevention, 6*, 62–68. (Original work published 1942, in *War Medicine, 2*, 586–596)

DiGuiseppi, C. G., Rivara, F. P., Koepsell, T. D., & Polissar, L. (1993). Bicycle helmet use by children: Evaluation of a community-wide helmet campaign. *Journal of the American Medical Association, 262*, 2256–2261.

Eads, G. C., & Reuter, P. (1983). *Designing safer products: Corporate responses to product liability law and regulation.* Santa Monica, CA: RAND.

Eriksen, M. P., & Gielen, A. C. (1983). The application of health education principles to automobile child restraint programs. *Health Education Quarterly, 10*, 30–55.

Ferguson, K. J. (1998). Community intervention programs. In R. B. Wallace (Ed.), *Public health and preventive medicine* (pp. 81–888). Stanford, CT: Appleton & Lange.

Fingerhut, L. A., & Warner, M. (1997). *Injury chartbook, Health United States, 1996–1997.* Hyattsville, MD: National Center for Health Statistics.

Frank, J., Fagan, M. M., & Ayers, K. A. (1987). Police attitudes toward DUI legislation. *Journal of Police Science and Administration, 15*, 307–320.

Friedman, M. (1997). On promoting a sustainable future through consumer activism. *Journal of Social Issues, 51*, 197–215.

Geller, E. S., Berry, T. D., Ludwig, T. D., Evans, R. E., Gilmore, M. R., & Clarke, S. W. (1990). A conceptual framework for developing and evaluating behavior change interventions for injury control. *Health Education Research, 5*, 125–137.

Gielen, A. C. (1992). Health education and injury control: Integrating approaches. *Health Education Quarterly 19*, 203–218.

Gielen, A. C., & Collins B. (1993). Community-based interventions for injury prevention. *Family and Community Health, 15*, 1–11.

Gielen, A. C., Joffe, A., Dannenberg, A. L., Wilson, M. E., & Beilenson, P. L. (1994). Psychosocial factors associated with the use of bicycle helmets among children in counties with and without helmet use laws. *Journal of Pediatrics, 1224*, 204–210.

Gielen, A. C., & McDonald, E. M. (1996). The PRECEDE–PROCEED planning model. In K. Glanz, F. M. Lewis, & B. K. Rimer (Eds.), *Health behavior and health education: Theory, research and practice* (2nd ed., pp. 359–385). San Francisco: Jossey-Bass.

Gielen, A. C., Wilson, M. E., Faden, R. R., Wissow, L., & Harvilchuck, J. (1995). In-home injury prevention practices for infants and toddlers. The role of parental beliefs, barriers, and housing quality. *Health Education Quarterly, 22*, 85–95.

Girasek, D. C. (1999). How members of the public interpret the word accident. *Injury Prevention, 5*, 19–25.

Girasek, D. C., Gielen, A. C., & Smith, G. S. (1998, May 18). *Public understanding of the injury/alcohol connection.* Poster presented at the Fourth World Conference on Injury Prevention and Control in RAI, Amsterdam, The Netherlands.

Glanz, K., Lewis, F. M., & Rimer, B. K. (1997). *Health behavior and health education: Theory, research and practice.* San Francisco: Jossey-Bass.

Glik, D., Kroenfeld, J., & Jackson, K. (1991). Predictors of risk perceptions of childhood injury among parents of preschoolers. *Health Education Quarterly, 18*, 285–301.

Green, L. W., & Kreuter, M. W. (1991). Health promotion planning: An educational and environmental approach. Mountain View, CA: Mayfield.

Green, L. W., Richard, L., & Potvin, L. (1996). Ecological foundation of health promotion. *American Journal of Health Promotion, 10*, 270–280.

Haddon, W., & Baker, S. P. (1981). Injury control. In D. Clarke & B. MacMahon (Eds.), *Preventive and community medicine* (pp. 109–140). New York: Little, Brown.

Hendrickson, S. G., & Becker, H. (1998). Impact of a theory-based intervention to increase bicycle helmet use in low income children. *Injury Prevention, 4*, 126–131.

Hingson, R., & Howland, J. (1989). Alcohol, injury and legal controls: Some complex interactions. *Law, Medicine & Health Care 17*, 58–68.

Hingson, R., McGovern, T., Howland, J., Heeren, T., Winter, M., & Zakocs, R. (1996). Reducing alcohol-impaired driving in Massachusetts: The Saving Lives Program. *American Journal of Public Health, 86*, 791–797.

Institute of Medicine, Committee on Injury Prevention and Control, Bonnie, R. J., Fulco, C. E., & Liverman, C. T. (Eds.). (1999). *Reducing the burden of injury, advancing prevention and treatment.* Washington, DC: National Academy Press.

Insurance Institute for Highway Safety. (1994). North Carolina safety belt law upgraded and plans set for more traffic law initiatives; Survey shows strong involvement of law enforcement. *Status Report, 29*, 7.

Insurance Institute for Highway Safety. (1996). Enforcement of purchasing age laws often not high priority. *Status Report, 31*, 4.

Irwin, C. E., Cataldo, M. F., Matheny, A. P., & Peterson, L. (1992). Health consequences of behaviors: Injury as a model. *Pediatrics 90*, 798–807.

Jacobs, L. R. (1992). The recoil effect: Public opinion and policy making in the U.S. and Britain. *Comparative Politics, 24*, 199–217.

Jason, L. A., & Rose, T. (1984). Influencing the passage of child passenger restraint legislation. *American Journal of Community Psychology, 12*, 485–495.

Johnston, I. R. (1992). Traffic safety education: Panacea, prophylactic or placebo? *World Journal of Surgery, 16*, 374–378.

Koltzow, K. (1993). Road safety rhetoric versus road safety politics. *Accident Analysis and Prevention, 25,* 647–657.

Kraus, J. F., Peek-Asa, C., & Vimalachandra, D. (1998). Injury control: The public health approach. In R. B. Wallace (Ed.), *Public health and preventive medicine* (pp. 1209–1222). Stamford, CT: Appleton & Lange.

Kraus, J. F., & Robertson, L. S. (1992). Injuries and the public health. In J. M. Last & R. B. Wallace (Eds), *Public health and preventive medicine* (pp. 1021–1034). Norwalk, CT: Appleton & Lange.

Langlois, J. A., Wallen, B. A. R., Teret, S. P., Bailey, L. A., Hershey, J. H., & Peeler, M. O. (1991). The impact of specific toy warning labels. *Journal of the American Medical Association, 265,* 2848–2850.

Lavelle, J. M., Hovell, M. F., West, M. P., & Wahlgreen, D. R. (1992). Promoting law enforcement for child protection: A community analysis. *Journal of Applied Behavioral Analysis, 25,* 885–892.

Lowenstein, S. R., Koziol-McLain, J., Satterfield, G., & Orleans, M. (1993). Facts versus values: Why legislators vote against injury control laws. *Journal of Trauma, 35,* 786–793.

Mallonee, S., Istre, G. R., Rosenberg, M. L., Reddish-Douglas, M., Jordan, F., Silverstein, P., & Tunell, W. (1996). Surveillance and prevention of residential fire injuries. *New England Journal of Medicine, 335,* 27–31.

Matheny, A. P. (1987). Psychological characteristics of childhood accidents. *Journal of Social Issues, 43,* 45–60.

McAlister, A. (1987). Social learning theory and preventive behavior. In N. D. Weinstein (Ed.), *Taking care: Understanding and encouraging self-protective behavior* (pp. 42–53). New York: Cambridge University Press.

McElroy, K. R., Bibeau, D., Steckler, A., & Glanz, K. (1988). An ecological perspective on health promotion programs. *Health Education Quarterly, 15,* 351–377.

McLoughlin, E. (1997). From educator to strategic activist for injury control. *Injury Prevention, 3,* 244–246.

McLoughlin, E., Langley, J. D., & Laing, R. M. (1986). Prevention of children's burns: Legislation and fabric flammability. *New Zealand Medical Journal, 99,* 804–807.

McLoughlin, E., Vince, C., Lee, A., & Crawford, J. (1982). Project Burn Prevention: Outcome and implications. *American Journal of Public Health, 72,* 241–247.

Mock, C. N., Maier, R. V., Boyle, E., Pilcher, S., & Rivara, F. P. (1995). Injury prevention strategies to promote helmet use decrease severe injuries at a Level 1 trauma center. *Journal of Trauma, 39,* 29–35.

National Center for Injury Prevention and Control, & Centers for Disease Control and Prevention. (1997). *10 leading causes of death, United States, 1997.* [Report]. Retrieved May 26, 2000 from the World Wide Web: http://webapp.cdc.gov

National Committee for Injury Prevention and Control. (1989). Injury prevention: Meeting the challenge. *American Journal of Preventive Medicine, 5*, 8.

National Safety Council. (1919, July 28). *Bulletin Board Series, 772.*

National Safety Council. (1998). *Accident facts, 1998 edition.* Itasca, IL: Author.

Nichols, J. L. (1994). Changing public behavior for better health: Is education enough? *American Journal of Preventive Medicine, 10*(Suppl. 1), 19–21.

Peterson, L., Ewigman, B., & Kilvahan, C. (1993). Judgements regarding appropriate supervision to prevent injury. *Child Development, 64*, 934–950.

Peterson, L., Farmer, J., & Kashani, J. H. (1990). Parental injury prevention endeavors: A function of health beliefs? *Health Psychology, 9*, 177–191.

Plumridge, E., McCool, J., & Chetwynd, J. (1996). Purchasing a cycle helmet: Are retailers providing adequate advice? *Injury Prevention, 2*, 41–43.

Pontell, H. N., Granite, D., Keenan, C., & Geis, G. (1985). Seriousness of crimes: A survey of the nation's chiefs of police. *Journal of Criminal Justice, 13*, 1–13.

Rice, R. E., & Atkin, C. F. (Eds.). (1989). *Public communication campaigns.* Newbury Park, CA: Sage.

Richards, N. D. (1975). Methods and effectiveness of health education: The past, present and future of social scientific involvement. *Social Science and Medicine, 9*, 141–156.

Rivara, F. P., Thompson, D. C., Thompson, R. S., Rogers, L.W., Alexander, B., Felix, D., & Bergman, A. B. (1994). The Seattle children's bicycle helmet campaign: Changes in helmet use and head injury admissions. *Pediatrics, 93*, 567–569.

Robertson, L. S., Kelley, A. B., O'Neill, B., Wixom, C. W., Eiswirth, R. S., & Haddon, W., Jr. (1975). Behavioral research and strategies in public health: A demur. *Social Science and Medicine, 9*, 165–170.

Robertson, L. S., Kelley, A. B., O'Neill, B., Wixom, C. W., Eiswirth, R. S., & Haddon, W. (1974). A controlled study of the effect of television messages on safety belt use. *American Journal of Public Health, 64*, 1071–1080.

Rogers, P. N., & Schoenig, S. E. (1994). A time series evaluation of California's 1982 driving-under-the-influence legislative reforms. *Accident Analysis and Prevention, 26*, 63–78.

Runyan, C. W. (1993). Progress and potential in injury control, editorial. *American Journal of Public Health, 83*, 637–639.

Sallis, J. F., & Owen, N. (1996). Ecological models. In K. Glanz, F. M. Lewis, & B. K. Rimer (Eds.), *Health behavior and health education: Linking theory, research and practice* (2nd ed., pp. 403–442). San Francisco, Jossey-Bass.

Schenk, A. P., Runyan, C. W., & Earp, J. A. L. (1985). Seat belt use laws: The influence of data on public opinion. *Health Education Quarterly, 12*, 365–377.

Seijts, G. H., Kok, G. J., Bouter, L. M., & Klip, H. A. (1995). Barriers to wearing bicycle safety helmets in the Netherlands. *Archives of Pediatrics and Adolescent Medicine, 149*, 174–180.

Shield, J. (1997). Have we become so accustomed to being passive that we've forgotten how to be active? *Injury Prevention, 3*, 243–244.

Simons-Morton, B. G., Brink, S. G., Simons-Morton, D. G., McIntyre, R. M., Chapman, M., Longoria, J., & Parcel, G. S. (1989). An ecological approach to the prevention of injuries due to drinking and driving. *Health Education Quarterly, 16*, 397–411.

Sleet, D. A. (1984). Introduction to occupant protection and health promotion. *Health Education Quarterly, 11*.

Sleet, D. A. (1987). Health education approaches to motor vehicle injury prevention. *Public Health Reports, 102*, 606–608.

Sleet, D. A, & Gielen, A. C. (1998). Injury prevention. In S. S. Gorin & J. Arnold (Eds.), *Health promotion handbook* (pp. 247–275). St. Louis, MO: Mosby.

Sleet, D. A., Hollenbach, K., & Hovell, M. (1986). Applying behavioral principles to motor vehicle occupant protection. *Education and Treatment of Children, 9*, 320–333.

Sleet, D. A., & Hopkins, K. (in press). *Behavioral science and unintentional injury prevention* (Draft Proceedings of an International Working Group). Atlanta, GA: Centers for Disease Control and Prevention, National Center for Injury Prevention and Control.

Smith, G. S. (1990). The physician's role in injury prevention. *Journal of General Internal Medicine, 5*(Suppl.), 567–573.

Smith, R. E., & Smoll, F. L. (1991). Behavioral research and intervention in youth sports. *Behavioral Therapy, 22*, 329–344.

Spiegel, C. N., & Lindaman, F. C. (1977). Children can't fly: A program to prevent childhood mortality from window falls. *American Journal of Public Health, 67*, 1143–1147.

Syme, S. L. (1992). Social determinants of disease. In J. M. Last & R. B. Wallace (Eds.), *Public health and preventive medicine* (pp. 687–700). Norwalk, CT: Appleton & Lange.

Tolsma, D. D. (1984). Health promotion approaches to occupant protection: An epidemiologic framework. *Health Education Quarterly, 11*, 133–140.

Towner, E. M. L. (1995). The role of health education in childhood injury prevention. *Injury Prevention, 1*, 53–58.

Wallack, L. M., Dorfman, L., Jernigan, D., & Themba, M. (1993). *Media advocacy and public health: Power for prevention*. Newbury Park, CA: Sage.

Wallack, L., & DeJong, W. (1995). Mass media and public health: Moving the focus from the individual to the environment. In S. Martin (Ed.), *The effects of the mass media on the use and abuse of alcohol* (Publication No. 95-3743). Rockville, MD: National Institutes of Health.

Wilson, M., & Baker, S. P. (1987). Structural approach to injury control. *Journal of Social Issues, 43*, 73–86.

Wilson, M. H., Baker, S. P., Teret, S. P., Shock, S., & Garbarino, J. (1991). *Saving children: A guide to injury prevention*. New York: Oxford University Press.

Winett, R. A., King, A. C., & Altman, D. G. (1989). *Health psychology and public health: An integrative approach.* New York: Pergamon Press.

Wintemute, G. J., & Wright, M. A. (1990). Swimming pool owners' opinions of strategies for prevention of drowning. *Pediatrics, 85,* 63–69.

Worden, R. E. (1989). Situational and attitudinal explanation of police behavior: A theoretical reappraisal and empirical assessment. *Law and Society Review, 23,* 667–711.

III

CONCEPTUAL AND METHODOLOGICAL CONSIDERATIONS IN THE INTEGRATION OF BEHAVIORAL AND SOCIAL SCIENCES WITH PUBLIC HEALTH

11

COMMUNITY MOBILIZATION FOR PREVENTION AND HEALTH PROMOTION CAN WORK

ABRAHAM WANDERSMAN

There are billions of dollars spent annually in the United States on community-directed disease prevention and health promotion activities conducted in schools and communities. No matter how successful research-directed programs are, such "community-directed" prevention reaches millions of people each day. Therefore, building a strong practice of community-directed prevention is the key to influencing the status of public health indicators, such as alcohol, tobacco, and other drug (ATOD) abuse; adolescent pregnancy; youth violence; AIDS; and mental illness.

According to social–ecological models of health and health promotion (e.g., Butterfoss, Wandersman, & Goodman, in press; Stokols, Allen, & Bellingham, 1996), the health of individuals is inextricably linked to the health of communities. The Healthy Cities/Healthy Communities public health movement defines a *healthy city or community* as "one that is continually creating and improving those physical and social environments and strengthening those community resources which enable people to mutually support each other in performing all the functions of life and achieving their maximum potential" (Hancock & Duhl, 1986, as cited in Hancock, 1993, p. 7). The public's health in the 21st century will be heavily influenced by the extent and quality of the programs delivered in schools and communities, and community mobilization is a major mechanism for achieving a healthy community.

In this chapter, I present major concepts about community mobilization, disease prevention, and health promotion. I discuss research-directed and community-directed community mobilization, as well as social–psychological and social–ecological approaches, and I consider community coalitions as a major example of mobilization strategies. Next I illustrate how behavioral and social sciences are making contributions toward more effective community mobilization. First, using coalitions as an example, I show how social science theory and research can be applied to understanding community mobilization at the individual, organizational, and community levels. Second, I illustrate how the behavioral and social sciences can be used to develop interventions that enhance the capacity of organizations for community mobilization and accountability.

COMMUNITY MOBILIZATION, DISEASE PREVENTION, AND HEALTH PROMOTION

There are many types of community intervention programs. Among those that are relevant for this chapter are (a) community-directed and research-directed activities and (b) programs oriented toward social psychology and toward social ecology.

Community- and Research-Directed Programs

As noted, there are prevention programs that are conducted every day in schools and other community settings that reach millions of people. Organizations within the community run these programs (e.g., safe and drug-free school programs, Center for Disease Control and Prevention [CDC] AIDS community prevention planning, maternal and child health programs, Center for Substance Abuse Prevention [CSAP] community coalitions). They generally have little, if any, direct contact with researchers. It is to this type of program that the term *community-directed prevention* (or *community-driven prevention*) generally refers. Community-directed prevention differs from research-directed prevention, which is typically conducted by university or research institute professionals. Typical examples of the latter are community trial interventions, such as the North Karelia study (Puska, Tuomilehto, Nissinen, & Vartianen, 1995; see also chapter 4 in this volume), the Stanford Heart Health study (Farquhar et al., 1990), and COMMIT (Community Intervention Trial for Smoking Cessation; COMMIT Research Group, 1995). These categories represent a typology rather than a dichotomy, and hybrids are possible and encouraged. One example of such a program is the CDC-funded Consortium for Immunization of Norfolk's Children (CINCH), which obtained statistically significant improvement in immunization rates and which began as research directed and evolved into a hybrid collaboration of researchers and government practitioners with community leadership (Butterfoss et al., 1998).

Social Psychology and Social Ecology Interventions

As Goodman, Wandersman, Chinman, Imm, and Morrissey (1996) noted, public health is experiencing a shift in emphasis from social psychology to social ecology. The traditional approach to community health development was grounded largely in social psychology, in which success often is measured in changes in the risk-producing behaviors of individuals (Hawkins & Catalano, 1992; McLeroy, Bibeau, Steckler, & Glanz, 1988; Steckler, McLeroy, Goodman, McCormick, & Bird, 1992). For example, the National Institutes of Health (NIH) funded several large-scale community health studies that extended from social psychology models, including the Stanford Five-Community, the Minnesota Heart Health, and the Pawtucket Heart Health studies (Elder et al., 1986; Farquhar et al., 1985; Jacobs et al., 1986). These projects used a combination of strategies (e.g., mass media, community organization, direct education) directed at different segments of communities (e.g., schools, work sites, physician offices). The project evaluations were directed largely at similar behaviorally based outcomes, however, such as weight reduction; modification of food-buying habits and other diet-related risk behaviors; reduction in blood pressure, cholesterol, pulse rate, smoking, and coronary heart disease; and mortality risk (Mittelmark, Hunt, Heath, & Schmid, 1993). Although reductions in risk-associated individual behaviors are desirable outcomes of community interventions, such changes often depend on larger social changes, that is, alterations in the social ecology (Stokols, 1992; Winett, 1995). Behavior is influenced by multiple factors, including biological, psychological, cultural, and environmental conditions. Therefore, to achieve behavior change, interventions must be directed to each of these levels. In this ecological perspective, the potential to change individual risk behavior is considered within the social and cultural context in which it occurs. Interventions that are informed by this perspective are directed largely at social factors, rather than only at individual motivations and attitudes. Such factors include community norms and the structure of community services, that is, their comprehensiveness, coordination, and linkages.

Community Coalitions

Community coalitions have become popular strategies for mobilizing communities to identify needs and develop solutions for their health problems. They tend to be community-directed and social–ecology oriented. *Community coalitions* have been defined as organizations "of diverse interest groups that combine their human and material resources to effect a specific change the members are unable to bring about independently" (Brown, 1984, p. 4).

Butterfoss, Goodman, and Wandersman (1993) discussed several reasons described in the literature that can explain the promise and popularity of coalitions. Coalitions allow individual organizations to

- become involved in new and broader issues without taking sole responsibility
- demonstrate widespread public support for issues and unmet needs
- maximize power through joint action
- minimize duplication of services
- help mobilize more talents than any one organization has
- provide an avenue for recruiting participants from diverse constituencies (business, schools, media).

Coalitions are widely used in public health. Some examples include CSAP, which has funded 250 community partnerships throughout the United States; the Fighting Back substance abuse programs funded by the Robert Wood Johnson Foundation; a newer generation of 10-year coalitions, America's Promise, begun with Robert Wood Johnson Foundation funding; SAFE KIDS, which are local, state, and national coalitions to prevent childhood injuries that are supported by Johnson and Johnson; the National Cancer Institute's COMMIT and ASSIST (American Stop Smoking Intervention Study) community tobacco control programs funded by the NIH; the PATCH (Planned Approach To Community Health programs) cardiovascular health promotion program funded by the CDC; the Native American health promotion efforts sponsored by the U.S. Office of Minority Health; the Health Resources and Service Administration's (HRSA's) Healthy Start program; and the AIDS community prevention planning program sponsored by CDC.

Stages

Butterfoss, Goodman, and Wandersman (1993) discussed coalition functioning by describing stages of development. These stages include formation, implementation, maintenance, and the accomplishment of goals or outcomes. Figure 11.1 illustrates a general model that is used for their development. It is an example based on work developed with CSAP coalitions (Goodman & Wandersman, 1994). The formation stage occurs at the initiation of the funding. The agency that is granted the funding (lead agency) convenes an ad hoc committee of local community leaders. The

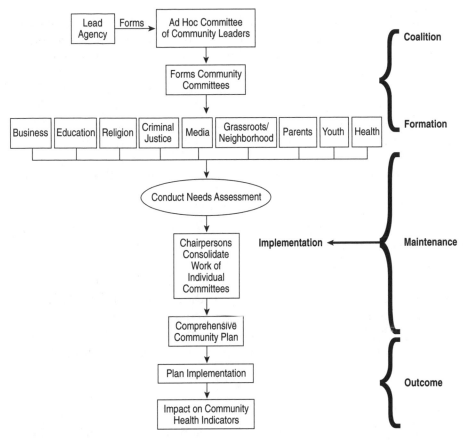

Figure 11.1. Overview of the development of a community coalition.

committee nominates influential citizens to serve on committees representing health care, business, education, religion, criminal justice, neighborhood organizations, the media, and other sectors of the community. Training on prevention goals, issues, and tasks takes place. The implementation stage occurs as each of the committees conducts a needs assessment to determine the extent and nature of its constituents' concerns and resources in regard to ATOD abuse. The needs assessment consists of archival data, as well as written questionnaires, town meetings, and interviews that are developed and conducted by the committees with input from the staff and evaluation teams. Implementation continues with committees using the results of the needs assessment to develop a community-wide intervention plan. The maintenance stage consists of the monitoring and upkeep of the committees and their planned activities. The outcome stage includes the evaluation of the impact of the prevention programs and strategies.

The coalition literature is relatively new and growing. There are additional frameworks of coalition structure and function (e.g., Hawkins & Catalano, 1992; Yin, Kaftarian, & Jacobs, 1996).

Some coalitions work well. A number of coalitions have had significant impact on community health indicators. Hingson et al. (1996) reported on the Saving Lives program in Massachusetts in which community coalitions of multiple city departments and private citizens engaged in program initiatives to reduce drunk driving and speeding. They found that as a result of coalition initiatives, the number of alcohol-impaired driving accidents, injuries, and deaths was significantly lower than in comparison communities. Another example of a successful coalition is the Gloucester (Massachusetts) Prevention Network, funded by CSAP. This program accomplished significant longitudinal changes in substance abuse outcomes among high school students, compared with national data trends (Shaw, Rosati, Salzman, Coles, & McGeary, 1997).

Nonetheless, many evaluations of coalitions have shown only modest evidence of outcomes and impacts. In a thoughtful review for the HRSA, Kreuter and Levin (1998) asked "Are consortia/collaboratives effective in changing health status and health systems?" Their answer, in short, was that there is some positive evidence that they work, and they provided six examples from the literature. They also concluded that there are many challenges and unrealistic expectations. Cross-site evaluations of multisite coalition interventions (e.g., Yin, Kaftarian, Yu, & Jansen, 1997) have shown a similar pattern of results.

Showing Results

The process and outcomes of community coalitions are very challenging (as suggested above). To follow are several reasons why it is difficult for coalitions to show results.

Process. Collaboration has been called "an unnatural act between unconsenting adults" (Wandersman, Goodman, & Butterfoss, 1997). Although this statement was made somewhat in jest, it is clear that the process of developing and implementing a coalition is complex. Wandersman et al. (1997) have used an open-systems framework to describe coalitions as organizations that require resources, organizational structure, activities, and outcomes. The framework suggests that coalitions are complex organizations that involve different partners to address complex issues and require considerable effort to run successfully.

Outcomes. Health outcomes of coalitions can be difficult to demonstrate. If expensive community trials (research-directed prevention), with all of their resources and special expertise, have difficulty demonstrating results, then it should not be surprising if community-directed interventions that often operate with smaller budgets would face even bigger challenges.

A review by Schooler, Farquhar, Fortmann, and Flora (1997) found that there are many challenges to community prevention trials and their evaluation. Their review included the classic North Karelia and Stanford Heart Health projects. They cited a number of challenges including the following:

- It can be difficult to demonstrate outcomes because of secular or contextual trends. It is expensive to get sufficient exposure in media campaigns that stand out from the everyday media (e.g., costly anti-tobacco messages may be overshadowed by tobacco use on television shows and movies and by cigarette advertising).
- There are components of the intervention that work but that do not affect the whole community. For example, a prevention intervention may be instituted in four schools and demonstrate outcomes. Because there are 20 schools in the community, however, community-level comparisons may not appear significant in the evaluation.

APPLYING SOCIAL AND BEHAVIORAL SCIENCES TO UNDERSTANDING AND ENHANCING PARTICIPATION IN COMMUNITY MOBILIZATION

Community mobilization is highly dependent on effective citizen participation. In this section, I illustrate how behavioral and social sciences are making contributions toward understanding citizen participation in community mobilization and how theory and research have been applied to developing interventions that achieve public health outcomes.

Much of this section is adapted from Wandersman, Goodman, and Butterfoss (1997) and Butterfoss, Wandersman, and Goodman (1998), and these references can be referred to for greater detail. Because the literature on community coalitions is still in an early phase, I have also relied on literature on block and neighborhood organizations to illustrate points about community mobilization.

Individual Level of Participation

A major puzzle in the citizen participation literature is "If participation is such a good thing, why don't more people participate?" Despite the desirable outcomes proposed as consequences of participation and exemplified in actual coalitions such as CINCH, relatively few people participate in government-initiated efforts, grassroots groups, or community partnerships (e.g., ISA Associates, 1992; Langton, 1978; Verba & Nie, 1972; Warren, 1963). The literature pertinent to individual characteristics and participation can be divided into demographic research and personality or social psychological research.

Demographic variables (e.g., age, race, and gender) have been used in political science, sociology, and psychological studies to predict participation. Nonetheless, they tend to predict relatively little variance. Two studies that used multiple demographic variables to predict participation predicted 9% of the variance or less (Edwards & White, 1980; Vassar, 1978).

Personality and social psychological variables offer interesting opportunities to understand and predict participation. For example, many psychologists agree that a complex interaction exists between the characteristics of the person and the environment that produces and sustains behavior. For this reason, an individual is likely to participate in only a few of the many organizations available. The organizations chosen are selected on the basis of the individual's own characteristics (e.g., needs, values, personality) and the characteristics of the organization (e.g., purposes, efficacy, location). Mischel (1973, 1977) suggested five cognitive social learning variables as potentially useful in conceptualizing how the qualities of the person influence the impact of situations and how each person generates distinct patterns of behavior in interaction with the conditions of his or her life. Florin and Wandersman (1984) operationalized the cognitive social learning variables to predict participation in community settings. The five cognitive social learning variables are (a) skills, (b) view of the situation, (c) expectations, (d) values, and (e) personal standards (Wandersman, Florin, Chavis, Rich, & Prestby, 1985). The set of cognitive social learning variables was compared with a larger set of traditional demographic and personality trait variables for ability to discriminate members from nonmembers, and they accounted for more of the variance in participation.

Based on a review of the literature, Widmer (1984) concluded that many of the studies on why citizens participate say little about the motives and benefits of participation and focus instead on the characteristics of who participates. One approach to the issue of why people participate is represented by the political economy theory (e.g., Moe, 1980; Olson, 1965; Rich, 1980), which suggests that a social exchange takes place in organizations in which participants will invest their energy only if they expect to receive some financial, social, or personal benefits. This can be related to social exchange theory in psychology. Chinman and Wandersman (1999) provided a detailed review of studies of costs, benefits, and incentives and their relationship to participation in community organizations and to the viability of the organizations (whether the organizations last). For example, in the Block Booster Project (a study of 29 neighborhood block associations), Prestby, Wandersman, Florin, Rich, and Chavis (1990) found that the most active participants reported receiving significantly more social or communal benefits and personal benefits than did less active participants, with personal benefits best distinguishing the most active participants. Prestby and colleagues proposed that personal benefits, such as learning new skills, are likely to be exclusive to the high-level participants because they are contingent on participation. Regarding costs and participation, Prestby et al. found that the least active participants reported experiencing significantly more social and organizational costs than did the active participants. In a study of participation in coalition committees, Butterfoss, Goodman, and Wandersman (1996) found that amount of participation was predicted by expectations of higher benefits and lower costs. In sum, social exchange and political economy theory was supported; the participation level was related to personal and social costs and benefits.

Taken as a whole, the social psychological and cost–benefit results lend empirical support to Henig's (1982) three-step model of mobilization wherein an individual (a) perceives a condition, (b) evaluates it as important to his or her well-being, and (c) calculates that something can be done about it. This points to the importance of understanding more fully the processes through which an individual engages in a decision to participate in a particular organization.

Organizational Level of Participation

As with any organization, a coalition needs resources, structure, activities, and accomplishments to survive. These are the essential elements of an open-systems framework, so named because it is open to and interacts with the environment (Katz & Kahn, 1978). The framework proposes that organizations can be seen as mechanisms for processing resources obtained from the environment into products that affect that environment. Using Katz and Kahn's work as a departure point, Prestby and Wandersman (1985) developed a framework of organizational viability that suggests that there are four components of organizational functioning: (a) resource acquisition, (b) maintenance subsystem (organizational structure), (c) production subsystem (actions or activities), and (d) external goal attainment (accomplishments). In this section, I apply this framework to coalitions (Wandersman, Goodman, & Butterfoss, 1997).

Resource Acquisition

The resources brought to a voluntary organization by its members represent the potential of the organization. Resources include the characteristics and expertise of the members, the amount of time they dedicate to the organization, and their connections with the rest of the community and beyond its frontier. Several variables related to the characteristics of members have been positively related to organizational maintenance (Prestby & Wandersman, 1985), including the size of the membership, depth of members' attachment to the mission of the organization, and members' personal and political efficacy. Clearly, the membership of a coalition is likely to be its greatest asset.

Coalitions benefit by linking with external resources, especially those related to policy, planning, and services (Butterfoss et al., 1993). The CINCH Coalition (Butterfoss et al., 1998) illustrated how external resources such as elected officials, government agencies, religious and civic groups, neighborhood and community development associations, and foundations were vital. In this and other coalitions, such resources provide expertise, meeting facilities, mailing lists, referrals, additional personnel for special projects, grant funding, loans or donations, equipment, supplies, and cosponsorship of events (Chavis, Florin, Rich, & Wandersman, 1987; Prestby & Wandersman, 1985).

Partnership Structure and Functioning

The maintenance subsystem of the open-systems framework involves organizational structure and functioning, which is the aspect of the partnership that obtains the resources and organizes the members. If partnerships are to be viable, they must be able to set goals, administer rewards, and mediate between members' individual needs and the task requirements of the organization. Examples of organizational structure and functioning include leadership, formalized rules, roles, and procedures, decision-making and problem-resolution processes, and organizational climate.

Strong central leadership is an important ingredient in the implementation and maintenance of partnership activities (Butterfoss et al., 1993). Formalization is the degree to which rules, roles, and procedures are precisely defined. Examples of formalization, used by coalitions such as CINCH, include written memoranda to assist understanding of bylaws, policy, and procedures manuals; clearly defined roles; mission statements, goals, and objectives; and regular reorientation to the purposes, goals, roles, and procedures of collaboration (Butterfoss et al., 1993; Goodman & Steckler, 1989).

Mizrahi and Rosenthal (1992) argued that conflict is an inherent characteristic of partnerships. It may arise between the coalition and its targets for social change or among coalition partners concerning issues such as leadership, goals, benefits, contributions, and representation. Mizrahi and Rosenthal identified four "dynamic tensions" that account for conflict in partnerships: (a) the mixed loyalties of members to their own organizations and to the partnership, (b) the autonomy a partnership requires and the accountability it has to its member organizations, (c) the lack of clarity about the partnership's purpose as either a means for specific change or a model for sustained interorganizational cooperation, and (d) the diversity of interests of its members.

Organizational climate assesses members' perceptions of the "personality" of an organization. Moos (1986) assessed organizational climate on 10 subscales: cohesion, leader support, expression, independence, task orientation, self-discovery, anger and aggression, order and organization, leader control, and innovation. Butterfoss et al. (1996) found that social climate characteristics (e.g., leader support, control) were related to satisfaction with the work, participation in the partnership, and costs and benefits.

Community Level of Participation

According to a symposium convened by the Division of Chronic Disease Control and Community Intervention of the CDC, community capacity consists of at least the following characteristics: participation and leadership, skills, resources, social and interorganizational networks, sense of community, community power, community values, and critical reflection (Goodman et al., 1997). Psychology has made important contributions to several of those areas, particularly participation and leadership, sense of community, and interorganization networks. (See Butterfoss et. al., 1998, for more details about the community level.)

APPLYING SOCIAL SCIENCE DEVELOPING TO INTERVENTIONS TO PROMOTE CAPACITY TO ACHIEVE PUBLIC HEALTH OUTCOMES

The behavioral and social sciences can be useful in designing, implementing, and evaluating interventions to enhance the capacities of organizations and agencies, helping them create programs and policies that enhance the public's health. Below we provide two examples: (a) building organizational capacity for efficacy and viability and (b) building an accountability system for state agencies to work with community systems for results.

Increasing Efficacy and Viability

Researchers have found it is difficult to maintain energy and long-term viability in voluntary organizations, especially in block and neighborhood organizations and community coalitions. For example, Yates (1973) found that more than 50% of the block organizations that he studied became inactive after they had performed initial simple tasks. In a study of 17 block organizations, Prestby and Wandersman (1985) found that only eight were still functioning 1 year later. Prestby and Wandersman used an open-systems framework from organizational psychology (Katz & Kahn, 1978) to show that differences in resources, organizational structure and functioning, action strategies, internal maintenance activities, and accomplishments predicted viability 1 year later. In a follow-up study, Florin, Chavis, Wandersman, and Rich (1992) used organizational development theory and tools to develop an organizational intervention designed to increase the viability and efficacy of block organizations. The organizational process—the Block Booster process—used organizational assessment of dimensions found to be related to viability, profiles of organizational strengths and weaknesses, feedback to organization leaders, matching profiles to suggestions for organizational improvement, action plans, and evaluation. Block organizations were randomly assigned to the Block Booster process or a control group. The results showed that organizations that went through the Block Booster process had a 50% higher survival rate than the organizations that did not.

Building an Accountability System

There have been two relatively recent Institute of Medicine reports related to the topics in this chapter: *Healthy Communities: New Partnerships for the Future of Public Health* (1996) and *Improving Health in the Community: A Role for Performance Monitoring* (1997). Using the two reports as a base, Stoto (1997) stated,

> The health of a community is a shared responsibility of many entities. Within this context, specific entities should identify, and be held accountable for, the actions they can take to contribute to the community's health. Governmental public health agencies, especially at the state and local levels, can take the lead in getting public and private community organizations to advance the health of the community, and should play a leadership role by developing partnerships with managed care organizations and community-based organizations. (p. 22)

Here is an example of how an interdisciplinary team including economists, social workers, political scientists, and psychologists worked to develop an accountability process in public agencies to promote public health in communities. In South Carolina, the Governor's Office for Health and Human Services and the Department of Health and Human Services worked with a University of South Carolina team to design and implement a program-improvement–program-effectiveness approach to accountability, PACE (Promoting Accountability: Committed to Effectiveness) (Imm et al., 1998). The PACE process provides a way to improve the effectiveness of programs and services while measuring progress toward results. This process includes building capacity of personnel to improve the planning and implementation of programs and services, assessing outcomes and results of programs and services, and using information to develop a continuous quality improvement approach to accountability. PACE members work with state agency personnel to develop and implement a results-oriented strategic planning process.

The PACE process has been used in two South Carolina agencies, the Department of Health and Human Services' Medicaid managed care program and the Department of Juvenile Justice. In the latter, PACE was used by the prevention department to assess new and continuing programs. For example, it was used for program development and evaluation of a camp for high-risk youth (who have a sibling or parent who has been incarcerated). In addition to providing staff and community volunteers with guidance for planning, implementation, and evaluation of the program, an evaluation of the PACE process itself was initiated (Morrissey-Kane, 1998). For example, PACE assessed whether staff have made changes in their practice of planning, implementation, and evaluation, comparing their practice at the beginning of the use of PACE and about 1 year later. This is a pilot evaluation with a small number of participants. A number of changes indicating increased use of planning, implementation, and evaluation skills were reported. In addition, comments about the PACE process were recorded. The comments below suggest that practitioners can appreciate accountability processes that are program-improvement–program-effectiveness oriented. Some of the comments included

> In the past 17 years or so I have been at this business, you folks have been the most effective, least obtrusive force for systemic change I have seen or been exposed to. Please stick around for a while and "see this thing through" with D.J.J. We will all be better for it.

> You have just touched the tip of the iceberg. The PACE mindset could, if committed to, result in fairly revolutionary change in the "way we do things." At best, it could move us past our "crisis management addiction" to a visionary, responsible, and realistic human services entity that weathers political and social whimsy, rather than being trashed by them.

CONCLUSION

As noted in the introduction, the public's health in the 21st century will be heavily influenced by the extent to which communities are able to mobilize its members and institute effective prevention programs. Community mobilization will be a key mechanism for achieving progress in preventing diseases and promoting health. To achieve their objectives, the community mobilization efforts must be launched by effective and efficient organizations, supported by adequate funding, and developed on research-based premises. They also must use appropriately the resources offered by their members.

The behavioral and social sciences have a great deal to contribute to these programs, both by applying theory and research to the programs and by testing the interventions that affect the community. Theoretically, psychologists can help understand when and where community mobilization efforts are an appropriate strategy, as well as the psychology of motivation to mobilize individuals, organize their efforts effectively, and evaluate the initiatives. The application of behavioral and social sciences knowledge can increase the success rate of these efforts.

REFERENCES

Brown, C. (1984). The art of coalition building: A guide for community leaders. New York: American Jewish Committee.

Butterfoss, F. D., Goodman, R. M., & Wandersman, A. (1993). Community coalitions for health promotion and disease prevention. *Health Education Research: Theory and Practice 8*, 315–330.

Butterfoss, F. D., Goodman, R. M., & Wandersman, A. (1996). Community coalitions for prevention and health promotion: Factors predicting satisfaction, participation and planning.

Butterfoss, F. D., Morrow, A. L., Rosenthal, J., Dini, E., Crews, R. C., Webster, J. D., & Louis, P. (1998). CINCH: An urban coalition for empowerment and action. *Health Education and Behavior 25*, 212–225.

Chavis, D., Florin, P., Rich, R., & Wandersman, A. (1987). *The role of block association in crime control and community development: The Block Booster Project* (Report to the Ford Foundation). New York: Citizen's Committee for New York City.

Chinman, M., & Wandersman, A. (1999). The benefits and costs of volunteering in community organizations: Review and practical implications. *Nonprofit and Voluntary Sector Quarterly, 28*, 46–64.

COMMIT Research Group. (1995). Community intervention trial for smoking cessation (COMMIT): I. Cohort results from a four-year community intervention. *American Journal of Public Health, 85*, 193–199.

Edwards, J. N., & White, R. P. (1980). Predictors of social participation: Apparent or real? *Journal of Voluntary Action Research, 9*, 60–73.

Elder, J., McGraw, S., Abrams, D., Ferreira, A., Lasater, T., Longpre, H., Peterson, G., Schwertfeger, R., & Carleton, R. (1986). Organizational and community approaches to community-wide prevention of heart disease: The first two years of the Pawtucket Heart Health Program. *Preventive Medicine, 15*, 107–117.

Farquhar, J., Fortmann, S., Flora, J., Taylor, C., Haskell, W., Williams, P., Maccoby, N., & Wood, P. (1990). The Stanford Five-City Projects: Effects of community-wide education on cardiovascular disease risk factors. *Journal of the American Medical Association, 264*, 359–365.

Farquhar, J., Fortmann, S., Maccoby, N., Haskell, W., Williams, T., & Flora, J.

(1985). The Stanford Five-City Project: Design and methods. *American Journal of Epidemiology, 22,* 323–334.

Florin, P., Chavis, D., Wandersman, A., & Rich, R. (1992). A systems approach to understanding and enhancing grassroots community organizations: The Block Booster Project. In R. Levine & H. Fitzgerald (Eds.), *Analysis of dynamic psychological systems* (pp. 215–244). New York: Plenum Press.

Florin, P., & Wandersman, A. (1984). Cognitive social learning variables and participation in community development. *American Journal of Community Psychology, 12,* 689–708.

Goodman, R. M., Speers, M. A., McLeroy, K., Fawcett, S., Kegler, M., Parker, E., Smith, S., Sterling, T., & Wallerstein, N. (1998). Identifying and defining the dimensions of community capacity to provide a basis for measurement. *Health Education and Behavior 25,* 258–278.

Goodman, R. M., & Steckler, A. (1989). A model for the institutionalization of health promotion programs. *Family and Community Health, 11,* 63–78.

Goodman, R. M., & Wandersman, A. (1994). FORECAST: A formative approach to evaluating community coalitions and community-based initiatives. *Journal of Community Psychology* [CSAP special issue], 6–25.

Goodman, R. M., Wandersman, A., Chinman, M., Imm, P., & Morrissey, E. (1996). An ecological assessment of community-based interventions for prevention and health promotion: Approaches to measuring coalitions. *American Journal of Community Psychology, 24,* 33–61.

Hancock, T. (1993, Spring). The evolution, impact and significance of the Healthy Cities/Healthy Communities movement. *Journal of Public Health Policy,* 5–18.

Hawkins, D., & Catalano, R. (1992). *Communities that care: Action for drug abuse prevention.* San Francisco: Jossey-Bass.

Henig, J. (1982). *Neighborhood mobilization: Redevelopment and response.* New Brunswick, NJ: Rutgers University Press.

Hingson, R., McGovern, T., Howland, J., Heeren, T., Winter, M., & Zakocs, R. (1996). Reducing alcohol-impaired driving in Massachusetts: The impact of the saving lives program. *American Journal of Public Health, 86,* 791–797.

Imm, P., Rowe, A., Wandersman, A., Saunders, L., Hallman, W., Blachman, M., & Appenzeller, G. (1998, August). Moving agencies toward effective programs using a results based accountability process. Paper presented at the annual meeting of the American Psychological Association, San Francisco, CA.

Institute of Medicine. (1996). *Healthy communities: New partnerships for the future of public health.* Washington, DC: National Academy Press.

Institute of Medicine. (1997). *Improving health in the community: A role for performance monitoring.* Washington, DC: National Academy Press.

ISA Associates. (1992). National evaluation of the community partnership demonstration program. Evaluation plan (Draft, in response to Contract No. 277-90-2003). Alexandria, VA: Author.

Jacobs, D., Luepker, R., Mittelmark, M., Folsom, A., Pirie, P., Mascioli, S., Hannan, P., Pechacek, T., Bracht, N., Carlaw, R., Kline, F., & Blackburn, H. (1986). Community-wide prevention strategies: Evaluation design of the Minnesota Heart Health Program. *Journal of Chronic Disease*, *39*, 775–788.

Katz, D., & Kahn, R. L. (1978). *The social psychology of organizations* (2nd ed.). New York: Wiley.

Kreuter, M., & Levin, M. (1998). *Are consortia/collaboratives effective in changing health status and health systems? A critical review of the literature.* Prepared for the Health Resources and Services Administration Office of Planning, Evaluation and Legislation.

Langton, S. (Ed.). (1978). *Citizen participation in America*. Lexington, MA: Heath.

McLeroy, K., Bibeau, D., Steckler, A., & Glanz, K. (1988). *An ecological perspective on health promotion programs*, *15*, 351–377.

Mischel, W. (1973). Toward a cognitive social learning reconceptualization of personality. *Psychological Review*, *80*, 252–283.

Mischel, W. (1977). The interaction of personality and situation. In D. Magnusson & N. S. Endler (Eds.), *Personality at the crossroads: Current issues in interactional psychology*. Hillsdale, NJ: Erlbaum.

Mittelmark, M., Hunt, M., Heath, G., & Schmid, T. (1993). Realistic outcomes: Lessons from community-based research and demonstration programs for the prevention of cardiovascular diseases. *Journal of Health Policy*, *14*, 437–462.

Mizrahi, T., & Rosenthal, B. (1992). Managing dynamic tensions in social change coalitions. In T. Mizrahi & B. Rosenthal (Eds.), *Community organization and social administration: Advances, trends and emerging principles*. Binghamton, NY: Haworth Press.

Moe, T. M. (1980). *The organization of interests: Incentives and the internal dynamics of political interest groups*. Chicago: University of Chicago Press.

Moos, R. (1986). *Group Environment Scale manual* (2nd ed.). Palo Alto, CA: Consulting Psychologists Press.

Morrisey-Kane, E. (1998). *Evaluation of the Camp Papui Win experience* (Report from the PACE Project). Columbia: University of South Carolina.

Olson, M. (1965). *The logic of collective action*. Cambridge, MA: Harvard University Press.

Prestby, J., & Wandersman, A. (1985). An empirical exploration of a framework of organizational viability: Maintaining block organizations. *Journal of Applied Behavioral Science*, *21*, 287–305.

Prestby, J., Wandersman, A., Florin, P., Rich, R., & Chavis, D. (1990). Benefits, costs, incentive management and participation in voluntary organizations: A means to understanding and promoting empowerment. *American Journal of Community Psychology*, *18*, 111–149.

Puska, P., Tuomilehto, J., Nissinen, A., & Vartiainen, E. (1995). *The North Karelia Project: 20 year results and experiences*. Helsinki, Finland: Helsinki University Printing House.

Rich, R. C. (1980). The dynamics of leadership in neighborhood organizations. *Social Science Quarterly*, *60*, 570–587.

Schooler, C., Farquhar, J., Fortmann, S., & Flora, J. (1997). Synthesis of findings and issues from community prevention trials. *Annuals of Epidemiology, 57*, 554–568.

Shaw, R. A., Rosati, M. J., Salzman, P., Coles, C., & McGeary, C. (1997). Effects on adolescent ATOD behaviors and attitudes of a 5-year community partnership. *Evaluation and Program Planning, 20*, 307–313.

Steckler, A., McLeroy, K. R., Goodman, R. M., McCormick, I., & Bird, S. T. (1992). Toward integrating qualitative and quantitative methods: An introduction. *Health Education Quarterly, 19*, 1–8.

Stokols, D. (1992). Establishing and maintaining health environments. *American Psychologist, 47*, 6–22.

Stokols, D., Allen, J., & Bellingham, R. (1996). The social ecology of health promotion: Implications of research and practice. *American Journal of Health Promotion, 10*, 247–251.

Stoto, M. (1997). Sharing responsibility for the public's health: A new perspective from the Institute of Medicine. *Public Health Management Practice, 3*, 22–34.

Vassar, S. (1978). *Community participation in a metropolitan area: An analysis of the characteristics of participants*. Unpublished doctoral dissertation, University of Illinois, Chicago.

Verba, S., & Nie, N. H. (1972). *Participation America*. New York: Harper & Row.

Warren, R. (1963). *The community in America*. Chicago: Rand McNally.

Wandersman, A., Florin, P., Chavis, D., Rich, R., & Prestby, J. (1985, November). Getting together and getting things done. *Psychology Today*, pp. 64–71.

Wandersman, A., Goodman, R., & Butterfoss, F. (1997). Understanding coalitions and how they operate. In M. Minkler (Ed.), *Community organizing and community building for health* (pp. 261–277). New Brunswick, NJ: Rutgers University Press.

Widmer, C. (1984). An incentive model of citizen participation applied to a study of human service agency boards of directors. Unpublished doctoral dissertation, Cornell University, Ithaca, NY.

Winett, R. A. (1995). A framework for health promotion and disease prevention programs. *American Psychologist, 50*, 341–350.

Yates, D. (1973). *Neighborhood democracy*. Lexington, MA: Heath.

Yin, R. K., Kaftarian, S. J., & Jacobs, N. F. (1996). Empowerment evaluation at federal and local levels: Dealing with quality. In D. Fetterman, S. Kafatrian, & A. Wandersman (Eds.), *Empowerment evaluation: Knowledge and tools for self-assessment and accountability* (pp. 188–207). Newbury Park, CA: Sage.

12

ASSESSING THE ECONOMIC COSTS AND BENEFITS OF BEHAVIORAL INTERVENTIONS

DAVID R. HOLTGRAVE AND STEVEN D. PINKERTON

Psychologists are concerned with a number of topics of importance to public health, including sexual behavior and its potentially adverse consequences, such as sexually transmitted diseases (including the virus that causes AIDS) and unplanned pregnancies; dependence on and abuse of alcohol, nicotine, and other substances; diet and nutrition; suicide prevention; childhood and adolescent problem behaviors; stress and coping; and general issues of mental health (e.g., depression). With the arrival of managed care and limits on health care spending at the national, state, and local levels, funding for the services that psychologists and other health behavior experts provide are coming into direct fiscal competition with more traditional medical services. Unfortunately, relatively little information is available about the cost-effectiveness of most public health–related psychological services.

In this chapter, we review the basics of economic efficiency (cost-effectiveness) analyses, focusing on the technique of cost–utility analysis. We present a detailed example of how cost-utility analysis can be applied to a specific public health problem—HIV prevention—and summarize the

249

results of several published analyses of relevance to the intersection of psychology and public health. In the concluding section, we offer some suggestions on the further involvement of behavioral scientists in the application and methodological refinement of these analytic techniques.

PUBLIC HEALTH DECISION MAKING DRIVES METHODS SELECTION

Public health decision makers at the local, state, and federal levels must make difficult choices about the allocation of scarce fiscal resources. In general, they are trying to use the available monies to the best public health benefit. They are not intentionally selecting inexpensive programs simply to "get by." Rather, these decision makers know that every dollar not used to its optimal potential is a dollar wasted, and wasting funds can cause real harm to public health (Holtgrave, Qualls, & Graham, 1996).

There are three central questions of interest to decision makers when allocating public health funds (Holtgrave et al., 1996):

1. *Affordability:* Are the resources available that are necessary to implement this program, or is the cost so high that it is not affordable in any case?
2. *Within-disease allocation:* What is the optimal level of funding for each type of intervention within a disease area? For example, is it better to reduce HIV infection by providing more street outreach prevention services, by sending a mailing to every household in the United States, or by implementing small-group behavioral interventions led by peers in areas of high HIV seroprevalence?
3. *Across-disease allocation:* What is the optimal level of funding for programs in each disease area? For example, is it better to spend some additional funds on cancer prevention campaigns or on interventions to raise adherence to tuberculosis treatment regimens?

Several evaluation methods have been devised that yield exactly the kind of information required to answer these three general questions. Answering the affordability question requires estimating the cost of a given intervention or program. Cost analysis is used to estimate or measure resources consumed by a public health activity and to express these resources in monetary terms (Gorsky, 1996). For instance, a cost analysis of a clinic-based smoking cessation intervention might calculate the average cost per client served by the intervention, including counseling costs, stop-smoking aids (nicotine gum, patches, or inhalers), overhead (rent, utilities), and other expenses. Notice that this type of analysis says nothing about the effectiveness of the intervention or the positive economic consequences of the intervention, only about the resources consumed.

Within-disease allocation questions can be answered using the standard economic efficiency evaluation technique of cost-effectiveness analysis (Haddix & Shaffer, 1996; Haddix, Teutsch, Shaffer, & Duñet, 1996). Cost-effectiveness analysis summarizes the impact of a program as a ratio of program costs to some naturally occurring health outcome, such as cost per case of lung cancer prevented. This is fine for comparing several types of lung cancer prevention interventions to each other. However, it is not possible to compare a cancer prevention intervention to, say, a tuberculosis treatment adherence intervention using this method.

To answer across-disease allocation questions requires that programs be evaluated in comparable units that do not depend on the particular disease or health condition under consideration. Cost-utility analysis, in which public health programs are compared in terms of cost per quality-adjusted life-year (QALY) saved, is well suited to this task. (Although we focus on QALYs here, other outcome measures, such as unadjusted life-years, could be used instead.) We can most easily define a QALY by example. A time period of 2 years spent alive but in a health state that diminishes perceived quality of life by 50% is taken to be worth 1 year of life in perfect health; both scenarios are considered to be worth 1 QALY. Theoretically, at least, it is possible to assess the cost of any public health program, ascertain its effectiveness in terms of QALYs saved, and summarize its impact as a cost per QALY saved.

At first blush, it may seem easier to compare programs across disease areas in terms of cost per year of life saved (without adjusting for quality of life). To do so would be to focus only on the benefits of interventions that increase longevity and ignore the positive consequences of interventions that increase the quality, but not necessarily length, of life. Health-related quality of life, which includes such factors as mobility, ability to care for one's self, and pain and discomfort, reflects both psychological and physical influences on subjective well-being. Some intervention programs, such as those that improve patients' overall mental health, have little or no effect on longevity but have substantial consequences for patients' quality of life, whereas others, such as smoking-cessation programs, potentially affect both quality and length of life. Because cost-utility analysis can be used to address both across-disease and within-disease allocation questions, it provides important flexibility that is not provided by the technique of cost-effectiveness analysis.

Two other types of economic evaluation are commonly cited in economic evaluation texts. The first is cost-minimization analysis, which is used to choose between two or more alternatives that have the same health effects (Drummond, Stoddart, & Torrance, 1987). In this situation, the most cost-effective alternative will be the one with the smallest cost.

Therefore, the evaluator need only determine the cost of each alternative. Cost-minimization analysis plays a much more limited role in answering policy makers' questions than do other economic evaluation techniques (e.g., cost-effectiveness and cost-utility analyses) because the specific type of question it answers ("which of several equally effective interventions costs the least?") arises only rarely.

In conducting economic analyses, it is important to distinguish between costs and charges. The cost of an intervention equals the value of resources consumed in producing the intervention; the charge is the price that the provider might ask a client or a funder to pay. To illustrate, although a hospital patient might be charged $2 for a pair of aspirin, the cost to the hospital is less than a dime. (The distinction between costs and charges is similar to that between production costs and retail prices.) Economic analyses of public health programs typically are concerned with the true cost of the intervention to society, rather than the amount that private providers might charge for their goods or services.

The last type of economic evaluation discussed here is cost-benefit analysis (Haddix, Clemmer, & Haddix, 1996). In this type of analysis, each health outcome is converted to a dollar value. For instance, if a specific intervention costs $5,000 per year of life saved, cost-benefit analysis would take another step and convert the year of life saved into a dollar value by determining how much money society would be willing to pay to save a life-year. Thus, both the cost of the intervention and the health benefits are in monetary units, and it is easy to state how much money the program saves, if any, by comparing the monetary costs with monetized benefits. Although this is appealing conceptually, both methodologically and politically it is very difficult to determine a universally acceptable way to convert, say, a year of life—or even an entire life saved—into a dollar value. These difficulties have served to limit the promulgation of the method of cost-benefit analysis. Nonetheless, some analysts still prefer cost-benefit analysis for theoretical reasons, such as its consistency with the social welfare foundations of economic efficiency analysis and its applicability to a wide range of public welfare issues (e.g., the decision of whether to build a new airport or to fund Head Start programs), as well as to health-related interventions (Gold, Siegel, Russell, & Weinstein, 1996; Haddix, Clemmer, & Haddix, 1996).

The evaluation techniques described above can be utilized while an intervention is being conducted or after it has concluded. In a prospective evaluation, the costs and health consequences of an intervention are empirically measured while the intervention is ongoing. In a retrospective analysis, costs and effects are measured, or estimated after the program is completed. Both types of analyses have been used extensively to evaluate the cost effectiveness of public health interventions.

These techniques can also be used a priori to estimate the potential cost-effectiveness of an intervention before it is broadly implemented. This type of analysis is especially important to decision makers who are considering expanding an intervention that was tested in a more limited geographic area. For instance, one recent analysis estimated the cost-effectiveness of a national implementation of a program to increase access to sterile syringes for injection drug users, so as to decrease HIV infection (Holtgrave, Pinkerton, Jones, Lurie, & Vlahov, 1998). Although the results of this analysis suggest that such a program would be highly cost-effective, the use of federal funds for needle exchange is actually banned by law. Still, data on the potential impact and cost-effectiveness of such a program would provide important information for national policy makers should it ever become a legal and viable policy option.

Although there are multiple types of economic evaluation techniques from which to choose, we emphasize cost-utility analysis throughout this chapter for three main reasons. First, as discussed below, it can be used to answer all three major types of policy questions listed above. Second, it is appropriate for interventions whose principal (or only) benefit is to improve quality of life, as well as for those that extend longevity. Third, the U.S. Panel on Cost-effectiveness in Health and Medicine, a federally sponsored, blue-ribbon panel of economic evaluation experts, recommends that all published economic efficiency studies include a cost-utility component to ensure comparability of economic analyses undertaken for interventions across a wide range of diseases and health-related interventions (Gold et al., 1996).

HEALTH-RELATED QUALITY OF LIFE

Some behavioral and mental health interventions have only small or nonexistent effects on mortality and instead exert their main effect by reducing morbidity or enhancing quality of life. For instance, a counseling intervention that helps adolescents alleviate anxiety over sexual orientation might markedly improve participants' quality of life while having no effect on the length of that life. The main issue is therefore not whether quality of life is an important outcome of psychological and other health-related interventions—it clearly is—but rather, what is the best way to conceptualize and measure it?

Historically, economic analysts have subsumed concerns about morbidity and quality of life under the rubric of "pain and suffering." In cost-benefit analysis, intervention-induced reductions in pain and suffering are assigned a monetary value that is intended to reflect the amount that people would be willing to pay for this reduction. Assigning a monetary value to changes in quality of life (and in health status more generally) has proved a difficult task, however.

In cost–utility analysis, health-related quality of life is not valued directly. Instead, a weight is assigned to each health state (e.g., severe depression, advanced AIDS, renal disease requiring dialysis) that reflects the quality of life associated with that state. The number of QALYs associated with spending n years in a health state with quality of life weight w is $n \times w$. Conventionally, the weights are between 0 (*death*) and 1 (*perfect health*). Most people, at most times, are not at perfect health, of course; indeed, one study suggests that at any given time, the health-related quality of life of the general population averages 0.94 (Patrick & Erickson, 1993).

The quality-of-life weight associated with a particular health state can be measured using any of several methods, including the standard-gamble technique, in which the individual is asked a series of lottery-type questions to compare their preference for different health-related outcomes; the time trade-off technique, in which the individual identifies the number of years in health state S that would be equivalent to a single year of full health; and survey methods, in which individuals are asked to judge how being in health state S would affect several dimensions of quality of life, such as mobility, physical activities, social activities, and physical discomfort. Several psychometrically validated quality-of-life assessment tools have been developed in the past decades and are in wide use (the standard-gamble and time trade-off techniques, although theoretically sound, are difficult to implement at the population level and are not commonly used). Among the most popular tools are the Quality of Well-Being Scale, the EuroQOL, and the Health Utility Index. The interested reader should consult the relevant literature (e.g., Drummond, O'Brien, Stoddart, & Torrance, 1997; Tolley, Kenkel, & Fabian, 1994).

COST–UTILITY ANALYTIC METHODS

In this section, we provide some additional detail on the conduct of cost–utility analysis. For a full treatment, we refer the reader to more comprehensive sources in the literature (Drummond, Stoddart, & Torrance, 1987; Gold et al., 1996).

The first step in conducting a cost–utility analysis requires the analyst to establish the following key characteristics of that analysis:

1. *The perspective.* The perspective determines which costs and consequences are included in the analysis. Possible perspectives include those of the individual, government, hospital, insurance company, and so forth. Most analyses of public health interventions adopt a comprehensive societal perspective in which all costs and consequences are included in the

analysis regardless of who pays them or who experiences them, respectively.

2. *The time horizon, index year, and discount rate.* The index year is the year in which the intervention begins. All future costs should be converted to equivalent index year dollars by discounting them at a standard discount rate, usually 3%. The time horizon is the period during which the effects and costs of the intervention are monitored. It should be long enough to capture all relevant costs and consequences of the intervention, starting in the index year.

3. *The appropriate comparison conditions.* Often, the intervention of interest is compared with the absence of that intervention or with an alternative intervention that addresses the same health condition.

4. *The prospective, retrospective, or a priori nature of analysis.* See above discussion.

Once these characteristics of the analysis are decided, information is gathered to determine the costs and effectiveness of the intervention, where effectiveness is measured as the number of QALYs saved (or gained) by the intervention, relative to the comparison condition. This information is then summarized via the cost–utility ratio, which is expressed as cost per QALY saved. For example, suppose we wanted to compare two behavioral interventions to prevent adolescents from initiating smoking, and suppose that Intervention 1 is both more costly and more effective (saves more QALYs) than is Intervention 2. To directly compare these interventions, we would first calculate the incremental cost–utility ratio: $R = (C_1 - C_2)/(E_1 - E_2)$, where C_k is the net cost and E_k is the number of QALYs saved by Intervention k. The incremental cost–utility ratio is a measure of the additional cost per additional QALY saved by one intervention relative to another. If, rather than comparing two interventions, a single intervention is compared with its absence, then the above equation simplifies to what is known as an average cost–utility ratio: $R = C/E$, where C is the net cost of the intervention under consideration and E is the number of QALYs it saves.

One might ask what values of the cost–utility ratio, R, are readily accepted by society as representing acceptable levels of economic efficiency, that is, when is an intervention cost-effective? If the numerator of R is negative, indicating a negative net cost, then the intervention would actually save societal resources in the long run (such an intervention is called cost-saving). The magnitude of a negative cost–utility ratio is not readily interpretable, and some would argue that if the net cost is negative, then the ratio need not be calculated; it suffices to say that the intervention is cost-saving (Ganiats & Wong, 1991).

If R has a positive value, then its magnitude is important. Between $0 and $40,000, most analysts and policy makers would agree that the intervention is cost-effective. Over $180,000, it would be highly difficult to justify the intervention as cost-effective. Between $40,000 and $180,000, the matter of cost-effectiveness is debatable. There are clearly some interventions in this range that society is willing to accept (e.g., certain types of cardiovascular surgery), but there are others that are not so readily accepted (Tengs et al., 1995). The boundaries of these three "zones" of relative acceptability are not precise, and there is not universal agreement as to what value of R is too big to be considered acceptable (Paltiel & Stinnett, 1998). Nonetheless, we believe that there is some general consensus that the boundaries of these three zones are very roughly those described above (Pinkerton & Holtgrave, 1998a).

Calculation of the cost–utility ratio requires assessing the net cost of and the QALYs saved by the intervention. The intervention cost calculations should capture all resources consumed by delivery of the intervention. Indeed, assessing the gross (as opposed to net) intervention cost is identical to the conduct of cost analysis as defined in the first section of this chapter. In general, cost analysis proceeds via the following steps:

1. identifying all categories of resources consumed by the intervention
2. measuring or estimating the number of units of each resource category consumed
3. assessing a dollar value of each unit of each resource category consumed
4. multiplying Item 2 by Item 3 for all resources categories identified in Item 1 and summing across resource categories to determine the total cost of the intervention.

Examples of resource categories consumed include staff time, supervisory time, materials, equipment, client time, client transportation, rent, utilities, and overhead costs. Detailed descriptions of cost-analytic methods can be found in the literature (e.g., Gorsky, 1996).

Unlike general methods of cost analysis, techniques for assessing the effectiveness of interventions (QALYs saved in the cost–utility framework) are necessarily specific to the particular health-related condition. We can use an HIV prevention intervention example to illustrate the main methodological points here (Pinkerton & Holtgrave, 1998a, 1998b). First, notice that if A is the number of infections prevented by an intervention (compared with its absence), then the total number of QALYs saved by the intervention is $A \times Q$, where Q is the number of QALYs lost whenever a person becomes infected with HIV (Q is discounted into present value per standard methodological practice in economic evaluation). Similarly, by preventing people from becoming infected, the intervention also averts

$A \times T$ dollars of future HIV-related medical care costs, where T is the discounted lifetime cost of caring for someone with HIV. Thus, if the gross cost of implementing the HIV prevention intervention is K, then the net cost is $K - A \times T$. The cost–utility ratio, R, therefore equals: $(K - A \times T)/(A \times Q)$.

The medical cost and QALY parameters (T and Q) can be estimated once and then used in multiple analyses. Holtgrave and Pinkerton (1997) have estimated the discounted HIV-related treatment costs averted and the number of QALYs saved each time an HIV infection is prevented. Both parameters were discounted into present value per standard economic evaluation practice. Once these parameters are adjusted for the average age of the client pool of the intervention of interest, they can be used in nearly any HIV prevention cost–utility analysis (Pinkerton & Holtgrave, 1998a, 1998b). This reduces the burden on intervention effectiveness researchers interested in applying cost–utility techniques to their studies. Further, it adds an important element of methodological standardization across interventions.

Estimating the number of HIV infections averted by an intervention relative to the absence of that intervention, A, is fairly straightforward if HIV incidence is directly measured in an intervention effectiveness trial. In all but a few exceptional cases, however, HIV prevention interventions are tested in trials that use behavioral outcome measures, such as changes in risky sexual or injection practices. This poses a methodological challenge, but one that is definitely surmountable. For instance, the cumulative probability, P, of a woman becoming HIV infected after n unprotected and k protected acts of receptive vaginal intercourse with each of m male partners can be approximated using the following Bernoullian equation: $P = 1 - [(1 - \pi) + \pi(1 - \alpha_n)^n(1 - \alpha_k)^k]^m$, where π is the prevalence of HIV among the male sex partners, α_n is the probability of HIV transmission per act of unprotected intercourse, and α_k is the per-act probability of HIV transmission for condom-protected intercourse (Pinkerton & Abramson, 1998). This equation can be used as the basis for estimating the number of infections prevented by the behavioral intervention (Pinkerton, Holtgrave, Leviton, Wagstaff, & Abramson, 1998). Of course, any model used in such a fashion should be validated. For instance, a Bernoullian model was recently used in an intervention trial that tested the effects of a spermicide when used by commercial sex workers to help prevent HIV transmission (Rehle et al., 1998). The model predicted an HIV incidence of 73 cases over a year, and the trial (which used behavioral and biological outcome measures) observed 78 cases, an impressive match. More exhaustive discussions of the Bernoullian model of HIV transmission are available in the literature (Pinkerton & Abramson, 1998; Weinstein, Graham, Siegel, & Fineberg, 1989).

Unless all parameters in the cost–utility ratio equation (and their constituent subcomponents) are known with certainty, it is critical to subject the cost–utility ratio calculations to sensitivity analyses (Gold et al., 1996). In sensitivity analyses, one or more parameters are varied separately or conjointly across a range of plausible values. For instance, let us assume that a cost–utility analysis is done retrospectively. We assume for illustration that T and Q are available from the literature, A is available from seroincidence measurements in an intervention trial, yet K can only be approximated. In this case, it is critical to vary K across a range of plausible values to determine the robustness of the cost–utility analysis results to changes in assumptions about intervention costs. Many times, it will be found that some uncertain elements have relatively little impact on the overall results and are not a source of concern. Other times, it will be found that the cost–utility ratio is quite sensitive to the value of one or more parameters; in such a situation, the results of the cost–utility analysis must be interpreted with extreme caution.

Threshold analysis is a special type of sensitivity analysis that is used to determine the cutoff value of a particular parameter, when others are left fixed, that would make the intervention cost-effective or cost-saving (Holtgrave et al., 1997; Norton, Martin & Wechsberg, 1998). For instance, in conducting a retrospective cost–utility analysis of an HIV prevention program, Norton and colleagues (1998) were able to ascertain the gross cost, K, with a high level of precision and to obtain a valid estimate of T from the literature, but data were not available to reliably estimate A. Recall that an HIV prevention intervention is cost-saving if the net cost, $K - A \times T$ is negative. Therefore, they sought to determine the value of A at which $A \times T$ was exactly equal to K and hence, the medical costs saved by the intervention exactly balance the costs of the program. Once this threshold value of A was determined, the researchers could attempt to assess whether true value of A was greater or less than that value, based on the available evidence. This type of threshold analysis can also be used to set performance standards for national prevention programs (Holtgrave & Pinkerton, 1998a, in press).

APPLICATIONS OF COST-EFFECTIVENESS AND COST–UTILITY ANALYSIS

Although the number of carefully conducted studies that have applied cost-effectiveness and cost–utility analysis to behavioral interventions designed to improve the public's health appears to be increasing, it is still relatively small. In recent years, several studies of smoking cessation (Klesges, Ward, & DeBon, 1996; Reid, 1996) and HIV prevention interventions have been published (Holtgrave & Pinkerton, 2000; Holtgrave et al., 1996), as well as smaller numbers of studies of behavior-based interventions such as physical exercise promotion, stress reduction, weight control, and psychological therapy (Groth-Marnat & Schumaker, 1995). In this section, we briefly review the findings of selected studies.

Kamlet and colleagues (1995) conducted a retrospective cost–utility analysis of maintenance treatments for recurrent depression. The analysis was based on the empirical results of a clinical trial that assessed the effectiveness of interpersonal therapy, imipramine drug therapy, and a hybrid of the two interventions. Compared with a placebo group, the drug therapy was found to increase QALYs and save medical costs; thus, the cost–utility ratio was negative, indicating that the intervention was cost-saving. In contrast, interpersonal maintenance therapy was found to increase QALYs but not to reduce medical costs when compared with the placebo group. Thus, the interpersonal therapy intervention was not cost-saving. Nonetheless, its cost–utility ratio was less than $5,000 per QALY saved, which suggests that the intervention was cost-effective by conventional standards. In sum, although both interventions would be economically attractive, the drug therapy would be the more economically efficient of the two options.

Holtgrave and Pinkerton (1998b) collaborated on a series of four cost–utility analyses of HIV prevention behavioral interventions. All four analyses were retrospective and built on empirical effectiveness studies designed to test the impact of HIV prevention interventions on HIV-related risk behaviors. Each study used a Bernoullian model of HIV transmission to estimate the number of HIV infections averted by the intervention, given the level of self-reported behavior change identified in the empirical effectiveness studies.

Three of the four analyses focused on HIV prevention interventions for gay men. Holtgrave and Kelly (1997) found that a 12-session, small-group, behavioral risk reduction intervention cost about $470 per client to deliver, yet was actually cost-saving to society as a result of the medical costs averted by the intervention. Pinkerton, Holtgrave, and Valdiserri (1997) found that adding a skills-training component to a lecture-based HIV prevention intervention cost an additional $40 per client and also averted sufficient medical costs that it can be considered cost-saving to society. Pinkerton and colleagues (Pinkerton, Holtgrave, DiFranceisco, Stevenson, & Kelly, 1998) examined the cost–utility of a community-level, peer-opinion leader, behavioral risk reduction intervention. They found that it cost only about $38 per client and reduced medical costs sufficiently that the intervention could be considered cost-saving. Each of these three studies on interventions for gay men included numerous sensitivity analyses and found that the results were robust to changes in parameter values. The fourth of the series of analyses found that a five-session, small-group, behavioral risk reduction intervention for at-risk women recruited through an urban primary health care center cost about $269 per client to deliver (Holtgrave & Kelly, 1996). The cost–utility ratio was approximately

$2,024 per QALY saved. Sensitivity analyses indicated that even under a broad range of parameter assumptions, the ratio was at a level easily considered cost-effective.

Two recent smoking-related intervention studies used cost-effectiveness analysis to evaluate the cost per life-year saved by smoking-cessation and prevention-delay programs. In the first study, Secker-Walker and colleagues (Secker-Walker, Worden, Holland, Flynn, & Detsky, 1997) examined the cost-effectiveness of a mass media intervention to prevent the onset of smoking among 10th to 12th graders. The intervention cost $41 per student exposed to the campaign's messages, $754 per student smoker averted, and $696 per discounted year of life saved. The study also included a modeling component that estimated the cost per discounted year of life that would be saved if the campaign were implemented in all major U.S. media markets.

In the second study, Meenan and colleagues (1998) evaluated the cost-effectiveness of a hospital-based smoking-cessation program. The intervention consisted of a 20-minute session with a trained counselor, a 12-minute video viewing, self-help materials, and one or two follow-up visits by the counselor. The incremental cost of this intervention, over and above the cost of usual care received in the hospital setting, was estimated at about $16 per patient for a typical 200-bed hospital, and the incremental cost per life-year saved was $381 (discounted at 3%). Thus, both of the smoking-prevention programs reviewed here were highly cost-effective.

The final example is provided by Erfurt and colleagues (Erfurt, Foote, & Heirich, 1992), who conducted a comparative cost-effectiveness analysis of four work-site wellness programs for hypertension control, weight loss, smoking cessation, and exercise. Site A offered only health education and served as the comparison condition; Site B set up a physical fitness center for use by employees that included extensive weight training and aerobic exercise equipment; similar to Site A, Site C provided health education but, in addition, this program included wellness counselors who provided semi-annual follow-up counseling to all employees with identified risk factors. In addition to the strategies used at Site C, Site D adopted a plant-wide, pro-exercise stance that stressed the positive aspects of exercise and fitness and included limited access to exercise equipment and a 1-mile walking course. The effectiveness of the four programs was evaluated 3 years after initial implementation. Surprisingly, perhaps, employees at the site with the physical fitness facility (Site B) were the least likely to engage in regular physical activity. In contrast, employees at Sites C and D were more likely to exercise than those at either Site A or B. Program costs ranged from $18 (Site A) to $39 (Site B) per employee. The authors of this study report a complex pattern of incremental cost-effectiveness results for the targeted behaviors, concluding that "these cost-effectiveness analyses justify the addition to wellness program designs of regular outreach, follow-up counseling, and a menu of health improvement programs, but do not justify the addition of fitness facilities without outreach and follow-up counseling" (Erfurt et al., 1992, p. 23).

FURTHER RELATIONSHIPS AMONG PSYCHOLOGY, PUBLIC HEALTH, AND ECONOMIC EVALUATION

We believe that the pressures of fiscal accountability and the use of economic evaluation factors in public health decision making will continue to grow. Therefore, psychologists working on the development, testing, and dissemination of behavioral intervention to improve the public's health likely will become increasingly involved in the economic evaluation of their interventions. We also believe that there will be increasing use of cost–utility analysis as the main referent methodology used in economic evaluation and that the roles for psychologists working on cost–utility analyses concomitantly will increase. We see these increased roles especially in the following areas.

Psychologists might want to include the conduct of cost–utility analysis in the routine course of intervention development (Holtgrave, 1998). This would have the benefit of making the results of their intervention studies even more relevant to policy makers. It would also allow for the expansion of the literature on prospective cost–utility analyses (of which there are now precious few; the field is dominated by retrospective analyses). If interested intervention researchers utilized common methods of cost–utility analysis in a standardized manner, then the results of the studies could be meaningfully compared; the development of such a literature of standardized, comparable studies is precisely what decision makers need to support their fiscal allocation efforts.

Psychologists have conducted pioneering work in the area of quality-of-life measurement (Kaplan, 1989; Kaplan, Feeny, & Revicki, 1993), and this is an area in need of further development. In particular, quality-of-life measurements are needed in an ever-increasing number of newly emerging disease areas; indeed, when the first psychological work was being done on quality-of-life issues, HIV was not a recognized disease. In addition, existing measurement tools for assessing quality of life are generally not sensitive enough to detect small changes, such as those that can result from psychological interventions (e.g., counseling; Chisolm, Healey, & Knapp, 1997). Psychometricians could play an important role in developing and validating more sensitive instruments to assess changes in health-related quality of life.

The U.S. Panel on Cost-Effectiveness in Health and Medicine (Gold et al., 1996) has recommended that quality-of-life measurements for a particular disease or health condition be taken from community-wide samples of people (as opposed to people currently experiencing the health state of interest). For instance, if a research team were interested in the quality of life of people with throat cancer, they would survey the community at large about the perceived decrement in quality of life due to this type of cancer (not just patients living with this disease). This recommendation by the panel is bold and somewhat controversial. If widely accepted and implemented, it will necessitate the conduct of many psychometrically difficult studies on quality of life.

Quantitative psychologists and other methodologists can also assist in the development of new techniques for the conduct and validation of cost-utility analyses. In particular, there is increasing interest in the development of statistical inference tests for cost–utility ratios and other decision analytic measures (Holtgrave, 1990). Existing methods for handling uncertainty in cost–utility analyses (e.g., sensitivity analysis) focus on uncertainty in the values of key parameters but do not adequately address the issue of sampling variability in the cost and effectiveness estimates. The task of estimating confidence intervals around the cost-utility ratio point estimate is complicated by the fact that this ratio is a nonlinear combination of quantities (cost and effects) that have separate, but possibly correlated, distributions (O'Brien, Drummond, Labelle, & Willan, 1994; Wakker & Klaassen, 1995). Fundamental statistical work is needed in this area.

In conclusion, cost–utility analysis will become an increasingly recognized and routine component in the development, testing, and promulgation of behavioral interventions for public health improvement, and psychologists have a number of key roles to play in this arena. We believe that this truly is a positive trajectory. Indeed, behavioral interventions are overlooked all too often in public health programs. Having scientifically sound information on their cost-effectiveness will increase their relevance to policy makers and will (if economically efficient) increase the likelihood that they are more centrally included in comprehensive public health programs. The scientific literature contains many instances of behavioral interventions that have been shown to be not only life-saving but cost-saving as well. To fail to widely implement such interventions would be to fail the public's health and well-being. When lives are at stake, one cannot waste time or all-too-limited fiscal resources.

REFERENCES

Chisolm, D., Healey, A., & Knapp, M. (1997). QALYs and mental health care. *Social Psychiatry and Psychiatric Epidemiology, 32*, 68–75.

Clemmer, B., & Haddix, A. C. (1996). Cost-benefit analysis. In A. C. Haddix, S. M. Teutsch, P. A. Shaffer, & D. O. Duñet (Eds.), *Prevention effectiveness:*

A guide to decision analysis and economic evaluation (pp. 103–129). New York: Oxford University Press.

Drummond, M. F., O'Brien, B., Stoddart, G. L., & Torrance, G. W. (1997). *Methods for the economic evaluation of health care programmes* (2nd ed.). New York: Oxford University Press.

Drummond, M. F., Stoddart, G. L., & Torrance, G. W. (1987). *Methods for the economic evaluation of health care programmes.* New York: Oxford University Press.

Erfurt, J. C., Foote, A., & Heirich, M. A. (1992). The cost-effectiveness of worksite wellness programs for hypertension control, weight loss, smoking cessation, and exercise. *Personnel Psychology, 45,* 5–27.

Ganiats, T. G., & Wong, A. F. (1991). Evaluation of cost-effectiveness research: A survey of recent publications. *Family Medicine, 23,* 457–462.

Gold, M. R., Siegel, J. E., Russell, L. B., & Weinstein, M. C. (Eds.). (1996). *Cost-effectiveness in health and medicine.* New York: Oxford University Press.

Gorsky, R. D. (1996). A method to measure the costs of counseling for HIV prevention. *Public Health Reports, 111,* 115–122.

Groth-Marnat, G., & Schumaker, J. (1995). Psychologists in disease prevention and health promotion: A review of the cost-effectiveness literature. *Psychology —A Quarterly Journal of Human Behavior, 32,* 1–10.

Haddix, A. C., & Shaffer, P. A. (1996). Cost-effectiveness analysis. In A. C. Haddix, S. M. Teutsch, P. A. Shaffer, & D. O. Duñet (Eds.), *Prevention effectiveness: A guide to decision analysis and economic evaluation* (pp. 130–142). New York: Oxford University Press.

Haddix, A. C., Teutsch, S. M., Shaffer, P. A., & Duñet, D. O. (Eds.). (1996). *Prevention effectiveness: A guide to decision analysis and economic evaluation.* New York: Oxford University Press.

Holtgrave, D. R. (1990). Evaluation of a statistical inference method for multi-criteria decision making [Abstract]. *Medical Decision Making, 11,* 70.

Holtgrave, D. R. (1998). A few reflections on the practicality of economic evaluation methods and conclusions. In D. R. Holtgrave (Ed.), *The handbook of economic evaluation of HIV prevention programs* (pp. 211–215). New York: Plenum Press.

Holtgrave, D. R., DiFranceisco, W., Reiser, W., Resenhoeft, R., Hoxie, N., Pinkerton, S. D., & Vergeront, J. (1997). Setting standards for the Wisconsin HIV counseling and testing program: An application of threshold analysis. *Journal of Public Health Management and Practice, 4,* 59–66.

Holtgrave, D. R., & Kelly, J. A. (1996). Preventing HIV/AIDS among high risk urban women: The cost-effectiveness of a behavioral group intervention. *American Journal of Public Health, 86,* 1442–1445.

Holtgrave, D. R., & Kelly, J. A. (1997). The cost-effectiveness of an HIV/AIDS prevention intervention for gay men. *AIDS and Behavior, 1,* 173–180.

Holtgrave, D. R., & Pinkerton, S. D. (1997). Updates of cost of illness and quality of life estimates for use in economic evaluations of HIV prevention programs. *Journal of Acquired Immune Deficiency Syndromes, 16*, 54–62.

Holtgrave, D. R., & Pinkerton, S. D. (1998a). Setting performance standards for a national HIV prevention program [Abstract]. *International Conference on AIDS, 12*, 944.

Holtgrave, D. R., & Pinkerton, S. D. (1998b). The cost-effectiveness of small group and community-level intervention. In D. R. Holtgrave (Ed.), *The handbook of economic evaluation of HIV prevention programs* (pp. 119–126). New York: Plenum Press.

Holtgrave, D. R., & Pinkerton, S. D. (2000). The economics of HIV primary prevention. In J. L. Peterson & R. J. DiClemente (Eds.), *Handbook of HIV prevention* (pp. 286–296). New York: Plenum Press.

Holtgrave, D. R., & Pinkerton, S. D. (in press). Implications of economic evaluations for national HIV prevention policy makers. In E. H. Kaplan & R. Brookmeyer (Eds.), *Quantitative evaluation of HIV prevention programs*. New York: Oxford University Press.

Holtgrave, D. R., Pinkerton, S. D., Jones, T. S., Lurie, P., & Vlahov, D. (1998). Cost and cost-effectiveness of increasing access to sterile syringes and needles as an HIV prevention intervention in the United States. *Journal of Acquired Immune Deficiency Syndromes, 18*(Suppl. 1), S133–138.

Holtgrave, D. R., Qualls, N. L., & Graham, J. D. (1996). Economic evaluation of HIV prevention programs. *Annual Review of Public Health, 17*, 467–488.

Kamlet, M. S., Paul, N., Greenhouse, J., Kupfer, D., Frank, E., & Wade, M. (1995). Cost utility analysis of maintenance treatment for recurrent depression. *Controlled Clinical Trials, 16*, 17–40.

Kaplan, R. M. (1989). Health outcome models for policy analysis. *Health Psychology, 8*, 723–735.

Kaplan, R. M., Feeny, D., & Revicki, D. A. (1993). Methods for assessing relative importance in preference based outcome measures. *Quality of Life Research, 2*, 467–475.

Klesges, R. C., Ward, K. D., & DeBon, M. (1996). Smoking cessation: A successful behavioral/pharmacologic interface. *Clinical Psychology Review, 16*, 479–496.

Meenan, R. T., Stevens, V. J., Hornbrook, M. C., La Chance, P.-A., Glasgow, R. E., Hollis, J. F., Lichtenstein, E., & Vogt, T. M. (1998). Cost-effectiveness of a hospital-based smoking cessation intervention. *Medical Care, 36*, 670–678.

Norton, E. D., Martin, R. F., & Wechsberg, W. (1998). Threshold analysis of AIDS outreach and intervention. In D. R. Holtgrave (Ed.), *The handbook of economic evaluation of HIV prevention programs* (pp. 195–209). New York: Plenum Press.

O'Brien, B. J., Drummond, M. F., Labelle, R. J., & Willan, A. (1994). In search of power and significance: Issues in the design and analysis of stochastic cost-effectiveness studies in health care. *Medical Care, 32*, 150–163.

Paltiel, A. D., & Stinnett, A. A. (1998). Resource allocation and the funding of

HIV prevention. In D. R. Holtgrave (Ed.), *The handbook of economic evaluation of HIV prevention programs* (pp. 13–32). New York: Plenum Press.

Patrick, D. L., & Erikson, P. (1993). *Health status and health policy: Allocating resources to health care*. New York: Oxford University Press.

Pinkerton, S. D., & Abramson, P. R. (1998). The Bernoulli-process model of HIV transmission: Applications and implications. In D. R. Holtgrave (Ed.), *The handbook of economic evaluation of HIV prevention programs* (pp. 35–152). New York: Plenum Press.

Pinkerton, S. D., & Holtgrave, D. R. (1998a). Assessing the cost-effectiveness of HIV prevention interventions: A primer. In D. R. Holtgrave (Ed.), *The handbook of economic evaluation of HIV prevention programs* (pp. 34–43). New York: Plenum Press.

Pinkerton, S. D., & Holtgrave, D. R. (1998b). A method for evaluating the economic efficiency of HIV behavioral risk reduction interventions. *AIDS and Behavior, 2*.

Pinkerton, S. D., Holtgrave, D. R., DiFranceisco, W. J., Stevenson, L. Y., & Kelly, J. A. (1998). Cost-effectiveness of a community-level HIV risk reduction intervention. *American Journal of Public Health, 88*, 1239–1242.

Pinkerton, S. D., Holtgrave, D. R., Leviton, L. C., Wagstaff, D. A., & Abramson, P. R. (1998). Model-based evaluation of HIV prevention interventions. *Evaluation Review, 22*, 155–174.

Pinkerton, S. D., Holtgrave, D. R., & Valdiserri, R. O. (1997). Cost-effectiveness of HIV-prevention skills training for men who have sex with men. *AIDS, 11*, 347–357.

Rehle, T. M., Saidel, T. J., Hassig, S. E., Bouey, P. D., Gaillard, E. M., & Sokal, D. C. (1998). AVERT: A user-friendly model to estimate the impact of HIV/sexually transmitted disease prevention interventions on HIV transmission. *AIDS, 12*(Suppl. 2), S27–S35.

Reid, D. (1996). Tobacco control: Overview. *British Medical Bulletin, 52*, 108–120.

Secker-Walker, R. H., Worden, J. K., Holland, R. R., Flynn, B. S., & Detsky, A. S. (1997). A mass media programme to prevent smoking among adolescents: Costs and cost-effectiveness. *Tobacco Control, 6*, 207–212.

Tengs, T. O., Adams, M. E., Pliskin, J. S., Safran, D. G., Siegel, J. E., Weinstein, M. C., & Graham, J. D. (1995). Five-hundred lifesaving interventions and their cost-effectiveness. *Risk Analysis, 15*, 369–390.

Tolley, G. L., Kenkel, D., & Fabian, R. (Eds.). (1994). *Valuing health for policy: An economic approach*. Chicago: University of Chicago Press.

Wakker, P., & Klaassen, M. P. (1995). Confidence intervals for cost/effectiveness ratios. *Economic Evaluation, 4*, 373–381.

Weinstein, M. C., Graham, J. D., Siegel, J. E., & Fineberg, H. V. (1989). Cost-effectiveness analysis of AIDS prevention programs: Concepts, complications, and illustrations. In C. F. Turner, H. G. Miller, & L. E. Moses (Eds.), *AIDS: Sexual behavior and intravenous drug use* (pp. 471–499). Washington, DC: National Academy Press.

13

TOWARD A PSYCHOSOCIALLY HEALTHY WORK ENVIRONMENT: BROADER ROLES FOR PSYCHOLOGISTS AND SOCIOLOGISTS[1]

ROBERT KARASEK

This chapter discusses the costs and benefits of emerging psychosocial characteristics of modern work life. It highlights some of the macrolevel political–economic implications of psychosocially health job redesign based on "new work organization" principles. Such work design processes normally occur at the level of the work station or work place but carry broader political–economic implications as well. The chapter claims that professionals who combine the humane well-being goals of public health professionals and psychological and sociological wisdom relating to working life and its effects have the necessary skills to allow them to take a leading role in developing humane alternative forms for workplace economic development in both the microlevel of the company and the macropolitical level. In a new form of work—here labeled conductive production—this knowledge is becoming central to the production process.

---

[1]This chapter uses "psychologists and sociologists" to include noneconomic social science disciplines (e.g., psychologists, sociologists, anthropologists, political scientists). I do, however, distinguish between professionals in these disciplines and those who work in neoclassical economics. Neoclassical economics is related to a very different conception of the work environment, for which this chapter proposes an alternative.

New skills relating to psychosocial working life are needed to meet the broad challenge of developing healthy work environments in a modern global economy. There are major transformations occurring in the organization of work activity in our global economy. These changes dramatically affect two relatively new areas of occupational health practice: psychosocial workplace health hazard analysis and work reorganization intervention to promote psychosocial well-being. Some claim that these areas of study also offer a means to understand certain changes in the workplace brought about by the changing global economy.

Although the audience of this chapter, and the book as a whole, is broad, it is also unique in that it has a set of broadly humane goals beyond profitability, which is often the priority of many social policy discussions. By contrast, the market-based model (neoclassical economics) that is driving many of the changes in the global economy is used by corporations to attain very specific private-sector profitability goals. Unfortunately, these private goals have become the central basis of almost all social policy discussions. Nonetheless, public health professionals, as well as many social sciences professionals, have broader goals that include, in addition to productivity, advocacy for human well-being and human developmental possibilities—at work and in other spheres of life. This set of goals is crucial because when it is combined with the social science wisdom about social and psychological organization in the workplace and its effects, it leads to a new perspective on the organization of economic life, with implications for public health.

This chapter is based on the assumption that work-related psychosocial factors—such as low decision latitude, high psychological demands, and low social support—are understood to be significant contributors to distress and chronic disease. It does not summarize the evidence for this conclusion, although a brief listing of some of the review articles is provided. Certainly not all readers would consider this point to be thoroughly proven at this time; many important research topics in this new area of study remain under investigation, and it will remain the subject of much future work. My comments about new forms of production also represent only a brief outline (see Karasek, 1997, 1999a, 1999b, for further discussion). The point of this chapter is to discuss the next step. Consider the apparent psychosocial costs of modern work activity and the new "psychosocial forms of productivity" that dominate growth areas of industrial development (briefly mentioned below). Given these issues, an entirely new perspective emerges regarding the public health consequences of modern economic development, as does a new set of roles for social scientists.

The conventional political policy approaches to occupational health issues that have until now provided the broad social context for work life change (both free-market-oriented and classic social welfare state approaches) are failing. I believe the reason for this is that they have insufficient understanding of the psychosocial side of working and of the political implications of so-called new work organizations. Policy makers must give consideration to humane economic growth strategies, job security and intensity, services provided by the workplace, and the relation between civil democracy and economy. Although many readers of this chapter may consider themselves either as scientists or health care providers and not policy makers, the psychosocial approach provides an important linkage to the broader social political debate relating to the alternative forms of production and their implications.

THE NEW WORK ORGANIZATION: A TIME OF TRANSITION

From a psychosocial perspective, there have been both positive and negative trends in work organizations in the global economy. On the positive side, work-organization changes that promote human development and that significantly affect psychosocial characteristics of work are occurring in many industries and on a global scale; some of these changes include increased skill breadth, reduced hierarchy, horizontal collaboration, customer engagement, and creative product development. Typical slogans used to describe the new work organization are "the end of hierarchy," "worker participation in decision making," and "intellectual capital as a major asset."

This new image of the future is certainly rhetorical in part, but it is supported by such powerful economic institutions that it could hardly be considered a utopian dream. The new ideas are seen in business books and magazines of every advanced industrial society, as well as in emerging corporate policies. For example, a *Business Week* cover story (Byrne, 1994) about horizontal organization highlights the fact that rigid vertical hierarchies with many levels of authority are being flattened, reducing power inequalities. These structures were insufficiently flexible to respond to customer needs in the global economy. They also restricted worker's abilities to use and develop their skills. Internet linkages and telecommuting add to the possibility of nonhierarchical work relationships. A second theme in the work reorganization process, designed to change organizations into more flexible forms, is the need to expand decision-making freedom for individuals. James Champy is a coauthor of a well-known corporate redesign program—re-engineering—which has swept U.S. corporations and is arriving in parts of Europe. Champy (1996) described how "putting employees in the driver's seat" will increase effectiveness of business organizations (p. 13). "Power to the people" is the unmistakable content of this message. Even the nature of investment capital in society is dramatically changed, according to *Fortune Magazine*'s cover story (Stewart, 1994) "Intellectual Capital: The New Wealth of Organizations." This article discussed the value of employees' skills, implying a major modification in the rules governing private property (Stewart, 1997).

On the negative side, psychosocial changes in job characteristics are also occurring; among these are increasing job insecurity (even in the context of high employment), high levels of work intensity, and an undermining of the social institutions for labor protection and social security. These changes are the result of ever-more-aggressive applications of free-market economic policies that focus solely on profitability. This is leading to a second, threatening set of headlines including the "End of the Job," "Rewriting the Social Contract," and "Productivity to Nowhere." In the United States, currently the model economy for many European market oriented policy (MOP) policy makers, the new power of employers over employees has brought increased work intensity (see Hancock, 1995, and Church, 1994), and decision making in production is moving farther from the shop floor and office cubicle.

The central institution of the "job," the basic social unit and thus the source of stability in modern society of specialized workers, is under threat. The "job" is ironically termed a "social artifact that has outlived its usefulness" in a *Fortune* Magazine cover story (*"The End of the Job,"* Bridges, 1994). This assault, coming with unprecedented speed in the United States, has created very high levels of job insecurity (over 40% of the workforce reporting insecurity in multiple surveys in the mid 1990s and currently acknowledged by Federal Reserve Chairman Alan Greenspan, in spite of low unemployment levels; Technology Is Heightening, 2000). It also undermines the social framework of communities with few compensating local advantages (Uchitelle & Klienfield, 1996). The social contract that has evolved as the industrial relations system, which relates to labor conditions, job stability, relative wages, labor union organization, and collective bargaining, is being rewritten. As Gleckman (1995) claimed in *Business Week*, international business is "rewriting the social contract," but he observed in the footnotes that the modern populations may not willingly be accepting this unilaterally negotiated bargain. Multinational capitalism is coming into a newly dominant position in the balance of power between capital and national democratic institutions and between capital and labor.

In many cases new forms of work organization are being applied in the context of old profits-only goals, for example "lean production" (see p. 279). This represents a new contradiction between means and ends and leads to confusion in social policy. I attempt to resolve this conflict here through development of a new definition of the "end goal" of production processes, that is, by providing a new definition of productivity called *conducive production* (see below). This new definition is more consistent with the humane development content of skills-based work organization change. It is consistent with new trends in economic development and, important for this audience, it is more consistent with the goal of promoting psychosocial health in the workplace.

THE UNINTENDED COSTS OF INDUSTRIAL PRODUCTION: THE EVOLVING CONTRIBUTIONS OF PSYCHOLOGISTS AND SOCIOLOGISTS

For most of this century, the unintended costs of mass production have been assumed to be primarily physical hazard based (and perhaps a numbing, but otherwise nontoxic boredom). Thus, emerging chronic diseases of populations in the 20th century, many of them with a possible stress-related etiology, were thought to have primarily nonwork causes. Only in more recent times, as stress-related disability and illness have become more prevalent, have social and psychological causes related to adult working life come into focus. In the past decade, however, work organization increasingly gained social recognition as the cause of many chronic conditions—at least in the most advanced counties. Nonetheless, many health care practitioners with social science backgrounds continue to be engaged in after-the-fact amelioration of patients' symptoms without exploring the new prevention-based possibilities that occur in relation to work environment redesign even if the work-related nature of these illnesses is confirmed. Rather than redesigning workplaces, the present role of health care providers is limited to "patching up" the unintended residues of increasingly more demanding economic competition, although institutional alternatives do exist, as discussed below. Thus, new, broadly preventative roles may exist for psychologists and sociologists.

A Brief Review of Evidence Supporting the Importance of the Psychosocial Work Environment to Public Health

Unfortunately, it is beyond the scope of this chapter to review the extensive research literature linking psychosocial job characteristics to illness. Briefly, the pathways to illness include lack of social support (both at work and outside work), job insecurity, insufficient reward for work (Siegrist, 1996), as well as research of the demand, control, and social support model to which this author has contributed, have altogether accumulated a voluminous literature (Belcik et al., 2000; Karasek, 1976; Karasek & Theorell, 1990). (The demand–control–support perspective is discussed in reviews by Kristensen, 1995, 1996; Schnall, Landsbergis, & Baker, 1994; Theorell & Karasek, 1996.) In summary, it can be stated that low decision latitude, low social support, and high psychological demands at work demonstrate substantial, but often variable, predictive validity with respect to a broad variety of stress-related chronic disease in international and U.S. research. Further research into the causes and extent of risk linkages has been and will continue to be a major role for psychologists and sociologists.

Associations between job strain (the combination of high demand coupled with low ability to control behavior in the face of those demands) and heart disease represent the broadest base of empirical support for the demand–control–support model. Questionnaire-based and occupationally linked job characteristic estimates associate significantly with cardiovascular mortality using a wide range of methodologies. Landsbergis (discussing his reviews in Schnall et al., 1994, and Belcik et al., 2000, by personal communication, December 1997) has tabulated 72 published studies of cardiovascular disease (CVD) or CVD risk factors to test associations with job strain. Of the 36 studies that investigated CVD or mortality, more than two thirds showed positive associations (i.e., either all significant or mixed significant positive results) with job strain (broadly interpreted as high demand, low control, or both), and many of these are positive cohort studies. The conventional coronary heart disease (CHD) risk factor associations among smoking, cholesterol, blood pressure, and job strain are much less consistent. The more sophisticated 24-hour blood-pressure-monitoring strategies do show much more consistently supportive results, however; perhaps advances in methodology will improve understanding of the risk factors. Of course, other pathways to heart disease, such as stress-induced arrhythmia, may be responsible for the more robust heart disease and mortality findings.

Associations between mental strain and the same job characteristics scales are also consistently reported (see Karasek & Theorell, 1990; Van der Doef & Maes, 1999), but differential effects of job characteristics are noted. Measures of exhaustion and burnout are more consistently associated with high psychological demands, whereas depression and anxiety measures are more strongly associated with low decision latitude.

Occupational psychosocial musculoskeletal illness prediction is reviewed for 30 first-generation studies by Bongers, DeWinter, Kompier, and Hildebrandt (1993), who found support for the predictive utility of the demand–control–support model, particularly for upper-extremity disorders. Many additional studies using the demand–control–support model and the JCQ scales have been undertaken since then. Recent studies of pregnancy disorders (Brandt & Neilsen, 1992; Fenster et al., 1995) also show job strain associations. More recently, studies testing associations between job strain and immune system dysfunctions are under way and show positive associations (Kawakami et al., 1997; Peters et al., 1998).

Difficult methodological challenges remain, such as effective measurement of psychological demands and the integration of job strain effects with the demand–control–support model's active behavior hypotheses. These challenges certainly imply a significant role for research in the future for psychologists and sociologists. Work psychology from northern Europe represents a potential new role model. In Sweden, Denmark, Norway, the Netherlands, Finland, and Germany, specialists in the behavioral and social sciences focus less on individual personality and coping than on environmental hazards of psychological and social character. This helps shift some of the burden of healthy adaptation from the worker to the workplace.

Psychosocial Workplace Questionnaires: Increasing Utility for Policy Issues

The first set of tools used by psychosocial workplace researchers are questionnaires that can measure aspects of work-related public health problems and test many of the trends noted above. Well-developed tools exist to measure psychological demands of work, task-related decision possibilities, skill utilization, influence at the organizational level, social relations with coworkers, social relations with supervisors, job insecurity, and other dimensions.

Without such new criteria about the quality of jobs created, competing economic development and labor relations strategies take on an increasingly beggar-thy-neighbor quality. Economic development policies based on free-market rationales have the goal of increasing material well-being by reducing production costs of manufactured goods, often relying on competition between countries to reduce wages and labor protections. In my own experience, visiting a number of European countries in 1990– 1991, I found that in country X, policy makers were worried that their automobile factories would be shut down by competition from country Y and that they would therefore need to cut social costs. Country Y said that because of their competition with country X, they also had to cut social costs to remain competitive or close their auto factories. Far from leading to the best of all possible worlds in which prices of manufactured goods were reduced, as has been taught by market-oriented economic policy, this competition was leading both countries to cut their social expenditures. However well people might do in terms of material well-being (e.g., cheaper cars), the people of each country would suffer from a major loss of social benefits and new forms of psychosocial suffering, which have not been tabulated in this social decision-making process.

Ironically, this is happening just as these "invisible" social losses are being demonstrated as measurable and comparable between countries. These measures provide suitable new criteria for international discussions of broader, "qualitative" social impact. For example, Dhondt (1998) reviewed workplace time constraints (psychological demand combined with low decision latitude) that could contribute to psychological stress measured in five European questionnaire studies from the 1970s through the mid-1990s. The results indicate that these stresses are increasing. These are important trends and further demonstrate that psychosocial factors are sufficiently measurable to contribute to broad social discussions.

One such questionnaire instrument for measuring the demand– control–support model—the Job Content Questionnaire (JCQ)—demonstrates substantial similarity in means and standard deviations across six broadly representative studies in four countries: the United States, Canada, the Netherlands, and Japan. The between-country variance on the job content scales is substantially smaller than the consistent between-occupational differences reported in other studies on a number of important dimensions (Karasek et al., 1998). Thus, working conditions in modern industrial countries appear to be significantly more similar across national boundaries than they are across occupational boundaries. A global economy for working conditions has arrived in industrialized countries.

Questionnaires such as the one cited above could give policy makers a much-needed new tool to use in international policy discussions affecting psychosocial working conditions, such as international free-trade agreements. Thus, one role for psychologists and sociologists is certainly to tabulate the cost of economic development both internationally and locally. Who else could provide these insights?

Broader use of such measurement tools could eventually help resolve a major challenge in the psychosocial area: the lack of general awareness about the work-relatedness of these hazards. The importance of additional public understanding of these hazards is illustrated in the *Dutch Monitor* survey covering ergonomic hazard estimates—by employee groups and separately by employers—for more than 700 companies (Houtman et al., 1998). There are major discrepancies in the report of psychosocial hazards at work between groups of employees and their employers. In the 700 companies, some employee groups report very high psychological risk, others report low-level risk, and many report a mid-level risk, yielding the expected binominal distribution with a mean of about 30% reporting significant problems at the company. On the other hand, managers for the same company report dramatically lower levels of psychosocial risks and a very skewed distribution, with a mean of fewer than 10% reporting significant problems at the company. Most of the companies report that they have no problem at all: "everything is fine here." The disagreement itself could represent an aspect of distrust and adds another level of psychosocial risk (Warren, 1997) that is important for predicting musculoskeletal disorders, for example. Thus, there needs to be more social dialogue about the nature of these risks, and psychologists and sociologists must lead it.

THE PRODUCTIVITY BENEFITS OF PRODUCTION

Psychosocial Work Redesign Interventions: A Dual Health and Productivity Focus

Human well-being is more than the absence of illness. The design of workplaces must promote positive goals for human capability development as well. Furthermore, because productivity is the primary goal of a company's workplace arrangements, major workplace reorganization rarely can be undertaken with health concerns as the only goal. Therefore, major workplace redesign must focus on both productivity consequences of new workplace solutions and their health consequences from both a human well-being and a company well-being perspective. To the extent that the worker's personal development can be consistent with company productivity goals, an additional, strong multiparty motivation for significantly redesigned workplaces can be created. This movement could gain the support of both health professionals and companies. This new set of roles for psychologists and sociologists already has been captured in part by management-oriented advocates of the new work organization, but in my view, a socially more responsible definition of this activity is needed.

The demand–control model demonstrates one relevant analytic model that shows the integrated link between productivity and health in terms of psychosocial job characteristics and is relevant to both cost and benefit analyses. It is discussed above with respect to cost-based hypotheses about health hazards of psychosocial working conditions (high-strain jobs). The model also has hypotheses about productivity benefits of highly motivating, learning-oriented working conditions (active jobs with high decision latitude and high, but not too high, demands). Consistent work organization policies to achieve both increased productivity and reduced incidence of illness (via increased decision authority and skill use, as well as improved coworker and supervisor relations) are predicted by the model. Nonetheless, to understand how both productivity and improved well-being might be achieved in a productive social process, a more detailed understanding of the social processes of production is required.

Historical Evolution of the New Forms of Production and Social Science Contributions

Of course, the conventional form of large-scale, mass production of physical objects (hereafter termed *commodity production*) still drives much of the world's economic policy making. But new evolutionary trends are significant. First, I contend that the nature of work coordination that most optimally produces this commodity value has a generalized, negative effect on psychosocial health. This occurs because the profitability of commodity-oriented production processes is maximized through mass production, which in turn rests on the contribution of specialized labor and machines. Furthermore, the most profitable mass production is based on large markets. The larger the market, the larger the production process and the more specialization of labor it supports (Smith, 1776/1976). This contributes to the productivity advantage of mass production in a global economy. But specialization of labor is, of course, the same as low-decision-latitude jobs. Skills are reduced and narrowed in specialized work, the control over activity at work is reduced for many lower status workers below the levels that were common for farmers and craft workers in earlier eras of production (Karasek & Theorell, 1990, p. 46). Thus, I contend that the conventional economic model of production applied in global markets would not lead to psychosocially healthy workplaces. This free-market-guided, "quantitative," physical-object-focused model has excluded appropriate attention to psychosocial factors that are relevant both to modern workplace health risks and to new forms of productivity.

The role of psychologists and sociologists in the most recent period of industrial production—since the advent of the automobile assembly line —has been to contribute insights about improving social behavior in physical-object-oriented, mass-production processes in large-scale hierarchical organizations. Sometimes it meant encouraging efficient participation in the boring jobs; other times it meant resolving leadership and communication bottlenecks in the rigid communication and authority structures. For example, social psychologists developed knowledge about leadership skills (Mayo, in Roethlisberger & Dickinson, 1939), and organizational charting (Gulick & Urwick, 1937) and about efficient participation in work groups (Homans, 1950). The "human relations" school that emerged in organization and management departments of business schools provided social skills for management and technical personnel that transcended the earlier quantitative-only assessment of task content and wage rates from Taylor's earlier "scientific management" era. Nonetheless, many managers continued to see these social skills as "charm course" supplements to the more prized information inputs from engineers and cost accountants about expensive mechanical investments, complex technical processes efficiency, and physical resource inputs. Even the more recent contributions of this type (March & Simon, 1958), which utilize new computer-based information systems to control worker motivation and steer corporate behavior, recommend management procedures that are independent of the social content of the job itself. In all the above cases, social-relations wisdom from psychologists and sociologists, important as it has become, remains basically peripheral; it simply facilitates material production.

But the economy has changed significantly since Adam Smith (1776/ 1976) first developed the original formulations of classical economics 200 years ago. Michael Porter (1990) from the Harvard Business School claimed that the pathway to economic development that worked for the 18th and 19th centuries, via national resource strength and cheap labor, was not the approach used in the 20th century. Human resources are the key ingredient in the 11 countries examined by Porter in the current decade. Today, workers' skills, communication and collaboration between companies, active demand of customers, and motivation are the pathways to an organization's success or failure (a similar view is advanced by Piore & Sable, 1984). Customers are not to be passively satisfied but must actively develop demands for goods and services. Otherwise, they will not drive economic development. Social relations therefore become more central to production.

A Psychosocially Healthy New Productivity Definition: Conducive Production

By contrast to commodity production, the new definition of conducive production model introduced here focuses on the quality of labor. New principles of psychosocial coordination at work are the foundation of this new skills-based and socially relational model. Such principles also are visible in many of the most dynamic current industrial examples. For example, the productivity of the Internet is based on social association and skills facilitation (see discussion on p. 283). These features are also central to most service sector industries. Conducive production implies dramatically different patterns of social coordination in production. Consistent with the above economic evidence, but more descriptive of the actual human behavioral process of production involving human resource development, conducive production is an alternative definition of production output and value (Karasek, 1981, 1999a, 1999b; Karasek & Theorell, 1990). It might be called a "psychosocial form of productivity."

Conducive production means a mode of producing that is "conducive" to the positive development of skills of the producer and the customers as well. In conducive production, skills are mutually induced in both the producer (and employees) and the customer. In the model, products and services are valuable (deserve social recognition) if they enable the growth of the customer's own productive capabilities. I call this a "tool-like" output. It relates to innovative products as well as to services. The value of the output is based on the developmental capacity it offers the customer. This is fundamentally different from biologically required output (i.e., a tuna sandwich one eats to satisfy hunger).

Consider an example of a conducive product that is computer software: a simple word processor. The word processor was produced for the customer who used it to grow and develop publishing skills. Perhaps the customer started by writing business letters but eventually became interested in producing—for other customers in turn—company newsletters or desktop graphics. The customer's growth and development means they moved to a new level in terms of needs for their own production process tools. The customer has grown, and the word processor tools must grow with these evolving capabilities. This growth process generates the demand for more of the same intellectually qualified production that produced the word processor in the first place. In the process of producing, exchanging, using, and redesigning, the transfer continually focuses on increasing skills —skills of both the producer's employees and its customers. "Consuming" such an output is not the end of the production process, nor is producing it the initial phase of consumption. Both are aspects of a continuing process of association and coordination through skill (i.e., the process of continually using and developing and then reusing and redeveloping human capabilities). This new form of economic activity is a systemic process with feedback loops, rather than a series of separate functional equations about means–end relationships. Figure 13.1 may help to illustrate conducive production.

The first step in the process is when a production group produces a tool-like output that facilitates the customer's development of new capabilities. This enables the successful attainment of the original customer's goal. In step 2 the customer's capabilities grow as the conducive product is used in new applications. This, in turn stimulates new production ideas in the customer. It stimulates the customer to return to the first producer group with a demand for an even more sophisticated tool (step 3). Thus, conducive products generate their own demand for tool-like products (step 4), sustaining this type of economic growth. It also sustains the demand for broadly skilled work, by contrast to the Smithian demand for specialized skill: an alternative growth dynamic.

Linking customers to producers and workers into production is accomplished in a decentralized manner, requiring much higher levels of communication between workers and customers. Psychologists and other social scientists should be engaged to teach the new production behaviors that utilize creative coordination. This way of socially oriented relations is markedly different from hierarchically coordinated behavior.

Conducive Value: A Production Value Form That Embodies Creative Social Relations

On this platform of new work coordination patterns, a new form of output value is defined. The distinction between the coordination pattern and the nature of output value is a significant distinction because many of the new work organization examples are applied toward the goal of profit maximization. This can lead to a complex form of work inhumanity, such as that observed in "lean production." In lean production, the breadth of worker skills is higher than assembly-line work, but not exceptionally high, and if old, centrally controlled decision structures are not replaced with decentralized ones, overall worker decision freedom declines through more elaborate process control, ultimately increasing stress.[2]

---

[2]In lean production, some "job-enriching" elements are joined with even more stringent management controls to eliminate production "slack" in an effort to increase quantity output and reduce inventories. This increased workload, combined with restricted control, can be an unfortunate combination for workers. Systems are driven to the constant point of failure, leading to working conditions discussed as "management by stress" (Parker & Slaughter, 1988) in which prevention of any waste eliminates workers' last "valid" reasons for a rest break.

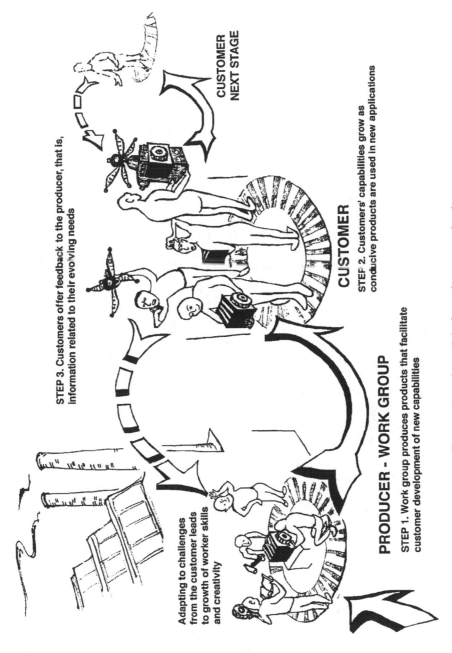

STEP 3. Customers offer feedback to the producer, that is, information related to their evolving needs

CUSTOMER
NEXT STAGE

CUSTOMER

STEP 2. Customers' capabilities grow as conducive products are used in new applications

Adapting to challenges from the customer leads to growth of worker skills and creativity

PRODUCER - WORK GROUP

STEP 1. Work group produces products that facilitate customer development of new capabilities

Figure 13.1. A model of conducive production.

Conducive value is a skills-based, associative value that develops in horizontally flexible, creative new production processes. This new form of value is particularly significant in innovative manufacturing industries and in service industries. This value is developed in both workers and customers as part of a new form of social exchange that emphasizes growth of capabilities of individuals and organizations.

Conducive production adds value to "growth-capable entities" rather than adding value to inanimate, physical objects that are commodities (e.g., wheat, oil, steel beams, computer chips, and automobiles). Current mass-production processes, for example, add value to an object by having laborers machine a piece of cast iron, and this object then becomes more "valuable" in the marketplace because of its desirable physical properties. But it is "dead," that is, it is a commodity, inanimate, with no developmental capability of its own. In the conducivity model, developing entities, such as people, organizations, and communities, occupy the central position. For example, when a teacher helps a young pupil read or a doctor teaches elderly patients how to care for their diabetes, human beings gain the value of the expended labor. Creative and interactive social relations are an inseparable component of conducive value but a meaningless characteristic for material objects. This value is thus much closer to the preventative and health-promoting goals of public health.

The physical-object focus of commodity value derives from an earlier era, when society's most valued outputs were indeed physical objects, often created by adding one's labor to natural resources, for example, by farming a field to produce crops. By contrast, today's challenge is to develop human resources while maintaining effective goods production.

Conventional economic goods must be scarce to satisfy the prerequisites of its "zero-sum" value; simply stated, what one person takes, another cannot have. The value of education cannot be considered in this way, however. Lessons may be taught over and over to many individuals without diminishing their utility because they have already been taught to someone else. Contrast the value of the skill of cake baking to the value in the cake itself. The cake itself has conventional zero-sum economic value that is reflected in the adage "you can't have your cake and eat it too." But one can teach cake baking to many pupils without losing the cake-baking skill in the process; indeed, the skill might be enhanced (i.e., the value of the skill is not removed from its producer during exchange).

Furthermore, skills, the capabilities of active entities like human beings, tend to associate by their nature. They are not bounded and limited like material objects, but expand and link to other skills as they are developed when individuals expand their goals and diversify experiences. For this new form of production, value is in the association; it is not in the objects themselves. It can be the association of capabilities that potentially can be integrated. It can be the value of a team of collaborators, the value of a well-integrated set of computer programs, or the value of each element in a good real estate investment package. Obviously, this value form incorporates interactive social relationships as the central basis of value creation—not as a peripheral aid.

Conducive Needs

A fundamental property of the conducivity model is that a need stems from human capabilities that "want to be used" in a socially constructive manner: "I am a carpenter. I want to build houses." Needs are not understood here as biological drives that must be satisfied; conducive needs are socially derived. Learning a skill increases the appetite for more knowledge (the need to know). Skills beget more skills and then lead to the desire to use these newly acquired capabilities; skills are their own source of motivation. All active organisms want to use their capabilities; they also want to use them in collaboration with others. The appropriate metaphor does not come from biological survival, but from making jazz music. Making jazz has been dubbed "collective improvisation," a "New England town meeting," and "a dialogue" among equals—the audience included (Marsalis, 1996). Consider jazz musician Curtis Fuller's description of his reaction to shouts from the audience:

> When I get that message, the guy in the audience is saying, "I'm still there. Come on, run it by me again." . . . Sometimes, I'll keep the thing going there. I'll deal with that phrase and expand on that, develop that. . . . And when I see those little interests tapering off, I'll say "All right now. Come on. Let's try something else and take it another way. . . . When I get that audience around that they won't let me off the stage." (Berliner, 1994, p. 468)

The producer and its employees are the musicians; the customer is the audience. Together, they collaborate to continually improve a product, just as the audience encourages Fuller to expand on a musical theme. Customers' needs are intermediate steps in a continuing process; they keep it going, rather than start or finish it. Of course, these developed needs are secondary in determining human behavior to biological needs for food, shelter, and security: The fundamental prerequisite for a conducive economy is that such basic needs must continue to be satisfied.

Conducive Production and Value in Services

Examples of conducive production and value can be found today in both the service and manufacturing industries (Karasek, 1999a). A Swedish service industry example shows that both the health status of elderly patients of nursing homes and the job satisfaction of nursing home employees is improved as the result of new work design solutions that focus on improving the capabilities of patients (capability increases represent increases in conducive value). In an example from an elderly care home in Sweden, researchers developed a plan to activate the patients by analyzing what employee actions could reinforce the patient's activity platform. One floor of patients was activated by interviewing them about what they had done in their active lifetimes in an effort to reconstruct that interest and increase their current level of activity. Health care employees would bring in magazines or books or talk to the patients about these interests. Sometimes they arranged activities at the nursing home. The control group had the socially passive treatment that derives from considering the patient as a biological entity only (i.e., meeting only biological needs not conducive needs), which was standard in the home.

In the following 8 months, the activity level of the patients in the experimental patient group increased. They became physiologically healthier (Arnetz, Eyre, & Theorell, 1982) and wanted to take over some aspects of policy administration of the home. This was conducive production because it focused on development of patient capabilities for active participation through communicative interaction with them, instead of providing a physical "improvement" (through medicine or a physical procedure) as in the case of conventional, object-oriented medical treatment, where health care providers monopolize decisions about prescriptions and treatment. Health improvement in a practical form was the outcome. Absenteeism was also lower among the employees, who felt motivated because they were finally actively caring for the patients in the professionally sophisticated manner for which they had been trained.

This experiment clearly demonstrated that a new, capability-related form of productivity is relevant to service industries. This more intensive and constructively supportive interaction with patients on the experimental floor is the type of productivity contribution that behavioral and social scientists can best support. Such capability measures make more common sense than cost-based productivity assessments of health care service provision, such as patient visits per hour, derived from a faulty application of the market model for commodity output. Such commodity output actually has nothing to do with the real productivity goals of an elderly home, which is to improve or at least maintain health (Karasek & Theorell, 1990), not just to reduce health care costs. Understanding productivity in health care has been a major economic dilemma in many countries precisely because of this attempt to redefine health in such a logically inconsistent manner. Contributions such as these will become increasingly important to the goal of maintaining public health.

Conducive Production and Value in Computers and Communication

A second example is taken from the core area of economic growth for the 21st century as forecasted by all leading business magazines: the computer and communications industry. In this area, new models of value are already in operation, even if the new model is not always clearly identified. The Internet is a clear example. As the presumed backbone for future economic growth, the Internet was not produced by a single company to increase its profits by triumphing over competitors. Instead, it was constructed by public agencies to promote skills-building interfaces between researchers in different parts of the world and by linking separate (and potentially competing) capabilities. Researchers wanted to work together as they do in conferences; the Internet promoted that collaborative form of productivity.

A related example is the software program Java, developed by Sun Microsystems and the "old-fashioned" policy that Microsoft applied to this program. Java allows programmers to write a software program and use it on many computer systems, facilitating integration of various programs. Microsoft's policy toward Java appeared to fit the old commodity model. In some ways, Microsoft, with its intense engagement in development in new software products, represents conducive production. However in other ways Microsoft has been criticized for failing to adapt to consumers and for attempting to unilaterally control product development in the computer industry. Whenever a Java program was to operate on a computer using a Microsoft operating system, the program would be altered so that it could only run on a computer with Microsoft software (from 1997 through 1999; Sun Microsystems 1997). Thus, Microsoft could gain control of and derive exclusive revenue from this program's future uses. In my opinion, Microsoft wanted to put the same possessive limited boundary around the product's value, the form of value created by scarcity and that is undermined by free, unlimited access, that is the core concept of the commodity model. The commodity model makes sense for physical production, but it does not work for the new kind of conducive production. It limits productivity to applying commodity production and distribution policies (such as lowering wage costs or limiting product knowledge). True productivity in this form of production relies on sophisticated knowledge of collaborative social interactions and social network communication, major contribution areas for psychologists and sociologists.

Such old-fashioned policy certainly limits the productivity of conducive products in the computer industry. Indeed, lack of dynamic connectedness between product components (i.e., lack of conducivity) is a cause of product death in the computer industry. The inability of a product to successfully integrate with its collaborating products from other producers (i.e., competitors) has been the cause of the most significant computer industry declines of the past two decades, leading to major market losses for both IBM in the early 1980s and Apple in the 1990s. Thus, conducive production policies are hardly utopian in these rapidly developing industrial sectors.

What is needed at this point are the humane orientations and a human relationship focus provided by public-health-oriented psychologists and sociologists to maintain the salience of the conducivity model's human development goals. Otherwise, the conventional economic rewards of such new production could otherwise dominate through tradition or reversion to older values. Just such a shift of goals could be seen after the speculative stock market price run-up of Internet companies in 1998 and 1999.

Psychosocial Tools for Participative Workplace Change

Redesign of work is not just an activity that requires analysis of problems at the workplace. It also requires social processes to develop and decide on alternative solutions to workplace problems (Karasek, 1992b). Certainly there have been many contributions from psychologists and sociologists starting with Eric Trist, in the 1950s and 1960s in Scandinavia (Trist, Jiggins, & Murray, 1963), who pioneered the Industrial Democracy and sociotechnical design approaches that continued with Gustavsen in the 1980s (Gustavsen, 1992). In all these contributions, the process of organizational change in mass-production-oriented companies has been based on democratically active and creative social relations tools, although these tools often have difficulty surviving in the "foreign cultures" of large-scale, hierarchically organized, mass-production industries. Indeed, in my opinion, the new social relations thinking embodied in these Industrial Democracy change methods have significantly contributed to the development of more conducive forms of production, via their examples of humanity and effectiveness at work.

Nevertheless, the conducive production methods above, with their explicit emphasis on adaptive production, require an even more sophisticated new set of tools for psychosocial workplace professionals. Below, a job redesign process example is discussed from the Nordnet project involving Swedish manufacturing firms (Karasek, 1992a). This was a conducive-production-based program intended to simultaneously increase (a) decision participation and skill development possibilities among workers and (b) the company's flexibility of production in network-based production processes. It was developed in the context of a "dialogue" between management and workers. Visual overview "tools" of social and psychological characteristics of work were needed to promote social processes that simultaneously increased the firm and the worker's capabilities.

Communication-enhancing, social-process-based tools facilitated the worker's ability to participate in meaningful decisions relating to work task reorganization. The fundamental requirement of a new division of labor is that the workers can get the overview, understand the potentials of new patterns of labor combination, and evaluate different alternatives so as to select the most feasible alternatives. Our job redesign activities have used visual and diagrammatic overview tools as their cornerstone. To achieve this goal, visual tools ("skill plates") showing the full range of skills of each worker were developed by workers in participatory sessions and assembled into images of new production processes (new work organization designs) to show social associations and skill relationships. The visual "overview" tools provided the "gestalt" (a right-brain aid) to organize concepts for verbal group discussions of alternative work designs to achieve both company goals and the worker's own goal of increased well-being and skill development. Special symbols on the skill maps represented skills the organization assigned the workers to use, whereas other symbols represented unused skills of the worker or new skills the workers planned to acquire as part of their own career development in the future. These latter two categories of skills, always more numerous than the assigned skills, were skills that persons had but the organization did not want to use or knew nothing about.

Participatory job redesign processes, with the goal of activating workers on the manufacturing floor, can use the overview tools to stimulate the worker's own action-based language development about work organization and thus bring workers into the communication process around redesign. We have used such overview tools in practice among manufacturing-floor workers with little formal education in small Swedish firms (Karasek, 1992a). These workers dramatically increased their engagement in redesign discussions. Workers are sometimes unaware of the power of this type of knowledge because they are normally discouraged from using it. But with supportive management and with the help of such overview tools, manufacturing-floor workers in these projects undertake complex work-planning initiatives. Creating the tools for local vocabulary development around new work organization is another role for psychologists and sociologists.

A Major Macrolevel Social Limitation: A Necessary Social Platform of Basic Economic Security and Social Trust

Conducive production is particularly relevant in the societal context in which satisfaction of basic biological needs for food and shelter is not problematic. Certainly, this is the case in most industrial countries.[3] The

[3]There are, of course, huge and increasing differences in material well-being in different countries. The motivation to seek conducive goals is posited to be stronger, and socially

fundamental prerequisite for a conducive economy is that basic needs must continue to be satisfied, otherwise more primitive motivations will return to dominate social behavior. Basic human needs have to be satisfied so the individuals in collaborative work roles can develop trusting relationships. Thus, the conducive society must diminish the responses of survival insecurity by making material necessities broadly available (diminishing biological needs in so doing) and by strengthening appropriate family and community security platforms. This establishes a political precondition for the creative forms of work activity above. A related requirement is social trust. Putnam (1993) contrasted trusting and economically prosperous northern Italy, together with its innovative production networks (which also developed capitalism's concepts of credit, derived from *credere*, to believe), with autocratic, fear-dominated, and economically backward southern Italy—both in the 1300s and today. This illustrates the reciprocal relationship between trusting associations in a civic context and economic innovation. These relationships facilitate creative, horizontal linkages between active individuals of relatively equal social status.

The Increasing Danger of Job Insecurity

Recent developments in the broad social context of employment relations have created increasing job insecurity and work-related exhaustion for many people. It has become increasingly clear that these new threats could undermine the feasibility of conducive production and are basically inconsistent with socially progressive goals. The microeconomic solution of conducive production calls forth a set of macroeconomic and macrosocial requirements.

To understand the nature of the macrolevel context of a conducive economy, an additional brief analysis of the causes of the present job insecurity is needed. Certainly a major source of this problem is the increasing mobility of capital, undermining the stability of local employment contracts. Perhaps an even more basic source of insecurity is the ever-narrowing definition of what should qualify as an "economically valuable" activity. The free-market definition is now evolving to the point that it

---

reinforced, in countries where material needs are securely met, as in the example from Scandinavia and the computer industry above. Nonetheless, this does not really limit the applicability of the conducivity model, and a broadly applicable model is certainly needed for a global economy. It is claimed to be a characteristic of the conducive economy model in general that it reduces the tendency toward material inequalities. The conducive economy implies a limitation on the degree of engagement in the free-market (the conducive section of the economy siphons work activity away from the pure free-market (commodity) economy, but remains linked to it as the "bridge model" below suggests; Karasek, 1999a, 1999b). This limitation of engagement both diminishes the potential degree of surplus generation and extraction (helping the income inequality problem in less-developed societies) and extends the degree of conducive development in all economies (particularly in developed economies, which further increases its likelihood there).

includes only those activities that can compete in the global economy marketplace—jobs in commodity production or commodity-like services. In this framework, many forms of locally valued social production lose their validity. The shrinking definition of valuable work, combined with a glut of production facilities in almost every commodity export market, means that workers in many countries face continual job loss pressures in many areas, particularly when capital is free to relocate these limited job opportunities to other locations. Advocacy of the importance of locally valued service production is needed from psychologists and sociologists who can best understand these contributions.

Thus, the conducive economy model must be built on a social–economic platform: It presumes a welfare state to maintain the base level of economic security for all members of society to allow individuals to enter into the trusting and collaborative relationships that conducive production requires. In the conducive economy, however, the welfare policies are the platform for, not the goal of, social development. The creative coordination goals would mean different operating principles for social institutions; certainly rigid centralized, bureaucratic operating procedures would be limited.

THE ROLE OF PSYCHOLOGISTS AND SOCIOLOGISTS: LINKING COMMODITY PRODUCTION AND CONDUCIVE PRODUCTION

Of course, the conventional commodity-based economic activity will continue to exist, so the major design challenge for conducive work organization solutions would be to examine the constructive linkages between old and new forms of productivity. Examining the model economists normally propose for commodity economy, I can be more specific about the design challenge. Economists usually illustrate the economy with a consumption side and a production side in the first chapter of basic textbooks. Workers contribute their labor and receive wages as compensation. Consumers purchase goods and services with their wages.

The conducive economy could be considered a second economy in parallel to the commodity economy, contributing the psychic and social benefits that have been missing for consumers and workers in the commodity economy. Meanwhile, the satisfaction of biologically based needs is provided, as is the case today, by the commodity economy. On the production side, the conducive economy generates the new technological ideas and the innovative products and training for the workforce. In return, the commodity economy contributes conventional capital investment resources and some operating resources to sustain the production structures of the conducive economy (e.g., machines, materials, start-up capital).

The linkages above also bind together social science disciplines in a new manner. They link the microlevel social phenomena relating to horizontal social relationship development to macrosociological concerns relating to equitable distribution of material rewards and to economists' conventional (neoclassical) conceptions of requirements for growth of material well-being in a market economy.

The combined conducive and commodity economy represents a metaphor for the need to broaden the conception of economic development beyond the commodity model. One might say this bridged model, with its adventurous conducive production, is a better description of some earlier positive forms of industrial society, such as organic small-town life when a broader range of social needs was met by local production and trade. This observation makes immediately clear the danger of further movement toward pure market-based commodity production in a global context and the need to immediately reverse this trend. As our conceptions of socially valuable economic activity narrow to only those that can create a profit in a global market, many locally valuable services that cannot survive large-scale competition are omitted. Such a definition is too narrow because it automatically limits what is a valuable job and eradicates many types of human service. Advocates of a more humane global economy must reintegrate some of the earlier positive societal forms with new understandings of humane economic development, and psychologists and other social scientists could be of help because of their broader, socially humane conceptions of value.

THE INCREASING IMPORTANCE OF PSYCHOSOCIAL WORKPLACE SKILLS

It can no longer be claimed that the contributions of behavior and social scientists in relation to working life are "residual." Their skills are relevant for much more than simply "patching up" the residues of otherwise beneficial productive activity—the unplanned but increasingly common wounded psyches of economic warfare and the related traumas, disabilities, and expanding dissatisfactions. Health care assistance must still be provided for these problems, but a preventative approach at the largest scale is a better alternative. Psychologists' and other social scientists' skills are now central to the economy. They define new norms of social production for the 21st century. For example, psychosocial understanding of work organization allows stimulation of new forms of productivity. Skills-based and social-relations-focused productivity are much closer to the true dynamics of economic development than are many economists' short-term labor cost-cutting strategies for older-style mass-produced commodities. These skills must be transmitted to other individuals for that kind of productivity to occur. For example, there is a need for teaching horizontally creative co-ordination behavior, development of work-related language for participatory processes, advocacy of locally valued services, and advocacy in public debates about broader social definition of value from production. In addition, psychologists and other social scientists understand the major hazards of the late 20th and early 21st centuries better than do economists, who are running the economic development debate. Still further contributions are needed in the areas of chronic disease etiology, social assessment methods, promotion of public understanding, and macrosocial tabulation of such costs. The cost side of the modern economy is no longer primarily material poverty. It must also include broadly defined psychosocial costs.

With such improved understanding of both the costs and the benefits of work so close at hand, why should psychosocial workplace understanding not be the very core wisdom for future workplace policy makers, replacing the dogmatic domination of free-market-oriented economists? This is certainly a topic for reflection. A more balanced view might suggest that the new development above is not relevant for just one profession in the behavior and social sciences. Instead, such insights would need to become part of the skill repertoire of professionals from a broad range of disciplines for coordinated workplace problem solving to occur. Also, the existing political partners—labor leaders, management, government officials, and researchers—must be trained in psychosocial perspectives for needed dialogues about the political–economic context of occupational health and safety to occur (Karasek, 1989). These activities must be the next steps if we are to realize the potential of the psychosocial work well-being and effectiveness approach.

In economic development discussions, psychosocial health practitioners and scientists who focus their efforts on the workplace should consider their skills equally valuable as those of professionals from other disciplines. Of course, there is a social division of labor, and with many economists and technical managers of companies already addressing these questions, many psychologists and sociologists may feel that this is simply "not their job." Although it is true that social scientists and health professionals would have much to learn about the workplace and about political process, the psychosocial core of their training embodies crucial wisdom for future work life development. If there is a vacuum of social understanding and broad social alternatives that is spreading as the global economy rapidly transforms, behavior and social scientists could partially fill this vacuum, bringing with them the broad-value focus that public health professionals have traditionally supplied.

REFERENCES

Arnetz, B. B., Eyre, M., & Theorell, T. (1982). Social activation of the elderly: A social experiment. *Social Science and Medicine, 16,* 1685–1690.

Belkic, K., Landsbergis, P., Schnall, P., Baker, D., Theorell, T., Siegrist, J., Peter, R., & Karasek, R. (2000). Psychosocial factors: review of the empirical data among men. In P. Schnall, K. Belkic, P. Landsbergis, & D. Baker (Eds.), *Occupational Medicine, State of the Art Reviews, The Workplace and Cardiovascular Disease*, Vol. 15, 7–68, January, 2000.

Berliner, H. (1994). *Thinking in jazz: The infinite art of improvisation*. Chicago: University of Chicago Press.

Bongers, P. M., DeWinter, C. R., Kompier, M. J., & Hildebrandt, V. (1993). Psychosocial factors at work and musculoskeletal disease. *Scandinavian Journal of Work Environment and Health*, 19, 297–312.

Brandt, L. P., & Neilsen, C. V. (1992). Job stress and adverse outcome of pregnancy: A causal link or recall bias? *American Journal of Epidemiology, 135*, 302–311.

Bridges, W. (1994, September 19). The end of the job. *Fortune*, p. 62.

Byrne, J. (1994, December 20). The horizontal organization: It's about managing across not up and down. *Business Week*, p. 26.

Champy, J. (1996, Summer). Putting employees in the driver's seat. *BJ's Journal, 7*, p. 3.

Church, G. (1994, October 24). We're #1, and it hurts. *Time*, p. 50.

Dhondt, S. (1998). *Time constraints and autonomy at work in the European Union*. Dublin, Ireland: European Foundation for the Improvement of Living and Working Conditions.

Fenster, L., Schaefer, C., Mathur, A., Hiatt, R. A., Pieper, C., Hubbard, A. E., Von Behren, J., & Swan, S. H. (1995). Psychologic stress in the workplace and spontaneous abortion. *American Journal of Epidemiology, 142*, 117–183.

Gleckman, H. (1995, November 20). Rewriting the social contract. *Business Week*, p. 120.

Gulick, L., & Urwick, L. (1937). Papers on scientific administration. New York: Columbia University, Institute of Public Administration.

Gustavsen, B. (1992). *Dialogue and development, Theory of communication, action research, and restructuring of working life*. Stockholm: Van Gorcum, Assen/Maastrict, and the Swedish Center for Working Life.

Hancock, L. (1995, March 6). Breaking point. *Newsweek*, p. 5 C.

Homans, G. (1950). *The human group*. New York: Harcourt, Brace.

Houtman, I. L. D., Goudswaard, A., Dhondt, van der Grinten, M., Hildenbrandt, V. H., & van der Poel, E. (1998). The Dutch Monitor on Stress and Physical Load: Risk factors, consequences and preventative action. *Occupational Environmental Medicine, 55*, 73–83.

Karasek, R. A. (1976). *The impact of the work environment on life outside the job* (Doctoral dissertation, Massachusetts Institute of Technology). Springfield, VA: U.S. Department of Commerce, National Technical Information Service (Thesis order no. PB 263-073./31).

Karasek, R. A. (1981). *New value*. New York: Columbia University, Department of Industrial Engineering and Operations Research.

Karasek, R. (1989). The political implications of the psychosocial work redesign: A model of the psychosocial class structure. *International Journal of Health Services, 19*, 481–508.

Karasek, R. (1992a). *The "NordNet" work reorganization process in manufacturing companies; The "Conducivity Game"; developing "worker coordination" vocabularies; and "Conducive Production" via creative coordination*, NordNet Project Documentation, Appendix 2–4, Department of Work Environment, University of Massachusetts, Lowell. (See also Swedish translation: Eriksson, K., Karasek, R., Uudelepp, & Weber, G. (1993). *Produktförnyelse och kreativt koordinerad produktion, Centrum for Arbetslivsutveckling, Högskolan i Halmstad*. Halmstad, Sweden: Center for Worklife Development, University College.)

Karasek, R. (1992b). Stress prevention through work reorganization: A summary of 19 international case studies. In *Conditions of work digest. Preventing stress at work* (pp. 23–41). Geneva: International Labour Office.

Karasek, R. (1997). Labor participation and job quality policy: Requirements for an alternative economic future. *Scandinavian Journal of Work Environment and Health, 4*(Suppl. 23):55–65.

Karasek, R. (1999a). The new work organization, conducive production, and work quality policy. In J. Ferrie, M. Marmot, & E. Ziglio (Eds.), *Labor market changes and job insecurity: A challenge for social welfare and health promotion* (WHO Regional Publications, European Series, No. 81, pp. 169–239). Copenhagen: World Health Organization, Regional Office for Europe.

Karasek, R. (1999b). The new work organization and conducive value. *Dutch Sociological Journal, 5*, 310–330.

Karasek, R., Brisson, C., Amick, B., Houtman, I., Bonger, P., & Kawakami, N. (1998). The job content questionnaire (JCQ): An instrument for internationally comparative assessments of psychosocial job characteristics. *Journal of Occupational Health Psychology, 3*, 322–355.

Karasek, R. A., & Theorell, T. (1990). *Healthy work: Stress, productivity, and the reconstruction of working life*. New York: Basic Books.

Kawakami, N., Tanigawa, T., Araki, S., Nakata, A., Sakurai, S., Yokoyama, K., & Morita, Y. (1997). Effects of job strain on helper-inducer (CD4+CD29+) and suppressor-inducer (CD4+CD45RA+) T cells in Japanese blue collar workers. *Psychotherapy and Psychosomatics, 66*, 192–198.

Kristensen, T. S. (1995). The demand–control–support model: Methodological challenges for future research. *Stress Medicine, 11*, 17–26.

Kristensen, T. S. (1996). Job stress and cardiovascular disease: A theoretic critical review. *Journal of Occupational Health Psychology, 1*, 246–260.

March, J., & Simon, H. (1958). *Organizations*. New York: Wiley.

Marsalis, W. (1996, January 2). *Making the music*. Washington, DC: U.S. National Public Radio, Jazz Program Series.

Parker, M., & Slaughter, J. (1988). Managing by stress. The dark side of the team concept. *ILR Report, 24*, 19–23.

Peters, M., Godaert, G., Ballieux, R., Vliet, M., Willemsen, J., Sweep, F., & Heijnen, C. (1998). Cardiovascular and endocrine responses to experimental stress: Effects of mental effort and controllability. *Psychoneuroendocrinology, 23*, 1–17.

Piore, M., & Sable, C. (1984). *The second industrial divide, possibilities for prosperity.* New York: Basic Books.

Porter, M. (1990). *Competitive advantage of nations.* London: Macmillan.

Putnam, R. D. (1993). *Making democracy work.* Princeton, NJ: Princeton University Press.

Roethlisberger, F. J., & Dickson, W. J. (1939). *Management and the worker.* Cambridge, MA: Harvard University Press.

Schnall, P. L., Landsbergis, P. A., & Baker, D. (1994). Job strain and cardiovascular disease. *Annual Review of Public Health, 15*, 381–411.

Siegrist, J. A. (1996). Adverse health effects of high-effort/low-reward conditions. *Journal of Occupational Health Psychology, 1*, 27–41.

Smith, A. (1976). *An inquiry into the nature and causes of the wealth of nations* (2 vols.). Chicago: University of Chicago Press. (Original work published 1776)

Stewart, T. (1994, October 3). Your company's most valuable asset: Intellectual capital. *Fortune Magazine*, p. 68.

Stewart, T. (1997). *Intellectual capital, the new wealth of organizations.* New York: Doubleday.

Sun Microsystems. (1997, June). Wake up and smell the JAVA: A new computing age has dawned [special advertising section]. *Byte*, pp. 55, 59.

Technology is heightening job worries, Greenspan says. (2000, July 12). New York Times, p. C2. Bloomberg News.

Theorell, T., & Karasek, R. A. (1996). Current issues relating to psychosocial job strain and cardiovascular disease research. *Journal of Occupational Health Psychology, 1*, 9–26.

Trist, E., Jiggins, G., & Murray, H. (1963). *Organizational choice.* London: Tavistock.

Uchitelle, L., & Kleinfield, N. (1996, March 3). On the battlefields of business, millions of casualties [first in series of eight articles]. *New York Times*, p. A1.

Van der Doef, M., & Maes, S. (1999). The job demands–control (–support) model and psychological well-being: A review of 20 years of empirical research. *Work & Stress, 13*, 87–114.

Warren, N. D. (1997). *The organizational and psychosocial bases of cumulative trauma and stress disorders.* University of Massachusetts Lowell Dissertation, UMI Number 2726279.

14

EVALUATION OF COMMUNITY-BASED HEALTH PROGRAMS: AN ALTERNATE PERSPECTIVE

ROBERT M. GOODMAN

In the temple of science are many mansions, and various indeed are
they that dwell therein and motives that have led them thither.
Albert Einstein (1934)

Public health and community psychology are applied disciplines
defined by their focus on population-based approaches to health. As
community-based initiatives are directed at populations often at risk for
undesirable health outcomes, such initiatives are fundamental to the professional practice of public health and community psychology. To demonstrate their effectiveness, community initiatives require sufficient evaluation. Experimental designs are considered the "gold standard" in ruling out
threats to internal validity (that is, to cause and effect—that the community initiative caused its intended outcomes). Quasi-experimental designs are considered next best when random assignment is not feasible.
The main contention of this chapter is that experimental and quasi-
experimental designs, in many instances, are neither feasible nor particularly informative in evaluating complex community health initiatives.
Therefore, the social and behavioral scientists that practice public health
and community psychology may benefit from alternative strategies of evaluation. This chapter first provides a rationale for an alternative perspective
and then suggests other evaluation design options.

Experimental and quasi-experimental evaluation approaches are referred to herein as classical designs in that they derive from the positivist tradition of research. In the late 19th and most of the 20th century, positivist principles guided laboratory, educational, agricultural, and behavioral studies (Campbell & Stanley, 1963; Cook & Campbell, 1979; Guba & Lincoln, 1989; Suchman, 1967). Today the application of classical designs to evaluating community initiatives may be inexact on at least two counts: First, positivist principles applied to research often do not translate well when applied to program evaluation studies (Patton, 1986). Second, research models derived from laboratory, agricultural, and behavioral studies often are limited models for community-focused evaluations (Kubisch et al., 1995; Murray, 1998). A brief overview of the criteria for judging internal validity is useful in illustrating the limitations of classical designs when applied to the evaluation of community-based health initiatives.

LIMITATIONS IN TRANSLATING POSITIVIST RESEARCH PRINCIPLES TO PROGRAM EVALUATION

Patton (1986) wrote

Before about 1978, the criteria for judging evaluation research could scarcely be differentiated from criteria for judging basic research in the traditional social and behavioral sciences. Technical quality and methodological rigor were the primary concerns of researchers. Use was not an issue. Methods decisions dominated the evaluation decision-making process. Methodological rigor meant experimental designs, quantitative data, and detailed statistical analysis. . . . Validity, reliability, measurability, and generalizability were the dimensions that received the greatest attention in judging evaluation research proposals and reports. (p. 24)

Along with Patton, several scientists note that evaluation and research are different in orientation and therefore dissimilar in their operationalization. For instance, whereas the classical design emphasizes generalizability through sample selection, program evaluation often is not concerned with external validity (Cronbach, 1980; Patton, 1986; Yin, 1994). Whereas the researcher in the classical tradition is an observer standing outside of the experiment so as not to influence it, the evaluator most often is deeply involved. The engaged evaluator provides the project with continuous data-based feedback to influence program operations (Patton, 1986; Wandersman et al., 1998). From the classical perspective, such active involvement is a threat to internal validity.

The last example illuminates the "fault line" between the alternative and classical perspectives concerning internal validity. In the positivist tradition, three criteria form the foundation for establishing internal validity:

(a) An association is demonstrated between the program and the outcomes produced, (b) the program's implementation occurs before evidence that the outcomes resulted (temporality), and (c) the association between the program and desired outcomes is not caused by some other factor (spurious results; Cook & Campbell, 1979). The use of random assignment in experimental designs rules out most internal validity threats to these criteria. Quasi-experimental designs that use equivalent comparisons without randomization are somewhat less rigorous in ruling out internal validity threats.

Community-based initiatives provide the evaluator with unique challenges in taking into account the three criteria for internal validity. Because community-based evaluations often focus on only one program, the unit of study lacks sufficient power for establishing statistical conclusion validity. Attaining sufficient statistical power may be too expensive for complex community programs to achieve (Newcomer, Hatry, & Wholey, 1994). Thus, where one or a limited number of programs form the unit of study, statistical correlation is an unlikely method for establishing an association between a community program and its impacts (Criterion 1). In addition, community programs are complex with many activities occurring at once that are directed at entire populations. Guba and Lincoln (1989) characterized these complexities as "mutual simultaneous shaping:" Program elements interact continuously, the elements most important in influencing others constantly shift depending on local circumstances, and the circumstances may never occur the same way more than once. Thus, establishing an orderly sequence of events (Criterion 2—temporality) can be an elusive task when evaluating complex community initiatives. Finally, community settings are not as conducive as are laboratory settings to regulating external conditions. Thus, spurious results, or "noise," (Criterion 3) are particularly difficult to rule out in community settings (Hollister & Hill, 1995).

The behavioral and social sciences can advance evaluation of community-based initiatives by embracing evaluation strategies that focus in depth on single, or few, communities. By so doing, evaluation can become a vehicle for community consultation by public health practitioners and community psychologists through which communities may build capacity for health-promoting action (Fetterman, Kaftarian, & Wandersman, 1996). Moreover, when evaluation strategies are developed to be flexible *during* application, behavioral and social scientists may better be able to account for the complexities associated with mutual simultaneous shaping and spurious factors. After all, behavioral and social scientists emphasize social context and its influence on health-promoting behaviors (McLeroy, Bibeau, Steckler, & Glanz, 1988). Therefore, evaluation approaches that illuminate context can add meaningful dimensions to the community consultation process.

LIMITATIONS IN TRANSLATING RESEARCH MODELS TO THE EVALUATION OF COMMUNITY INITIATIVES

According to Scheirer (1994),

> Variability and change in program delivery complicates the use of an experimental research model for program evaluation. Within the classical experimental model, one assumes that the so-called "treatment" is controlled by the researcher. . . . This assumption cannot be made for program evaluation. (p. 42)

The quote suggests that even when a sufficient number of programs are funded and community trials are possible, comparison groups remain difficult to establish. Baseline equivalence across treatment conditions frequently is neither feasible nor desirable. Because each community is unique, programs invariably operate differently across communities. Flexibility within the program is desirable for it to adapt to the distinct conditions and realities of each community (Kubisch et al., 1995). Murray (1998) cited the Minnesota Heart Health Program as an example of a community-based intervention that was tailored to the differences in communities. He noted that such adaptations of interventions to site specifications are problematic for maintaining reliability of the intervention, a condition that is integral to classical designs. Murray further noted that group-randomized trials are particularly susceptible to unreliability as a threat to internal validity.

Figure 14.1 is an implementation model for a community mobilization project to prevent diabetes in an urban, African American community in the South. On what basis would we expect such a complex model, one that is culturally and contextually based, to operate the same way in a rural Hispanic community in the Southwest or any other community with different demographics, culture, local history, and sense of community? In experimental design research, fidelity to the intervention model across all cases within a treatment condition is a virtue, but community health programs should be purposely flexible and responsive to changing local needs and conditions. Thus, even when communities are assigned to the same treatment condition, the desired variability of the intervention across communities runs counter to the reliability (fidelity) required within classical designs. Designs that test community programs as a whole for outcomes may not be sensitive to their complex inner workings, to how each aspect of the program contributes to the whole and to how each part interacts with the others (Scheirer, 1994; Steckler, 1989). Scheirer contended that, in such instances, "process data may be more useful than comparative experimental or quasi-experimental designs . . . particularly when aggregate programs have different program components in multiple sites" (p. 42). Scheirer recommended a "breaking down" of cause and effect into "micro

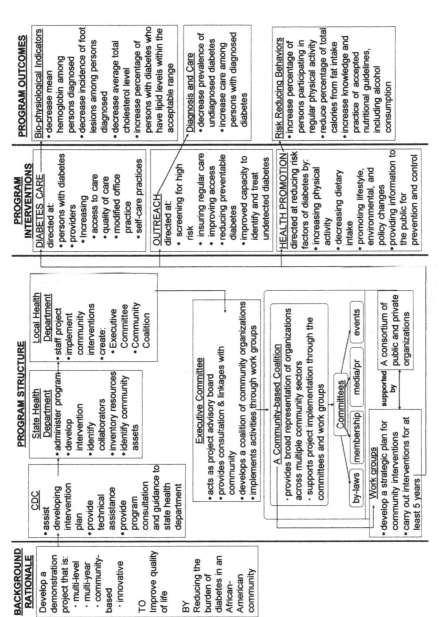

Figure 14.1. Project DIRECT model of operations.

steps." For community evaluation studies, establishing internal validity may depend on examination of these "micro-connections" within a program.

In sum, community health programs often have broad and multiple goals, have complex intervention designs, take many years to produce results, and require multiple data collection and analysis methods extended over long periods of time. Given these complexities and the costs associated with large-scale community intervention trials, evaluation of the individual program may be a wise and necessary approach, especially before wider program dissemination. In the following section, several guidelines are offered for evaluating complex community health programs from an alternate perspective to classical design. An extended discussion of these guidelines can be found elsewhere (Goodman, 1998).

GUIDELINE 1: USE OF LOGIC MODELS

To begin a complex community intervention, the intended program should be diagrammed well in advance of implementation to illustrate how each constituent part interconnects. The literature often terms such diagrams as *logic models*, which is defined as "a fancy term for what is merely a succinct, logical series of statements that link the problems your program is attempting to address, how it will address them, and what the expected result is" (Kumpfer et al., 1993, pp. 7–8). As in Figure 14.1, such models break the complex intervention down to micro steps of cause and effect and provide a framework for testing internal validity (Patton, 1986; Scheirer, 1994). When logic models are developed together with community members, the process reinforces consensus building among stakeholders regarding the assumptions underlying the program. Additional information on the development of logic models can be found in the literature (Goodman, 1998).

GUIDELINE 2: DEVELOPMENT MEASURES WITH THE LOCAL COMMUNITY IN MIND

The alternate perspective holds that evaluation should stem from the information needs of the program's primary stakeholders, and these needs differ across communities even when they implement the same program (Patton, 1986). Classical designs require equivalence of measures across cases. In evaluating community programs, measures may be more valid if they are contoured to the information needs of each individual community, thus increasing cultural sensitivity and potentially reducing cultural bias. For instance, I was involved in designing an evaluation for a maternal and child health clinic. A questionnaire with strong psychometric properties was proposed. It contained questions regarding mental health status, including one that asked the client to agree or disagree to the following statement: "Other people have difficulty understanding me." In many instances, agreement to a series of such questions may suggest mental distress. Because the clientele served by the maternal and child health clinic had recently arrived in the community and largely were Hispanic, an "agree" response to the question posed most likely reflects a language barrier and not mental distress.

The example illustrates that psychometrically tested measures may not be pertinent if they are not sensitive to the presenting conditions of different locales. The tension between the desirability of using a tried and tested measure as opposed to one contoured specifically to each program is evident in the community evaluation literature. For instance, Kumpfer and colleagues (1993) maintained that standardized evaluation instruments should be sought out, but they also noted that locating such measures can be frustrating because the instruments must conform to the language skills, age appropriateness, cultural relevance, and attention span of local audiences. Padilla and Medina (1996) asserted that cultural sensitivity should span the entire evaluation process including the adaptation, translation, and administration of measures, along with the analysis, scoring, and interpretation of results. Without such cultural adaptations, biases may occur that can lead to misinterpretation of a program's results (Keitel, Kopala, & Adamson, 1996). To reduce culturally induced bias, Suzuki, Meller, and Ponterotto (1996) offered the following suggestions: develop alternative measures and procedures for diverse populations, understand the norms of ethnic groups to which evaluations are applied, increase collaboration with bilingual and bicultural professionals in developing evaluations, increase racial and ethnic community involvement in the assessment process, and consult the literature and research available regarding multicultural assessment procedures.

GUIDELINE 3: TRIANGULATION AND USE OF QUALITATIVE APPROACHES

Community health programs, with their multiple and complex activities, require multiple measures to gauge results. Triangulation is the strategic application of multiple methods. It is alternatively termed multioperationalism, combined operations, mixed strategies, and multiple strategies (Blaikie, 1991). Triangulation can enrich both construct and internal validity, the former by triangulating methods at data collection and the latter by triangulating at data analysis (Denzin, 1978; Yin, 1994). When evaluating a limited number of programs, the convergence of analysis methods can be a strategic alternative to establishing internal validity through random assignment or comparison groups (Cook, 1987; Patton, 1990).

In triangulating for data analysis, qualitative methods may be particularly useful as they focus on "how" and "why" questions. For instance, how did the program work, or why did the program deviate from its implementation model? Quantitative evaluation methods often focus on questions concerning who, what, where, and how much (Yin, 1994). In evaluating single and complex community programs, "how" or "why" an intervention worked (or did not work) often is sine qua non, and qualitative case study designs are considered as optimum in such evaluations (Caudle, 1994; Yin, 1994). From the classical perspective, qualitative approaches often are considered as "weak" designs (Boruch, 1994; Boruch & Wothke, 1985; Suchman, 1967). In fact, they offer strengths that complement quantitative approaches. In triangulated designs, deciding what evaluation questions are important is probably the best guide for selecting complementary quantitative and qualitative approaches.

GUIDELINE 4: IMPORT OF SOCIAL ECOLOGY CONCEPTS ON COMMUNITY ASSESSMENTS

From a social ecology perspective, complex health conditions such as diabetes are viewed as interwoven into the social fabric. Effective programs intervene at multiple social levels simultaneously and often develop in stages; their sequenced development needs to be orchestrated deliberately. For instance, the Figure 14.1 model reflects several developmental steps that require deliberation, including hiring staff, forming a plan, developing community committees, and implementing services. It also reflects multiple levels of outcomes, such as influencing community members' knowledge, attitudes, and behaviors regarding diabetes; individual social support systems and practitioner networks; and community capacity to mobilize effective initiatives and policy change through media and lobbying. In assessing the staged development of a program, Patton (1986) emphasized the shifting nature of the evaluation question depending on the current stage of interest. As the evaluation shifts to a new stage, it also focuses on different social units. For example, in the early development of Figure 14.1 when the program was forming, evaluation might emphasize the development of the interorganizational arrangements necessary for developing the diabetes initiative. Once formed, the evaluation may shift its focus to implementation and emphasize skills for delivering the program. When the program becomes routine and enters a maintenance stage, the focus of the evaluation may shift again to client outcomes. Examples of assessment designs informed by social ecology principles are in the published literature (Shinn, 1996).

GUIDELINE 5: ROLE OF EVALUATOR AS STAKEHOLDER

The evaluator's involvement as a program stakeholder is an important distinction between community evaluation and classical research. The evaluator is committed to intervene early and often in a program's development so that if a program does not achieve its long-term outcomes, knowing which intermediate outcomes were not met helps identify possible weak links in the program. Such an approach is consistent with the importance that Patton (1986), Guba and Lincoln (1989), and others place on evaluation validity, or constituent validity to stakeholders. When providing continuous feedback during each stage of a community program's development, the evaluator becomes a program stakeholder, collaborator, and builder of capacity for the community initiative. Such involvement requires that the evaluator possess an array of core skills that, although desirable attributes, are not as fundamental to most classical research approaches (Patton, 1986). These skills focus on community building and include the ability to gain entrée, cooperation, and trust among various community groups; competencies in team building, group process, negotiation, teaching, and interpersonal communication; and the acquisition of political acumen (Brown, 1995; Israel 1992). Some evaluation approaches incorporate these skills into the assessment process. Participatory evaluation (Israel et al., 1995) aids community constituents define the evaluation questions, participate in data gathering, and use the data analysis as feedback for suggesting program improvements. Empowerment evaluation (Fetterman et al., 1996) supports community groups in developing skills for self-evaluation and consciousness raising. Participatory and empowerment evaluations are compatible with community development practices that are aimed at citizen participation and ownership.

CONCLUSION

The alternative perspective presented above reflects the community conditions that often make classical designs unlikely. Nonetheless, the perspective does not promote the abandonment of classical designs from community assessments—quite to the contrary. Murray (1998) illustrated how and under what conditions randomized community trials are optimal. From my perspective, they should be encouraged for both internal and external validity reasons. On the other hand, many community programs may not be appropriate candidates for group-randomized trials. Some of the reasons include interest in assessing only a single program, different demographic and cultural makeup across communities, the desire for flexibility when implementing a program in different locales, and the importance to program quality for the evaluator to continuously interact with the program.

Some argue that the distinctions between the classical and alternative perspective are paradigmatic and therefore irreconcilable (Blaikie, 1991; Guba & Lincoln, 1989). I think of Einstein's "many mansions" observation as a truer representation of science. Variety in approaches to science should be desirable, and evaluation science can benefit from a greater acceptance of the alternative perspective, for it can enrich our understanding of complex social phenomena such community health initiatives.

REFERENCES

Blaikie, N. W. H. (1991). A critique of the use of triangulation in social research. *Quality & Quantity, 25,* 115–136.

Boruch, R. F. (1994). The future of controlled randomized experiments: A briefing. *Evaluation Practice, 15,* 265–274.

Boruch, R. F., & Wothke, W. (1985). Seven kinds of randomization plans for designing field experiments. In R. F. Boruch & W. Werner (Eds.), *Randomization and field experimentation* (pp. 95–113). San Francisco: Jossey-Bass.

Brown, P. (1995). The role of the evaluator in comprehensive community initiatives. In J. P. Connell, A. C. Kubisch, L. B. Schorr, & C. H. Weiss (Eds.), *New approaches to evaluating community initiatives: Concepts, methods, and context* (pp. 201–225). Washington, DC: Aspen Institute.

Campbell, D. T., & Stanley, J. C. (1963). *Experimental and quasi-experimental designs for research.* Chicago: Rand McNally.

Caudle, S. L. (1994). Using qualitative approaches. In J. S. Wholey, H. P. Hatry, & K. E. Newcomer (Eds.), *Handbook of practical program evaluation* (pp. 69–95). San Francisco: Jossey-Bass.

Cook, T. D. (1987). Postpositivism critical multiplism. In W. R. Shadish & C. S. Reichardt (Eds.), *Evaluation studies: Review annual, Volume 12* (pp. 458–499). Newbury Park, CA: Sage.

Cook, T. D., & Campbell, D. T. (1979). *Quasi-experimentation: Design and analysis issues for field settings.* Boston: Houghton Mifflin.

Cronbach, L. J. (1980). *Toward reform of program evaluation.* San Francisco: Jossey-Bass.

Denzin, N. K. (1978). *The research act: A theoretical introduction to sociological methods.* New York: McGraw-Hill.

Fetterman, D. M., Kaftarian, S. J., & Wandersman, A. (Eds.). (1996). *Empowerment evaluation: Knowledge and tools for self-assessment and accountability.* Thousand Oaks, CA: Sage.

Goodman, R. M. (1998). Principles and tools for evaluating community-based prevention and health promotion programs. *Journal of Public Health Management and Practice, 4,* 37–47.

Guba, E. G., & Lincoln, Y. S. (1989). *Fourth generation evaluation.* Newbury Park, CA: Sage.

Hollister, R. G., & Hill, J. (1995). Problems in the evaluation of community-wide initiatives. In J. P. Connell, A. C. Kubisch, L. B. Schorr, & C. H. Weiss (Eds.), *New approaches to evaluating community initiatives: Concepts, methods, and context* (pp. 127–172). Washington, DC: Aspen Institute.

Israel, B. A. (1992). Conducting action research: Relationships between organization members and researchers. *Journal of Applied Behavioral Science, 28,* 74–101.

Israel, B. A., Cummings, K. M., Dignan, M. B., Heaney, C. A., Perales, D. P., Simons-Morton, B. G., & Zimmerman, M. A. (1995). Evaluation of health education programs: Current assessment and future directions. *Health Education Quarterly, 22,* 364–389.

Keitel, M. A., Kopala, M., & Adamson, W. S. (1996). Ethical issues in multicultural assessment. In L. A. Suzuki, P. J. Meller, & J. G. Ponterotto (Eds.), *Handbook of multicultural assessment: Clinical, psychological, and educational applications* (pp. 29–48). San Francisco: Jossey-Bass.

Kubisch, A. C., et al. (1995). Introduction. In J. P. Connell et al. (Eds.), *New approaches to evaluating community initiatives: Concepts, methods, and context.* Washington, DC: Aspen Institute.

Kumpfer, K. L., Shur, G. H., Ross, J. G., Bunnelle, K. K., Librett, J. J., & Millward, A. R. (1993). *Measurements in prevention: A manual on selecting and using instruments to evaluate prevention programs.* (U.S. Department of Health and Human Services, Center for Substance Abuse Prevention Technical Report 8.) Rockville, MD: U.S. Government Printing Office.

McLeroy, K. R., Bibeau, D., Steckler, A., & Glanz, K. (1988). An ecological perspective on health promotion programs. *Health Education Quarterly, 15,* 351–377.

Murray, D. M. (1998). *Design and analysis of group-randomized trials.* New York: Oxford University Press.

Newcomer, K. E., Hatry, H. P., & Wholey, J. S. (1994). Meeting the need for practical evaluation approaches: An introduction. In J. S. Wholey, H. P. Hatry, & K. E. Newcomer (Eds.), *Handbook of practical program evaluation* (1–14). San Francisco: Jossey-Bass.

Padilla, A. M., & Medina, A. (1996). Cross-cultural sensitivity in assessment using tests in culturally appropriate ways. In L. A. Suzuki, P. J. Meller, & J. G. Ponterotto (Eds.), *Handbook of multicultural assessment: Clinical, psychological, and educational applications* (pp. 3–28). San Francisco: Jossey-Bass.

Patton, M. Q. (1986). *Utilization-focused evaluation* (2nd ed.). Beverly Hills, CA: Sage.

Patton, M. Q. (1990). *Qualitative evaluation and research methods* (2nd ed.). Newbury Park, CA: Sage.

Scheirer, M. A. (1994). Designing and using process evaluation. In J. S. Wholey, H. P. Hatry, & K. E. Newcomer (Eds.), *Handbook of practical program evaluation* (pp. 40–68). San Francisco: Jossey-Bass.

Shinn, M. (1996). Ecological Assessment [Special issue]. *American Journal of Community Psychology, 24*(1).

Steckler, A. (1989). The use of qualitative evaluation methods to test internal validity: An example in a work site health promotion program. *Evaluation and the Health Professions, 12,* 115–133.

Suchman, E. A. (1967). *Evaluative research: Principles and practice in public service and social action programs.* New York: Russell Sage Foundation.

Suzuki, L. A., Meller, P. J., & Ponterotto, J. G. (1996). Multicultural assessment: Present trends and future directions. In L. A. Suzuki, P. J. Meller, & J. G. Ponterotto (Eds.), *Handbook of multicultural assessment: Clinical, psychological, and educational applications* (pp. 673–684). San Francisco: Jossey-Bass.

Wandersman, A., Morrissey, E., Davino, K., Seybolt, D., Crusto, C., Nation, M., Goodman, R. M., & Imm, P. (1998). Comprehensive quality programming: Eight essential strategies for implementing successful programs. *Journal of Primary Prevention, 19,* 3–30.

Yin, R. K. (1994). *Case study research: Design and methods* (2nd ed.). Thousand Oaks, CA: Sage.

15

EFFICACY AND EFFECTIVENESS TRIALS IN HEALTH PROMOTION AND DISEASE PREVENTION: DESIGN AND ANALYSIS OF GROUP-RANDOMIZED TRIALS

DAVID M. MURRAY

Behavioral and social sciences are becoming increasingly integrated with public health in the area of health promotion and disease prevention. Behavioral and social science methods are used to try to change behavioral and social risk factors for disease to improve the public health. Health promotion and disease prevention research targets the major public health problems of our time, including heart disease, cancer, AIDS, trauma, and other problems affecting the health of large segments of the population. They address behavioral and social risk factors such as tobacco, alcohol, and drug use; eating patterns; physical activity; and violence. Effective health promotion and disease prevention efforts require strong interventions and good evaluations; inadequacies in either domain will only yield disappointing results.

The purpose of this chapter is to outline strategies that can be useful in building good evaluation programs for health promotion and disease

EXHIBIT 15.1
Flay's (1986) Suggested Phases in Health Promotion and Disease Prevention Research

I	Basic research
II	Hypothesis development
III	Pilot tests
IV	Prototype studies
V	Efficacy trials
VI	Treatment effectiveness trials
VII	Implementation effectiveness trials
VIII	Demonstration studies

prevention research. Following an introduction to the several phases of health promotion and disease prevention research, it will focus on efficacy and effectiveness trials. These trials are used to determine whether a particular intervention has the desired effect under both controlled and more realistic conditions.

Particular attention is given to group-randomized trials, which are comparative studies in which identifiable groups are randomly assigned to study conditions. Members of those groups are observed to assess the effect of the intervention. Group-randomized trials are often the best comparative designs available to evaluate an intervention that operates at a group level, manipulates the social or physical environment, or cannot be delivered to individuals. Because so many of the interventions designed to change behavioral and social risk factors to improve the public health have exactly these characteristics, group-randomized trials are widely applicable in health promotion and disease prevention research.

PHASES OF RESEARCH

Flay (1986) described eight phases in health promotion and disease prevention research (Exhibit 15.1). Basic research leads to hypothesis development and preparation of draft materials and protocols for both intervention and evaluation. Pilot tests evaluate the feasibility and acceptability of those materials and protocols. Prototype studies provide preliminary testing of those materials and protocols as they would be used in later efficacy trials, but they do so in small studies that are not designed to assess either efficacy or effectiveness. Instead, they are designed to provide a preliminary estimate of the magnitude of the intervention effect. The methods used in these phases are the focus of Robert Goodman's contribution (chapter 14) to this volume.

Efficacy trials are designed to test whether the intervention causes the observed effect under carefully controlled conditions in which the investigator has control over the assignment of study conditions, the content of the intervention, the delivery of the intervention, and the conduct of the evaluation. Treatment and implementation effectiveness trials are used to determine whether the treatment will remain effective when implemented under more realistic conditions. Treatment effectiveness trials relax control over the content of the intervention, whereas implementation effectiveness trials relax control over both content and delivery of the intervention. Finally, demonstration studies include only minimal evaluation activities and are reserved for intervention programs that have already been proven efficacious and effective.

CLINICAL TRIALS AND GROUP-RANDOMIZED TRIALS

There are two types of efficacy and effectiveness trials commonly used in health promotion and disease prevention research. *Clinical trials* are comparative studies in which individuals are randomly assigned to study conditions and observed to assess the effect of the intervention. Examples include drug and surgical trials, some weight and smoking trials, and other trials with individual assignment. By contrast, *group-randomized trials* are comparative studies in which identifiable groups are randomly assigned to study conditions. Members of those groups are observed to assess the effect of the intervention. Examples include school-based studies, work-site studies, community-based studies, and other trials with group assignment. The design and analytic issues common to clinical trials are well known, and there are many textbooks devoted to them (e.g., Meinert, 1986); as a result, they will not be discussed in this chapter. The design and analytic issues common to group-randomized trials are less well known, although there has been increased attention to these issues over the past decade, and the first textbook on these issues appeared recently (Murray, 1998). The focus of this chapter will be on the design and analysis of group-randomized trials because they have broad application in the context of efficacy and effectiveness studies in health promotion and disease prevention research.

There is no question that efficacy and effectiveness trials that use group-randomized designs are often large and expensive. As a result, they should be initiated only after successful completion of the earlier phases described by Flay (1986). Unfortunately, this doesn't always happen. Efficacy trials in health promotion and disease prevention often start without the benefit of prototype studies and often even without the benefit of adequate pilot studies. This has happened in large part because the funding agencies have been reluctant to support pilot and prototype studies, preferring instead to fund efficacy and effectiveness trials. Unfortunately, the interventions that lead to group-randomized trials in health promotion and disease prevention tend to be more complicated than are those in other areas or that lead to clinical trials. Interventions that lead to group-randomized trials are more complicated because they often rely on social processes, environmental change, mass media, and other components that cannot be delivered to individuals. As such, it is even more important to subject them to adequate testing in pilot and prototype studies. These earlier phases of research can uncover important weaknesses in the intervention content or implementation methods. Moving too quickly to efficacy trials risks wasting substantial time and resources on interventions that could have been substantially improved through the experience gained in those pilot and prototype studies. It is hoped that funding agencies will recognize this point and begin to provide better support for pilot and prototype studies.

AN EXAMPLE

Group-randomized trials may be used with any identifiable group; the nature of the group will generally be dictated by the nature of the intervention, which in turn will generally be dictated by the nature of the problem and target audience. To change adolescent smoking patterns, researchers naturally think about school-based interventions and trials. To change the way physicians interact with their patients regarding cholesterol, we naturally think about clinic-based interventions and trials. To change the way the general public responds to early symptoms of heart attack, we naturally think about a mass media campaign and community-based trials.

Consider as an example the Pathways study. This study was funded by the National Heart, Lung, and Blood Institute in 1993 as a 3-year Phase I planning study with four field centers (University of Minnesota, University of New Mexico, Johns Hopkins University, Gila River Community) and a coordinating center (University of North Carolina). The purpose of the Phase I study was to develop the design, analytic plan, intervention materials, and evaluation protocols for a Phase II study to evaluate an intervention to prevent obesity among American Indian children. Phase II was funded in 1996 for 5 years to allow the investigators to conduct the trial planned during Phase I.

The Phase II study design is described by C. E. Davis et al. (1999). At each field center, schools that met the study's eligibility requirements were recruited for Phase II. Each school completed a baseline survey of second-grade students in the spring of 1997. Using the results of that survey, schools were rank ordered on median predicted percent body fat (PBF) based on a regression equation developed in Phase I (Lohman et al., 1999). Schools in the upper half of the distribution in a center were placed into one block, whereas schools in the lower half of the distribution in that center were placed in a second block. Schools within each block were assigned at random to the intervention condition or to the control condition. Posttest measures were taken at the end of the fifth grade in the spring of 2000. This design is similar to that used previously in the Child and Adolescent Trial for Cardiovascular Health (CATCH; Zucker et al., 1995).

The intervention program includes a classroom curriculum, a physical activity program, and a school lunch program (C. E. Davis et al., 1999). Behavioral and social scientists designed all the programs to improve eating patterns and physical activity among the participants. Special attention was given to ensure that the intervention program would be culturally appropriate for American Indian school children.

The research question is whether the children in the intervention and control conditions will differ at the end of the study in their level of obesity. The null hypothesis is that they will not. The alternative hypothesis is that the children in the intervention condition will display a lower average level of obesity than will the children in the control condition at the end of the fifth grade. The primary endpoint is the value for predicted PBF. The prediction equation relies on measures of height, weight, bioelectric impedance, and skinfold thickness for each child. The values obtained from the prediction equation have been shown to have good agreement with a criterion measure based on assessment of total body water (Lohman et al., 1999).

The Pathways study is a sophisticated group-randomized trial designed to promote health and prevent disease among American Indian school children. Identifiable groups (schools) were matched and randomized to intervention and control conditions. Members within those groups (students) are being followed as a cohort to assess the impact of the intervention. Behavioral and social scientists collaborated to develop a state-of-the-art intervention program that is culturally appropriate for American Indian school children. Given another health problem and another target population, a different intervention and design might be required, but other trials face a set of design and analytic issues that are common to group-randomized trials. The rest of this chapter addresses those issues.

DISTINGUISHING CHARACTERISTICS OF GROUP-RANDOMIZED TRIALS AND THEIR IMPLICATIONS

There are four characteristics that distinguish a group-randomized trial from a clinical trial. First, the unit of assignment is an identifiable group rather than an individual. Such groups are not formed at random but rather through some physical, social, geographic, or other connection among their members. Second, different groups are allocated to each study condition, creating a nested or hierarchical structure for the design and for the data. Third, the units of observation are members of those groups so that they are further nested within the groups. Fourth, group-randomized trials typically involve only a small number of groups in each study condition, usually less than 10. (By contrast, a clinical trial can include large numbers of individual participants.) Together, these characteristics set the stage for the special design and analytic issues common to group-randomized trials.

With a limited number of groups in each condition, the opportunity for randomization to evenly distribute all potential sources of bias is more limited than when there are many individual participants in each condition. As a result, bias is more of a concern in group-randomized trials than in many clinical trials. This increases the need to use design strategies that limit bias.

In addition, the members of the same group will share some physical, geographic, social, or other connection (Kish, 1965). That connection will create a positive intraclass correlation (ICC) that reflects an extra component of variance attributable to the group:

$$\text{ICC}_{m:g:c} = \text{corr}(y_{i:k:l}, y_{i':k:l}) = \frac{\sigma_{g:c}^2}{\sigma_e^2 + \sigma_{g:c}^2}$$

Here $\sigma_{g:c}^2$ is the component of variance attributable to the unit of assignment, σ_e^2 is the residual error variance, and $\sigma_y^2 = \sigma_e^2 + \sigma_{g:c}^2$.

Whenever this intraclass correlation is positive, the variance of any group-level statistic will be larger when identifiable groups rather than individuals are assigned to conditions. With a limited number of groups in each condition, the degrees of freedom available to estimate the group-level component of variance also will be limited. Any test that ignores either the extra variation or the limited degrees of freedom will have a Type I error rate that is inflated, often badly (Cornfield, 1978; Murray, Hannan, & Baker, 1996; Zucker, 1990).

Disappointing results for several large trials have led some to question the value of group-randomized trials. To question group-randomized trials in general based on the results from a small group of studies is both short sighted and impractical, however. Whenever an investigator wants to evaluate an intervention that operates at a group level, that manipulates the social or physical environment, or that cannot be delivered to individuals, the group-randomized trial is the best design available. The challenge is to create trials that are (a) sufficiently rigorous to address these issues, (b) powerful enough to provide an answer to the research question of interest, and (c) inexpensive enough to be practical. The question is not whether to conduct group-randomized trials, but how to do them well.

THREATS TO THE DESIGN AND THEIR DEFENSES

There are four primary sources of bias in group-randomized trials (Koepsell et al., 1992; Murray, 1998). Selection bias refers to baseline differences among the study conditions that might explain the results of the trial. This may result from nonrandom assignment, or from random assignment of a limited number of groups to each condition. Selection bias can mask or mimic an intervention effect. Differential history refers to some external influence that operates differentially among the conditions; like selection bias, it may mimic or mask an intervention effect. Differential maturation reflects uneven secular trends among the groups in the trial favoring one condition or another; it can also mask or mimic an intervention effect. Bias due to contamination occurs when intervention-like activities find their way into the comparison groups; it can bias the estimate of the intervention effect toward the null hypothesis.

These threats to the validity of the design are best avoided by randomization of a sufficient number of groups to each study condition. This will increase the likelihood that potential sources of bias are distributed evenly among those conditions, regardless of whether those sources might cause selection bias or bias due to differential history or differential maturation. Careful matching or stratification can increase the effectiveness of randomization, especially when the number of groups is small. As a result, all group-randomized trials planned with fewer than 20 groups per condition would be well served to include careful matching or stratification before randomization. Of course randomization will not protect against contamination. Although investigators often can control access to their intervention materials, there often is little that they can do to prevent the outside world from introducing similar materials into their control groups. As a result, monitoring exposure to events that could affect the trial's endpoints in both the intervention and comparison groups is especially important in group-randomized trials because this will allow the investigators to detect and respond to contamination. Objective measures and evaluation personnel who have no connection to the intervention are also important strategies to limit bias. Finally, analytic strategies, such as regression adjustment for confounders measured at baseline, can be helpful in dealing with bias if it is detected.

THREATS TO THE ANALYSIS AND THEIR DEFENSES

There are two major threats to the validity of the analysis of a group-randomized trial (Murray, 1998). Misspecification of the analytic model will occur if the investigator ignores a measurable source of random variation, misrepresents a measurable source of random variation, or misrepresents over-time correlation in the data. Low power will occur if the investigator uses weak interventions, has insufficient replication of groups and time intervals, has high variance or intraclass correlation in the endpoints, or has poor reliability of intervention implementation.

To avoid model misspecification, the investigator should plan the analysis concurrent with the design, plan the analysis around the primary endpoints, anticipate all sources of random variation, anticipate the error distribution for the primary endpoint, anticipate patterns of over-time correlation, consider alternate structures for the covariance matrix, consider alternate models for time, and assess potential confounding and effect modification (Murray, 1998; Murray et al., 1996, 1998; Murray & Wolfinger, 1994; Wolfinger, 1993; Zucker, 1990).

To avoid low power, investigators should plan a large enough study to ensure sufficient replication, choose endpoints with low variance and intraclass correlation, use matching or stratification before randomization, use more and smaller groups instead of a few large groups, use more and smaller surveys or continuous surveillance instead of a few large surveys, use repeat observations on the same groups or on the same groups and members, use strong interventions with good reach, and maintain the reliability of intervention implementation. In the analysis, they should use regression adjustment for covariates, model time if possible, and consider post hoc stratification (Koepsell et al., 1991; Murray, 1998; Murray & Short, 1995, 1996, 1997).

ANALYTIC STRATEGIES APPROPRIATE FOR GROUP-RANDOMIZED TRIALS

Selection and proper implementation of the analysis in a group-randomized trial has proven to be one of the more difficult issues, in part because the familiar methods are often inappropriate. Generally, analyses based on the general linear model (Searle, 1971) and on the generalized linear model (McCullagh & Nelder, 1989) will not be appropriate for one-stage analyses of data from group-randomized trials. Both provide for only one source of random variation, whereas group-randomized trials will always have at least two (groups and members). In contrast, The general linear mixed model (Donner, 1984; Harville, 1977; Laird, Lange, & Stram, 1987; Laird & Ware, 1982; Stiratelli, Laird, & Ware, 1984; Ware, 1985) and generalized linear mixed model (Breslow & Clayton, 1993; Wolfinger & O'Connell, 1993) are appropriate for one-stage analyses of data from group-randomized trials because they allow for multiple sources of random variation.

Properly implemented, the mixed-model analysis of variance/analysis of covariance (ANOVA/ANCOVA) will provide a valid analysis of data from a posttest-only control group design or a pretest–posttest control group design (Feldman & McKinlay, 1994; Koepsell et al., 1991; Murray, 1998; Murray & Hannan, 1990). This analysis requires application of the general or generalized linear mixed model, with both the groups and members identified as nested random effects. Regression adjustment for covariates can reduce confounding due to unevenly distributed covariates and can improve precision by removing variation due to extraneous factors. Given only one or two time intervals, there is no opportunity to misrepresent the pattern of over-time correlation in the data. Simulations have shown that mixed-model ANCOVA with only two time intervals has the nominal Type I error rate across a wide range of conditions common in group-randomized trials (Murray et al., 1996; Murray & Wolfinger, 1994; Zucker, 1990).

Murray et al. (1998) found that the mixed-model ANOVA/ANCOVA will not provide a valid analysis of data from a group-randomized trial that has more than two time intervals and measurable variation in the group-specific time trends. The mixed-model ANOVA/ANCOVA assumes that the time trends are homogenous, which is to assume that the component of variance for those trends is zero. Where the group-specific trends are heterogeneous, that component of variance will be measurable, the error variances from the mixed-model ANOVA/ANCOVA will be too small, and application of mixed-model ANOVA/ANCOVA will result in an inflated Type I error rate. Murray et al. (1998) found that the random coefficients analysis avoids this problem. This analysis provides for a component of variance for group slopes, linear or otherwise. If variation among those slopes exists, the random coefficients analysis will reflect it in the estimation of the error variance for the intervention effect. Murray et al. reported that the random coefficients analysis had a nominal Type I error rate regardless of the degree of slope heterogeneity across a wide range of conditions common to group-randomized trials. The random coefficients analysis is relatively new and is being used for the first time in a group-randomized trial in health promotion and disease prevention in the Rapid Early Action For Coronary Treatment (REACT) Trial (Feldman et al., 1998).

Fixed-effects methods based on the general linear model (Searle, 1971) and the generalized linear model (McCullagh & Nelder, 1989) are appropriate for data from a group-randomized trial if they are used in two stages (cf. Skinner, Holt, & Smith, 1989). This approach was first introduced as the means analysis for nested designs in the 1950s. In the first stage, group means, slopes, or other statistics are computed without regard to treatment condition but with regression adjustment for individual-level covariates if desired. In the second stage, the group-level statistics are used as the data in an analysis of treatment effects, with additional adjustment for group-level covariates if desired. Hopkins (1982) showed that this means analysis is identical to the mixed-model, ANOVA-given balanced data. It can be adapted for use with random coefficients analyses by computing group slopes rather than means. It was the primary analysis reported for the Minnesota Heart Health Program (Murray et al., 1994) and for CATCH (Zucker et al., 1995). Importantly, the two-stage approach is often the only possible model-based analysis when software for a one-stage analysis is not available.

Gail, Mark, Carroll, Green, and Pee (1996) suggested an alternative to model-based methods based on the randomization or permutation test. In this test, the intervention effect is estimated for all possible allocations of groups to conditions. Under the null hypothesis, the observed effect is but one result of a proper randomization. The probability of an effect as large as the observed effect is the proportion of possible intervention effects as large as the observed effect. Gail and colleagues reported that randomization tests had nominal Type I and Type II error rates across a variety of conditions common to group-randomized trials. One attraction of this approach is that it is often thought to involve fewer assumptions than do the model-based methods described above. Nonetheless, when regression adjustment for covariates is included, this approach requires many of the same assumptions as the model-based methods. It is also important to note that randomization tests for group-randomized trials are computer intensive, and software is not readily available. Even so, it is an approach that has much to offer, and it was the primary analysis used in the Community Intervention Trial for Smoking Cessation trial (COMMIT Research Group, 1995a, 1995b).

ANALYTIC STRATEGIES THAT ARE GENERALLY INAPPROPRIATE FOR GROUP-RANDOMIZED TRIALS

Murray (1998) reviewed a number of alternative strategies that have been suggested for or applied to the analysis of data from a group-randomized trial. Most were judged inappropriate for general use, although some could be appropriate under limited conditions, and others may be judged appropriate at a later time, pending the results of additional research.

Skinner and colleagues (1989) presented methods for the post hoc correction of the usual fixed-effect F test, t tests, chi-squares, and so forth so as to reflect extra variation often found in data collected using complex survey designs, especially those that involve multistage cluster sampling. Such designs are observational counterparts to the group-randomized trial because both involve measurements taken from members of identifiable groups, with the expectation that the observations from the members of the same group will be correlated. As such, it is not a great leap to consider application of their post hoc correction methods to the data from a group-randomized trial. Here, the data would be analyzed via the familiar fixed-effects methods, with correction post hoc for the extra variation reflected in the positive intraclass correlation. The difficulty with this approach is that it requires an external estimate of that intraclass correlation and would rely on the strong assumption that the external estimate is valid for the data at hand.

Moreover, there is no consensus on the degrees of freedom that would be used to evaluate the corrected test statistic (Hannan, Murray, Jacobs, & McGovern, 1994). As more information on the consistency of intraclass correlations across populations becomes available, this approach may prove useful.

A variety of other methods have been developed for data from complex surveys, and one can think of many ways to apply these methods in the context of group-randomized trials. These methods are generally based on resampling techniques to estimate standard errors and perform well given a large number of groups. Unfortunately, these methods do not perform well when the number of groups is limited (Skinner et al., 1989). These methods generally will not be appropriate except in larger trials.

Liang and Zeger (1986) combined the empirical sandwich formula for estimation of error variances with methods for correlated data based on generalized estimating equations (GEE). The empirical sandwich estimator is asymptotically robust against misspecification of the random-effects covariance matrix, and that makes the GEE approach attractive in group-randomized trials in which the structure of the random-effects covariance matrix is often complex.

Unfortunately, simulations have shown that when the degrees of freedom are limited (<40), the empirical sandwich estimator has an unreliable Type I error rate (Murray et al., 1998; Thornquist & Anderson, 1992). These findings suggest that use of the GEE approach in group-randomized trials should be limited to large trials with enough groups per condition to provide *at least* 40 degrees of freedom.

Some have suggested dividing groups into subgroups or batches for analysis at that level (Feldman, McKinlay, & Niknian, 1996). This approach rests on the strong assumption that the subgroup captures all of the variation within the group. Unfortunately, there is not sufficient data for a good test of this assumption in small trials involving only a few groups per condition. Moreover, simulations have shown that this approach has an inflated Type I error rate even when the subgroup captures as much as 80% of the group variation (Murray et al., 1996). As a result, the use of subgroups or batches is not likely to have broad application in group-randomized trials.

Many investigators would like to test for the significance of the group component of variance and simply ignore it if that test yields a nonsignificant result. This is a perfectly reasonable strategy, but only if the test performed is sensitive to the magnitude of intraclass correlation that can inflate the Type I error rate in a group-randomized trial if the correlation is ignored. The difficulty is that most tests are not sensitive, especially in small trials. For example, the z statistic that tests the variance component against its asymptotic standard error is highly insensitive when degrees of freedom are limited or when the correlation is small; of course those are exactly the conditions in a small group-randomized trial with modest intraclass correlation. The prudent course is to retain group as a nested random effect in the analysis and let the data dictate both the magnitude of the problem and the severity of the penalty. Simulations have shown that this is the course required to preserve the nominal Type I error rate (Murray et al., 1996; Zucker, 1990).

PROTOTYPE STUDIES

Having strongly recommended that the funding agencies support prototype studies, it is essential to address the question of how best to analyze the data from such studies. Prototype studies typically will be based on only one or two groups per condition and thus are particularly problematic if the investigator wants to make causal inferences relating the intervention as delivered to the outcomes as observed. Studies based on only one group per condition cannot estimate variation due to the group independent of variation due to condition. Studies based on only a few groups per condition cannot estimate that component of variance with much accuracy. Some of the methods described in the previous section can be applied, but all would require strong assumptions. For example, application of a post hoc correction would require the strong assumption that the external estimate of intraclass correlation is valid for the data at hand. Application of the subgroup or batch analysis would require the strong assumption that the subgroup captures the group variance. Application of the usual fixed-effects methods would require the strong assumption that the group component of variance is zero. This situation has led some statisticians to argue that there is no valid analysis in this situation.

Does this mean that we should not do prototype studies? The answer is clearly no, and, more to the point, the answer must be that such studies simply should not be used to make causal inferences relating the intervention and the outcome. Studies involving only one or two groups per condition are prototype studies, not efficacy trials, and must be analyzed with that in mind. With only one or two groups per condition, the investigator can estimate the magnitude of the intervention effect, but it will not be possible to estimate a standard error for that effect with any degree of accuracy. As a result, it will not be possible to put a confidence bound around the intervention effect or to draw any conclusions about the statistical significance of that effect. Even so, if the effect is much smaller than expected, that finding should push the investigators to rework their intervention because it is not likely that a reasonably sized efficacy trial would show such a small intervention effect to be significant. If the effect is as large as expected or larger, that finding should provide good support to the investigator in seeking support for the efficacy trial required to establish the causal link between the intervention and the outcome.

FUTURE EFFICACY AND EFFECTIVENESS TRIALS BASED ON GROUP-RANDOMIZED DESIGNS

A well-designed and properly-executed group-randomized trial remains the method of choice in public health and medicine when the purpose of the study is to establish the efficacy or effectiveness of an intervention that operates at a group level, manipulates the social or physical environment, or cannot be delivered to individuals. Nonetheless, efficacy and effectiveness trials should occur in proper sequence. They should occur only after pilot studies have established the feasibility and acceptability of the materials and protocols for the intervention and evaluation. They should occur only after prototype studies have shown that the magnitude of the intervention effect is large enough to warrant the larger trials. Efficacy and effectiveness trials should be large enough to ensure sufficient power, with groups assigned at random from within well-matched or stratified sets to protect against bias. Investigators should measure exposure and other process variables in all conditions. They should select a model for the analysis that reflects the design of the study and the nature of the endpoints. Investigators should be cautious of strategies that appear to easily solve or avoid the design and analytic problems that are inherent in group-randomized trials because those methods are likely to prove to be inappropriate.

REFERENCES

Breslow, N. E., & Clayton, D. G. (1993). Approximate inference in generalized linear mixed models. *Journal of the American Statistical Association, 88,* 9–25.

COMMIT Research Group. (1995a). Community intervention trial for smoking cessation (COMMIT): I. Cohort results from a four-year community intervention. *American Journal of Public Health, 85,* 183–192.

COMMIT Research Group. (1995b). Community intervention trial for smoking cessation (COMMIT): II. Changes in adult cigarette smoking prevalence. *American Journal of Public Health, 85,* 193–200.

Cornfield, J. (1978). Randomization by group: A formal analysis. *American Journal of Epidemiology, 108,* 100–102.

Davis, C. E., Hunsberger, S., Murray, D. M., Fabsitz, R., Himes, J. H., & Stephenson, L. K. (1999). Design and statistical analysis for Pathways. *American Journal of Clinical Nutrition, 69*(Suppl. 4), 760S–763S.

Davis, S. M., Going, S. B., Helitzer, D., Teufel, N. I., Snyder, P., Gittelsohn, J., Metcalfe, L., Arviso, V., Evans, M., Smyth, M., Brice, R., & Altaha J. (1999). Pathways: A culturally appropriate obesity-prevention program for American Indian schoolchildren. *American Journal of Clinical Nutrition, 69*(Suppl. 4), 796S–802S.

Donner, A. (1984). Linear regression analysis with repeated measurements. *Journal of Chronic Diseases, 37,* 441–448.

Feldman, H. A., & McKinlay, S. M. (1994). Cohort versus cross-sectional design in large field trials: Precision, sample size, and a unifying model. *Statistics in Medicine, 13,* 61–78.

Feldman, H. A., McKinlay, S. M., & Niknian, M. (1996). Batch sampling to improve power in a community trial: Experience from the Pawtucket Heart Health Program. *Evaluation Review, 20,* 244–274.

Feldman, H. A., Proschan, M., Murray, D. M., Goff, D., Stylianou, M., Dulberg, E., McGovern, P. G., Chan, W., Mann, C., & Bittner, V. (1998). Statistical design of REACT (Rapid Early Action for Coronary Treatment), a multi-site community trial with continual data collection. *Controlled Clinical Trials, 19,* 391–403.

Flay, B. R. (1986). Efficacy and effectiveness trials (and other phases of research) in the development of health promotion programs. *Preventive Medicine, 15,* 451–474.

Gail, M. H., Mark, S. D., Carroll, R. J., Green, S. B., & Pee, D. (1996). On design considerations and randomization-based inference for community intervention trials. *Statistics in Medicine, 15,* 1069–1092.

Hannan, P. J., Murray, D. M., Jacobs, D. R., & McGovern, P. G. (1994). Parameters to aid in the design and analysis of community trials: Intraclass correlations from the Minnesota Heart Health Program. *Epidemiology, 5,* 88–95.

Harville, D. A. (1977). Maximum likelihood approaches to variance component estimation and to related problems. *Journal of the American Statistical Association, 72,* 320–338.

Hopkins, K. D. (1982). The unit of analysis: Group means versus individual observations. *American Education Research Journal, 19,* 5–18.

Kish, L. (1965). *Survey sampling.* New York: Wiley.

Koepsell, T. D., Martin, D. C., Diehr, P. H., Psaty, B. M., Wagner, E. H., Perrin, E. B., & Cheadle, A. (1991). Data analysis and sample size issues in evaluations of community-based health promotion and disease prevention programs: A mixed-model analysis of variance approach. *Journal of Clinical Epidemiology, 44,* 701–713.

Koepsell, T. D., Wagner, E. H., Cheadle, A. C., Patrick, D. L., Martin, D. C.,

Diehr, P. H., & Perrin, E. B. (1992). Selected methodological issues in evaluating community-based health promotion and disease prevention programs. *Annual Review of Public Health, 13,* 31–57.

Laird, N., Lange, N., & Stram, D. (1987). Maximum likelihood computations with repeated measures: Application of the EM algorithm. *Journal of the American Statistical Association, 82,* 97–105.

Laird, N. M., & Ware, J. H. (1982). Random-effects models for longitudinal data. *Biometrics, 38,* 963–974.

Liang, K. Y., & Zeger, S. L. (1986). Longitudinal data analysis using generalized linear models. *Biometrika. 73,* 13–22.

Lohman, T. G., Caballero, B., Himes, J. H., Hunsberger, S., Reid, R., Stewart, D., & Skipper, B. (1999). Body composition assessment in American Indian children. *American Journal of Clinical Nutrition, 69*(Suppl.), 764S–766S.

McCullagh, P., & Nelder, J. A. (1989). *Generalized linear models* (2nd ed.). London: Chapman & Hall.

Meinert, C. L. (1986). *Clinical trials.* New York: Oxford University Press.

Murray, D. M. (1998). *Design and analysis of group-randomized trials.* New York: Oxford University Press.

Murray, D. M., & Hannan, P. J. (1990). Planning for the appropriate analysis in school-based drug-use prevention studies. *Journal of Consulting and Clinical Psychology, 58,* 458–468.

Murray, D. M., Hannan, P. J., & Baker, W. L. (1996). A Monte Carlo study of alternative responses to intraclass correlation in community trials: Is it ever possible to avoid Cornfield's penalties? *Evaluation Review, 20,* 313–337.

Murray, D. M., Hannan, P., Jacobs, D., McGovern, P. J., Schmid, L., Baker, W. L., & Gray, C. (1994). Assessing intervention effects in the Minnesota Heart Health Program. *American Journal of Epidemiology, 139,* 91–103.

Murray, D. M., Hannan, P. J., Wolfinger, R. D., Baker, W. L., & Dwyer, J. H. (1998). Analysis of data from group-randomized trials with repeat observations on the same groups. *Statistics in Medicine, 17,* 1581–1600.

Murray, D. M., & Short, B. J. (1995). Intraclass correlation among measures related to alcohol use by young adults: Estimates, correlates and applications in intervention studies. *Journal of Studies on Alcohol, 56,* 681–694.

Murray, D. M., & Short, B. (1996). Intraclass correlation among measures related to alcohol use by school aged adolescents: Estimates, correlates, and applications in intervention studies. *Journal of Drug Education, 26,* 207–230.

Murray, D. M., & Short, B. J. (1997). Intraclass correlation among measures related to tobacco use by adolescents: Estimates, correlates, and applications in intervention studies. *Addictive Behaviors, 22,* 1–12.

Murray, D. M., & Wolfinger, R. D. (1994) Analysis issues in the evaluation of community trials: Progress toward solutions in SAS/STAT MIXED. *Journal of Community Psychology* [CSAP special issue], 140–154.

Searle, S. R. (1971). *Linear models.* New York: Wiley.

Skinner, C. J., Holt, D., & Smith, T. M. F. (1989). *Analysis of complex surveys*. New York: Wiley.

Stiratelli, R., Laird, N., & Ware, J. H. (1984). Random-effects models for serial observations with binary response. *Biometrics, 40*, 961–971.

Thornquist, M. D., & Anderson, G. L. (1992, November). *Small sample properties of generalized estimating equations in group-randomized designs with Gaussian response*. Paper presented at the 120th Annual Meeting of the American Public Health Association, Washington, DC.

Ware, J. H. (1985). Linear models for the analysis of longitudinal studies. *American Statistician, 39*, 95–101.

Wolfinger, R. (1993). Covariance structure selection in general mixed models. *Communications in Statistics, Simulation and Computation, 22*, 1079–1106.

Wolfinger, R., & O'Connell, M. (1993). Generalized linear mixed models: A pseudo-likelihood approach. *Journal of Statistics and Computational Simulation, 48*, 233–243.

Zucker, D. M. (1990). An analysis of variance pitfall: The fixed effects analysis in a nested design. *Educational and Psychological Measurement, 50*, 731–738.

Zucker, D. M., Lakatos, E., Webber, L. S., Murray, D. M., McKinlay, S. M., Feldman, H. A., Kelder, S. H., & Nader, P. R. (1995). Statistical design of the Child and Adolescent Trial for Cardiovascular Health (CATCH): Implication of cluster randomization. *Controlled Clinical Trials, 16*, 96–118.

16

EMPOWERMENT EVALUATION AND SELF-DETERMINATION: A PRACTICAL APPROACH TOWARD PROGRAM IMPROVEMENT AND CAPACITY BUILDING

DAVID FETTERMAN

Empowerment evaluation involves the use of evaluation concepts, techniques, and findings to foster improvement and self-determination. It uses both qualitative and quantitative methodologies. Although it can be applied to individuals, organizations,[1] communities, societies, or cultures, the focus is usually on programs. Traditional evaluations typically place the evaluator in charge of the design, implementation, and reporting stages of an evaluation. An empowerment evaluation turns this process on its head. Program participants are primarily responsible for evaluating their own programs. They learn, with the assistance of an evaluation coach, to continually assess their program toward self-determined goals and to reshape their

---

[1] See Stevenson, Mitchell, and Florin (1996) for a detailed explanation about the distinctions concerning levels of organizations. See also Zimmerman (in press) for more detail about empowerment theory focusing on psychological, organizational, and community levels of analysis.

plans and strategies according to this assessment. In the process, self-determination is fostered, illumination is generated, and liberation is actualized.

Empowerment evaluation has been adopted in higher education, government, inner-city public education, nonprofit corporations, and foundations throughout the United States and abroad. A wide range of program and policy sectors use empowerment evaluation, including substance abuse prevention, HIV prevention, crime prevention, welfare reform, battered women's shelters, agriculture and rural development, adult probation, adolescent pregnancy prevention, tribal partnership for substance abuse, self-determination for individuals with disabilities, doctoral programs, and accelerated schools. Descriptions of programs that use empowerment evaluation appear in *Empowerment Evaluation: Knowledge and Tools for Self-assessment and Accountability* (Fetterman, Kaftarian, & Wandersman, 1996). *Empowerment Evaluation* (Fetterman, 2000) provides additional insight into this new evaluation approach, including information about how to conduct workshops to train program staff and participants to evaluate and improve program practice (see also Fetterman, 1994a, 1994b). In addition, this approach has been institutionalized within the American Evaluation Association[2] and is consistent with the spirit of the standards developed by the Joint Committee on Standards for Educational Evaluation (Fetterman, 1995; Joint Committee on Standards for Educational Evaluation, 1994).[3]

Empowerment evaluation is attentive to empowering processes and outcomes. Zimmerman's work on empowerment theory provides the theoretical framework for empowerment evaluation. According to Zimmerman (in press),

> A distinction between empowering processes and outcomes is critical in order to clearly define empowerment theory. Empowerment processes are ones in which attempts to gain control, obtain needed resources, and critically understand one's social environment are fundamental. The process is empowering if it helps people develop skills so they can become independent problem solvers and decision makers. Empowering processes will vary across levels of analysis. For example, empowering processes for individuals might include organizational or community involvement, empowering processes at the organizational level might include shared leadership and decision making, and em-

---

[2]Empowerment evaluation has been institutionalized as part of the Collaborative, Participatory, and Empowerment Evaluation Topical Interest Group (TIG). TIG chairs are David Fetterman and Jean King. All interested evaluators are invited to join the TIG and attend our business meetings, which are open to any member of the association.

[3]Although there are many problems with the standards and the application of the standards to empowerment evaluation, coupled with the fact that they have not been formally adopted by any professional organization, they nonetheless represent a useful tool for self-reflection and examination. Empowerment evaluation meets or exceeds the spirit of the standards in terms of utility, feasibility, propriety, and accuracy (see Fetterman 1996a, for a detailed examination).

powering processes at the community level might include accessible government, media, and other community resources.

Empowered outcomes refer to operationalization of empowerment so we can study the consequences of citizen attempts to gain greater control in their community or the effects of interventions designed to empower participants. Empowered outcomes also differ across levels of analysis. When we are concerned with individuals, outcomes might include situation-specific perceived control, skills, and proactive behaviors. When we are studying organizations, outcomes might include organizational networks, effective resource acquisition, and policy leverage. When we are concerned with community-level empowerment, outcomes might include evidence of pluralism, the existence of organizational coalitions, and accessible community resources.

Empowerment evaluation has an unambiguous value orientation; it is designed to help people help themselves and improve their programs using a form of self-evaluation and reflection. This approach to evaluation has roots in community psychology and action anthropology. It has also been influenced by action research and action evaluation. Program participants —including clients—conduct their own evaluations; an outside evaluator often serves as a coach or additional facilitator depending on internal program capabilities.

Zimmerman's (in press) characterization of the community psychologist's role in empowering activities is easily adapted to the empowerment evaluator:

> An empowerment approach to intervention design, implementation, and evaluation redefines the professional's role relationship with the target population. The professional's role becomes one of collaborator and facilitator rather than expert and counselor. As collaborators, professionals learn about the participants through their culture, their worldview, and their life struggles. The professional works *with* participants instead of advocating *for* them. The professional's skills, interest, or plans are not imposed on the community; rather, professionals become a resource for a community. This role relationship suggests that what professionals do will depend on the particular place and people with whom they are working, rather than on the technologies that are predetermined to be applied in all situations. While interpersonal assessment and evaluation skills will be necessary, how, where, and with whom they are applied can not be automatically assumed as in the role of a psychotherapist with clients in a clinic.

Empowerment evaluation also requires sensitivity and adaptation to the local setting. It is not dependent on a predetermined set of technologies. It is necessarily a collaborative group activity, not an individual pursuit. An evaluator does not and cannot empower anyone; people empower themselves, often with assistance and coaching. This process is fundamentally democratic in the sense that it invites (if not demands) participation, examining issues of concern to the entire community in an open forum.

As a result, the context changes: The assessment of a program's value and worth is not the endpoint of the evaluation, as it often is in traditional evaluation, but is part of an ongoing process of program improvement. This new context acknowledges a simple but often overlooked truth: that merit and worth are not static values. Populations and goals shift, knowledge about program practices and their value change, and external forces are highly unstable. By internalizing and institutionalizing self-evaluation processes and practices, a dynamic and responsive approach to evaluation can be developed to accommodate these shifts. Both value assessments and corresponding plans for program improvement, developed by the group with the assistance of a trained evaluator, are subject to a cyclical process of reflection and self-evaluation.

Value assessments are also highly sensitive to the life cycle of the program or organization. Goals and outcomes are geared toward the appropriate developmental level of implementation. Extraordinary improvements are not expected of a project that will not be fully implemented until the following year. Similarly, seemingly small gains or improvements in programs at an embryonic stage are recognized and appreciated in relation to their stage of development. In a fully operational and mature program, moderate improvements or declining outcomes are viewed more critically.

ROOTS, INFLUENCES, AND COMPARISONS

Empowerment evaluation has many sources. The idea first germinated during preparation of another book, *Speaking the Language of Power: Communication, Collaboration, and Advocacy* (Fetterman, 1993b). In developing that collection, I wanted to explore the many ways that evaluators and social scientists could give voice to the people they work with and bring their concerns to policy brokers. It was found that socially concerned scholars in myriad fields increasingly are making their insights and findings available to decision makers. These scholars and practitioners address a host of significant issues, including conflict resolution, the dropout problem, environmental health and safety, homelessness, educational reform, AIDS, American Indian concerns, and the education of gifted children. The aim of these scholars and practitioners was to explore successful strategies, share lessons learned, and enhance their ability to communicate with an educated citizenry and powerful policy-making bodies. Collaboration, participation, and empowerment emerged as common threads throughout the work and helped crystallize the concept of empowerment evaluation.

Empowerment evaluation has roots in community psychology, action anthropology, and action research. Community psychology focuses on people, organizations, and communities working to establish control over their affairs. The literature about citizen participation and community development is extensive. Rappaport's (1987) article "Terms of Empowerment/Exemplars of Prevention: Toward a Theory for Community Psychology" is a classic in this area. Sol Tax's (1958) work in action anthropology focuses on how anthropologists can facilitate the goals and objectives of self-determining groups, such as Native American tribes. Empowerment evaluation also derives from collaborative and participatory evaluation (Choudhary & Tandon, 1988; Oja & Smulyan, 1989; Papineau & Kiely, 1994; Reason, 1988; Shapiro, 1988; Stull & Schensul, 1987; Whitmore, 1990; Whyte, 1990).

Empowerment evaluation has been influenced strongly by and is similar to action research. Stakeholders typically control the study and conduct the work in action research and empowerment evaluation. In addition, practitioners empower themselves in both forms of inquiry and action. Empowerment evaluation and action research are characterized by concrete, timely, targeted, pragmatic orientations toward program improvement. They both require cycles of reflection and action and focus on the simplest data collection methods adequate to the task at hand. Nonetheless, there are conceptual and stylistic differences between the approaches. For example, empowerment evaluation is explicitly driven by the concept of self-determination. It is also explicitly collaborative in nature. Action research can be either an individual effort documented in a journal or a group effort. Written narratives are used to share findings with colleagues (see Soffer, 1995). A group in a collaborative fashion conducts empowerment evaluation, with a holistic focus on an entire program or agency. Empowerment evaluation is never conducted by a single individual. Action research is often conducted on top of the normal daily responsibilities of a practitioner. Empowerment evaluation is internalized as part of the planning and management of a program. The institutionalization of evaluation in this manner makes it more likely to be sustainable rather than sporadic. Despite these differences, the overwhelming number of similarities between the approaches has enriched empowerment evaluation.

Another major influence was the national educational school reform movement with colleagues such as Henry Levin, whose Accelerated School Project (ASP) emphasizes the empowerment of parents, teachers, administrators, and students to improve educational settings. We worked to help design an appropriate evaluation plan for the ASP that contributes to this effort (Fetterman & Haertel, 1990). The ASP team and I also mapped out detailed strategies for districtwide adoption of the project to help institutionalize the project in the school system (Stanford University and American Institutes for Research, 1992).

Dennis Mithaug's (1991, 1993) extensive work with individuals with disabilities to explore concepts of self-regulation and self-determination provided additional inspiration. A 2-year grant (funded by the Department of Education) supported this study on self-determination and individuals with disabilities; the research was designed and conducted to help both providers for students with disabilities and the students themselves become more empowered. Important lessons were learned about self-determined behavior and attitudes and environmentally related features of self-determination by listening to self-determined children with disabilities and their providers. Using specific concepts and behaviors extracted from these case studies, a behavioral checklist was developed to assist providers as they work to recognize and foster self-determination.

Defined as the ability to chart one's own course in life, *self-determination* forms the theoretical foundation of empowerment evaluation. It consists of numerous interconnected capabilities, such as the ability to identify and express needs, establish goals or expectations and a plan of action to achieve them, identify resources, make rational choices from various alternative courses of action, take appropriate steps to pursue objectives, evaluate short- and long-term results (including reassessing plans and expectations and taking necessary detours), and persist in the pursuit of those goals. A breakdown at any juncture of this network of capabilities, as well as various environmental factors, can reduce a person's likelihood of being self-determined (see also Bandura, 1982, concerning the self-efficacy mechanism in human agency).

A pragmatic influence on empowerment evaluation is the W. K. Kellogg Foundation's (1992) emphasis on empowerment in community settings. The foundation has taken a clear position concerning empowerment as a funding strategy:

> We've long been convinced that problems can best be solved at the local level by people who live with them on a daily basis. In other words, individuals and groups of people must be empowered to become changemakers and solve their own problems, through the organizations and institutions they devise. . . . Through our community-based programming, we are helping to empower various individuals, agencies, institutions, and organizations to work together to identify problems and to find quality, cost-effective solutions. In doing so, we find ourselves working more than ever with grantees with whom we have been less involved—smaller, newer organizations and their programs. (p. 6)

This foundation's work in the areas of youth, leadership, community-based health services, higher education, food systems, rural development, and families and neighborhoods exemplifies this spirit of putting "power in the hands of creative and committed individuals—power that will enable them to make important changes in the world" (p. 13). For example, one project, Kellogg's Empowering Farm Women to Reduce Hazards to Family Health and Safety on the Farm, involves a participatory evaluation component. The work of Sanders, Barley, and Jenness (1990) on cluster evaluations for the foundation also highlighted the value of giving ownership of the evaluation to project directors and staff members of science education projects.

These influences, activities, and experiences form the background for this new evaluation approach. An eloquent literature on empowerment theory by Zimmerman (in press); Zimmerman, Israel, Schulz, and Checkoway (1992); Zimmerman and Rappaport (1988); and Dunst, Trivette, and LaPointe (1992) also informs this approach. A brief discussion about the pursuit of truth and a review of empowerment evaluation's many steps and facets will illustrate its wide-ranging application.

PURSUIT OF TRUTH AND HONESTY

One of the most important principles to guide empowerment evaluation is a commitment to truth and honesty. This is not a naive concept of one absolute truth but instead a sincere intent to understand an event in context and from multiple worldviews. The aim is to understand what is going on in a situation from the participant's own perspective as accurately and honestly as possible and then to proceed to improve it with meaningful goals and strategies and credible documentation. There are many checks and balances in empowerment evaluation, such as having a democratic approach to participation (i.e., involving participants at all levels of the organization), relying on external evaluators as critical friends, and so on.

Empowerment evaluation is like a personnel performance self-appraisal. Employees come to an agreement with their supervisor about goals, strategies for accomplishing them, and credible documentation to determine if they are meeting them. The same agreement is made with a program's clients. If the data are not credible, program leaders lose their credibility immediately. If the data at the end of the year are positive, they can be used to advocate for the program and its leaders. Empowerment evaluation applies the same approach to the program and community level. Advocacy, in this context, becomes a natural by-product of the self-evaluation process if the data merit it. Advocacy is meaningless in the absence of credible data. In addition, external standards and requirements can significantly influence any self-evaluation. To operate without consideration of these external forces is to proceed at one's own peril. Nonetheless, the process must be grounded in an authentic understanding and expression of everyday life at the program or community level. A commitment to the ideals of truth and honesty guides every step and facet of empowerment evaluation.

STEPS OF EMPOWERMENT EVALUATION

There are three steps involved in helping others learn to evaluate their own programs: (a) developing a mission, vision, or unifying purpose; (b) taking stock or determining where the program stands, including its strengths and weaknesses; and (b) planning for the future by establishing goals and helping participants determine their own strategies to accomplish program goals and objectives. In addition, empowerment evaluators help program staff members and participants determine the type of evidence required to document and monitor progress credibly toward their goals. These steps combined help to create a "communicative space" (Vanderplaat, 1995) to facilitate emancipatory and "communicative action" (Habermas, 1984).

Defining a Mission

The first step in an empowerment evaluation is to ask program staff members and participants to define a mission. An empowerment evaluator facilitates an open session with as many staff members and participants as possible. They are asked to generate key phrases that capture the mission of the program or project. The evaluator records these phrases, typically on a poster sheet or chalkboard, and asks a workshop participant to volunteer to transcribe these telescopic phrases into a paragraph or two. This document is shared with the group, revisions and corrections are made, and then the group is asked to accept the document on a consensus basis. The mission statement represents the values of the group and, as such, represents the foundation for the next step, which is taking stock.

Taking Stock

The second step in an empowerment evaluation is taking stock, which is comprised of two parts. The first involves generating a list of current key activities that are crucial to the functioning of the program. Once again, the empowerment evaluator serves as a facilitator, asking program staff members and participants to list the most significant features and activities associated with the program. After generating this list, it is time to prioritize and determine which are the most important activities presently meriting evaluation.

The second phase of taking stock involves rating the activities. Program staff members and participants are asked to rate how well they are doing concerning each activity on a 1 to 10 scale, with 10 as the highest level and 1 as the lowest. The rating process sets the stage for dialogue, clarification, and detailed definition about the activities rated. Typically, staff and participants rate each activity on a piece of paper. Then they are asked to come to the front of the room and record their ratings on the board or poster sheet. There is nothing confidential about the process; contrary to most research designs, this system generally is designed to ensure that everyone knows and is influenced by each other's ratings records. The taking-stock phase of an empowerment evaluation is conducted in an open setting for three reasons: (a) it creates a democratic flow of information and exchange of information, (b) it makes it more difficult for managers to retaliate because it is in an open forum, and (b) it increases the probability that the disclosures will be diplomatic because program staff members and participants must remain in that environment after the exercise.

It is important that program staff members and participants be asked to begin by assessing individual program activities. The ratings can be totaled and averaged by person and activity. This provides some insight into routinely optimistic and pessimistic participants. It allows participants to see where they stand in relation to their peers, which helps them calibrate their own assessments in the future. The more important rating, of course, is across the matrix or spreadsheet by activity. Each activity receives a total and average. Combining the individual activity averages generates a total program rating, often lower than an external assessment rating. This represents the first baseline data concerning that specific program activity. This can be used to compare change over time.[4]

All of this work sets the tone for one of the most important aspects of the empowerment evaluation process: dialogue. The empowerment evaluator facilitates a discussion about the ratings. A survey would have accomplished the same task up to this point. Participants are asked to explain their rating and provide evidence or documentation to support the rating. This plants the seeds for the next stage of empowerment evaluation, planning for the future, in which they will need to specify the evidence they plan to use to document that their activities are helping them accomplish their goals. The empowerment evaluator serves as a critical friend during this stage, facilitating discussion and making sure that everyone is heard, while at the same time being critical and requesting additional clarification and substantiation about a particular rating or viewpoint for both the positive and negative ratings.

Participants are reminded that they can change their ratings throughout the dialogue and exchange stage of the workshop, based on what they hear and learn from their peers. As noted earlier, the significance of this process, however, is not the actual rating so much as it is the creation of a baseline from which future progress can be measured. In addition, it

---

[4]Program staff members and participants should return to these activity ratings on a routine basis. In some cases, a monthly comparison is needed. Most programs return to these ratings at 3-, 6-, or 12-month intervals, however.

sensitizes program participants to the necessity of collecting data to support assessments or appraisals.

This process is superior to surveys because it generally has a higher response rate—close to 100% depending on how many staff members and participants are present—and allows participants to discuss what they mean by their ratings and recalibrate and revise their ratings based on what they learn. This minimizes participants "talking past each other" about certain issues or other miscommunications, such as defining terms differently and using radically different rating systems.

Planning for the Future

After rating their program's performance and providing documentation to support that rating, program participants are asked where they "want to go from here." They are asked how they would like to improve both what they do well and what they do less well. The empowerment evaluator asks the group to use the list of activities from the taking-stock phase as the basis for their plans for the future so that the group mission guides the taking-stock phase, and the taking-stock phase shapes the planning-for-the-future phase. This creates a thread of coherence and an audit trail for each step of their evaluation and action plans.

Program staff members and participants are asked to list their goals based on the results of their taking-stock exercise. They set specific goals associated with each activity and define strategies to accomplish each goal. They are also asked to generate forms of evidence to monitor progress toward specified goals. Program staff members and participants supply all of this information.

The empowerment evaluator is not superior or inferior because staff members, participants, and evaluators are equals in the process. The empowerment evaluator adds ideas as deemed appropriate without dominating the discussion. The primary role is to serve as a coach, facilitator, and critical evaluative friend. The evaluator also must be analytical and critical, asking or prompting participants to clarify, document, and evaluate what they are doing, to ensure that specific goals are achieved.

In planning for the future the following aspects need to be considered.

Setting Goals

The selected goals should be established in conjunction with supervisors and clients to ensure relevance from both perspectives. In addition, goals should be realistic, taking into consideration such factors as initial conditions, motivation, resources, and program dynamics. They should also take external standards into consideration (e.g., accreditation agency standards, superintendent's 5-year plan, board of trustee dictates, board standards, and so on).

In addition, it is important that goals be related to the program's activities, talents, resources, and scope of capability. In empowerment evaluation, program participants are encouraged to select intermediate goals that are directly linked to their daily activities. These activities can then be linked to larger, more diffuse goals, creating a clear chain of reasoning and outcomes.

Program participants are encouraged to be creative in establishing their goals. A brainstorming approach is often used to generate a new set of goals. The list generated from this activity is refined, reduced, and made realistic after the brainstorming phase through a critical review and consensual agreement process.

There are a bewildering number of goals for which to strive at any given time. As a group begins to establish goals based on this initial review of their program, they realize quickly that a consensus is required to determine the most significant issues on which to focus. These are chosen according to significance to the operation of the program, such as teaching and educational settings; timing or urgency, such as recruitment or budget issues; and vision, including community-building and learning processes.

Goal setting can be a slow process when program participants have a heavy work schedule. Sensitivity to the pacing of this effort is essential. Additional tasks of any kind and for any purpose may be perceived as simply another burden when everyone is fighting to keep their heads above water.

Developing Strategies

Program participants are also responsible for selecting and developing strategies to accomplish program goals in the future. The same process of brainstorming, critical review, and consensual agreement is used to establish a set of strategies. These strategies are routinely reviewed to determine their effectiveness and appropriateness. Determining appropriate strategies, in consultation with sponsors and clients, is an essential part of the empowering process. Program participants are typically the most knowledgeable about their own jobs, and this approach acknowledges and uses that expertise. In the process, it puts them back in the "driver's seat."

Documenting Progress

Program staff members and participants are asked what type of documentation or evidence is required to monitor progress toward their goals. This is a critical step, and each form of documentation is scrutinized for relevance to avoid devoting time to collecting information that will not be useful or pertinent. Program participants are asked to explain how a given form of documentation is related to specific program goals. This review process is difficult and time-consuming but prevents wasted time and disillusionment at the end of the process. In addition, documentation must be credible and rigorous if it is to withstand the criticism that an evaluation is self-serving. (See Fetterman, 1994a, 1994b, for additional discussion on this topic.)

Creating a Program Theory

The entire process of establishing a mission, taking stock, and planning for the future creates an implicit logic model or program theory, demonstrating how there is "nothing as practical as a good theory" of action (grounded in participants' own experiences). For additional discussion about program theory, see Bickman (1987); Chen (1990); Connell, Kubisch, Schorr, and Weiss (1995); Cook and Shadish (1994); McClintock (1990); Patton (1994); Weiss (1998); and Wholey (1987).

FACETS OF EMPOWERMENT EVALUATION

Training, facilitation, advocacy, illumination, and liberation are all facets—if not developmental stages—of empowerment evaluation. The emphasis is on program development, improvement, and lifelong learning. These facets, or demarcation points, help empowerment evaluators know where they are along the continuum of empowerment evaluation. They should be viewed as similar to a Maslowian hierarchy, as developmental stages or building blocks. Training and facilitation are the most fundamental forms of interaction in empowerment evaluation. They build a foundation on which the remaining facets or development stages can emerge. Once program staff members and participants learn how to assess themselves, they can use the findings for advocacy. In addition, being a part of the evaluation process is a precondition for illumination and liberation. A meta-evaluation of an empowerment evaluation can use these facets as benchmarks to determine the type or level of empowerment evaluation observed. They can also be used to assess the developmental stage of an empowerment evaluation appropriately.

Training

In one facet of empowerment evaluation, evaluators teach people to conduct their own evaluations and thus become more self-sufficient. This approach desensitizes and demystifies evaluation and ideally helps organizations internalize evaluation principles and practices, making evaluation an integral part of program planning. Too often, an external evaluation is an exercise in dependency rather than an empowering experience: In these instances, the process ends when the evaluator departs, leaving participants without the knowledge or experience to continue for themselves. In contrast, an evaluation conducted by program participants is designed to be ongoing and internalized in the system, creating the opportunity for capacity building.

In empowerment evaluation, training is used to map out the terrain, highlighting categories and concerns. It is also used in making preliminary assessments of program components while illustrating the need to establish goals, strategies to achieve goals, and documentation to indicate or substantiate progress. Training a group to conduct a self-evaluation can be considered equivalent to developing an evaluation or research design (because that is the core of the training), a standard part of any evaluation. This training is ongoing because new skills are needed to respond to new levels of understanding. Training also becomes part of the self-reflective process of self-assessment (on a program level) in that participants must learn to recognize when more tools are required to continue and enhance the evaluation process. This self-assessment process is pervasive in an empowerment evaluation, built into every part of a program, even to the point of reflecting on how its own meetings are conducted and feeding that input into future practice.

Training is important because, in essence, empowerment evaluation applies the concept of "give people fish and you feed them for a day; teach them to fish, and they will feed themselves for the rest of their lives." In empowerment evaluation, the evaluator and the individuals benefiting from the evaluation are typically on an even plane, learning from each other. (See Dugan 1996; Fetterman, 1997; Linney & Wandersman, 1991, 1996; and Mayer, 1996, for a sample of useful training tools.)

Facilitation

Empowerment evaluators serve as coaches or facilitators to help others conduct a self-evaluation. In their role as coaches, they provide general guidance and direction to the effort, attending sessions to monitor and facilitate as needed. It is critical to emphasize that staff members and participants are in charge of the effort; otherwise, program staff members and participants initially tend to look to the empowerment evaluator as expert, which makes them dependent on an outside agent. In some instances, the evaluator's task is to clear away obstacles and identify and clarify miscommunication patterns. (See Fetterman, 1996a, p. 11, for an example of working with an internal team at the Oakland Unified Public School System.)

An empowerment evaluation coach also can provide useful information about how to create facilitation teams (balancing analytical and social skills briefly discussed above), work with resistant (but interested) units, develop refresher sessions to energize tired units, and resolve various protocol issues. Simple suggestions along these lines can keep an effort from backfiring or being seriously derailed. Participants and staff members may also ask a coach to help create the evaluation design with minimal additional support.

Whatever the contribution, the empowerment evaluation coach must ensure that the evaluation remains in the hands of program personnel. The coach's task is to provide useful information, based on his or her training and past experience, to keep the effort on course.

Advocacy

A common workplace practice can provide a familiar illustration of self-evaluation and its link to advocacy on an individual level. Employees in a company often collaborate with both supervisor and client to establish goals, strategies for achieving those goals, and documenting progress on realistic time lines. Employees collect data on their own performance and present their case for their performance appraisal. Self-evaluation thus becomes a tool of advocacy. This individual self-evaluation process is easily transferable to the group or program level.

Sponsors and program administrators invest in a program and would like to see a return on their investment. They are not interested in requests for a blank check or a "free ride" from program staff members or participants. They are interested in seeing appropriate processes and specific outcomes; they typically are interested in funding programs that can demonstrate effectiveness. Program staff members and participants are in a better position to request funding when they have the data—specifically, a record of desired results they can share with sponsors and administrators. Program staff members and participants are also in a better position to share negative findings about performance with a sponsor and request funding to improve their performance when they can demonstrate how effective they have been with funded efforts. These are forms of legitimate advocacy. In 1959, Mills wrote:

> There is no necessity for working social scientists to allow the potential meaning of their work to be shaped by the "accidents of its setting," or its use to be determined by the purposes of other men [or women]. It is quite within their powers to discuss its meaning and decide upon its use as matters of their own policy. (p. 177)

The same sentiment applies to program staff members and participants as they engage in the process of self-evaluation and chart their own future. (See Fetterman, 1993b, 1996a; Hess, 1993, Hopper, 1993; Parker & Langley, 1993; and Weeks & Schensul, 1993, for examples of research and evaluation based-advocacy.)

Illumination

Illumination is an eye-opening, revealing, and enlightening experience. Typically, individuals develop new insight or understanding about roles, structures, and program dynamics in the process of determining worth and striving for program improvement (see Partlett & Hamilton, 1976). Empowerment evaluation is illuminating on a number of levels. For example, an administrator in one empowerment evaluation, with little or no research background, developed a testable, researchable hypothesis in the middle of a discussion about indicators and self-evaluation. It was not only illuminating to the group (and to her), it also revealed what they could do as a group when given the opportunity to think about problems and come up with workable options, hypotheses, and tests. This experience of illumination holds the same intellectual "intoxication" each researcher experienced the first time he or she came up with a researchable question. This experience also applies to evaluators trained in another tradition who suddenly see the power of this approach. As one colleague exclaimed in the middle of a presentation, "I get it. It is not formative, it is transformative!" The process creates a dynamic community of learners (for all of us) as people engage in the art and science of evaluating themselves. (See Fetterman, 1996a, pp. 15–16, for additional examples in the Oakland Unified Public School System. See also chapter 4, this volume, for case examples.)

Liberation

Illumination often sets the stage for liberation. It can unleash powerful, emancipatory forces for self-determination. Liberation is the act of being freed or freeing oneself from pre-existing roles and constraints. It often involves new conceptualizations of oneself and others. Empowerment evaluation can also be liberating. Many examples in this discussion demonstrate how helping individuals take charge of their lives—and finding useful ways to evaluate themselves—liberates them from traditional expectations and roles, leading to a full participation in their communities. They also demonstrate how empowerment evaluation enables participants to find new opportunities, see existing resources in a new light, and redefine their identities and future roles.

For example, school nurses in the Oakland public school system used this approach to help them understand their own evolving role in the school district. They are very highly educated professionals, but they were underutilized, essentially placing bandages on children's arms. The contrast of using such a highly educated work force to conduct menial tasks conflicted with their own sense of self-worth and the administration's financial capacity to support them. The nurses used empowerment evaluation to help define their role in the future. Instead of focusing exclusively on individual children, they became more involved in assessing the life circumstances of the entire student population. This liberated them from their highly confining roles. It also enabled them to generate more effective efforts, which were appreciated and valued by school administration. For example, instead of providing a generic health program throughout the district (with little impact), they developed highly specific health packages targeting issues such as asthma or AIDS. This targeted approach was more effective than a generic health care approach. Administrators appreciated the change because it demonstrated specific measurable outcomes (which also made them look good; Fetterman, 1996a).

Liberation takes on another level of significance when working in townships in South Africa. Community members used empowerment evaluation with a broad range of community participation health care programs. They used self-evaluation to monitor and build on successes and failures. This commendable work took place in a context of poverty and violence (Fetterman 1993a).

Program staff members and participants engaged in personally liberating experiences every day, even with the backdrop of the now-outlawed system of apartheid. Many of their daily activities, particularly those associated with self-determination and taking one's life into one's own hands, were illegal before apartheid was abolished. One impoverished Black community near Cape Town is now implementing and evaluating smoking-cessation, hypertension, and teenage pregnancy prevention programs. This progressive, self-reflective community reflects the real spirit of hope for democracy and the reconstruction of South Africa (Fetterman, 1993a; Fetterman, Kaftarian, & Wandersman, 1996).

It should also be noted that liberation applies to the empowerment evaluator in evaluations. I recall one township meeting where I had a suggestion about how to design the community gardens (for self-sufficiency) and was told "not right now David." A traditional evaluator might have viewed this as an inefficient use of resources—failure to use the evaluator, who has traveled a great distance to facilitate the evaluation. Personally, the traditional evaluator might even have been insulted. As an empowerment evaluator, I viewed this experience with great pleasure. They were "getting it"; they didn't need me in the same way anymore. They were taking charge of their own lives. This can be a liberating experience for evaluators, as we learn a new, less dominant but more powerful role: nurturing and fostering self-determination.

CALIFORNIA INSTITUTE OF INTEGRAL STUDIES: A CASE EXAMPLE

The California Institute of Integral Studies is an independent graduate school in San Francisco. It has been accredited since 1981 by the

Commission for Senior Colleges and Universities of Schools and Colleges. The accreditation process requires periodic self-evaluations, and the institute adopted an empowerment evaluation approach as a tool to institutionalize evaluation. It became part of planning and management operations while responding to the accreditation self-study requirement. The evaluation had three parts, as outlined above. The first stage focused on identifying the program mission. The second, taking stock, examined and assessed the merit of a unit. The third was designed to establish goals and strategies to improve program practice. In addition, evidence was specified to monitor change over time. This third stage was part of strategic planning and was built on the collaborative foundation of understanding informed by mission and taking-stock activities.

All units in the institute—including academic, governing, and administrative units—conducted self-evaluations. The purpose of these self-evaluations was to improve operations and to build a base for planning and decision making. In addition to focusing on improvement, these self-evaluations contributed to institutional accountability.

Workshops were conducted throughout the institute to provide training in evaluation techniques and procedures. All unit heads attended the training sessions held over 3 days. Then they served as facilitators in their own groups. Training and individual technical assistance was also provided throughout the year for governing and other administrative groups, including the office of the president and the development office. (See Fetterman, 2000, for additional detail.)

The self-evaluation process required thoughtful reflection and inquiry. The units described their purpose and listed approximately 10 key activities that characterized their unit. Members of the unit democratically determined the top 10 activities that merited consideration and evaluation. Then each member of a unit evaluated each activity by rating the activities on a scale of 1 to 10. Individual ratings were combined to produce a group or unit rating for each activity and one for the total unit. Unit members reviewed these ratings. A sample matrix is provided in Table 16.1 to illustrate how this process was implemented.

Unit members discussed and dissected the meaning of the activities listed in the matrix and the ratings given to each activity. This exchange provided unit members with an opportunity to establish norms concerning the meaning of terms and ratings in an open and collegial atmosphere. They also were required to provide evidence or documentation for each rating and to identify areas in which additional documentation was needed.

These self-evaluations represented the first baseline data about program and unit operations concerning the entire institute. This process was superior to survey methods for four reasons: (a) unit members determined what to focus on to improve their own programs, improving the validity of the effort and the buy-in required to implement recommendations; (b)

TABLE 16.1
Sample Self-Evaluation Worksheet

STL Wide Self-Evaluation Worksheet (Subpopulation Sample for Demonstration)

Activities	EK	KK	YT	DE	BH	MT	EG	DF	JA	MC	Subtotal	Average
1 Building capacity	7	5	7	5	5	7	5	6	7	8	62	6.2
2 Teaching	5	6	8	8	6	8	8	8	8	9	74	7.4
3 Research	5	7	7	3	6	6	3	8	7	6	58	5.8
4 Transformative learning	8	6	6	5	5	7	9	7	7	8	68	6.8
5 Dissemination—scholarly	3	6	7	4	6	6	5	8	5	5	55	5.5
6 Enhance health relationship CIIS	7	6	8	6	6	8	5	7	5	7	65	6.5
7 Community building	6	6	7	6	7	7	6	6	6	8	65	6.5
8 Curriculum dev/refin/eval	8	6	7	7	7	7	8	8	8	8	74	7.4
9 Experimental pedagogy	8	6	9	8	8	8	8	8	8	9	80	8
10 Diversity	5	4	8	6	5	7	5	4	4	6	54	5.4
Subtotal	62	58	74	58	61	71	62	70	65	74	655	65.5
Average (activity)											65.5	6.55
Average (person)	6	6	7	6	6	7	6	7	7	7	6.55	
Unit Average												6.55

Note. This is a sample matrix used from an actual empowerment evaluation session for the institute. It is a sample of a subpopulation for demonstration purposes. The top line labeled STL is the name of one of the schools in the Institute (School for Transformative Learning). On the left side is an abbreviated list of critical activities associated with the school. In the middle of the matrix are initials of members of the school on top (e.g., EK, KK, YT, etc.). Under the initials are the person's ratings concerning the activities listed on the left side of the matrix. Each person's rating is totaled on the right side under Subtotal. Then each subtotal is averaged at the far right of the matrix. Similarly, each individual's ratings are totaled and averaged to determine who is optimistic and who is pessimistic to facilitate the norming process within the group. At the far right bottom of the matrix is the average of the scores (both the average of the activities and the average of each individual) to create an overall unit or program average. Program participants are more likely to give a realistic overall average after being given the opportunity to state where they are doing well and where they are not doing well concerning program performance.

a majority of members of the community were immersed in the evaluation experience, making the process of building a culture of evidence and a community of learners as important as the specific evaluative outcomes; (b) members of the community entered into a dialogue about the ratings, helping them establish norms and common understandings; and (c) there was a 100% return rate (as compared with typically low return rates for surveys).

These self-evaluations were used to implement specific improvements in program practice. This process was used to reexamine and reframe existing problems, leading to solutions, adaptations, and new activities for the future. It was also used to reframe existing data from traditional sources, enabling participants to give meaningful interpretation to data they already collect. In addition, self-evaluations were used to ensure programmatic and academic accountability. For example, the psychology program decided to discontinue its PhD program as part of the self-evaluation process, a significant measure of internal or external accountability. The viability of the program was a significant and long-standing concern to both the accreditation agency and the institute, and the core of the problem was that there were not enough faculty to properly serve the number of matriculating students in their program. The empowerment evaluation process provided a vehicle for the faculty to come to terms with this problem in an open, self-conscious manner and make the appropriate decision. The faculty had complained about the workload and working conditions before, but they had never consciously analyzed, diagnosed, and documented this problem because they did not have the time or a simple, nonthreatening mechanism to assess themselves. They were dedicated to serving students properly, but when they analyzed faculty–student ratios and faculty dissertation loads, the problem became self-evident. Empowerment evaluation provided institute faculty with a tool to evaluate the program in light of scarce resources and make an executive decision to discontinue the program. Similarly, one of the institute's online PhD programs was administratively merged with another distance-learning program as a result of this self-evaluative process. This was done to provide greater efficiencies of scale, improved monitoring and supervision, and more face-to-face contact with the institute faculty. (See Fetterman 1996b and 1996c for a description of one of these online educational programs.)

The last stage of empowerment evaluation involved building plans for the future based on these evaluations. All units at the institute completed their plans for the future, and these data were used to design an overall strategic plan. Goals and strategies were specified, as was relevant evidence to monitor progress toward selected goals. This process ensures community involvement and commitment to the effort, generating a plan that is grounded in the reality of unit practice. The provost institutionalized this process by requiring self-evaluations and unit plans on an annual basis to facilitate program improvement and contribute to institutional accountability.

CAVEATS AND CONCERNS

The following are common questions with regard to self-evaluation.

Is Research Rigor Maintained?

The above case study presented a picture of how research and evaluation rigor is maintained. Mechanisms used to maintain rigor included workshops and training, democratic participation in the evaluation (ensuring that majority and minority views are represented), quantifiable rating matrices to create a baseline to measure progress, discussion and definition of terms and ratings (norming), scrutinizing documentation, and questioning findings and recommendations. These mechanisms help ensure that program participants are critical, analytical, and honest.

Empowerment evaluation is one approach among many being used to address social, educational, industrial, and health care dilemmas, as well as many other problems. As with the exploration and development of any new frontier, this approach requires adaptations, alterations, and innovations. This does not mean that significant compromises must be made in the rigor required to conduct evaluations. Although I am a major proponent of individuals taking evaluation into their own hands, I recognize the need for adequate research, preparation, and planning. These first discussions need to be supplemented with reports, texts, workshops, classroom instruction, and apprenticeship experiences if possible. Program personnel new to evaluation should seek the assistance of an evaluator to act as coach, assisting in the design and execution of an evaluation. Further, an evaluator must be judicious in determining when it is appropriate to function as an empowerment evaluator or in any other evaluative role.

Does Empowerment Evaluation Abolish Traditional Evaluation?

New approaches require a balanced assessment. A strict constructionist perspective may strangle a young enterprise; too liberal a stance is certain to transform a novel tool into another fad. Colleagues who fear that we are giving evaluation away are right in one respect; we are sharing it with a much broader population. But those who fear that empowerment evaluators are educating themselves out of a job are only partially correct. Like any tool, empowerment evaluation is designed to address a specific evaluative need; it is not a substitute for other forms of evaluative inquiry or appraisal. The main purpose is to educate others to manage their own affairs in areas they know or should know better than do the external evaluators. At the same time, new roles are being created for evaluators to help others help themselves.

How Objective Can a Self-Evaluation Be?

Objectivity is a relevant concern. We need not belabor the obvious point that science and specifically evaluation have never been neutral. Anyone who has had to roll up his or her sleeves and get involved in program evaluation or policy arenas is aware that evaluation, like any other dimension of life, is influenced by the political, social, cultural, and economic perspectives. It rarely produces a single truth or conclusion. In the context of a discussion about self-referent evaluation, Stufflebeam (1994) stated,

> As a practical example of this, in the coming years U.S. teachers will have the opportunity to have their competence and effectiveness examined against the standards of the National Board for Professional Teaching Standards and if they pass to become nationally certified. (p. 331)

Regardless of one's position on this issue, evaluation in this context is a political act. What Stufflebeam considered an opportunity, some teachers consider a threat to their livelihood, status, and role in the community. This can be a screening device in which social class, race, and ethnicity are significant variables. The goal is improvement, but the questions of for whom and at what price remain valid. Evaluation in this context or any other is not neutral; it is for one group a force of social change, for another a tool to reinforce the status quo.

According to Stufflebeam (1994), "Objectivist evaluations are based on the theory that moral good is objective and independent of personal or merely human feelings. They are firmly grounded in ethical principles, strictly control bias or prejudice in seeking determinations of merit and worth" (p. 326). To assume that evaluation is all in the name of science or that it is separate, above politics or "mere human feelings" (indeed, that evaluation is objective), is to deceive oneself and to do an injustice to others. Objectivity functions along a continuum; it is not an absolute or dichotomous condition of all or none. Fortunately, such objectivity is not essential to being critical. For example, one can support programs designed to help dropouts pursue their education and prepare for a career yet be highly critical of program implementation efforts. If the program is operating poorly, it is doing a disservice both to former dropouts and to taxpayers.

One needs only to scratch the surface of the objective world to see that values, interpretations, and culture shape it. Whose ethical principles are evaluators grounded in? Do evaluators all come from the same cultural, religious, or even academic tradition? Such an ethnocentric assumption or assertion flies in the face of the accumulated knowledge about social systems and evaluation. Similarly, assuming that we can "strictly control bias or prejudice" is naive, given the wealth of literature available on the subject ranging from discussions about cultural interpretation to reactivity in experimental design.

What About Participant or Program Bias?

The process of conducting an empowerment evaluation requires the appropriate involvement of stakeholders. The entire group—not a single individual, not the external evaluator, not an internal manager—is responsible for conducting the evaluation. The group thus can serve as a check on individual members, moderating their various biases and agendas.

No individual operates in a vacuum. Everyone is accountable in one fashion or another and thus has an interest or agenda to protect. A school district may have a 5-year plan designed by the superintendent, a graduate school may have to satisfy requirements of an accreditation association, or an outside evaluator may have an important but demanding sponsor pushing either timelines or results or may be influenced by training to use one theoretical approach rather than another.

In a sense, empowerment evaluation minimizes the effect of these biases by making them an explicit part of the process. The example of a self-evaluation in a performance appraisal is useful again here. An employee negotiates with his or her supervisor about job goals, strategies for accomplishing them, documentation of progress, and even the timeline. In turn, the employee works with clients to come to an agreement about acceptable goals, strategies, documentation, and timelines. All of this activity takes place within corporate, institutional, and community goals, objectives, and aspirations. The larger context, like theory, provides a lens in which to design a self-evaluation. Self-serving forms of documentation do not easily persuade supervisors and clients. Once an employee loses credibility with a supervisor, it is difficult to regain it. The employee thus has a vested interest in providing authentic and credible documentation. Credible data (as agreed by supervisor and client in negotiation with the employee) serve both the employee and the supervisor during the performance appraisal process.

Applying this approach to the program or community level, superintendents, accreditation agencies, and other "clients" requires credible data. Participants in an empowerment evaluation thus negotiate goals, strategies, documentation, and timelines. Credible data can be used to advocate for program expansion, redesign, or improvement. This process is an open one, placing a check on self-serving reports. It provides an infrastructure and network to combat institutional injustices. It is a highly self-critical process because program staff members and participants are typically more critical of their own program than an external evaluator, often because they are more familiar with their program and would like to see it serve its purposes more effectively.[5] Empowerment evaluation is successful because it adapts and responds to existing decision-making and authority structures on their own terms (see Fetterman, Kaftarian, & Wandersman, 1996). It also provides an opportunity and a forum to challenge authority and managerial facades by providing data about actual program operations from the ground up. The approach is particularly valuable for disenfranchised people and programs to ensure that their voices are heard and that real problems are addressed.

CONCLUSION

Empowerment evaluation is grounded in my work with the most marginalized and disenfranchised populations, ranging from urban school systems in the United States to community health programs in South African townships, who have educated me about what is possible in communities overwhelmed by violence, poverty, disease, and neglect. They have also repeatedly sensitized me to the power of positions of privilege. One dominant group has the vision, makes and changes the rules, enforces the standards, and need never question its own position or seriously consider any other. In such a view, differences become deficits rather than additive elements of culture. People in positions of privilege dismiss the contributions of a multicultural world. They create rational policies and procedures that systematically deny full participation in their community to people who think and behave differently.

Evaluators cannot afford to be unreflective about the culturally embedded nature of the profession. There are many tacit prejudgments and omissions embedded in the primarily Western thought and behavior. These values, often assumed to be superior, are considered natural. Western philosophies, however, have privileged their own traditions and used them to judge others who may not share them, disparaging such factors as ethnicity and gender. In addition, they systematically exclude other ways of knowing. Some evaluators are convinced that there is only one position and one sacred text in evaluation, justifying exclusion or excommunication for any "violations" or wrong thinking (see Stufflebeam, 1994). Scriven's (1991,

---

[5]There are many useful mechanisms to enhance a self-critical mode. Beginning with an overall assessment of the program often leads to inflated ratings. Asking program participants to assess program components before asking for an overall assessment facilitates the self-critical process, however. In addition, allowing individuals to comment on successful parts of the program typically enables them to comment openly on problematic components.

pp. 260–261) discussion about perspectival evaluation is instructive in this context, highlighting the significance of adopting multiple perspectives, including new ones.

It is important to keep open minds, including alternative ways of knowing, but not empty heads. Skepticism is healthy; cynicism, blindness, and condemnation are not, particularly for emerging evaluative forms and adaptations. New approaches in evaluation and even new ways of knowing are needed if we, as evaluators, are to expand our knowledge base and respond to pressing needs. As Campbell (1994) stated, we should not "reject the new epistemologies out of hand. . . . Any specific challenge to an unexamined presumption of ours should be taken seriously" (p. 293). Patton (1994) might be right "that the world will not end in a subjective bang, but in a boring whimper as voices of objectivity [drift] off into the chaos" (p. 312).

Evaluation must change and adapt as the environment changes, or it will either be overshadowed by new developments or—as a result of its unresponsiveness and irrelevance—follow the path of the dinosaurs to extinction. People are demanding much more of evaluation and are not tolerant of the limited role of the outside expert who has no knowledge of or vested interest in their program or community. Participation, collaboration, and empowerment are becoming requirements, not recommendations, in many community-based evaluations. Program participants are conducting empowerment and other forms of self- or participatory evaluations with or without the evaluation community. It is healthier for all parties concerned to work together to improve practice rather than ignore, dismiss, and condemn evaluation practice; otherwise, we foster the development of separate worlds operating and unfolding in isolation from each other.

Empowerment evaluation is fundamentally a democratic process. The entire group—not a single individual, not the external evaluator or an internal manager—is responsible for conducting the evaluation. The group thus can serve as a check on its own members, moderating the various biases and agendas of individual members. The evaluator is a coequal in this endeavor, not a superior and not a servant; as a critical friend, the evaluator can question shared biases or "group think."

As is the case in traditional evaluation, everyone is accountable in one fashion or another and thus has an interest or agenda to protect. Empowerment evaluations, like all other evaluations, exist within a context. Nonetheless, the range of intermediate objectives linking what most people do in their daily routine to their macro goals is almost infinite. People often feel empowered and self-determined when they can select meaningful intermediate objectives that are linked to larger, global goals.

Empowerment evaluation is a dynamic community of leaders, and many elements must be in place for empowerment evaluation to be effective and credible. Participants must have the latitude to experiment, taking both risks and responsibility for their actions. An environment conducive to sharing successes and failures is also essential. In addition, an honest, self-critical, trusting, and supportive atmosphere is required. Conditions need not be perfect to initiate this process, but the accuracy and usefulness of self-ratings improve dramatically in this context. An outside evaluator who is charged with monitoring the process can help keep the effort credible, useful, and on track, providing additional rigor, reality checks, and quality controls throughout the evaluation. Without any of these elements in place, the exercise may be of limited utility and potentially self-serving. With many of these elements in place, the exercise can create a dynamic community of transformative learning.

Despite its focus on self-determination and collaboration, empowerment evaluation and traditional external evaluation are not mutually exclusive; to the contrary, they enhance each other. In fact, the empowerment evaluation process produces a rich data source that enables a more complete external examination. In the empowerment evaluation design developed in response to the California Institute of Integral Studies' accreditation requirement that was presented in this chapter, a series of external evaluations were planned to build on and enhance self-evaluation efforts. A series of external teams were invited to review specific programs. They determined the evaluation agenda in conjunction with department faculty, staff, and students. They operated as critical friends, providing a strategic consultation rather than a compliance or traditional accountability review. Participants agreed on the value of an external perspective to add insights into program operation, serve as an additional quality control, sharpen inquiry, and improve program practice. External evaluators can also help determine the merit and worth of various activities. An external evaluation is not a requirement of empowerment evaluation, but it is certainly not mutually exclusive. Greater coordination between the needs of the internal and external forms of evaluation can provide a reality check concerning external needs and expectations for insiders and a rich data base for external evaluators.

The external evaluator's role and productivity is also enhanced by the presence of an empowerment or internal evaluation process. Most evaluators operate significantly below their capacity in an evaluation because the program lacks even rudimentary evaluation mechanisms and processes. The external evaluator routinely devotes time to the development and maintenance of elementary evaluation systems. Programs that already have a basic self-evaluation process in place enable external evaluators to begin operating at a much more sophisticated level.

A matrix (such as Table 16.1) or similar design to further systematize internal evaluation activity facilitates comparison and analysis on a larger scale. Another approach involves a more artistic approach using green and red dots to signify progress or deterioration concerning specific topics of concern. The dots have a strong visual impact and can be quantified. Any system can work if it provides participants with (a) straightforward, user-friendly tools to make credible judgments about where they are at any given point in time; (b) consistent patterns (including those with a strong visual impact) that are meaningful to them; (c) the ability to facilitate comparison across individuals, categories, and programs; and (d) the motivation to stimulate constructive activity to improve program practice.

Finally, it is hoped that empowerment evaluation will benefit from the artful shaping of our combined contributions rather than follow any single approach or strategy. As Cronbach (1980) urged more than two decades ago, "It is better for an evaluative inquiry to launch a small fleet of studies than to put all its resources into a single approach" (p. 7).

REFERENCES

Bandura, A. (1982). Self-efficacy mechanism in human agency. *American Psychologist, 37,* 122–147.

Bickman, L. (1987). *New directions for program evaluation: No. 33. Using program theory in evaluation.* San Francisco: Jossey-Bass.

Campbell, D. T. (1994). Retrospective and prospective on program impact assessment. *Evaluation Practice, 15,* 291–298.

Chen, H. (1990). Issues in constructing program theory. In L. Bickman (Ed.), *New directions for program evaluation: No. 47. Advances in program theory* (pp. 7–18). San Francisco: Jossey-Bass.

Choudhary, A., & Tandon, R. (1988). *Participatory evaluation.* New Delhi: Society for Participatory Research in Asia.

Connell, J. P., Kubisch, A. C., Schorr, L. B., & Weiss, C. H. (Eds.). (1995). *New approaches to evaluating community initiatives: Concepts, methods, and contexts.* Washington, DC: Aspen Institute.

Cook, T., & Shadish, W. (1994). Social experiments: Some developments over the past fifteen years. *Annual Review of Psychology, 45,* 545–580.

Cronbach, L. J. (1980). *Toward reform of program evaluation.* San Francisco: Jossey-Bass.

Dugan, M. (1996). Participatory and empowerment evaluation: Lessons learned in training and technical assistance. In D. M. Fetterman, S. Kaftarian, & A. Wandersman (Eds.), *Empowerment evaluation: Knowledge and tools for self-assessment and accountability* (pp. 277–303). Thousand Oaks, CA: Sage.

Dunst, C. J., Trivette, C. M., & LaPointe, N. (1992). Toward clarification of the meaning and key elements of empowerment. *Family Science Review, 5,* 111–130.

Fetterman, D. M. (1993a, October 3). Confronting a culture of violence: South Africa nears a critical juncture. *San Jose Mercury,* pp. 1C, 4C.

Fetterman, D. M. (1993b). *Speaking the language of power: Communication, collaboration, and advocacy (translating ethnography into action)*. London: Falmer Press.

Fetterman, D. M. (1994a). Empowerment evaluation. Presidential address. *Evaluation Practice, 15,* 1–15.

Fetterman, D. M. (1994b). Steps of empowerment evaluation: From California to Cape Town. *Evaluation and Program Planning, 17,* 305–313.

Fetterman, D. M. (1995). In response to Dr. Daniel Stufflebeam's Empowerment Evaluation, Objectivist Evaluation, and Evaluation Standards: Where the Future of Evaluation Should Not Go and Where It Needs to Go. *Evaluation Practice, 16,* 179–199.

Fetterman, D. M. (1996a). Empowerment evaluation: An introduction to theory and practice. In D. M. Fetterman, S. Kaftarian, & A. Wandersman (Eds.), *Empowerment evaluation: Knowledge and tools for self-assessment and accountability* (pp. 3–48). Thousand Oaks, CA: Sage.

Fetterman, D. M. (1996b). Ethnography in the virtual classroom. *Practicing Anthropology, 18,* 36–39.

Fetterman, D. M. (1996c). Videoconferencing: Enhancing communication on the Internet. *Educational Researcher, 25,* 23–27.

Fetterman, D. M. (1997). Empowerment evaluation and accreditation in higher education. In E. Chelimsky & W. Shadish (Eds.), *Evaluation for the 21st century: A handbook* (pp. 381–395). Thousand Oaks, CA: Sage.

Fetterman, D. M. (2000). *Foundations of empowerment evaluation: Step by step.* Thousand Oaks, CA: Sage.

Fetterman, D. M., & Haertel, E. H. (1990). *A school-based evaluation model for accelerating the education of students at-risk* (ERIC Document Reproduction Service No. ED 313 495). Clearing House on Urban Education.

Fetterman, D. M., Kaftarian, S., & Wandersman, A. (1996). *Empowerment evaluation: Knowledge and tools for self-assessment and accountability.* Thousand Oaks, CA: Sage.

Habermas, J. (1984). *The theory of communicative action* (Vol. I). Boston: Beacon Press.

Hess, F. A., Jr. (1993). Testifying on the Hill: Using ethnographic data to shape public policy. In D. M. Fetterman (Ed.), *Speaking the language of power: Communication, collaboration, and advocacy (Translating ethnography into action)* (pp. 38–49). London: Falmer Press.

Hopper, K. (1993). On keeping an edge: Translating ethnographic findings and putting them to use: NYC's homeless policy. In D. M. Fetterman (Ed.), *Speaking the language of power: Communication, collaboration, and advocacy (translating ethnography into action)* (pp. 19–37). London: Falmer Press.

Joint Committee on Standards for Educational Evaluation. (1994). *The program evaluation standards.* Thousand Oaks, CA: Sage.

Levin, H. M. (1995). Empowerment evaluation and accelerated schools. In D. M. Fetterman, S. Kaftarian, & A. Wandersman (Eds.), *Empowerment evaluation:*

Knowledge and tools for self-assessment and accountability (pp. 49–64). Thousand Oaks, CA: Sage.

Linney, J. A., & Wandersman, A. (1991). *Prevention Plus III: Assessing alcohol and other drug prevention programs at the school and community level. A four-step guide to useful program assessment.* Rockville, MD: U.S. Department of Health and Human Services, Office of Substance Abuse Prevention.

Linney, J. A., & Wandersman, A. (1996). Empowering community groups with evaluation skills: The Prevention Plus III Model. In D. M. Fetterman, S. Kaftarian, & A. Wandersman (Eds.), *Empowerment evaluation: Knowledge and tools for self-assessment and accountability* (pp. 259–276). Thousand Oaks, CA: Sage.

Mayer, S. (1996). Building community capacity with evaluation activities that empower. In D. M. Fetterman, S. Kaftarian, & A. Wandersman (Eds.), *Empowerment evaluation: Knowledge and tools for self-assessment and accountability* (pp. 332–378). Thousand Oaks, CA: Sage.

McClintock, C. (1990). Administrators as applied theorists. In L. Bickman (Ed.), *New directions for program evaluation: No. 47. Advances in program theory* (pp. 19–33). San Francisco: Jossey-Bass.

Mills, C. W. (1959). *The sociological imagination.* New York: Oxford University Press.

Mithaug, D. E. (1991). *Self-determined kids: Raising satisfied and successful children.* New York: Lexington.

Mithaug, D. E. (1993). *Self-regulation theory: How optimal adjustment maximizes gain.* New York: Praeger.

Oja, S. N., & Smulyan, L. (1989). *Collaborative action research.* Philadelphia: Falmer Press.

Papineau, D., & Kiely, M. C. (1994). Participatory evaluation: Empowering stakeholders in a community economic development organization. *Community Psychologist, 27,* 56–57.

Parker, L., & Langley, B. (1993). Protocol and policy-making systems in American Indian tribes. In D. M. Fetterman (Ed.), *Speaking the language of power: Communication, collaboration, and advocacy (translating ethnography into action).* London: Falmer Press.

Partlett, M., & Hamilton, D. (1976). Evaluation as illumination: A new approach to the study of innovatory programmes. In D. Hamilton (Ed.), *Beyond the numbers game.* London: Macmillan.

Patton, M. Q. (1994). Developmental evaluation. *Evaluation Practice, 15,* 311–320.

Rappaport, J. (1987). Terms of empowerment/exemplars of prevention: Toward a theory for community psychology. *American Journal of Community Psychology, 15,* 121–148.

Reason, P. (Ed.). (1988). *Human inquiry in action: Developments in new paradigm research.* Newbury Park, CA: Sage.

Sanders, J. R., Barley, Z. A., & Jenness, M. R. (1990). *Annual report: Cluster evaluation in science education.* Unpublished report. Western Michigan State University.

Scriven, M. (1991). *Evaluation thesaurus* (4th ed., pp. 260–261). Thousand Oaks, CA: Sage.

Shapiro, J. P. (1988). Participatory evaluation: Toward a transformation of assessment for women's studies programs and projects. *Educational Evaluation and Policy Analysis, 10,* 191–199.

Soffer, E. (1995). The principal as action researcher: A study of disciplinary practice. In S. E. Noffke & R. B. Stevenson (Ed.), *Educational action research: Becoming practically critical.* New York: Teachers College Press.

Stanford University & American Institutes for Research. (1992). *A design for systematic support for accelerated schools: In response to the New American Schools Development Corporation RFP for designs for a new generation of American schools.* Stanford & Palo Alto, CA: Author.

Stevenson, J. F., Mitchell, R. E., & Florin, P. (1996). Evaluation and self-direction in community prevention coalitions. In D. M. Fetterman, S. Kaftarian, & A. Wandersman (Eds.), *Empowerment evaluation: Knowledge and tools for self-assessment and accountability* (pp. 208–233). Thousand Oaks, CA: Sage.

Stufflebeam, D. L. (1994). Empowerment evaluation, objectivist evaluation, and evaluation standards: Where the future of evaluation should not go and where it needs to go. *Evaluation Practice, 15,* 321–338.

Stull, D., & Schensul, J. (1987). *Collaborative research and social change: Applied anthropology in action.* Boulder, CO: Westview.

Tax, S. (1958). The Fox Project. *Human Organization, 17,* 17–19.

Vanderplaat, M. (1995). Beyond technique: Issues in evaluating for empowerment. *Evaluation, 1,* 81–96.

W. K. Kellogg Foundation. (1992). *Transitions.* Battle Creek, MI: Author.

Weeks, M. R., & Schensul, J. J. (1993). Ethnographic research on AIDS risk behavior and the making of policy. In D. M. Fetterman (Ed.), *Speaking the language of power: Communication, collaboration, and advocacy (translating ethnography into action)* (pp. 50–69). London: Falmer Press.

Weiss, C. (1998). *Evaluation* (2nd ed.). Englewood Cliffs, NJ: Prentice Hall.

Whitmore, E. (1990). Empowerment in program evaluation: A case example. *Canadian Social Work Review, 7,* 215–229.

Wholey, J. (Ed.). (1987). *Organizational excellence: Stimulating quality and communicating value.* Lexington, MA: Lexington Books.

Whyte, W. F. (Ed.). (1990). *Participatory action research.* Newbury Park, CA: Sage.

Zimmerman, M. A. (in press). Empowerment theory: Psychological, organizational, and community levels of analysis. In J. Rappaport & E. Seldman (Eds.), *Handbook of community psychology.* New York: Plenum Press.

Zimmerman, M. A., Israel, B. A., Schulz, A., & Checkoway, B. (1992). Further explorations in empowerment theory: An empirical analysis of psychological empowerment. *American Journal of Community Psychology, 20,* 707–727.

Zimmerman, M. A., & Rappaport, J. (1988). Citizen participation, perceived control, and psychological empowerment. *American Journal of Community Psychology, 16,* 725–750.

17

PUBLIC HEALTH AND RELIGION

DIANE M. BECKER

Religion has been proposed as a modifier of health status, as well as a vector for public health strategies, yet its potential is poorly defined and not universally accepted. Personal beliefs of scientists and academicians have affected the ways in which religion and health have been perceived, as well as how they have been studied. One could argue that the common good is best served if personal religious beliefs do not obscure scientific judgments about how religion may have an impact on health. Evidence from population surveys indicates a strong desire of people to have their spiritual needs addressed in concert with their health needs. The public often perceives state-of-the-art public health and medical care strategies as unresponsive to their spiritual perspective. The discrepancy between population perceptions and service-based reality provides a challenge for public health professionals to better develop and understand strategies that effectively integrate the religious, social, and physical aspects of health.

In the 1992 opening plenary sessions of the American Psychological Association Annual Convention, it was noted that most of the members described themselves as atheists or agnostics and that religion was of

Gratitude is expressed to Rev. Herbert W. Watson, Jr., for his thoughtful discussion of this chapter and assistance with scriptural references and to Christine Holzmueler for editorial assistance.

351

minimal interest to psychologists. This widely held belief is supported by data demonstrating that the prevalence of belief in a divine power has been much lower among psychologists and other mental health professionals, generally only about 40%, compared with the general population, 83% (American Psychiatric Association, 1975; Ragan, Malony, & Beit-Hallahmi, 1980). Until recently, the gap between the belief systems of health professionals and those of the general public has not been breached, and public health in the United States has avoided religion (Jones, 1995). In the past two decades, however, we have entered an era in which mind–body medicine is emerging as an important paradigm, opening the gate to a more holistic approach to health and religion (Bunk, 1998; Matthews & Larson, 1997). Models of health care delivery that include holistic and integrative medicine now exist in both the academic and private health care sectors. The rapidly changing scientific and social milieu of the past two decades, in which exploration of novel technological and genetic approaches to health have flourished, provides an opportunity to revisit the science and philosophy of public health and religion (Koenig, 1999).

THE HISTORICAL PERSPECTIVE

Spiritual practices applied to physical health were an integral part of ancient culture and Western Judeo-Christian society for centuries (Amundsen, 1996). In ancient Greece, healers, called *theraputae*, were providers of both spiritual counseling and physical health care; religious-based systems of public health addressed food preparation and lifestyle, as well as sanitation. In the 4th century BC, with the advent of the Hippocratic tradition, healing and health entered the era of "modern medicine" (Lloyd, 1978). Physicians coexisted with religious leaders as caretakers of the body and the spirit. In the early 17th century, Rene Descartes profoundly influenced the importance placed on the role of religion in health by promulgating a philosophy that separated the mind from the body and the physical from the spiritual (Wozniak, 1992). The Cartesian Age of Reason challenged the strong role of the church by mandating that certainty and science drive the way the human body was viewed. A dichotomy emerged between the church and physicians; physical health became the domain of physicians, the practitioners of mechanistic science. The concept of duality of mind and body suppressed any major credible role of religion in the "science" of public health for the next three centuries.

During the early 20th century, the relationship of religion to health was reexamined. What emerged initially was an extremely negative perspective. Sigmund Freud, considered by many as the founder of modern psychiatry, espoused a professional philosophy that religion "caused" mental illness, calling it the "universal neurosis of humanity" (Freud, 1962). Many of Freud's influential professional colleagues, including Albert Ellis, supported the belief that religion was injurious to health (Ellis, 1988). Religion was no longer disassociated from health but was perceived as having a serious harmful impact that could be "treated" only by divesting people of religious beliefs. Most of these observations were based solely on case studies of individuals with mental illness. More recently, evidence-based approaches have been applied to understanding the role of religion in both physical and mental health (Pargament, Maton, & Hess, 1992). A large body of data now suggests a fairly consistent and strong link between well-being and religiosity, although the "evidence" has been generically criticized by some as methodologically flawed (Sloan, Bagiella, & Powell, 1999).

Many scientists never viewed science and religion as discordant, however. "Science without religion is lame; religion without science is blind," noted Albert Einstein (1949, pp. 28–29) in his landmark 20th-century treatise on science, philosophy, and religion. In the 21st century, the United States appears to be in an era of conciliation, in which the role of religion is being examined empirically and evaluated. In the first quarter of 1999, more than 150 published articles on religion and health were identified on a Medline search. Recent articles such as "Do You Believe in God?" (Parmley, 1999) and "Getting Religion Seen as Help in Being Well" (Mitka, 1998) were published in highly credible medical journals (*Journal of The American College of Cardiology* and *Journal of the American Medical Association*, respectively). This is emblematic of the fact that the topic is now open for discussion and debate. Although religion as a viable approach to health and well-being is no longer shunned, it remains poorly understood. The public debate has become part of a dialogue in major health journals (McBride, 1998; Orr & Genesen, 1998; Stotland, 1999).

From an organizational perspective, religious-based hospitals existed both in Europe and the United States, independent of the discordant health-religion philosophical dialogue. Religious organizations often trained health care professionals and established complex systems of health care for acutely ill people. Medical care of the public was quietly sustained by religious orders throughout the Cartesian era, in which spirituality and health remained divorced from one another conceptually. Hospitals with religious affiliations often bore the responsibility for care of the poor and underserved populations in the United States during the 19th century (Pascover, 1998). Religious-based health care systems still exist in the United States today, although their future remains uncertain. The advent of competitive for-profit commercial managed care services has forced many religious-based health care organizations from the marketplace, leaving care systems that do not bear the same humanity-oriented ethos (Foege, 1998; Gunderson, 1998). Religious health care institutions are falling prey to a powerful "for-profit" motive that diminishes their potential to tackle today's major public health issues. Religion as an acceptable public health strategy could, in part, be undermined by the disappearance of an informed expert health care delivery system linked to religious organizations.

RELIGION, FAITH, SPIRITUALITY, AND DIVINITY DEFINED

The lexicon of religion is elusive. The literature is replete with the words "spirituality," "faith," "religion," and "divinity." The concepts often are confused with one another, making interpretation of studies and understanding of ideas difficult. These concepts are certainly related, although not interchangeable. For the purpose of understanding their role in public health, definitions are summarized from several dictionaries of the English language. *Spirituality* refers to the soul or mind and aspects of human nature that are not corporeal or tangible. One cannot see or touch spirituality because it is a personal and highly subjective experience. *Divinity* pertains to the presence of a divine power, a deity, to God in the Judeo-Christian faith or Allah in Islamic traditions, for example. *Faith* is defined as unconditional confidence in the principle of something, of trust in things unknown. Perhaps it best explained from a biblical perspective: "Faith is the substance of things hoped for, the evidence of things not seen" (Hebrews 11:1). Faith can exist without belief in a divine power. Finally, *religion* is a system of beliefs unified by acceptance of a divine or superhuman power. Western society is, in general, monotheistic, believing in one God.

In many recent studies of health, religion is the object of interest, inclusive of the notion of divinity. People may be spiritual and even have faith yet still reject religious belief systems or the presence of a divine power. One can be religious and reject formal organized religions. Religion, as a term, encompasses virtually all personal systems of belief to which a divine power is central. Religion may also be a collective entity that organizes shared beliefs among people into formal denominations, attendant institutional structures, administrative operations, and political units. Different intra- and interpersonal faith systems and religious systems also may have a specific effect on health systems and on their unique practices and beliefs. Further, the degree of religious involvement has been shown to have a relationship to health outcomes, including mortality (Matthews et al., 1998). People with intensive personal commitment, such as Catholic nuns, monks, orthodox Jews, and priests in the Mormon tradition, have among the lowest rates of premature mortality (de Gouw, Westndrop, Junst, Mackenbach, & Vandenbrouke, 1996; Friedlander, Kark, & Stein, 1986; Gardner & Lyon, 1982; Timio et al., 1997). Some critics have attributed these findings to a measurably better diet, lifestyle, and reduced stress in these populations. This fact does not negate the findings or the potential of religion and the degree of devotional commitment to improve health outcomes (Sloan et al., 1999).

THE PERVASIVENESS OF RELIGION IN THE UNITED STATES

In U.S. communities, the pervasiveness of organized religion is notable. Surveys conducted by the Princeton Religion Research Center (1996) show that 96% of Americans indicate belief in a universal spirit or divine power, and 83% accept a monotheistic God. The number of people who believe in God has remained relatively stable over the past 50 years. In general, women, people older than age 50, African Americans, people of lower income, and individuals of lower educational attainment have a greater prevalence of belief in a divine power. The prevalence of belief in any divine faith-based presence is above 90% for people younger than age 30. More than 80% of teenagers in the United States identify with an organized religious denomination. Most people indicate that the divine power, or God, is revealed to them through prayer (84%) or miracles (79%).

According to a compilation of annual Gallup polls published in the Princeton Religion Research Center's 1996 report, 31% of the American population attends religious services at least weekly. An additional 12% attend religious services almost weekly, and 16% attend about once a month, for a total of 59% of American adults indicating that they attend worship services at least monthly. In 1994, there were an estimated 900,000 Bible study groups and 800,000 adult Sunday school classes; 40% of Americans said they belonged to at least one religious support group extrinsic to usual worship services. The majority of religious attendees (69%) indicated that they are members of a specific church or synagogue. In the United States, most people were Christian, with 2% of the population identifying themselves as Jews, and 1% each as Muslim, Hindu, and Buddhist.

Prayer is prevalent in the United States; 90% of adults say that they pray daily. The majority of Americans (90%) indicate that religion is important in their personal lives, with older Americans finding it to be considerably more important than do younger individuals (Princeton Religion Research Center, 1996). It is not clear if this is a cohort effect or a function of a change in belief systems with aging. Religion appears to play a special role in coping with aging, with people returning to the church after absences in their younger years (Koenig, 1994). Religion holds an even stronger place among African Americans, among whom almost 100% indicate belief in a divine power (Ferraro & Koch, 1994). Although Americans have the highest rates of church attendance in the world, atheism, agnosticism, and total abstinence from any religious involvement is differentially represented among American health professionals and scientists (Princeton Religion Research Center, 1996). As early as medical school, future physicians have been found to be notably less spiritually oriented and religious than the patients for whom they provide care (Goldfarb, Galanter, McDowell, Lifshutz, & Dermatis, 1996).

Prayer is commonly used as a coping mechanism (Koenig, 1999). Among people with known illnesses, 40% indicated that prayer was their single most important coping mechanism, whereas 90% indicated that it played at least some role. Among African Americans, prayer often is identified as the major daily coping mechanism. Even though religion appears to be important to a large percentage of the American population, prayer and organized religious systems rarely play a role in contemporary public health strategies. This discrepancy is even recognized by health care practitioners. In a recent study of the attitudes and practices of family physicians relative to spiritual concerns of patients, 96% of physician respondents to a mailed survey (response rate 74%) had a high level of spirituality on the Ellison Spiritual Well-Being Scale, and nearly all physician respondents indicated that spiritual well-being was an important component of physical health (Ellis, Vinson, & Ewigman, 1999). More than 58% of physicians in the survey believed that physicians should address patients' spiritual concerns, but less than 20% reported ever doing so. Barriers cited were lack of time, inadequate training, and difficulty in communicating with patients about these issues. Referrals to hospital chaplains were also infrequent despite the belief among family practitioners that this was important. This study supports the premise that the current health care milieu does not enable the integration of religion and health through its physician leaders, despite considerable enthusiasm from a relatively small contingent in the medical profession (Dossey, 1996).

Further, the general population has expressed a greater desire for the integration of faith or religion into their health care considerations. In April 1998, a *CBS News* poll indicated that 80% of the general population believed in personal prayer or other spiritual practices as an adjunct to medical treatment in people who are seriously ill. In the same poll, 22% of respondents said that they had been cured of an illness as a result of prayer; and 63% indicated that doctors should join patients in prayer if the person requests it. In a February 1996 *USA Weekend* faith and health poll, 79% of the general U.S. public said they believed that faith can help people recover from illness; 56% indicated a personal experience with faith and recovery; and in accordance with the CBS poll, 63% believed it was good for doctors to talk with patients about spiritual faith. In this poll, only 10% said that a health professional had ever asked them about their spiritual faith as a factor in their physical health.

There are a number of other public polls reported in the media that provide similar data. The quandary, then, is whether or how people with a science background can, will, or should participate in any spiritual or religious aspects of an individual's experience with physical health. To some extent, this quandary may be a function of the "evidence" that this is a beneficial undertaking.

HEALTH AND RELIGION: THE "EVIDENCE"

An increasing number of studies examining the relationship of religion to health and the response of illness to religious belief systems have appeared in the past two decades. Systematic reviews have been published. Many studies are not designed explicitly to examine religion but are more general inquiries in which religion has been included as a variable. Most show a salutary effect of religion on health; several show a trend for religion to be associated with decrements in risks for major health problems (Levin, 1994). Out of 27 studies of health and religion that Levin considered, 22 showed a beneficial relationship. A four-volume series of publications (Larson, 1994; Matthews & Larson, 1995; Matthews, Larson, & Barry, 1993; Matthews & Saunders, 1995) on the relationship of faith and religion systematically reviewed the clinical literature. The majority of the more than 180 studies reviewed in the series showed religion or aspects of religion to be beneficial in some way. Nonetheless, studies of this nature are often called into question in regard to both their validity and their salience (Sloan et al., 1999). Further, there are few systematic reviews that present the negative studies. Indeed, negative studies may never be published. Questionable issues exist in most studies, many of which are small and dependent on modestly standardized measures. Doubt about results often is fueled by a preponderance of ecological studies in which the effects of religious practices cannot be parsed out of other aspects of the social culture.

Examination of larger rigorous prospective epidemiological studies supports the positive effects of religion. The Alameda County Study, a prospective study of 5,286 adults followed for 28 years, showed that frequent church attendees had 36% lower mortality rates compared with nonattendees (Strawbridge, Cohen, Shema, & Kaplan, 1997). The effect was strongest in women. Although adjustments for health status did not affect this relationship, adjustments for health practices and social connections slightly lowered the magnitude of the religious attendance–mortality relationship. Church attendees were more likely to stop smoking, exercise, and remain married. Thus, the beneficial impact was most likely to be at least partially mediated by healthier lifestyles in church attendees, even controlling for sociodemographic and health status factors. This finding has been replicated often in many other populations, including a large study of middle-aged men in Finland, in which premature cardiovascular mortality rates are extremely high (Rasanen, Kauhanen, Lakka, Kaplan, & Salonen, 1996). A 16-year prospective study of total mortality in 11 religious and 11 sociodemographically matched nonreligious kibbutzim in Israel showed that rates were significantly higher in the secular group (Kark et al., 1996). Multivariate adjustment for sociodemographic and behavioral variables showed that mortality from each of the major causes of death was higher in the nonreligious kibbutzim. It was concluded that belonging to a religious collective was protective and that this effect could not be explained by any health status or social variables. These are but a few of the many examples that show a lower mortality rate prospectively in population-based studies. There is a paucity of research that offers specific insight into the mechanism of this protective effect.

One could contend, counter to the Freudian position, that religion's greatest potential benefit would be on mental health. A systematic review of the recent literature and meta-analyses concluded that religious approaches to counseling can be (at least) as effective as standard approaches to counseling depressed patients (McCullough, 1999). In this review, five recent trials randomly assigned patients with depression to receive religious support and positive religious imagery for people who wished it or to usual care without religious support. Depression levels were measured periodically. There was a notable, but not statistically significant, improvement in the 1-week measures of depression. In longer follow-up studies, effects were more distinguishable. One study showed a decrement in relapse from depression in people who received religious counseling, whereas another showed that depressed patients with strong faith were more likely to recover from a depressive episode. In a study of 1,900 female twins, lower rates of depression, cigarette smoking, and alcoholism were found among twins who were religious compared with those who were not, independent of calculated heritability effects (Kendler, Gardner, & Prescott, 1997). A compendium of several clinical epidemiological studies provides hypothesis-generating results that support the positive role of religion (Koenig, Larson, & Weaver, 1998). These are summarized briefly. In 4,000 healthy elderly people, a study by the National Institute on Aging showed that those who attended church more often had a 0.50 relative risk for depression, meaning that their rates of depression were half those of people who were not religious. In multivariate analysis controlling for health status, age, and social support, the protective effect persisted. In a study of hospitalized patients with serious physical illness accompanied by depression, recovery from depression was significantly faster in those with strong religious beliefs, independent of the progress of the physical illness. Similarly, a study of 850 persons hospitalized for acute physical illness showed that those with religious coping skills were significantly less depressed, even when adjusting for illness severity. These studies are exploratory and highlight the need for more intensive, longer trials, as well as a study of the potential social and psychological mediators of the effect.

Many have posited that religion, collective forms in particular, results in improved health status because it addresses the major behavioral risk factors. Smoking, eating high-fat meats (beef and pork), sexual promiscuity, and alcohol consumption are often proscribed. In U.S. society, these high-risk behaviors are associated with high-prevalence diseases including heart attacks, stroke, cancer, liver disease, sexually transmitted diseases, and pulmonary diseases. From a preventive perspective, avoiding these behaviors is likely to result in a marked decrement in risk. It is also possible that social support and tangible support are associated with religious affiliation.

In specific illnesses, the salutary impact of religion is often seen. In a study of risk factors for death 6 months after coronary bypass surgery, for example, the absence of religious beliefs in the recovery process was a powerful predictor of mortality in older people, independent of age and measures of the severity of illness (Oxman, Freeman, & Manheimer, 1995). Several studies have shown that religious involvement is inversely related to the development of hypertension morbidity and mortality in African Americans (Levin, 1996).

In the environment of modern medicine, patients who use religion as a coping mechanism indicate disappointment that their physicians do not become involved in spiritual issues. In one study, 77% of hospital inpatients thought that their doctors should consider spiritual needs, and slightly more than one third felt that they should discuss religious beliefs with them more frequently (King & Bushwick, 1994). A 1997 Consensus Report on Scientific Research on Spirituality and Health presented the ideas of 70 researchers, physicians, and scholars who addressed the state of the art and future directions in a national conference forum (Larson, Swyers, & McCullough, 1998). In many well-conducted studies, it was concluded that there was a salutary effect of religion, spirituality, or faith, whatever the mechanism.

MODELS OF HEALTH AND RELIGION

Religion as an organized entity may be viewed from complementary perspectives that facilitate understanding the instrumental role of both personal and collective belief systems. The social–psychological perspective offers insight into the ways that faith influences collective and individual health behaviors, while, on the other side of the spectrum, biological models explain the ways that personal faith influences human psychology, including immunity and responses to stress.

A Social–Psychological Perspective

The social environment of the church may provide role models who help others avoid unhealthy behaviors, such as smoking and alcohol use. Prayer may be perceived as a powerful support for undertaking difficult behaviors that may enhance health. Among Christians, for example, guidelines for a healthy and collectively beneficial lifestyle reside in biblical scriptures. Exemplary of the many lessons about healthful eating is a story from the Book of Daniel:

> Please test your servants for ten days, and let them give us vegetables to eat and water to drink. Then let our appearance be examined before you, and the appearance of the young men who eat the portion of the King's delicacies. . . . So he consented with them in this matter and tested them ten days. And at the end of the ten days, their features appeared better and fatter in the flesh than all the young men who ate the portion of the king's delicacies. Thus the steward took away their portion of the delicacies and the wine that they were to drink and gave them vegetables. (Daniel 1:8–16)

People of faith exposed to scriptural messages to promote healthy behaviors may have a higher probability of incorporating the concepts into their daily lives. There are many faith-based scriptures that are used for coping. Consider the following: "And the prayer of the faith shall save the sick, and the Lord shall raise him up" (James 5:15). Religious writings can be very potent support in times of difficulty and stress for people who are believers.

When examining the ways in which faith or religion can be supportive, the concept of health locus of control seems to be an issue. As health professionals, we encourage self-care and accountability for one's own health behaviors. Some studies show that an internal locus of control (belief that one is responsible for one's own actions) is strongly associated with positive health behaviors and outcomes. Because religion is faith based, religious individuals often give "control" to a divine power. Research has shown, however, that health locus of control is not necessarily related to the use of prayer or the belief in a divine power (Saudia, Kinney, Brown, & Young-Ward, 1991). An equal number of people with an internal locus of control and an external locus use prayer and perceive it to be helpful. It is thus unlikely that faith-based religion would encourage people to abrogate responsibility for their own health. In the case of individuals who do not wish to alter health behaviors, virtually anything might be used as an excuse to avoid changing, including the fatalistic perspective that a divine power will define their fate. Denial and cognitive dissonance resolution may take many forms, including the use of religion.

Many would maintain that psychosocial models are neither useful nor necessary when examining the religion–health link. People with strong religious beliefs may attribute any beneficial impact of religion explicitly to the direct impact of a divine power. Attempting to delineate a universally accepted theory or model of causality related to religion and health is unlikely to be successful and will be considered by some to be heretical and by others to be weak science.

Biological Models

We are at the cusp of a scientific revolution that no longer requires that psychosocial models of health be separated from biological models. Recent discoveries offer exciting opportunities to examine the interactions among environmental, social, psychological, and biological models of health. A total body communication system has been discovered that may explain why religious belief systems "work."

The Cartesian mechanistic view of the body as an entity separate from the mind created a science where research was narrow and focal. Until the 20th century, few even believed that there was any direct biological interaction between the central nervous system and the autonomic nervous system. Clearly the discovery that strong internal mind–body links do in fact exist has led scientists to conclude that emotions are not separate from human physiology. Virtually all human cells have receptors or sensors that allow transmission of the "signals" of emotions to cells, influencing all organ systems in the body (Moyers, 1993). In the 1970s, the seminal work of Candace Pert and Solomon Snyder sparked a new science of mind–body medicine. The discovery of the opiate receptor in the brain and its relationship to "feelings" was a recent landmark event, just 25 years ago (Pert & Snyder, 1973). Emotions are now examined, in part, as biological processes. Pert and colleagues published the key findings in a 1985 *Journal of Immunology*, summarizing the molecular basis of emotions as follows: "Neuropeptides and their receptors join the brain, glands, and immune system in a network of communication between brain and body, probably representing the biochemical substrate of emotion" (Pert, Ruff, Weber, & Herkenham, 1985). Body processes can thus be regulated by emotions. Even immune system cells have receptors for neuropeptides, and further, they also appear to produce biochemical substances that affect mood. Information exchange between mind and body systems is bidirectional. Mood can affect immunity; immune responses can affect mood. Finally, there is at least theoretical evidence that chronic emotional stress could potentially cause changes in immune activity that produces allergies, inflammation, fatigue, and autoimmune diseases (Sternberg, 1997a, 1997b). Stressful emotions may influence the biological substrate for serious illness. One study examined 32 "stressed" spouse caregivers of people with Alzheimer's disease, and compared immune responses related to exposure to an influenza virus vaccine to 32 matched control participants without the caregiving responsibility (Kiekholt-Glaser, as cited in Bunk, 1998). On two assays, stressed caregivers consistently had significantly lower levels of the virus-induced cytokines interleukin-1 and interleukin-2 (immune molecules that control communication with the central nervous systems), suggesting a depression of the immune system in people exposed to a chronic stressor. Epidemiological studies have shown religious coping to be a mediator of stress-related mortality (Krause, 1998). Religion should be included as a potentially important modifier of the chronic stress–immune relationship in future clinical and population studies.

The discovery of the mind–body connection represents a radical 20th-century paradigm shift that may explain why some people remain healthy if surrounded by salutary circumstances, such as social support, family stability, personal accomplishments, and religious environments. Likewise, serious physical consequences can result from social and psychological disturbances. There is now a biologically plausible mechanism that could explain why strong personal beliefs in a divine power or prayer might work to produce health benefits. This finding in no way negates the potential for the existence of a divine power. In fact, some might contend that this elegant complex human system has an origin that can be explained only by the existence of a superhuman power. Spirituality has the ability to influence health, and the mechanisms might now be best explained by a more integrated psychological, social, and biological model. The emergent model is likely to be beyond fully testable hypotheses, although the reductionist perspective may parse out aspects that would be useful for furthering the public's health.

Levin (1996) published a scholarly review of the literature on health and its relation to religion. Using the "epidemiology of religion," Levin pointed out important misinterpretations of the existing literature that may lead to discord and the failure to consider the importance of religion in health. Two important misinterpretations or overinterpretations are perhaps the dominant cause for mistrust of the literature. The first is that "there is empirical evidence of a supernatural force on health" (p. 856). Levin indicated that this is the failing of "sympathetic religious partisans" to scientifically critique the findings of studies. Research only shows that religion as a system of beliefs influences health and does not prove the presence of a supernatural power. Detractors suggest that other factors can explain a religion–health association. These other factors, however, are most likely to be mechanisms of the effect. Observed relationships are not "confounding," but valid pathways for an impact. Levin proposed that the study of the protective effects of religion needs to be more methodologically sound and should include the concept of salutogenesis (positive factors affecting health), the natural history of disease, and host resistance. All may be the vectors through which religion may have a beneficial impact on health. Host resistance is a particularly important concept that melds such ideas as hope, forgiveness, support, and empathy with the new mind–body science. Thus, there are many ways that religion, spirituality, or faith might be operationalized, conceptualized, and even organized to address health issues and attendant research. It is not necessary to prove divinity; certainly there is no reason to deny its potential as a mediator of health. The desire for more in-depth understanding of this phenomenon should be an impetus for hypothesis-driven research and clinical studies.

APPLICATION OF FAITH-BASED APPROACHES TO PUBLIC HEALTH

The American Public Health Association has a professional interfaith caucus for people with an interest in faith issues to explore, develop, and implement health projects in the United States. *Strong Partners*, a monograph produced in 1998 by the Carter Interfaith Center in Atlanta, presented a series of cogent dialogues on how faith can be integrated into public health in hospitals, as well as in community-based activities. Parish nursing, faith-based outreach, religious health care systems, and community partnerships that allow inclusion of faith into public health programs, often tackle the difficult issues of care for poor and underserved populations, as well as immunization, violence prevention, home care for elderly people, and the creation of new types of nurturing practitioners from communities of faith. The impact of these efforts has never been well evaluated.

The leaders of faith-based programs may hold sufficiently strong beliefs that they are serving humanity and that their initiatives require no "proof." Further, such issues as cost-effectiveness evaluation may have little meaning in faith-based religious institutions that exist primarily to serve. Traditional science-based outcomes evaluation may be of little interest. Most of these institutions cannot afford the cost of evaluation, and grant awarding is limited because there is an amendment to the U.S. Constitution that mandates the separation of church and state, making it difficult to award government funds to large religion-oriented demonstration projects or even to smaller trials. Recently, however, the National Center for Complementary and Alternative Medicine has noted an interest in the impact of religion on health and even the potential role of pastoral counseling. To truly understand the role of religion in the health of the public and to convince doubting health professionals of its utility in improving health, it may be necessary to rigorously evaluate programs and to conduct studies that elucidate both tangible and theoretical mechanisms. The nature of such research will be considered too weak by some and unnecessary by others.

ARE RELIGION AND THE SCIENCE OF PUBLIC HEALTH ANTITHETICAL?

Can anyone truly prove the presence of a divine power? Some have maintained that it can be examined inferentially using epidemiological principles that attribute causality. Conversely, many people would maintain that the ability to determine the true presence of divinity is beyond human comprehension. If one believes in divinity, this belief must then, by definition, be faith based. It may make little pragmatic difference if the impact of religion on health or quality of life occurs because of divine intervention, because of social mechanisms, the biochemistry or psychology of strongly held beliefs, or any combination thereof.

There is enormous potential for religion and religious organizations to serve as vectors for public health messages and to provide helping services through hospitals, community outreach, and parish nursing (Cook, 1997; Ford, Edwards, Rodriguez, Gibson, & Tilley, 1996; Jackson, 1990; Smith, Merritt, & Patel, 1997). The sheer scope of religious involvement in the population simply cannot be relegated to the obscure mystical position it holds among many scientists and health professionals, nor can it be assigned a neutral position in the lives of the people for whom it is integral. It is important to recognize the difference between understanding religion, working with religious organizations, and evangelizing. The evangelical movement generally remains the purview of the church. Few public health professionals would advocate converting nonbelievers to people of religion or faith. Nonetheless, novel health and religion partnerships may serve the well-being of the public. Design and evaluation of public health interventions integrating religion and health requires mutual respect and understanding between health care professionals and religious leaders. For religious leaders, faith reigns supreme and evaluation or understanding is not necessary. For scientists and health professionals, evaluation and understanding are crucial.

There are powerful opportunities in the 21st century for religion and science to coalesce for the purpose of improving the public's health. Can we ever evaluate the presence of a divine power in a way that would meet the requirements of modern science to define theory and test it? We probably cannot. Are religion and science antithetical? I would maintain that this issue is not operationally important because both the public health and the religious communities share an interest in the common good and well-being of humanity.

> Draw if thou canst the mystic line,
> Severing rightly His from thine,
> Which is human, which is divine.
> (Ralph Waldo Emerson)

REFERENCES

American Psychiatric Association. (1975). *Task force report on the psychiatrists' viewpoint on religion and their services to religious institutions and the ministry.* Washington, DC: Author.

Amundsen, D. W. (1996). *Medicine, society, and faith in the ancient media and medieval world.* Baltimore: Johns Hopkins University Press.

Bunk, S. (1998). Mind and body: What's the connection? *Scientist, 12,* 1–5.

Carter Interfaith Center. (1998). *Strong partners: A report on realigning religious health assets for community health.* Atlanta, GA: Author.

Cook, C. (1997). Faith-based health needs assessment: Implications for empowerment of the faith community. *Journal of Health Care for the Poor and Underserved, 8,* 300–301.

de Gouw, H. W., Westndrop, R. G., Junst, A. E., Mackenbach, J. P., & Vandenbrouke, J. P. (1996). Decreased mortality among contemplative monks in the Netherlands. *American Journal of Epidemiology, 141,* 771–775.

Dossey, L. (1996). *Prayer is good medicine.* San Francisco: HarperCollins.

Einstein, A. (1949). *The world as I see it.* New York: Philosophical Library.

Ellis, A. (1988). Is religiosity pathological? *Free Inquiry, 18,* 27–32.

Ellis, M. R., Vinson, D. C., & Ewigman, B. (1999). Addressing spiritual concerns of patients: Family physicians' attitudes and practices. *Journal of Family Practice, 48,* 105–109.

Ferraro, K. F., & Koch, J. R. (1994). Religion and health among Black and White adults: Examining social support and consolidation. *Journal for the Scientific Study of Religion, 33,* 362–375.

Foege, W. (1998). On values and vulnerability. In *Strong partners: A report on realigning religious health assets for community health.* Atlanta, GA: Carter Interfaith Center.

Ford, M. E., Edwards, G., Rodriguez, J. L., Gibson, R. C., & Tilley, B. C. (1996). An empowerment-centered, church-based asthma education program for African American adults. *Health & Social Work, 21,* 71–75.

Freud, S. (1962). *Future of an illusion.* London: Hogarth Press. (Original publication 1927)

Friedlander, Y., Kark, D., & Stein, Y. (1986). Religious orthodoxy and myocardial infarctions in Jerusalem; A case control study. *International Journal of Cardiology, 10,* 33–41.

Gardner, J. W., & Lyon, J. L. (1982). Cancer in Utah Mormon men by lay priesthood level. *American Journal of Epidemiology, 116,* 243–257.

Goldfarb, L. M., Galanter, M., McDowell, D., Lifshutz, H., & Dermatis, H. (1996). Medical student and patient attitudes toward religion and spirituality in the recovery process. *American Journal of Alcohol Abuse, 22,* 549–561.

Gunderson, G. (1998). On faith, science and hope. In *Strong partners: A report on realigning religious health assets for community health.* Atlanta, GA: Carter Interfaith Center.

Jackson, A. L. (1990). Operation Sunday School—Educating caring hearts to be healthy hearts. *Public Health Report, 105,* 85–88.

Jones, T. L. (1995). Religion's role in health. What's God got to do with it? *Texas Medicine, 91,* 24–29.

Kark, J. D., Shemi, G., Friedlander, Y., Martin, O., Manor, O., & Blondheim, S. H. (1996). Does religious observance promote health? Mortality in secular versus religious kibbutzim in Israel. *American Journal of Public Health, 85,* 341–346.

Kendler, K. S., Gardner, C. O., & Prescott, C. A. (1997). Religion, psychopathology, and substance use and abuse: A multimeasure genetic-epidemiologic study. *American Journal of Psychiatry, 154,* 322–329.

King, D. E., & Bushwick, B. (1994). Beliefs and attitudes of hospital inpatients about faith healing and prayer. *Journal of Family Practice, 39,* 349–352.

Koenig, H. G. (1994). *Aging and God.* Binghamton, NY: Haworth Press.

Koenig, H. G. (1999). *The healing power of faith—Science explores medicine's last great frontier.* New York: Simon & Schuster.

Koenig, H. G., Larson, D. B., & Weaver, A. J. (1998). Research on religion and serious mental illness. In New Directions in Mental Health Services (Ed.), *Spirituality and religion in recovery from mental illness* (p. 80). San Francisco: Jossey-Bass.

Krause, N. (1998). Stressors in highly valued roles, religious coping, and mortality. *Psychology of Aging, 13,* 242–255.

Larson, D. B. (1994). *The faith factor bibliography series: Vol. II. Annotated bibliography of systematic reviews and clinical research on spiritual subjects.* Rockville, MD: National Institute for Healthcare Research.

Larson, D. B., Swyers, J. P., & McCullough, M. E. (1998). *Scientific research on spirituality and health: A consensus report.* Rockville, MD: National Institute for Healthcare Research.

Levin, J. S. (1994). Religion and health: Is there an association, is it valid, and is it causal? *Social Science and Medicine, 38,* 1475–1482.

Levin, J. S. (1996). How religion influences morbidity and health: Reflections on natural history, salutogenesis, and host resistance. *Social Science and Medicine, 43,* 849–864.

Lloyd, G. E. R. (1978). *Hippocratic writings.* New York: Penguin Books.

Matthews, D. A., & Larson, D. B. (1995). *The faith factor bibliography series: Vol. III. Enhancing life satisfaction.* Rockville, MD: National Institute for Healthcare Research.

Matthews, D. A., & Larson, D. B. (1997). Faith and medicine: Reconciling the twin traditions of healing. *Mind Body Medicine, 2,* 3–6.

Matthews, D. A., Larson, D. B., & Barry, C. P. (1993). *The faith factor bibliography* series: Vol. I. Annotated bibliography of clinical research on spiritual subjects. Rockville, MD: National Institute for Healthcare Research.

Matthews, D. A., McCullough, M. E., Larsen, D. B., Koenig, H. G, Swyers, J. P., & Milano, M. G. (1998). Religious commitment and health status. *Archives of Family Medicine, 7*, 118–124.

Matthews, D. A., & Saunders, D. M. (1995). *The faith factor bibliography series: Vol. IV. Prevention and treatment of illness, addictions, and delinquency.* Rockville, MD: National Institute for Healthcare Research.

McBride, J. L. (1998). The new focus on spirituality in medicine. *Journal of the Medical Association of Georgia, 87*, 281–284.

McCullough, M. E. (1999). Research on religion-accommodative counseling: Review and meta-analysis. *Journal of Consulting Psychology. 46*, 1–7.

Mitka, M. (1998). Getting religion seen as help in being well. *Journal of the American Medical Association, 280*, 1896–1897.

Moyers, B. (1993). *Healing and the mind.* New York: Doubleday.

Orr, R. D., & Genesen, L. B. (1998). Medicine, ethics and religion: Rational or irrational? *Journal of Medical Ethics, 24*, 385–387.

Oxman, T. E, Freeman, D. H., & Manheimer, E. D. (1995). Lack of social participation or religious strength and comfort as risk factors for death after cardiac surgery in the elderly. *Psychosomatic Medicine, 57*, 5–15.

Pargament, K. I., Maton, K. I., & Hess, R. E. (1992). *Religion and prevention in mental health: Research, vision, and action.* Rockville, MD: National Institute for Healthcare Research.

Parmley, W. W. (1999). Do you believe in God? *Journal of the American College of Cardiology, 33*, 583.

Pascover, D. (1998). On following new paths. In *Strong partners: A report on realigning religious health assets for community health.* Atlanta, GA: Carter Interfaith Center.

Pert, C. B., & Snyder, S. H. (1973). Opiate receptor: Demonstration in nervous tissue. *Science, 179*, 1011–1014.

Pert, C. B., Ruff, M. R., Weber R. J., & Herkenham, M. (1985). Neuropeptides and their receptors: a psychosomatic network. *Journal of Immunology, 135*(Suppl. 2), 820S–826S.

Princeton Religion Research Center. (1996). *1996 report: Will the vitality of the church be the surprise of the 21st century?* Princeton, NJ: Princeton Religion Research Center.

Ragan, C., Malony, H. N., & Beit-Hallahmi, B. (1980). Psychologists and religion. Professional factors and personal belief. *Review of Religious Research, 21*, 208–217.

Rasanen, J., Kauhanen, J., Lakka, T. A., Kaplan, G. A., & Salonen, J. T. (1996). Religious affiliation and all-cause mortality: A prospective populations study in middle-aged men in eastern Finland. *International Journal of Epidemiology, 25*, 1244.

Saudia, T. L., Kinney, M. R., Brown, K. C., & Young-Ward, L. (1991). Health locus of control and helpfulness of prayer. *Heart and Lung, 20,* 60–65.

Sloan, R. P., Bagiella, E., & Powell, T. (1999). Religion, spirituality, and medicine. *Lancet, 353,* 664–667.

Smith, E. D., Merritt, S. L., & Patel, M. K. (1997). Church-based education: An outreach program for African Americans with hypertension. *Ethnicity and Health, 2,* 243–253.

Sternberg, E. M. (1997a). Neural-immune interactions in health and disease. *Journal of Clinical Investigation, 1,* 2641–2647.

Sternberg, E. M. (1997b). Emotions and disease. From balance of humors to balance of molecules. *Nature Medicine, 3,* 264–267.

Stotland, N. L. (1999). When religion collides with medicine. *American Journal of Psychiatry, 15,* 304–307.

Strawbridge, W. J., Cohen, R. D., Shema, J., & Kaplan, G. A. (1997). Frequent attendance at religious services and mortality over 28 years. *American Journal of Public Health, 87,* 957–961.

Timio, M., Lippi, G., Venanzi, S. Gentili, S., Quintaliani, G., Verdura, C., Monarca, C., Saronio, P., & Timio, F. (1997). Blood pressure trend and cardiovascular events in nuns in a secluded order: A 30-year follow-up study. *Blood Pressure, 6,* 81–87.

Wozniak, R. H. (1992). *Mind and body: Rene Descartes to William James.* Bethesda, MD: National Library of Medicine and American Psychological Association.

AUTHOR INDEX

SUBJECT INDEX

Measurement (*continued*)
of demands of psychosocial workplace, 272–274
and evaluator as stakeholder, 301
of impact of violence, 101–103
Media campaigns
as component of North Karelia project, 83–84
to encourage breast cancer screenings, 182–183
and injury control, 218–219
Medicare, 183
Mental health
and exposure to violence, 100–101
and male violence against women, 117
and religion, 358
Microsoft, 282–283
Mind–body connection, 362
Minnesota Heart Health program, 296
Mithaug, Dennis, 325–326
Molecular genetics, 41
Morbidity rates, 6
Mortality rates, 4–6, 87–88
Mothers Against Drunk Driving, 213–214
MRFIT studies, 11–12

National Center for Complementary and Alternative Medicine, 363
National Coalition of Gay STD Services, 162
National Committee for Injury Prevention and Control, 207
National demonstration projects, 82–83
National Gay Health Coalition, 162
National Gay Task Force, 162
National Health and Nutrition Examination Survey (NHANES), 32
National High Blood Pressure Education Program, 11
National Institute of Drug Abuse (NIDA), 169–170
National Institute of Mental Health (NIMH), 169, 170
National Institute on Aging, 358
National Institutes of Health (NIH), 167, 170, 177, 233, 234
National Research Council, 120–123
Needle-exchange programs, 14

Needs, community/social
in conducive production model, 280, 285
and evaluation of community-based health initiatives, 298–299
Netherlands, 208
New Haven (Connecticut), 150, 152
Newton, Isaac, 4
New York City, 146, 152, 162
NHANES (National Health and Nutrition Examination Survey), 32
NIDA. *See* National Institute of Drug Abuse
NIH. *See* National Institutes of Health
NIMH. *See* National Institute of Mental Health
North Karelia project, 74–92
conduct of community programs in, 80–83
description of problem and initial response, 78–79
goals of, 79–80
interventions within, 83–85
results of, 85–90
and risk factors, 86–87
and smoking cessation, 85–86
Norway, 217

Obesity, 31–45
behavioral approaches to, 33–36
and body image, 38
clinical definition of, 32
and dietary intake, 33
environmental-level influences on, 43–44
genetic determinants of, 40–43
as major public health challenge, 32–33
and physical activity, 33–34
preventive measures with, 44–45
and psychological impact of weight loss, 39
psychological treatment approaches with, 38–39
and psychopathology, 36–37
and quality of life, 38
and self-esteem, 37
and thought patterns surrounding weight/eating, 37–38
transdisciplinary approach to, 32

Ob gene, 41–42
Occupational health. *See* Work environment
Orlistat, 42
Oslo Heart Study, 11
Overeating, 37–38

PACE, 242–243
"Pain and suffering," 253
Partner violence, 116–117
Past Exposure to Violence survey, 102
PATCH, 234
Pathological ecology, 103–104
Pathways study, 308–309
Patton, M. Q., 294
Pervasive community violence, 99
Pharmacological therapies, for obesity, 42
Planned behavior, theory of, 15
Pneumonia, 7
Police Athletic League, 105
Positivism, 294–295
Posttraumatic stress disorder, 117
Prader-Willi syndrome, 40, 41
PRECEDE–PROCEED model, 16–18,
187, 190, 209–210
Preventive measures
cardiovascular disease, 64–67
individual vs. population-based approaches, 8–10
obesity, 44–45
Primary prevention, 9, 64
Primordial prevention, 9–10, 65
Protection motivation theory, 77
Prototype studies, 316–317
Psychoactive drugs, "licit," 143
Psychopathology, among obese, 36–37
Psychosocial work environment, 271–
274, 287–289

QALY. *See* Quality-adjusted life-year
Qualitative research, 300
Quality-adjusted life-year (QALY), 251,
254–257, 259
Quality of life, and obesity, 38
Quasi-experimental designs, 13–14
"Quit and Win" smoking cessation program, 84, 86, 90

Randomized clinical trials, 13
Rape, 118
Rapid Early Action for Coronary Treatment (REACT), 313
Reasoned action, theory of, 15
Recent Exposure to Physical Violence
survey, 102
Reductionism, 3–4, 8
Religion, 351–364
and application of faith-based approaches to public health, 363
appropriateness of, in public health initiatives, 364
biological models of health and, 361–363
and divinity, 354
and faith, 354
historical background of health and,
352–356
pervasiveness of, in United States,
355–357
positive health effects of, 357–359
social–psychological perspective on
health and, 360–361
and spirituality, 354
Reppucci, N. D., 123
Residual risk behavior, 147
Risk factors
for cardiovascular disease, 53, 75, 86–87
identification of, 5–6
Russia, 168

Sanders, Robert, 217
San Francisco, 162
San Francisco AIDS Foundation, 162–163
Sarason, S. B., 118
Saving Lives program, 236
Scarlet fever, 4
Scheirer, M. A., 296
Schools
group-randomized trial in, 308–309
violence in, 100–101
Science, 118
Seat belts, 208, 211
Secondary prevention, 9, 64
Sedentary behavior, 43, 57–59
Self-determination, 326

and empowerment evaluation, 323
Very-low-calorie diets (VLCDs), 34
Violence
    communal, 99
    community, 99
    definition of, 98
    health consequences of, 98–99
    partner, 116–117
    urban. *See* Urban violence
    against women. *See* Male violence
        against women
Viruses, 4
VLCDs (very-low-calorie diets), 34

W. K. Kellogg Foundation, 326–327
War on Drugs, 153
Weight loss
    long-term, 35
    psychological impact of, 39
    success rates for, 34–35
Weight-loss surgery, 42
WHO. *See* World Health Organization
Within-disease allocation, 251
Women
    breast cancer screening for. *See* Breast
        cancer screening
    male violence against. *See* Male vio-
        lence against women

Work environment, 267–289
    and chronic conditions, 270–272
    and commodity production model,
        275–276, 286–287
    and conducive production model, 276–
        287
    and current social policy discussions,
        267–268
    and job insecurity, 269–270, 285–286
    in North Karelia project, 84
    psychosocial, 271–274
    and psychosocial workplace skills,
        287–289
    psychosocial work redesign interven-
        tions for improvement of, 274–
        275
    sexual/gender harassment in, 116
    and trends in global economy, 268–
        270
World Health Organization (WHO), 83,
    147, 148

Youth projects (North Karelia project),
    83–84

Zimmerman, M. A., 322–323

ABOUT THE EDITORS

Neil Schneiderman, PhD, is the James L. Knight Professor of Psychology, Medicine, Psychiatry and Behavioral Sciences, and Biomedical Engineering at the University of Miami. He is also director of the university's Behavioral Medicine Research Center and the director of the Division of Health Psychology in the department of psychology. He is program director of the National Institute of Mental Health's (NIMH) "Behavioral Management and Stress Responses in HIV/AIDS" program and for NIMH's research training grant "Psychoneuroimmunology and HIV/AIDS." He is also program director for the National Heart, Lung, and Blood Institute's (NHLBI) "Biobehavioral Bases of CHD Risk and Management" program and for NHLBI's research training grant "Behavioral Medicine Research in Cardiovascular Disease." Dr. Schneiderman is principal investigator of the Miami Clinical Unit for the NHLBI multicenter trial "Enhancing Recovery in Coronary Heart Disease (ENRICHD)." In 1994, he was awarded the Distinguished Scientific Award from the American Psychological Association (APA), and in 1997, he received the Distinguished Scientific Contribution Award from the Society of Behavioral Medicine. He has served as editor-in-chief for the journals *Health Psychology* and *International Journal of Behavioral Medicine*, was president of APA's Academy of Behavioral Medicine Research and of APA's Division of Health Psychology (Division 38), and has received APA Division 38's Award for Outstanding Contributions to Health Psychology. Currently, he chairs APA's Board of Scientific Affairs and is president of the International Society of Behavioral Medicine.

For the past 34 years, Dr. Schneiderman's research has been funded by the National Institutes of Health and the National Science Foundation. His research has ranged from single neuronal recordings in the rabbit medulla, through studies of psychosocial contributions to disease progression, to primary prevention of physical illness and the behavioral management of chronic disease in clinical patients. Dr. Schneiderman has published more than 300 books, chapters, and journal articles.

Marjorie A. Speers, PhD, is the deputy associate director for science for the Centers for Disease Control and Prevention (CDC). She also serves as the human subjects coordinator and the behavioral and social sciences coordinator at the CDC and is the first behavioral scientist to hold this newly created position. Previously, as director of the CDC's Division of Chronic Disease Control and Community at the National Center for Chronic Disease Prevention and Health Promotion, she supervised public health programs in cardiovascular health, aging, physical activity promotion, and health education. Other positions she has held at the CDC include chief of the Aging and Statistics Branch and epidemiologist in the Cancer Prevention and Control Branch. Prior to joining the CDC, Dr. Speers was an assistant professor in the Department of Preventive Medicine and Community Health at the University of Texas in Galveston, and was an instructor in the department of psychology at the University of Connecticut.

Dr. Speers has earned doctoral degrees in psychology and epidemiology from Yale University and has earned a bachelor's degree in arts from Dickinson College. She has published widely on a variety of subjects, including cardiovascular disease, cancer, aging, and public health practice. She is a consulting editor for the *Journal of Behavioral Medicine*, and she is regional editor for the journal *Health Promotion International*.

Julia M. Silva, is the project development officer for the American Psychological Association's (APA) early violence prevention project "ACT Against Violence." Previously, she was manager of the national conference "Public Health in the 21st Century: Behavioral and Social Science Contributions," which was organized by the APA in collaboration with 13 professional organizations and funded by the Centers for Disease Control and Prevention, the Office of Juvenile Justice and Delinquency Prevention, the Substance Abuse and Mental Health Services Administration, and several institutes and offices of the National Institutes of Health. Prior to joining the APA, Ms. Silva worked as a consultant on international education projects for the Academy for Educational Development in Washington, DC, and has held positions with the Brazilian government at the Ministry of Labor, the National Research Council, and the National School of Public Administration.

Ms. Silva has longstanding international experience and has held positions in France, the United States, and her native Brazil. She earned a masters degree in sociology from the University of Paris III and a bachelor's degree in psychology from the Catholic University of Sao Paulo in Brazil. She has provided leadership for projects addressing behavioral science and public health, violence prevention, professional development for public servants and school staff, training for community leaders, women's issues, and immigrant's issues.

Henry Tomes, PhD, received a BS in psychology from Fisk University in Nashville, Tennessee in 1957 and a PhD in clinical psychology from Pennsylvania State University in 1963. Since 1991, he has served as the executive director of the American Psychological Association's (APA) Public Interest Directorate. Before joining the APA, Dr. Tomes has held positions with Meharry Medical and Dental College in Nashville and the State of Washington's Division of Mental Health. From 1986 to 1991, he was appointed by Governor Michael Dukakis to serve first as deputy commissioner, then commissioner, of the Massachusetts Department of Mental Health.

In a career spanning over 30 years, Dr. Tomes has received numerous grants and contracts for training and administration in health and mental health and has published professional articles pertaining to a variety of health, mental health, and social issues. He has been presented with honorary doctoral degrees from the Massachusetts School of Professional Psychology, was honored by the Chicago School of Professional Psychology, and was elected to the Phi Beta Kappa Honorary Society. The APA has honored him with an award for Distinguished Professional Contributions to Public Service. Dr. Tomes has provided leadership in a number of organizations, most notably the APA and the Association of Black Psychologists, for which he served as cochair from 1966 to 1970. He is married with four children and six grandchildren.

Jacquelyn H. Gentry, PhD, is director of Public Interest Initiatives for the American Psychological Association (APA) where she coordinates APA-wide activities pertaining to violence awareness. She was staff director for the APA Commission on Violence and Youth, and she is one of the editors of *Reason to Hope: A Psychosocial Perspective on Violence and Youth*, the commission's scientific volume and full report. She directed the work of the APA's Presidential Task Force on Violence and the Family and developed a behavioral science research agenda on violence as part of the Human Capital Initiative. As part of her duties at the APA, she is involved in projects on aging, adolescent health, emergency medical services for children, and the interface of public health and behavioral science.

Before joining the APA in 1989, Dr. Gentry worked for 22 years in the National Institute of Mental Health (NIMH) communications program. As chief of NIMH's Science Communications, she directed a program to produce and market professional and public education materials about mental health. She earned her bachelor's degree from Stetson University in DeLand, Florida; her master's degree from Syracuse University in Syracuse, New York; and her doctoral degree from the University of Maryland, College Park.